In the Heart of the Whore

The story of
apartheid's death squads

Jacques Pauw

JONATHAN BALL PUBLISHERS
Johannesburg & Cape Town

Originally published in 1991 by Southern Book Publishers (Pty) Ltd.
This edition published by
JONATHAN BALL PUBLISHERS
A division of Media24 (Pty) Ltd
PO Box 33977
Jeppestown
2043

ISBN 978-1-86842-894-6
ebook ISBN 978-1-86842-895-3

*Every effort has been made to trace the copyright holders and to obtain their permission
for the use of copyright material. The publishers apologise for any errors or omissions and
would be grateful to be notified of any corrections that should be incorporated in future
editions of this book.*

Twitter: www.twitter.com/JonathanBallPub
Facebook: www.facebook.com/JonathanBallPublishers
Blog: http://jonathanball.bookslive.co.za/

Cover image: detail from *The Interrogators*, a triptych by Paul Stopforth, reproduced
by permission of Iziko National Gallery, Cape Town

Cover design by Anton Sassenberg
Typesetting by Wouter Reinders
Reproduction of cover and picture section by Kohler Carton & Print (Natal)

Printed by **novus print**, a Novus Holdings company

Acknowledgements

THIS book is the culmination of a two-year investigation into state-sponsored death squads that led to the publication of a series of articles in *Vrye Weekblad* and other publications around the world, the appointment of a judicial commission of inquiry and a Supreme Court libel case.

There are many people I wish to thank. All of them have contributed to the success of my investigation and the writing of this book.

Firstly, I wish to thank *Vrye Weekblad* editor Max du Preez for the incredible courage that led him to publish the death squad story and for his never-nding encouragement. I am indebted to him for granting me leave of absence from daily journalism to write this book.

Many thanks also go to:

All the lawyers who represented *Vrye Weekblad* with dedication at the Harms Commission and during *Vrye Weekblad*'s defamation case: Bobby Levin, Eberhard Bertelsmann, Martin Luitingh, Frans Rautenbach, Mark Rosin, Lauren Jacobson and David Hoffe.

Martin Welz, a friend and a journalist I have always admired and learned much from. He introduced me to Dirk Coetzee and assisted me throughout the investigation and in the writing of this book.

Andre Zaaiman, for his courage in helping Dirk Coetzee to leave the country and assisting me in my investigations.

The ANC's Jacob Zuma, who played an invaluable role behind the scenes make publication of the death squad allegations possible.

Ben Coetzee, brother of Dirk Coetzee, for allowing me to use and to quote from his unpublished biography of his brother.

Dr Frederik Van Zyl Slabbert, for writing the foreword.

All my colleagues at the *Sunday Star* and the *Weekly Mail* who contributed to unearthing the truth. I particularly want to pay tribute to *Sunday Star* journalist Kitt Katzin.

The firm of attorneys Bell, Dewar and Hall, the Independent Board of Inquiry into Informal Repression, the Human Rights Commission and Lawyers for Human Rights for generously providing me with court, inquest and commission records and opening their files to me.

This book would have been impossible without the help of many people who provided information, introductions, leads, suggestions, advice and guidance. Without the support of friends and colleagues, this investigation would never have been possible.

I wish that I had twice the time and twice the space to include everything that I originally intended. But in the end I hope I will have succeeded in contributing something to the understanding of what has happened in my country.

This book is about the death squad operatives and their victims. I wish to pay special tribute to the memory of all the victims of apartheid's death squads. Amongst them were some of South Africa's finest and brightest individuals.

I have met and come to know many SAP and SADF operatives whose personalities and characters I have described and sketched in this book as honestly as I could. I remain aghast and saddened at what I saw and heard.

Yet I remain deeply indebted to Dirk Coetzee, who has enabled me to publish his story. I want to thank him for his honesty and wish him forgiveness and happiness. He made tremendous personal sacrifices to tell his story and I truly believe that in future we will look back at Dirk Coetzee with gratitude.

Finally, I dedicate this book to Elize Viljoen.

Foreword

ANTON Lubowski was my friend. Once we travelled to New York and back in one weekend to see if we could bring about a reconciliatory meeting between Sam Nujoma of the South West Africa People's Organisation (Swapo) and Dirk Mudge of the Democratic Turnhalle Alliance (DTA). That was quite some time before the implementation of Resolution 435 began, which culminated in the Constituent Assembly elections that led to Namibia's independence. According to the following account, his assassination was probably part of a campaign to disrupt Swapo's participation in those elections. One of the CCB operatives involved called it a "terrible mistake" – a gross misstatement. His death was a mindless, brutal, senseless act of terror. Many of those are recorded in the pages of this book.

On such a long weekend flight to New York and back, a friendship deepens and explores many confidential and intimate contours of the other's existence – marriage, children, fidelity, politics, Africa, music, existential angst – the whole "sense of it all". Anton was a bighearted, lovable paradox of a man. His total absence of malice and calculation was not enough to protect those close to him from the hurt he caused them and that he himself experienced because of it. If anything, it was the consequence of a powerful zest for life and an inability to deny himself any opportunity to experience it with others. He was incapable of deliberately hurting any living thing and was filled with a deep rage by those who did. He died at the hands of such.

July 1987, Dakar, Senegal: A group of about 60 predominantly Afrikaner South Africans sit around a table with ANC executive members. Mac Maharaj talks about the ANC's armed struggle. He says: "Before I went to Robben Island I could kill in anger; when I left it, I could kill in cold blood." A chill went through the gathering and then passionate debate exploded which dominated the whole period of our interaction over the next ten days: When, if ever, is violence as a political instrument justified? What about innocent lives? When has one explored every possible non-violent source? The meeting ended without resolution except to agree to differ. The day before my return to South Africa from the Dakar meeting a bomb went off outside the Witwatersrand High Command, injuring scores of innocent civilians. The ANC accepted responsibility.

Much later, perhaps two years afterwards, in Lusaka, ANC President Oliver Tambo drew me aside and apologised for any embarrassment the bombing may have caused me, assuring me that it was not calculated to coincide with my return. The Minister of Law and Order, Adriaan Vlok, later blamed a young Afrikaner from an impeccable establishment family, Hein Grosskopf, for leading the bombing mission on behalf of Umkhonto we Sizwe (MK). This led to an outcry because Hein Grosskopf had neither been arrested nor formally charged.

I joined in the outpouring of indignation and wrote a letter of sympathy to his parents, who are well known to me. After the Tambo meeting, another Institute for a Democratic Alternative for South Africa (Idasa) conference between members of MK and those involved with the South African Defence Force took place in Lusaka. At this meeting Hein Grosskopf acknowledged that he was a member of MK and, without accepting responsibility for the High Command bombing, said he was quite willing and able to lead such a mission, even if innocent bystanders got killed.

I am not a pacifist – I can well imagine when, out of anger, fear or in a warlike situation, I might kill. But then, and now, I cannot justify cold-blooded, premeditated murder for political purposes. I lack the ideological dogmatism and moral certitudes to make this likely, and in fact, have no desire to be cursed with either. But if I cannot justify, I have come to understand how it is possible. This book deepens such understanding.

It explores how successive governments used the State apparatus to change the victims of its policies into enemies and to fashion any conceivable instrument to eliminate them. It records how some of the agents of State security can "kill in cold blood" without regard for "innocent bystanders". South Africa is not unique in this respect. Many authoritarian regimes have been exposed in their use of death squads, political assassinations and destabilisation. Almost without exception they adopted omniscient ideological delusions of grandeur of "our own total strategy" versus "total onslaught" variety. When this happens, legal accountability becomes capricious; civil liberties are crushed; society polarises; and brutality and barbarism replace the rule of law. This is true for Chile, Colombia, Romania, Uganda and South Africa.

In our case, funny little grey men wear Afro wigs, dark glasses and play 007 games with their fellow citizens. Drunk with limitless power, they decide on a whim who to "take out", "neutralize" or "eliminate" in order to save the "Fatherland" or protect themselves. They live in pockets of moral vacuity, insulated from the expository influence of the civil society they systematically set out to destroy. Some of them end up consuming endless bottles of cough mixture to stay awake from their own nightmares whilst society stumbles on in the heart of darkness.

Now, the political leaders of South Africa, from inside and outside the regime, have declared a common commitment to move away from such darkness. They tell us we hover on the threshold of a "new South Africa".

This book, like a bucket of cold water in the face, serves to remind us how fragile such a commitment is if the instruments of State security do not understand, support or are possibly even hostile to a new order. The transition to "a non-racial democratic" South Africa is incapable of being negotiated if the instruments of State security are not clearly under control and accountable to civilian authority, providing non-partisan and legitimate stability and law and order. This will have to be demonstrably evident before any serious negotiations can begin. If not, our transition will simply regress to a new kind of autocracy where, once again, laws without justice will be enforced by secret groups of people accountable only to themselves.

It is in the nature of a negotiated transition that society is denied the fresh, clean start which some believe a dramatic historical rupture provides. The legacies of the past have to be recognized and transformed; in the process the future will be created. One such legacy is the security system. We cannot afford to ignore it or pretend it does not have a history and a culture. Because if we do, we will not be able to transform it and make it serviceable to the non-racial and democratic future to which our politicians have dedicated themselves, and to us. There is no point in "a new South Africa" if innocents like Anton Lubowski are to be killed in cold blood and youngsters like Hein Grosskopf are prepared to accept responsibility for similar incidents because of the actions of State security. Such a transition is simply a gearshift into madness.

Jacques Pauw is to be commended for his resolution and courage in writing this book. Max du Preez, editor of *Vrye Weekblad*, for the same qualities and for supporting Jacques Pauw. Theirs has been a lonely and lonesome journalistic task but I have no doubt that should South Africa move into a nonracial, democratic mode of existence with a non-partisan security system constrained by and committed to the finest principles of the rule of law, future generations will look back also to the likes of them with gratitude and pride.

Dr Frederik van Zyl Slabbert

Former leader of the Official Opposition in Parliament and co-founder and director of the Institute for a Democratic Alternative for South Africa (IDASA).

June 1991

Johannesburg

Contents

"The fact that such things could take place among us is a humiliation we must henceforth face."
Albert Camus

CHAPTER ONE

Stalkers of the night

IT was late afternoon on the banks of the Komati River, between Komatipoort and the Mozambique border. A small group of men stood around two prisoners, watching as the drug at last took effect. The prisoners, manacled together, were dull-eyed and slack-jawed, swaying slightly. As they finally lapsed into unconsciousness one of their captors, well built, blond, stepped forward, in his hand a Russian-made Makarov pistol fitted with a silencer. He placed his foot against the neck of one of his captives, pressed the barrel to his head and pulled the trigger. The body gave a slight jerk, then lay still, blood oozing from the wound. Seconds later, the other was executed in the same manner.

In a dry ditch on the slightly elevated river bank, a shallow grave was dug and filled with bushveld wood and tyres. The two corpses were lifted onto the pyre and as the sun set over the Eastern Transvaal lowveld two fires were lit, one to burn the bodies to ashes, the other for the security policemen and their askaris to sit around, drinking their beer and brandy and grilling meat. All night long they drank, boasted and cracked jokes as they waited for the bodies to be cremated. They slapped the executioner on the back and commended his neat craftsmanship.

Every hour or so, one of them got up to add a new pile of wood to the fire and turn the bodies over. It took about seven hours for the dead men to be reduced to ashes, and early the next morning their remains were scooped into the river.

By midday – dirty, tired, hungover – the executioner and his friends had returned to base near Pretoria. Their commander reported a successful mission: the "terrorists" had been eliminated; no tracks and no traces had been left behind.[1]

In the months of October and November 1981 the murder of Vuyani Mavuso and Peter Dlamini went unnoticed, as did those of Eastern Cape student activist Sizwe Kondile and an unnamed Lesotho diamond dealer, but a raid into Botswana and another act of extraordinary violence and brutality made world news.

Durban, 19 November 1981. Prominent human rights lawyer and political activist Griffiths Mxenge bade a colleague goodnight and left his Victoria Street law firm. It was almost eight o'clock and a thick blanket of mist and rain looked like slowing his journey home to Umlazi. He was a worried man.

Griffiths Mxenge had fought a tireless campaign against apartheid in South Africa. The former Robben Island prisoner – affectionately known as "the ANC lawyer" – had become famous for his stand in the trials of anti-apartheid activists and for the defence of hundreds of black people arrested, detained and charged with offences under the Suppression of Communism Act, the Group Areas Act, the Terrorism Act, the Influx Control Act, the Police Act and the Pass Laws Act.

These were particularly dangerous times for opponents of the government. Mxenge's telephone was tapped, there had been threats against his life. Driving through the ghostly grey night, he turned over an ominous incident in his mind. That morning he had been awakened by the screams of his children: one of the family's bull terriers was dead on the front lawn, the other writhing in agony next to it. Rushed to the local vet, it died on the examination table. Tests revealed strychnine poisoning.[2]

"Why might someone want to poison my dogs?" he had asked colleagues at tea time. It had dearly been a professional job. Bitter-tasting strychnine cannot be rubbed onto meat; exact amounts had been inserted into little cuts.

Mxenge's rumination was disturbed by the presence of a grey pick-up van parked in the road ahead with its bonnet open. A man stepped out into the headlights, waving. Mxenge stopped his white Audi and wound his window down as the stranger approached.[3]

"Can you help us? There is something wrong with the bakkie. Don't you have jumper leads or something?"

As Mxenge got out of his car two more figures loomed out of the shadows. The man drew a pistol and pointed it straight at him. "Do as I say. Get into the back of the car."

Mxenge was pushed into the back seat of his car. One of the men slid in after him, holding a pistol against him, while another got into the driver's seat and started the car. They drove back the way he had come, with the bakkie following behind.

"Where are you taking me? Please don't kill me. You can take everything I have. You don't have to shoot me," Mxenge pleaded. There was no answer.

After a few minutes the driver turned into a dirt road and stopped the car. They were next to the Umlazi cycling stadium.

"Get out!" – a pistol jab to his ribs. Behind them, the bakkie too came to a standstill. The driver emerged with a knife in his hand.

It was very dark and wet underfoot as Mxenge was pulled from his car. The next moment, the blade of a hunting knife sank into his flesh. He fell to the ground, stabs raining down on him.

The Durban lawyer, blinded by pain and shock, managed to struggle to his feet. The driver of the bakkie stepped forward and drove the 30-centimetre blade of his Okapi knife deep into Mxenge's chest.

As the stabber tried to pull the knife from his victim's chest, Mxenge pushed him away and drew the bloody blade out of his own body. Okapi in his hand, he stumbled towards the man who only a few minutes earlier had asked him for help. The man held a tyre spanner with a sharpened end high in the air. He knocked the knife out of Mxenge's hand, stepped forward and hammered him over the head.

This time Mxenge didn't get up again. The killer pack pounced on him, hitting, kicking and stabbing. When the job was finished they removed his jacket, watch and wallet and drove off with their victim's brand-new car into the dark.

By this time, Nonyamezelo Victoria Mxenge already feared that something terrible had happened to her husband. She had left the law practice shortly before Griffiths, expecting him home a few minutes after her. Earlier that day, he had told her that he was frightened by the death of the dogs and that he would try to get others from a friend as soon as possible.

The couple knew that they were both prime targets for right-wing violence. Another possibility that tormented Victoria was that Griffiths might once again have been incarcerated by the police's Security Branch.

At eight-thirty, having phoned friends and colleagues to find out if they knew where her husband was, she decided to drive back to Durban to look for him. Her younger son, Viwe, accompanied her. She went to the office, but found no sign of him. She went back home, made some more calls and then waited up through the night.[4]

Griffiths Mlungisi Mxenge was born in King William's Town and obtained a BA degree from the University of Fort Hare, the same institution ANC leaders Nelson Mandela and Oliver Tambo had graduated from 20 years earlier.[5]

No teenager of his generation could escape the influence of the Defiance Campaign of 1952, the historic Congress of the People in 1955, the Pound-a-Day Campaign, or the State of Emergency of 1960. Like thousands of others, Mxenge had become a member of the outlawed ANC's Youth League.

By March 1966, when Griffiths was slammed with his first banning order, he had already served 190 days in political detention. Victoria was expecting their first child at the time. The baby, a boy they named Mbasa, was born in May 1966.[6]

A year later, Griffiths was convicted under the Suppression of Communism Act for furthering the aims of the ANC and sentenced to two years' imprisonment on Robben Island. Upon his release in 1969, he was banned for another two years.

3

Further problems arose when, on completion of his articles, Mxenge sought admission as an attorney. Because of his conviction under the Suppression of Communism Act he could not gain admission automatically. Eventually, in 1974, after many representations, Justice Minister Jimmy Kruger relented and gave him special permission to practise his profession. One of the first cases he accepted concerned whether or not the word "kaffir" is offensive. He lost the battle in the magistrate's court, but won on appeal before the Judge-President of Natal.

In March 1976, Mxenge was taken into custody again. This time, after being detained for 109 days, he was subpoenaed to give evidence in a case he himself had been instructed to handle. He refused, arguing that since the person he was called to testify against was a client he would be guilty of a breach of ethics if he gave evidence against him. The court ruled in his favour.

During 1978 he appeared for some of the accused in the mammoth Pan Africanist Congress trial in the southeastern Transvaal town of Bethal. He also featured in the case of Joseph Mduli and Mapetla Mohapi – both of whom died in police cells while being detained by the security police.

Mxenge served on the Release Mandela Committee, was a member of Lawyers for Human Rights and a founder member of the South African Democratic Lawyers' Association, which is an affiliate of the International Society of Jurists.

Victoria Mxenge, born in a dusty village in the Eastern Cape, chose nursing as a profession and trained at Victoria Hospital near Fort Hare and Durban's King Edward VII before working at a clinic in Umlazi. It was only in 1974 that she enrolled for a law degree at the University of South Africa. She began working with her husband in 1975 and became a fully fledged attorney in February 1981.[7]

As dawn broke at five o'clock on the morning of 20 November, Victoria could wait no longer. She drove to the King Edward VII Hospital, then to St. Aidan's Hospital and the CR Swart Police Station to make enquiries about her husband. Nobody knew anything about his whereabouts and she went home again. Just after eight, she phoned Brigadier Jan van der Hoven, head of the Security Branch in Natal, who told her that his men had not detained her husband.

She finally drove to the government mortuary in Durban, where she was shown the body of an "unknown black male" brought in earlier that morning in the back of a police van. The corpse was naked and covered with a piece of cloth. It was the mutilated body of Griffiths Mxenge.

Shortly after identifying his body, Victoria had to inform family, friends and colleagues of the brutal murder. "My husband died in great pain. His throat was slashed, his stomach ripped open and his ears almost cut off. The rest of his body was covered with stab wounds. I don't believe this is the work of ordinary thugs, it was done by someone who was opposed to what he stood for," she said.[8]

News about the murder of Griffiths Mxenge spread rapidly. One of the first to offer his condolences was ANC president Oliver Tambo: "Agents of the Pretoria regime have brutally assassinated Griffiths Mxenge. Fare well, dear brother and comrade. Your sacrifice is not in vain," his message read.[9]

The chief of the Security Branch, General Johan Coetzee, appeared to agree that it was no ordinary murder, but he pointed a finger at the ANC itself. It was known, he said in a statement, that there was dissatisfaction within the ANC about the manner in which Mxenge had been managing funds sent by a number of overseas support organisations. Authorities had looked into the alleged misappropriation and, he continued, "Police are investigating various theories surrounding the death of Mr Mxenge, including the possibility that the ANC may have acted against him."[10]

Victoria dismissed Coetzee's allegations and took a pledge never to rest until she had found her husband's assassins. "When people have declared war on you, you cannot afford to be crying. You have to fight back. As long as I live, I will never rest until I see to it that justice is done, until GM's killers are brought to book."

Three days after the murder, a forester in the Piet Retief district on the Swazi border investigated the source of a cloud of black smoke rising over his farm, and found Mxenge's burning car.

Griffiths Mxenge was laid to rest a week after he was slain. From far and near, workers, professional and business people, students and peasants converged on the tiny hamlet of Rayi, just outside King William's Town, to pay their last respects.

At dawn on the day of burial, 15 000 mourners gathered to pay tribute to the dead man. Speaker after speaker stood up to tell the sombre throng that Mxenge's death must not be in vain. It was a day of rededication, of unity and of resolve.

Albertina Sisulu, patron of the United Democratic Front (UDF) and wife of the then jailed ANC leader, Walter Sisulu, told the crowd: "It is true that Mr Mxenge died for all the oppressed people of this country. But there is a particular group of people who have suffered a more immediate loss. These are the hundreds of black people who are daily arrested and detained . . . he had dedicated his whole life to the defence of these people."[11]

Bishop Desmond Tutu, then Secretary-General of the South African Council of Churches, told the mourners: "Our liberation is going to be costly. Many more will be detained. Many more will be banned. But we shall be free."[12]

As Mxenge's coffin, draped in the colours of the ANC, was lowered into the ground, a Transkei security policeman was found covertly tape recording the proceedings. Desmond Tutu and another priest tried in vain to shield Detective-Constable Albert Gungqwama Tafile from a frenzied mob screaming: "Kill, kill the *impimpi* (sell-out)!"

"Have you come here to bury Griffiths or kill one another?" shouted the bishop, his white robes splattered with blood, as the battered policeman lay dying behind the makeshift VIP platform.[13]

Two days after burying her husband, Victoria Mxenge was back in Durban, sitting behind his desk. "I want to run this office the way GM would have liked it to be run. I cannot just give up his work. I'll continue where he left off. If by killing my husband they thought the work he was doing would come to an end, they have made a mistake. I'll continue even if it means I must also die. A rough life is part and parcel of me now."[14]

As telling of the times was the official inquest held in the Durban magistrate's court six months later. If Victoria Mxenge feared a sinister official hand in her husband's death, the way the inquest was conducted can have done nothing to put her mind at ease. To an increasingly incredulous and outraged world South African inquests into the deaths of suspected activists were coming to display an almost ant-like unity of purpose among the officers of the state.

Forensic pathologist Barend van Straaten told the court that 45 wounds had been found on the deceased's body and that the cause of death was "multiple clean-cut injuries to the lungs, liver and heart". The majority of wounds had been caused by a knife or knives but a number of wounds on the head had been inflicted by a blunt-edged instrument "like a hammer".[15]

State Counsel André Oberholzer chose to pursue the allegations linking Mxenge and his death to the ANC. He immediately gave expression to the white government's obsession with the defenders of black liberation movements – and particularly those evading the ever-widening scope of measures to cut off their funding.

Oberholzer: "Where did the money come from to defend these people [Mxenge's clients]?"

Mrs Mxenge: "From various sources."

Oberholzer: "From the ANC?"

Mrs Mxenge: "No."

Oberholzer: "There was an allegation that your husband was involved in the misappropriation of ANC funds. Do you know anything of that?"

Mrs Mxenge: "That allegation has no foundation whatsoever."

Oberholzer: "You like to make bold statements. Why do you say that it is impossible for the ANC to have killed your husband?"

Mrs Mxenge: "Why would they kill him?"

Oberholzer: "Don't ask me questions, answer my questions."

Mrs Mxenge: "Because there was absolutely no reason why they would kill him."

Oberholzer: "Who do you think killed him?"

Mrs Mxenge: "I am not able to point at people. People who hated him are people who alleged that he was leftist. Those are the people who hated him so they are the only people who could have killed him as far as I am concerned."

Oberholzer: "Don't the ANC have right-wing activists as well?"

. . .

Oberholzer: "And the general [Johan Coetzee] also lied when he said that [Mxenge might have been killed by his own comrades]?"

Mrs Mxenge: "Yes, I can face the general, he is sucking it from his thumb."

On the poisoning of the two dogs –

Oberholzer: "Did [Mxenge] reveal that his life was also in danger?"

Mrs Mxenge: "It could be inferred from the killing of the dogs that there was somebody who wanted to get into the house to do some sinister thing."

Oberholzer: "It's a well-known fact that very recently several animals were poisoned in the Pinetown [a white suburb] area. I can't see that your husband will now say there is a sinister plan to get to him."

Mrs Mxenge: "We are not staying in the Pinetown area and no dogs had been killed in Umlazi."

During the inquest, Victoria testified that the owner of a sauna parlour next to the Mxenges' law practice had told them that she had been approached by security policemen who said they wanted to bug the law firm's telephones from her business premises.

Under cross-examination, the investigating officer, Detective Sergeant Christopher Shange, could not explain what had happened to Mxenge's shirt, which could have provided valuable evidence, why the lawyer's body had been removed from the scene without photographs being taken and why a written statement from the last man to see Mxenge alive was only taken five months after the murder.

At this point, Counsel for the Mxenge family, Louis Skweyiya, exclaimed: "Your Worship, there is a complete lack of investigation. I'm going to argue in the end that this case was never investigated."

Here, at least, the magistrate, Victor Patterson, agreed – up to a point: "I do not say there was a complete lack of investigation. I said that it is apparent to me that the investigations were not done the same as you and I would have expected."

The investigation, it appeared, had been left to the inexperienced and frightened Christopher Shange, who had clearly been more completely on his own than he realised. He confessed that the pocketbook he had been using at the time of his investigation into the murder had disappeared into thin air from the filing room of the police station.

"This is the difficulty we have in this whole saga," Skweyiya protested. "This is an important piece of information which we could have used to help us determine the truth of this matter and now it is missing."

In September 1983, nearly two years after the slaying of Griffiths Mxenge, the magistrate gave his findings: death was caused by "the act of some unknown person or persons".

Patterson added: "I know that criticism has been levelled at the police but I think that they did try. If they had known that there was going to be such a cross-examination, that every action was going to be placed under the searchlight, perhaps more would have been done under the circumstances."

Certain inconsistencies had arisen and certain matters had not been properly explained, Patterson said, but he did not elaborate. He dismissed as speculation the assertion that Mxenge had been assassinated for political reasons.

Victoria Mxenge, who had been present throughout the inquest hearing, said that she had expected such a finding. However, she said, she was convinced that some day she would discover the identity of her husband's killers.

On 20 July 1985 a crowd of 50 000 people packed the dusty Lingelihle Stadium near Cradock to pay their last respects to four community leaders brutally killed three weeks before.

The coffins of Matthew Goniwe and Fort Calata were covered in red velvet, and those of Sparrow Mkontho and Sicelo Mhlawuli in the black, yellow and green colours of the ANC. The four, all prominent members of the UDF, had gone missing on 27 June after attending a meeting. Their bodies were found days later dumped in the veld near Port Elizabeth.

Victoria Mxenge spoke at the funeral, describing the murders as a "dastardly act of cowardice". During her visit to the Eastern Cape she had visited her husband's grave and recalled the anger and grief that had surrounded his death and drawn thousands of mourners to his funeral, too. The dead, she told the mourners, had gone as messengers to the forefathers. "Go well, peacemakers. Tell your great grandfathers we are coming because we are prepared to die for Africa," she cried out.[16]

Those were prophetic words. Twelve days later Victoria Mxenge was stabbed and shot by four men who ambushed her as she arrived at her home in Umlazi. She died in hospital that same evening, her own brutal death as much a mystery as that of her husband.[17]

Victoria was killed as she got out of a car driven by the Reverend Mcebisi Xundu, chairperson of the UDF in Natal and an old family friend.

"We had just returned from Pietermaritzburg at about seven o'clock and I was helping her collect her parcels from my car when four men came rushing from the bushes across the road into the driveway," the Reverend said. At first he thought it was her children's friends playing a silly game but then he heard the murderers shouting as they rushed towards her. She grabbed her parcels and fled down the driveway screaming for help. Two shots went off. Xundu, who was still seated behind the steering wheel of his car, reversed out of the driveway at great speed and rushed to the police station.

The men caught up with Victoria as she reached the side of the house. The children were in the front garden when their mother was attacked. Victoria's 19-year-old son, Mbasa, said that one of the killers pointed a gun at his head, asking if he would have to shoot him as well. Mbasa fled across the road and seconds later heard two shots and his mother screaming. He returned to see his mother lying face down in a pool of blood. He rushed her to hospital but it was too late.[18]

The killing of Victoria Mxenge, and the manner in which it was done, drew outraged reaction. The United Democratic Front and the Azanian People's Organisation, the two major black anti-apartheid organisations within the country at that time, blamed "agents of apartheid" for the murder. The UDF described it as a cold-blooded assassination, a devilish act aimed at wiping out the leadership of the organisation.

Even the Reagan Administration condemned the killing. In an unusually strong reaction, a State Department spokesman said: "Mrs Mxenge was well known in South Africa and to many American diplomats who had served there as a dedicated, humane person. Her killing is a heinous and horrible crime. We call on the South African Government to bring to book the perpetrators of the crime."[19]

In a glowing tribute, the celebrated black newspaper editor Percy Qoboza wrote: "Victoria Mxenge was a special person. So special that even my young kids, who have never met her personally but only through newspaper columns, wept hysterically. In a strange way, they identified with her emotionally. What appals me most is the deafening silence on the part of the Government over this latest incident. No message of condolence to the children of this tragedy, nothing – just silence. I am not suggesting that the Government offer its condolences at the drop of a hat, but Victoria was not just anybody. Or should I assume, like Steve Biko, they did not know who she was? I doubt it."[20]

On Griffiths Mxenge's death, Victoria had been elevated from obscurity to the forefront of black politics in Natal. Once a virtual unknown in politics, now she sat on the executive of the Natal Organisation of Women and the

United Democratic Front, and was a member of the Release Mandela Committee.

However, her real influence was among the youth who loved her as their adopted mother. Two years before her death, she had successfully defended students against the confiscation of their examination results by the Department of Education and Training. The day after her death students took to the streets in their thousands in protest, calling for a week-long boycott of classes in mourning.[21]

Victoria Mxenge was gunned down a few days before 16 UDF and Natal Indian Congress members were due to appear in the Pietermaritzburg Supreme Court on charges of treason. As a member of the defence team she had spent months collecting evidence and many felt her death was connected to the trial. At the opening of the trial, Natal's Judge President, Mr Justice Milne, acknowledged the public mood when he deplored the killing in a personal statement to the packed courtroom.

"It grieves me to have to record that one of the most recent of the tragic and deplorable acts of violence that are afflicting this country is Mrs Mxenge's death," Milne said.[22]

Victoria Mxenge was buried next to her husband in the small cemetery at Ryai. Messages in tribute from Nelson Mandela and Oliver Tambo were read out at the funeral. More than 10 000 mourners listened as the array of speakers condemned the murder.

The anger of the crowd found sudden expression in one more act of violence. On the way to the cemetery a Ciskeian army truck carrying three soldiers – ignorant stooges of a sell-out government, in the eyes of the mourners – overtook the funeral procession. As youths threatened the apparently bewildered black soldiers and pelted them with stones, one of the men leapt from the truck and ran for the veld. Corporal Mnyamezeli Bless, shouting "Amandla" in a desperate and pathetic bid to appease the incensed crowd, was caught, beaten and stoned. A tyre was put around his body, doused with petrol and set alight.[23]

More than two years later, a Durban magistrate refused to allow a formal inquest into the death of Victoria Mxenge. A formal inquest would have allowed witnesses and policemen to be called and cross-examined. Magistrate FM Vorster said that it was "not the court's function to examine police on the course of their investigation". His ruling: "Victoria Mxenge died of head injuries and was murdered by a person or persons unknown."[24]

The magistrate's findings are typical. At least six anti-apartheid activists were assassinated in South Africa before Griffiths Mxenge, and a further 81 have died in mysterious circumstances since then (see Annexure A). In each case, an inquest court has made the predictable finding: murdered by a person or persons unknown, and in each case there has been a conspicuous failure on the part of the South African Police to apprehend the killers.

To the mourners of Griffiths and Victoria Mxenge and those who tried to keep a tally of unsolved murders of liberal and radical opponents of the government, it was evident that something singularly unwholesome had taken root in the country.

But the magistrates had ruled and the dockets were closed. Or so everyone thought.

CHAPTER TWO

Testimony of an assassin

NOVEMBER 7, 1989. It was a warm and sunny day on the tropical island of Mauritius. A few metres away children were splashing in the crystal-clear water of the Indian Ocean. Further along the beach, sundrenched holiday-makers looked like multicoloured speckles on the snow-white sand.

Sitting cross-legged next to me on the beach under a swaying palm tree, slowly sipping a frosty beer, was Dirk Johannes Coetzee, his handsome face tanned and clean-shaven, a slick of hair over his forehead. Two days before, we had booked into a tourist hotel on the southern tip of the island. On the face of it, we were just two ordinary holidaymakers enjoying the ambiance of the island that has become one of South Africa's most popular vacation destinations.

But this was no holiday. We were booked into the hotel under false names. Every night after dinner, we would retreat to our rooms and Dirk Coetzee would start talking into my tape-recorder. Three times a day, we had to book urgent calls to London and Johannesburg.

The trip to Mauritius was the culmination of weeks of secret planning, of late-night meetings, cryptic messages smuggled to the Political-Military Council of the ANC and clandestine visits to the organisation's headquarters in Lusaka.

Dirk Coetzee is a former security policeman, holder of a police medal for faithful service, the best student of his police college intake nearly 20 years earlier. But Dirk Coetzee was no ordinary policeman.

"I was the commander of a South African Police death squad. I was in the heart of the whore. My men and I had to murder political and security opponents of the police and the government. I know the deepest secrets of this special unit, which acted above the law and enjoyed very special protection."

The man sitting in front of me had planned and commanded the assassination of Griffiths Mxenge.[1]

During those three days in Mauritius, Coetzee would describe to me, in the grimmest detail, the death squad's murder missions in South Africa, Swaziland, Lesotho and Botswana. Wherever Coetzee and his squad went, they left a bloody rail of death and destruction. People were shot, poisoned, harassed, burnt, stabbed and blown to pieces. Cars were stolen, dogs poisoned and houses bombed.

Dirk Coetzee admitted his involvement in at least 23 serious crimes committed in "the line of duty" as a member of the South African security police. It was a bloodcurdling tale that spanned three countries and included six murders, attempted murder and conspiracy to murder, arson, sabotage, kidnapping, housebreaking and various incidents of car theft. All these crimes had been committed between January 1977 and December 1981. Besides the six murders he "officially" committed, he was also involved in the murder of a Lesotho national during an abortive illicit diamond deal. Most of the serious crimes were committed between September and December 1981 when, in an orgy of violence, four murders, the attempted murder, arson and some of the car thefts were committed. The diamond dealer was also murdered during this period.

Some of South Africa's top policemen were implicated, among them the former Commissioner of Police, General Johan Coetzee, the police's forensic expert and third highest ranking officer, General Lothar Neethling, and various security police brigadiers and colonels.

Dirk Coetzee had turned against his former comrades in the police force, his Afrikaner "Volk" and his government. He knew that when his death squad allegations were published he would be branded a traitor and a liar.

And while we were sitting on the beach drawing up a statement, the ANC – the dreaded communists and terrorists he had hated, hunted and fought – were preparing to meet the 44-year-old death squad commander in London to take him into their protection and give him sanctuary.

The former policeman, who had killed and maimed supporters of the ANC "for Volk and Vaderland, for my wife and my children and my mother and my father", was about to walk into the enemy's lair and beg for mercy and forgiveness.

"Make a plan with Griffiths Mxenge," Brigadier Jan van der Hoven, chief of the Security Branch in Natal, gave the order. "He is a former Robben Island convict and an attorney who gives us a lot of trouble. Mxenge defends accused in terrorist trials and more than R100 000 from the ANC recently passed through his account. We tried to build up a case against him, but failed. We just do not have enough evidence to charge him."

Captain Dirk Coetzee, commander of a security police counter-insurgency unit based at Vlakplaas, a secret police farm just outside Pretoria, had never heard of Mxenge. "What do you want us to do with him?"

"Don't shoot or abduct him. It must look like a robbery," was Van der Hoven's instruction. A few minutes later, Coetzee left the brigadier's office to report to a local security police captain who would give him more information on the whereabouts and daily routine of his target.

Coetzee and his team of "askaris" – former ANC and Pan Africanist Congress guerrillas who had been captured, "turned" and drafted into the security police – had come to Durban for surveillance work. The ostensible task of the ANC and PAC defectors was to identify their former comrades and arrest them. But over the years, only a few ANC and PAC guerrillas had been apprehended by the Vlakplaas contingents. This secret unit was involved in a much more secret and dirty campaign against supporters and members of the ANC. As Coetzee explained, "We were fighting fire with fire. They killed us, and we killed them. It was a war without rules."

Coetzee said that was why he never questioned the command of his superior officer when he was told to eliminate the Durban attorney, who according to the brigadier was a "blatant ANC perpetrator" and revolutionary. If they couldn't catch him, they could always kill him.

Shortly after this briefing Coetzee called his team of askaris (a Swahili word meaning black soldier) together and explained their mission. The askaris were David "Spyker" Tshikalange (his nickname means "nail" in Afrikaans), Almond Nofemela and Brian Ngqulunga. Coetzee had already asked Van der Hoven to send another askari, Joe Mamasela, down to Durban to assist them.

"Joe and Almond did not smoke or drink and were both intelligent, fit and in my judgement had a killer instinct. I intended these two to form the core of the death squad assigned to kill Mxenge," Coetzee said. Ngqulunga was a Zulu and knew the Umlazi area; Tshikalange – whom Coetzee had drafted into the security police – was his former gardener and trusted friend. Two white security policemen based at Vlakplaas, Captain Koos Vermeulen and Warrant Officer Paul van Dyk, were also involved in the planning.

For the next day or two, the squad did surveillance on Mxenge, following him from his house to his office, around Durban and back home at night. Nofemela and Mamasela worked out the details of the murder plan. Coetzee told them that it had to look like a robbery and that therefore they should stab or club their man to death, take some of his personal possessions and leave in his car.

Coetzee cautioned them to wear old shoes and clothes that could be destroyed afterwards and also to empty their pockets before the attempt so that nothing could be lost at the scene of the crime. He gave the four askaris a big hunting knife and two Okapi knives.

The askaris decided to kill Mxenge as he arrived home from work, but they were worried about the presence of the bull terriers and asked Coetzee to get rid of them. He obtained a chunk of meat from the local police mess, which he cut into four pieces, inserting a small amount of strychnine into each. That night, they drove to Mxenge's home, where Nofemela got out and threw the meat over the wall.

The askaris decided to kill Mxenge the following night, as heavy rain in the Durban area meant that they would leave virtually no tracks. Coetzee arranged to pick them up at a Durban bar just after the murder. "When I arrived at the bar at about ten o'clock that Thursday night, the four had already changed into other clothes and were waiting for me. Joe was wearing Mxenge's jacket and his silver watch, and held his wallet in his hand. I called them outside, where they told me that at the last minute they had changed their murder plan and eventually killed Mxenge near a stadium in Umlazi. David told me his Okapi got stuck in Mxenge's chest."

Coetzee took the clothes they had worn during the attack, the knives and Mxenge's belongings and put them in the boot of his car. The askaris gave him Mxenge's car keys and told him that the Audi was parked at the CR Swart Police Station. That same night, they fitted false number plates to the car and Paul van Dyk left for northern Natal.

Coetzee reported to Jan van der Hoven late that night. "Have you left any traces?" the brigadier asked. Coetzee told him not to worry, they were going to destroy all possible evidence. The next morning, Van der Hoven told him that the askaris must immediately return to Vlakplaas. As the askaris returned to base, Coetzee left Durban to team up with Van Dyk.

They burnt the wallet and jacket near the Pongola River and threw the watch and original number plates into the water. Coetzee cannot remember what they did with the hunting knives. Returning to Pretoria with Mxenge's car, he was instructed by the chief of the Security Branch in the Northern Transvaal, Brigadier Jan du Preez, to get rid of it – burn it – as soon as possible.

The next day, a Sunday afternoon, Coetzee, Van Dyk, Koos Vermeulen and Sergeant Koos Schutte, foreman at Vlakplaas, left for the Swazi border in Mxenge's car. They were cheerful, Coetzee said, drinking brandy and beer as Schutte played his mouth organ and guitar in the back of the car.

Near the Swazi border, they turned into a forestry road and parked the car a few metres from the border fence in an opening between two plantations. Van Dyk, who had previously served on the Swazi border, knew the spot well and told them that it was famous for ANC guerrillas entering and leaving the country illegally. Before they poured petrol into the boot, on the seats and on the engine, Schutte removed the car radio and speakers. As they drove away, they could see the red glow of the burning car in the distance.

The next morning, Coetzee had a meeting with Du Preez and the head of the ANC-PAC desk at Security Branch headquarters, Brigadier Willem Schoon, who was also in charge of the Vlakplaas units. They decided that Nofemela, Tshikalange and Mamasela should each receive a bonus of R1 000 for the excellent work they had done. Nofemela bought Lionel Richie records, clothes and gifts for his eight siblings while Tshikalange gave his bounty to Coetzee for safekeeping. Ngqulunga, who according to the others played a passive role in the murder, did not receive any award. The brand-new radio from Mxenge's car was installed in Jan du Preez's state-subsidised Mercedes-

Benz. Sitting on the beach in Mauritius, the truth about the death of Griffiths Mxenge was no surprise to me. For the past month, I had listened time and time again to the same story as Coetzee tried to persuade me, my editor and a representative of the ANC that he was indeed a murderer. In fact, it was a story that I had first heard five years earlier.

I was introduced to Dirk Coetzee by my friend and colleague Martin Welz towards the end of 1984. At first glance he struck me as an open-faced Afrikaner, no different from many thousands with whom I would rub shoulders on a daily basis in Pretoria. But I soon discovered that he was a strange man with an extraordinary story.

Coetzee had compiled a report about telephone tapping by the security police and sent it to the then leader of the official opposition in the House of Assembly, Dr Frederik van Zyl Slabbert. The report caused a sensation in Parliament, but a few days later, Coetzee was suspended and had to face an internal police inquiry.

Coetzee was clearly embittered against the security police. During our first encounter, he told me that they were waging a terrible vendetta against him, not only tapping his telephone, but also breaking into his house to look for official police documents. He therefore kept a deadly puff-adder in a small backyard storeroom to guard some valuable documents he intended to produce at his internal trial.

To show me with how much contempt he regarded the tapping of his private telephone, he picked up the instrument and started swearing. He described in the most vivid detail and obscene language which members of the force were sleeping with whose wives. He called a senior general a scoundrel and an adulterer for having a sleazy affair with the wife of a well-known Supreme Court judge.

He explained that as soon as he lifted the handset – before even dialling a number – the tape recorder at Security Branch headquarters would start turning and the policeman monitoring his calls would have had to listen to his vulgar diatribe. It was clear to me that these one-sided telephone conversations provided him much merriment.

Coetzee's telephone manners landed him in deep trouble soon afterwards when he told the senior police officer listening to his calls that his wife was having a red-hot love affair with a close friend, who was also a security policeman! Both men instituted civil proceedings against Coetzee, and in the end he had to pay them R100 each and legal costs of R20 000. His offensive language over the telephone would also be used to discredit him at his internal police inquiry.

A few days after this absurd meeting, Martin and I saw the rebel cop again. He was very talkative that night, tattling endlessly about his escapades in the police force. Coetzee was regaling us with the security police's torture skills when I asked him: "Come now, Dirk, we all know they torture people.

But tell us about the other things they do. What did you do when you were there?"

For the next hour, I listened in awe and almost total disbelief. It was a story reminiscent of a political thriller, but Coetzee assured me it was all too real. He told us about "a Durban attorney" they had stabbed to death, about a young anti-apartheid activist from Port Elizabeth who had mysteriously disappeared after being poisoned by security police, and how they had stolen an Eastern Cape labour union's microbus from a Johannesburg hotel.

At that time I was a reporter with the Afrikaans Sunday newspaper *Rapport*, and being a typical Afrikaner from a fairly conservative Pretoria background, I had no recollection of activists who had disappeared or been murdered in mysterious circumstances.

I remembered the Soweto uprising of 1976, but had been much more interested in the current All Black rugby tour. Black kids being gunned down by white policemen were far removed from my privileged surburban existence. I knew that Steve Biko, the Black Consciousness leader, had died a year later in police custody, but the anger and bitterness surrounding his death never touched me.

In fact, at that time the only political assassination that had ever made an impression on me was when I was six years old and my sister came running towards me sobbing hysterically. "Doctor Hendrik Verwoerd has just been murdered!" she informed me and my friend Heinrich where we were playing Robinson Crusoe in our tree house. That night, my mother and father cried when they listened to the news over the radio. I suppose I cried as well. The morning after the assassination, I had to attend a prayer meeting where everybody cried again. The Afrikaner nation was torn apart by grief and bitterness over the death of their beloved prime minister.

It was only after I had met Dirk Coetzee that I realised how many times South Africa's black people must have grieved about yet another detainee who had slipped on soap in a police cell shower, fractured his own skull on an interrogation room wall, fallen out of a window, disappeared from the face of the earth – or simply been assassinated.

The morning after Coetzee told me about security police atrocities, I looked at newspaper clippings about assassinations and disappearances of anti-apartheid activists and soon recognised the "Durban attorney" as Griffiths Mxenge and the young Eastern Cape activist as Siphiwo Mtimkulu. Their names were new to me. When the events took place in late 1981, I had just started my career in journalism and their fate was simply not important to me or to the Afrikaans daily newspaper for which I worked.

I discussed Coetzee's allegations with Martin Welz and suggested that we should try to do something with our newly acquired knowledge. Welz said it was an off-the-record conversation, we couldn't possibly jeopardise Coetzee's safety and there was no prospect that *Rapport*, which supported the government, would publish the allegations. In any case, the political climate in 1984 was not conducive to the exposure of security force atrocities. It was dangerous knowledge we had obtained and we should keep it to ourselves. I discovered years later that Coetzee had told Welz in much more detail about his involvement and had also mentioned the existence of death squads to some very prominent parliamentary politicians.

I saw Coetzee regularly during his police trial and until early 1986, when he received his medical discharge from the force. I later questioned him again about Vlakplaas and his death squad, but he was evasive, saying that I might do something irresponsible and get him into deep trouble. For the next three years, I kept my knowledge secret, knowing what the security police are capable of doing if they regard somebody as an enemy.

One Monday night in September 1989, Coetzee and I had dinner at a Portuguese restaurant in Pretoria. It was a few days after the assassination of Anton Lubowski, a Namibian advocate and prominent white member of the South-West Africa People's Organisation. Earlier that year Dr David Webster, anthropologist and prominent foe of apartheid, had been shot dead outside his home in Johannesburg. Because of what Coetzee had told me four years before, I knew that there was a strong possibility that death squads, operating with the consent of the state, were responsible for the elimination of Lubowski and Webster. I asked Coetzee to give me more information about death squads and to tell me exactly what his involvement had been. I had plans then to write a novel based on his life and times in the security police.

Coetzee had just become involved in a new business venture to trace the owners of cars that had been stolen and recovered and did not want to jeopardise the scheme. His partner in the new venture was a police general's son. However, after I had vowed never to reveal or publish what he was about to tell me without his consent, he gave me a full account of his personal involvement. Coetzee told me in explicit detail how Griffiths Mxenge was eliminated and how he had also murdered two ANC members on a farm near Komatipoort and burnt their bodies after poison obtained from General Lothar Neethling at the police's forensic laboratory had failed to work.

He said that the parcel bomb that killed Ruth First, wife of South African Communist Party Secretary-General Joe Slovo, had been sent to her by the security police's foreign section. He described how a murder mission to kill ANC exile Marius Schoon had been called off at the last minute, though his wife and daughter, Jeanette and Katryn, were eventually killed in 1984 by a parcel bomb sent to them in exile. He described various operations in Swaziland and Botswana, how an ANC member's hand had been blown away when he opened a post box and how he had killed an infiltrator and a child with a powerful bomb placed against the wall of a house. In Botswana,

18

a woman had been shot point-blank when the squad attacked her house in Gaborone.

Coetzee described his past friendship with superspy and later member of the President's Council, Major Craig Williamson, who had told him that the security police were responsible for the 1982 bomb blast at the ANC's European headquarters in London. The explosives used in the attack had been smuggled into the British capital in a diplomatic bag.

I asked Coetzee whether he felt any remorse. "I don't know," he replied. "I did it for Volk and Vaderland and I believed then that it was the right thing to do. After I was kicked out of the force, I realised that I had been used to do their dirty work."

I also asked him under what circumstances he would be prepared to have his allegations investigated and finally published in a newspaper. "Well, get me out of the country and find me a safe place where my family and I can live in peace. Then I will tell the whole world what I did and what I know."

South Africa had changed substantially since the middle eighties. The South Africa of September 1989 was not the South Africa of 1984 or 1985. The repressive and authoritarian rule of State President PW Botha had come to a merciful end and South Africa was slowly moving towards a more open, free and just society.

My own position had changed dramatically. From working for newspapers loyal and devoted to the government's policies, I had become a founder member of the independent and free-thinking *Vrye Weekblad*, which was part of the so-called alternative press and the only Afrikaans newspaper to the left of the government. The editor of *Vrye Weekblad*, Max du Preez (in some circles known as "Mad Max"), is a daring and fearless editor. If there was one newspaper with the guts to publish Coetzee's allegations, it was *Vrye Weekblad*.

Since its inception in November 1988, *Vrye Weekblad* had been a controversial newspaper, challenging the government on issues such as conscription, security legislation and state corruption. The government regarded us as a threat to state security and *Vrye Weekblad* had to pay the highest deposit in South African newspaper history before being allowed to register and publish.

We started the newspaper with only the savings of the five journalists involved and a R10 000 overdraft from a friendly but nervous bank manager. Conservative Afrikaners accused us of being traitors to the cause of Afrikaner nationalism. In some circles we were described as woolly-headed Afrikaner revolutionaries.

The first edition of *Vrye Weekblad* was filled with the issues and personalities that the Afrikaans media had been sweeping under the carpet for more than a generation. Splashed across the front page was an assessment of the positive role that the release of jailed ANC leader Nelson Mandela could have on South African politics. We alleged that former State President PW Botha had connections with a notorious Mafia boss. The State President promptly threatened to sue for defamation, but never pursued the matter.

In the next edition we published an article debating an economic argument by Joe Slovo, who according to security legislation at that time could not be quoted. Du Preez was convicted under the Internal Security Act and a long and bitter state campaign against the newspaper started. We became the most persecuted and prosecuted newspaper of the decade, leaving Max du Preez with a criminal record. Legal costs became the newspaper's highest single expense.

There was no advertising forthcoming. Within three months, the unpaid-for computers were repossessed and the newspaper skipped an edition. (Fortunately, it was Labour Day, which gave us an excuse.) By the end of six months, *Vrye Weekblad* had received substantial foreign funding, and things looked better.

The morning after my conversation with Dirk Coetzee, I told Du Preez about the death squad allegations and that the only way we could ever hope to expose the security police was if we could find Coetzee refuge outside South Africa. We realised that even if we could find the money to sponsor such a venture, it would be virtually impossible for Coetzee to live anywhere in the world if it was known that he had been a death squad commander. He might have to flee the rest of his life from both the South African Police and the ANC, and would always run the risk of being extradited back to South Africa.

There was only one way out: the African National Congress. If we could get Coetzee to the ANC and if it was willing to protect and harbour him, we could expose one of the most taboo political stories of the decade. Allegations of shadowy death squads had been around for years, but with harsh laws making it an offence to publish untested allegations about police conduct, no South African newspaper had seriously tackled the issue.

It was at once a frightening, exciting and terribly dangerous suggestion. In October 1989, the ANC was still a banned and outlawed organisation. Handing Coetzee over to "the enemy" constituted a very serious criminal offence and, according to past judgements, furthering the aims of the ANC warranted a long jail sentence.

But how would Coetzee react to such a suggestion? I knew that he had voted for the Conservative Party in the general election less than a month before. It was almost impossible to contemplate an apartheid assassin joining ranks with his former enemy.

And the ANC? What had it to gain? For many years, its leaders had claimed that they had evidence of the existence of apartheid death squads. Coetzee could corroborate their suspicions and information. They could, of course, also use him for propaganda purposes. But would they be prepared to protect and harbour a former death squad operator? How would they explain it to their supporters?

Max and I considered our options, but each time came back to the ANC as the logical solution. We realised then that before we could publish any allegations, we would need some corroboration for Coetzee's story. The ANC was the only organisation other than the South African security services with the intelligence capabilities to verify at least some of his allegations.

Why was it so important to publish this story? Let's face it, it was a hell of a newspaper story, the kind of exposé and scoop that every journalist and editor dreams about. But there was another, more important reason. This was a story that South Africans had the right to hear. We were dealing here with allegations that struck to the very heart of government ethics and morality. Death squads were a blot on all of us.

After all, Du Preez argued, an Afrikaner government was responsible for creating death squads: therefore we as Afrikaners had a duty to open and clean up this festering sore in our society. This was our kind of story. This was what *Vrye Weekblad* was all about and why a year earlier we had been prepared to suffer incredible hardships to establish a voice for those Afrikaners who had broken ranks with the establishment.

Although we realised that we might land up in jail or ultimately destroy the newspaper's credibility, we decided that this was a story for which we would lay everything on the line. We knew that if the story failed, the government would grasp the opportunity to close us down.

But we also knew that if the story succeeded and we could claim credit for exposing death squads, it would probably guarantee *Vrye Weekblad*'s future existence, safeguarding foreign funds for years to come.

We had to find a trustworthy go-between to establish whether the ANC would be interested in talking to Coetzee. We approached a regional director of the Institute for a Democratic Alternative for South Africa (Idasa), Andre Zaaiman, who we knew had excellent contacts with the ANC and frequently visited the organisation's headquarters in Lusaka.

Zaaiman was both excited and concerned. Was this not perhaps a set-up to get a trained assassin within close range of very senior ANC intelligence and military personnel? Was this not a deadly trap, a high-risk operation executed by an expendable assassin? His first assessment of the situation was smuggled by a special courier out of South Africa to members of the ANC's Political-Military Council in Lusaka, requesting permission to proceed with the project. When the courier returned, we were informed that the project needed further evaluation and was classified as a high security risk.

The time had arrived for Zaaiman to meet Coetzee and to inform the former security policeman that the only way he could ever hope to start a new life in another country was to meet the ANC and try to make a deal. But before I could even arrange a meeting, a sensational incident in Pretoria's

Central Prison changed everything.On the eve of his execution, a death row prisoner made an affidavit.

"Almond has talked. I'm in shit. You must come and see me." When I saw Dirk Coetzee an hour later, he hardly greeted me before showing me a copy of that Friday's *Weekly Mail*. The heading read: "Death-row policeman tells of Special Branch hit-squad". The publication of Butana Almond Nofemela's sworn statement had caused a stir in the security establishment and was the first major lead to emerge from the series of political assassinations in recent years.[2]

Nofemela, then aged 32, made a last-minute appeal for clemency to the Minister of Justice the night before he was due to hang. He identified himself as a former security policeman, claiming to be a member of a police death squad who had participated in several assassination missions on the orders of senior policemen.

Sentenced to death in September 1987 for murdering a Brits farmer – not a political crime, but a cold-blooded killing – Nofemela had hoped that his colleagues in the security police would save him from the gallows. Senior policemen had sent messages to him in his death cell asking him not to talk about his role in the death squads. They had promised to save his life in return for his absolute silence. Three days before he was due to meet the hangman, he was visited by a security police officer who told him that there was nothing they could do for him. He would have to "take the pain". Nofemela realised that he had been betrayed, called his attorney at Lawyers for Human Rights and made an affidavit.[3]

"I am a 32-year-old male presently under sentence of death. My execution is scheduled for tomorrow morning, 20 October 1989, at 07h00. I wish to hereby reveal facts about my past which, I respectfully contend, might very well have had a bearing on my conviction and sentence of death had they been known to the trial court, Appeal Court and the Minister of Justice.

"During the period of my service in the security branch, I served under station commander Brigadier [Willem] Schoon. In 1981, I was appointed a member of the Security Branch's assassination squad, and I served under Captain Johannes Dirk Coetzee, who was my commanding officer in the field.

"Some time during late 1981 I was briefed by Brigadier Schoon and Captain Coetzee to eliminate a certain Durban attorney, Griffiths Mxenge. I was told by these superiors that Mxenge was to be eliminated for his activities within the African National Congress. They instructed me to travel to Durban in the company of Brian Justice Ngqulunga, David Tshikalange and Joseph Mamasela, colleagues of mine in the assassination squad. I was the leader of this group that had to eliminate Mxenge . . .

"I was involved in approximately eight other assassinations during my stint in the assassination squad, and also numerous kidnappings. At this stage, I do not recall the names of any of the victims. Some of the assassinations, four in fact, took place in Swaziland, one in Botswana, one in Maseru and one in Krugersdorp. The victims were all ANC members, except in Krugersdorp where the victim was the brother of an ANC terrorist."

Nofemela's affidavit, coming within six months of David Webster's murder and less than two months after the assassination of Anton Lubowski, confirmed the view of those people who had always believed that the state employed assassins to murder its opponents.

The fact that Nofemela was on death row lessened the credibility of his allegations. It was unclear whether the confession was genuine, or merely a cunningly hatched plot to escape the noose. But for Max du Preez and myself, the confessions provided much-needed corroboration. Coetzee had mentioned Nofemela's name to us, and their accounts converged in nearly all respects. The few discrepancies could be expected after a time lapse of eight years. The same men who did the actual killing were named, in both accounts the dogs were poisoned, Mxenge was stabbed to death after being ambushed near his home and the assassins took his car and his valuables to make it look as though it was a common crime.

When I saw the ashen-faced Coetzee that Friday morning, he said: "This is it. I think I've had enough. I told them a long time ago to look after Nofemela because he could bring all of us down with him. What are we going to do?"

Coetzee had been haunted for years by the possibility of the death squads being exposed. The day he dreaded had finally arrived. He said he was tired of living under the stress of possible prosecution and future persecution by a new, black government.

I told him: "We have already made contact with the ANC in Lusaka. They are interested in what you have to say. Would you be willing to meet them, talk to them, maybe in the end even join them? They are the only people who can really help and protect you."

We discussed his options. He said he could join in the cover-up and discrediting of Nofemela that were certain to follow, but that he thought there was a real risk of being isolated with his former colleague. Even if they succeeded in branding Nofemela a liar, how long before another death squad member spilt the beans?

"What do I do if the police turn against me and say: 'Coetzee, you killed Mxenge, but you did it on your own account and we are going to charge you with his murder.' The legal costs would be impossible; I am a sequestrated man. Because of the very nature of our operations, there are no records of instructions of superiors. I would have no hope of being believed if I stayed in South Africa," Coetzee said.

It seemed that the moment for getting it all out in the open had finally arrived. If he was going to expose the death squads, Coetzee swore, it had to be the full story and it had to be made fully public. He agreed to meet Andre Zaaiman.

Two days later, the first of a series of meetings took place between Coetzee, Zaaiman, Max du Preez and me. We met late at night in a small thatched cottage belonging to Frederik van Zyl Slabbert (who at that time was a visiting fellow at Oxford University), situated on a smallholding between Johannesburg and Pretoria. The smallholding was fairly isolated from other homesteads, with a breathtaking view of the Johannesburg skyline. We decided to meet there because it would be easy to detect any surveillance.

The discussions between Zaaiman and Coetzee got off to a shaky start. Both were jittery as they considered the serious repercussions that could flow from the meeting. Moreover, Coetzee felt uneasy dealing with the "enemy", although Zaaiman was not an official representative of the ANC.

We sat for hours as Coetzee elaborated his story, going through the long list of events over and over again, checking and rechecking all possible problem areas, inconsistencies and inaccuracies. Pacing nervously around the lounge as we prepared bottomless cups of coffee, Coetzee seemed desperate to be believed, and Zaaiman told me afterwards that it was this sincere anxiety of the former policeman that made him feel he was telling the truth. We unplugged all telephones to guard against possible tapping as Zaaiman proceeded to cryptically document Coetzee's claims.

From then on, living with the fear that the scheme might be exposed became a nerve-wracking experience. For Zaaiman, who had to live alone in the cottage, it was even worse. He changed bedrooms frequently and often slept in the bath or the passage. The sense of fear was aggravated by the fact that Coetzee had not omitted to inform us that the notorious Vlakplaas, home of the death squads, was only a few kilometres away from the cottage.

After a few meetings, and having secured funds through the ANC underground, Zaaiman travelled via Botswana to Lusaka to brief members of the Political-Military Council on developments. He concealed his notes on Coetzee in a fictitious Idasa project report, blending and intermixing the important details of Coetzee's story. The ANC's Chief of Intelligence, Jacob Zuma, took personal charge of the project.

By that time, the Minister of Justice, Kobie Coetsee, had appointed a commission consisting of the Free State Attorney-General, Advocate Tim McNally, and the head of the CID, General Alwyn Conradie, to investigate Nofemela's claims. Many people doubted the objectivity of the commission assisted by senior police officers briefed to investigate the conduct of fellow police officers.

Coetzee's fear of being made the scapegoat grew by the hour as the commission failed to contact him. By the end of October they had interviewed most of the policemen implicated by Nofemela, with the exception of Coetzee

– who was, after all, named as the death squad's field commander. Coetzee sat at home day after day, waiting for the commission to reel him in.

By that time he had already visited his guardian in the police force, Brigadier Jan du Preez, for advice. The brigadier did not appear in the least concerned. Deny everything, he said, as nobody is going to believe a black man anyway. Coetzee had also called his old colleague and friend, Captain Paul van Dyk, who had been mentioned by both him and Nofemela as being involved in the Mxenge murder. Van Dyk, who had just returned from Namibia, came to see Coetzee and told him not to worry, the McNally Commission was a cover-up and they were certain to discredit Nofemela.

Van Dyk said that one of the senior policemen assisting the commission, was expected to visit the policemen who were implicated to tell them to deny any knowledge of Nofemela's allegations. Van Dyk said Nofemela had incorrectly described most of the wounds they inflicted on Mxenge, giving the commission good reason to find that the condemned man was lying to save his own neck. Van Dyk promised to contact Coetzee again a few days later.

When Zaaiman got back from Lusaka, he told us that the ANC had decided that the project should continue and that provisional arrangements had been made for Coetzee's flight from South Africa. Coetzee had insisted that the ANC agree to certain conditions, including securing a job and a house for himself in a safe country. He also wanted an assurance that the ANC would never expect him to participate in its armed struggle.

The ANC replied that it would undertake to ensure his safety in so far as it was humanly possible and give him sanctuary, on the condition that he was telling the truth and did not attempt any dirty tricks. It promised not to use him in its military, but apart from that, could make no guarantees. He was, after all, a self-confessed hitman.

Coetzee was distraught at the ANC's lack of commitment. When we came back from the meeting, he told me that his almost blind father was dying and would certainly not survive the shock of his son leaving his fatherland and turning against his own people. Then there was his youngest son, Kalla, a diabetic and terribly dependent on his father. He might not see his family for a long, long time.

Coetzee told me that he would under no circumstances go to the ANC alone. He wanted his trusted friend and former security policeman, David "Spyker" Tshikalange, to go with him. The next day, Tshikalange arrived from the homeland of Venda, ready and excited at the prospect of leaving the country with his former boss. That night, as we sat in the dark outside the thatched cottage, Tshikalange sketched his involvement in the Mxenge killing. Speaking slowly, in a low-pitched, emotionless voice, he gave us a cold-blooded account of how he drove the blade of the Okapi into Mxenge's chest. Always remember to turn the knife in your victim's body in order to cause more injury and damage, he told us, and if you slit somebody's throat, don't stop slashing until you feel the bone.

Zaaiman went to Lusaka again the next day, and the ANC instructed that we should proceed in earnest with Coetzee's and Tshikalange's escape. We decided that it would be safer to conduct the final newspaper interviews in Mauritius, en route to London, where Coetzee would meet the ANC. The ANC made an undertaking that if it found his story unacceptable, it would assist him for a period of four months to enable him to find political asylum and a job in exile. Tshikalange was to travel to Zimbabwe, where the ANC would meet up with him.

By now Coetzee was a nervous wreck. Paul van Dyk had not made contact and he became more and more convinced that the police were going to make a scapegoat out of him. We decided to leave for Mauritius on Saturday, 4 November 1989. Zaaiman secured R20 000 from ANC underground funds and proceeded to make the necessary arrangements for Coetzee's flight and stay in London.

However, early that Saturday morning, Coetzee phoned me. He said he could not leave his family behind and had had second thoughts. The enormity of leaving his country and entrusting his life to the ANC had finally caught up with him. He had never been overseas and was scared. When we saw Zaaiman later that morning, Coetzee chain-smoked and looked exhausted.

We were all wearing a bit thin by then. Zaaiman explained to Coetzee that he had nothing to fear from the ANC, that the organisation had given its word that he would not be killed and that it would look after him, but that he had to make up his own mind and accept responsibility for his own decisions. Encouragingly, we said that although this looked like an enormous decision, looking back at our discussion in two or three years from then, he would feel only relief and happiness.

Coetzee was unconvinced. He said that he had to go and speak to his older brother, Ben, whom he had always trusted with the important decisions of his life and who knew about his death squad involvement. The afternoon was torture, but later that evening, I received a call: "I am ready to go. See you tomorrow morning."

At six o'clock the next morning Coetzee stood waiting for me outside his house next to two suitcases. His wife Karin embraced him, and he picked up his two little poodles and gave each of them a kiss. "I am going to miss the dogs. I am so fond of them," he said as he got into the car. On our way to the airport, he confessed that Karin did not know what was going on or where he was going. He had told her that he had to leave and did not know when he would be back again. The previous night, he had taken his two boys, Dirkie and Kalla, to stay with friends because he couldn't face saying goodbye to them. He was too distraught to call his parents and tell them he was going away.

Coetzee did not have any money on him, having left everything he had behind for his family. Before we got to the airport, he took an enormous box of Valium tranquillisers out of his suitcase and told me that this was the start of a new life: he wouldn't need them any more. He left the box behind.

Checking through customs at Jan Smuts Airport was a nerve-wracking experience. Zaaiman had taken up a position in the look-out lounge to monitor our progress. If we did not board the plane, he had instructions to go and call Max du Preez who would contact an attorney we had on standby to assist us. But two hours later, we were on our way. Before we were properly airborne, Coetzee called a stewardess and ordered a bottle of champagne.

It was ironic to think that a white South African, a member of the privileged elite in my country, was doing what thousands of black people had been obliged to do for decades before him to escape persecution and join the ranks of the ANC. Going into exile, many had to leave families behind, facing a future of uncertainty. At least in Coetzee's case, he had a planned and comfortable escape route and a high-ranking reception committee awaiting him on the other side.

En route to Mauritius, I had mixed feelings about what we were trying to achieve. In a country so desperately in need of justice, we were helping an apartheid assassin to escape exactly that. Only time would tell whether we had done the right thing.

At ten o'clock on 10 November 1989, Captain Dirk Coetzee came face to face with the enemy in a small London hotel. He was unceremoniously introduced to Intelligence Chief Jacob Zuma and senior members of Umkhonto we Sizwe, the military wing of the ANC.

He had arrived the day before aboard a British Airways flight. At Heathrow Airport, Andre Zaaiman had met a calm and collected Coetzee leaning with his back against a pillar, one foot up against the wall, smiling when he saw his South African contact. I had warned Zaaiman that Coetzee left Mauritius in a fairly rattled state and we were nervous that he might not make it through the notorious British customs. But it seemed that by then Coetzee had resigned himself to his fate.

The three days in Mauritius had been hectic. Apart from our tape-recorded interviews, we had drawn up a lengthy statement, taken photographs, made phone calls to Zaaiman in London and Max du Preez in Johannesburg, and rushed into the capital of Port Louis to pick up Coetzee's air ticket and money.

Coetzee had asked me time and time again whether he should go ahead and meet the ANC in London. He already missed home, and his youngest son's birthday was only days away. We did the last of our interviews on the way to the airport. It was an emotional farewell. As I embraced Coetzee I realised that over the weeks, I had grown very close to this man whom I probably would otherwise have despised. I did not leave the airport until the aircraft had taken off and disappeared in the distance.

When Coetzee phoned me two days later, he was elated. The ANC had believed his story and were going to protect him and look after him. When

I asked him what the people he had met were like, he said: "Well, ordinary people, you know. Not what I thought they would be. Highly intelligent, well informed and very civilised."

Coetzee expressed his shock that the ANC seemed so far removed from the images that for so many years had been conjured up by the state and its supreme instruments of propaganda, the South African Broadcasting Corporation and the government-supporting Afrikaans press.

He said that despite the hardships he had inflicted on the ANC, there was an amazing lack of bitterness or hatred towards him. Afterwards, he described his debriefing to me: "I had decided not to go about matters in a half-hearted manner and opened up completely. As I spluttered and stuttered to relate the murders and atrocities that I helped to perpetrate, I began to sense an atmosphere of understanding and sympathy. This lasted throughout the long debriefing. They listened intently and patiently, never pressing for information, never bombarding me with questions and hardly ever speaking other than to enquire about my comfort and needs."

Zaaiman returned to South Africa two days later, having said goodbye to Coetzee on a rainy and misty London afternoon. Coetzee had begun to understand the terrible nature of what he had done, he said, and was telling the ANC over and over again that he wanted to do everything possible to make up for his horrible actions of the past.

A few months later, Coetzee described the decision he had to take: "I had to take this calculated risk and walk straight into the laager of the enemy, the African National Congress, tell them of my involvement in the atrocities against them, and hope to heaven they would accept me as a victim of the apartheid system and a fighter in a dirty, unconventional war. By going to the ANC and assisting them, I might to some extent be able to make good for what I had done to their supporters and their families."

Zaaiman said that Coetzee did not make any dramatic contribution to the ANC's knowledge about police death squads. They were well informed and could corroborate most of what he told them and even fill him in on the parts he had forgotten. They could furnish him with the identities of nameless victims. They even had a photograph and historical background on him.

Vrye Weekblad decided to proceed with the story and publish as soon as possible. A major problem was that the State of Emergency was still in force and the state could legally either stop us from publishing or confiscate the newspaper. We could not ask the police for comment for fear of state action.

We had planned the story for the edition of 24 November, which would have given us enough time to transcribe the hours of tape recordings and properly plan our strategies. It would also give the ANC the opportunity to move Coetzee to a place of safe-keeping and for Ben Coetzee to prepare his parents and Karin Coetzee for the shock.

The Tuesday after I returned from Mauritius, I took Tshikalange to the Northern Transvaal, from where he would enter Zimbabwe. The following day I received a phone call from a reporter at the *Weekly Mail* asking whether it was true that we had taken Coetzee out of the country. The story was blown: we had to publish that same Friday.

We received legal advice to proceed with publication, but were warned that we could expect a frenzied state and police response. Our trusted attorney, Lauren Jacobson, advised us to remove the name of General Lothar Neethling as he was a highly respected forensic scientist and would certainly sue for defamation. To her absolute astonishment, Max du Preez took out a coin, asked me to choose head or tails, flipped it in the air and declared: "Tails, we win. His name goes in!"

In the event of the story leaking out and *Vrye Weekblad* being seized, we informed some foreign correspondents we thought we could trust about the allegations we were going to publish. Just before publication, we furnished them with translated copies of the articles.

We followed the newspaper from the office to the printers, waited for it to be printed and followed the trucks to the airport from where it would be distributed around the country.

On Friday, 17 November *Vrye Weekblad* published Coetzee's story. The dramatic front page carried a larger-than-life portrait of Dirk Coetzee, with the stark words in Afrikaans: "BLOODY TRAIL OF THE SAP". It continued: "Meet Captain Dirk Johannes Coetzee, commander of a police death squad. He exclusively reveals the full sordid tale of political assassinations, poison drinks, letter bombs and attacks in neighbouring states."[4]

Coetzee's allegations were simultaneously the lead stories on the front pages of leading British, European and American newspapers, while other foreign correspondents picked up the interview and sent it around the world.

The story inflicted a devastating blow to the South African Police and government of State President FW de Klerk. Ironically, the Minister of Law and Order, Adriaan Vlok, had denied on television the very night before that a police death squad ever existed.

Opposition politicians, black political leaders and organisations, human rights lawyers and foreign diplomats demanded a judicial commission of inquiry, the immediate resignation of Adriaan Vlok, and that all the policemen implicated by Coetzee and Nofemela be charged with murder. The British Embassy drew up a report that was presented to Prime Minister Margaret Thatcher.

The police were quick to respond. Police public relations chief General Herman Stadler vehemently denied that there was a police death squad, admitted that Vlakplaas did exist but said that the "rehabilitated terrorists" were only used to detect their former ANC and PAC cadres and arrest them. "Like any policeman, they have orders to arrest ANC and PAC terrorists, certainly not to murder them. It seems strange that Captain Coetzee, who several years ago was suspended by the SAP, now makes these unfounded, untested and wild allegations from a foreign country where he cannot be questioned to verify his claims.

"The essence of these allegations was previously made by several critics of the SAP. The Minister of Law and Order and the Commissioner of Police stated that no so-called hit squads exist in the SAP and in isolated cases policemen who had taken the law into their own hands, had to carry the punishment. It is regrettable that a registered newspaper chose to publish Captain Coetzee's one-sided allegations without even asking the SAP for comment," Stadler said.[5]

Journalists were hastily taken to Vlakplaas and introduced to some "rehabilitated" ANC and PAC renegades who had seen the result of their wrongdoings and were now co-operating with the police. Journalists were invited to talk to some of the askaris, who flatly denied that a death squad ever operated from the farm.

A week after we had published the allegations, General Lothar Neethling sued us for defamation, demanding damages of R1 million. It was a court case that could have destroyed *Vrye Weekblad*. It was also, however, an opportunity to prove that Dirk Coetzee was not a raving lunatic and *Vrye Weekblad* not an irresponsible newspaper.

That was the beginning of a long, uphill battle. We knew that the police would never admit their complicity in the assassination of anti-apartheid activists and would go to extreme lengths to discredit Coetzee. In the months that followed, he had to repeat his story to an array of journalists and international television networks, to a judicial commission of inquiry and to a senior judge.

It took more than a year before the South African Supreme Court found that Dirk Coetzee had been telling the truth and that a police death squad did exist.

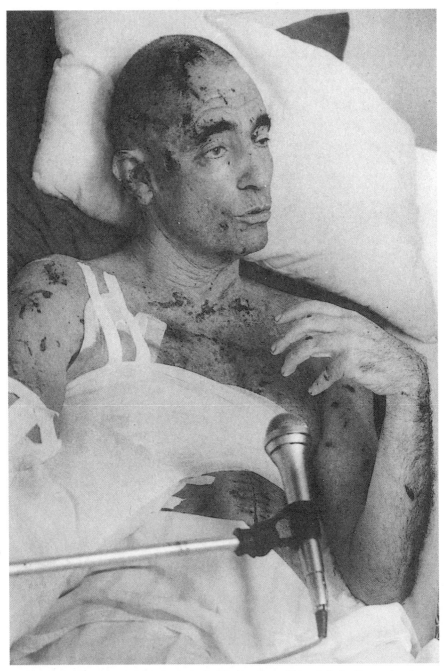

ANC lawyer and academic Albie Sachs in the Maputo Central Hospital after the car bomb explosion that failed to kill him but severed his right arm from his body.

(*Photo: Agência de Informaçao de Moçambique*)

Dirk Coetzee served in the Rhodesian Special Branch in 1974. *Above*: SB members digging shallow graves in which to burn and then bury killed guerrillas; *below*: a group of policemen standing around the body of a man killed by guerrillas.

Dirk Coetzee in exile in London.

Part of a security police agent's arsenal:
plastic assassination revolver with six built-in
bullets that is disposed of after the operation
is completed, throwing knife and 7,65
millimetre assault rifle bullets.

Above: Vlakplaas operative Ronald
Bezuidenhout, who claimed he was part
of a group of Vlakplaas security policemen
who planned to kill Dirk Coetzee with a
parcel bomb.

(Photo: Ruvan Boschoff)

Above right: The head of the Scientific and
Technical Section of the SAP, General Lothar
Neethling, who is also in charge of the
forensic laboratory. In 1991 a Supreme Court
judge found that he had provided former
security police captain Dirk Coetzee with
poison to kill ANC activists.

(Photo: Vrye Weekblad)

Right: CCB operative Abram "Slang" van Zyl,
a former lieutenant at Brixton Murder and
Robbery, admitted that he blew up an early
learning centre in Cape Town, victimised
Archbishop Desmond Tutu and conspired to
kill anti-apartheid activists.

(Photo: The Star)

Above: Marthinus Grobler, the young Piet Retief police constable who fled to Lusaka and joined the ANC. He was present in the charge office on the night in June 1988 when four alleged ANC infiltrators were shot by a Vlakplaas death squad.

(*Photo: Jaques Pauw, Vrye Weekblad*)

Above right: The Reverend Frank Chikane, Secretary General of the South African Council of Churches, who was targeted by the CCB and was poisoned in 1988.

(*Photo: Peter Williams, World Council of Churches*)

Above: ANC Chief Representative in France, Dulcie September, was gunned down by an assassin in front of her Paris office in 1988.

(*Photo: International Defence and Aid Fund*)

Above left: Human rights lawyer Griffiths Mxenge, who was stabbed to death in November 1981 by alleged robbers. Eight years later three security policemen confessed that they were members of the death squad that assassinated him.
(*Photo: International Defence and Aid Fund*)

Above: Victoria Mxenge, human rights lawyer, UDF leader and wife of Griffiths Mxenge. She was assassinated four years later.
(*Photo: International Defence and Aid Fund*)

Left: Almond Butana Nofemela, former Vlakplaas security policeman who admitted his part in a police death squad in an affidavit from death row in the Pretoria Central Prison.

UDF leader Matthew Goniwe, who disappeared with three other UDF officials in the Eastern Cape in June 1985. Their bodies were found a few days later.

(*Photo: International Defence and Aid Fund*)

Above left: Swapo leader Hidipo Hamutenya, who was on the CCB death list in an attempt by the SADF to disrupt Swapo before the November 1989 independence elections. Today Hamutenya is Namibia's Minister of Information.

(Photo: John Liebenberg)

Above: Swapo leader and human rights lawyer Anton Lubowski, who was shot dead with an AK-47 assault rifle in front of his Windhoek home in September 1989. Members of the internal region of the CCB are wanted by the Namibian authorities for his murder.

(Photo: Anne Day, Afrapix)

Left: Anthropology lecturer and anti-detentions campaigner Dr David Webster, assassinated outside his Johannesburg home in May 1989.

(Photo: International Defence and Aid Fund)

Above left: Staal Burger, former Brixton Murder and Robbery commander who resigned to become manager of the internal region of the CCB. Wanted in Namibia for the murder of Swapo advocate Anton Lubowski.

(*Photo: The Star*)

Above: CCB operative and convicted murderer Ferdi Barnard, a former narcotics bureau detective who joined the CCB after being released from jail.

(*Photo: The Star*)

Left: General Johan Coetzee, former Commissioner of Police and Head of the Security Branch.

(*Photo: Vrye Weekblad*)

Right: Calla Botha, former member of the CCB's internal region. Before he joined the CCB he was a member of the Brixton Murder and Robbery Unit.

(Photo: The Star)

Below: Pieter Botes, CCB operative who maimed Albie Sachs and assassinated six other people in Mozambique.

(Photo: The Pretoria News)

Below right: General Eddie Webb, commander of the SADF's Special Forces and chairman of the CCB.

(Photo: Vrye Weekblad)

Pictures taken of South African academic Rob Davies in Maputo. From the only CCB death file ever fully revealed: the photographs, taken by the CCB operator planning the murder, show Davies, his Volkswagen, his wife at her car and a map of exactly where he lives in Maputo.

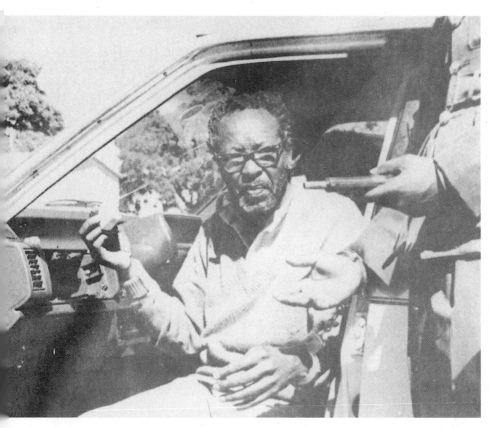

From the intelligence files of the Zimbabwean Central Intelligence Organisation: CCB assassin Leslie Lesia showing members of the CIO the secret compartment in his car which contained a bottle of poison, a pistol with a silencer, explosives and spying equipment.

Above: Anti-apartheid activist Jeanette Schoon and her six-year old daughter, Katryn were killed by a letter bomb in Angola in 1984.
(*Photo: International Defence and Aid Fund*)

Above right: Ruth First, professor at the Eduardo Mondlane University in Maputo and wife of South African Communist Party leader Joe Slovo. She was killed by a letter bomb in August 1982.
(*Photo: International Defence and Aid Fund*)

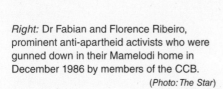

Right: Dr Fabian and Florence Ribeiro, prominent anti-apartheid activists who were gunned down in their Mamelodi home in December 1986 by members of the CCB.
(*Photo: The Star*)

CHAPTER THREE

An assassin's apprenticeship

THE murder of the two prisoners, Peter Dlamini and Vuyani Mavuso, with which this book began was witnessed by Dirk Coetzee, although he was not the one to pull the trigger. Whatever it was that made him turn and scan the horizon on occasions like this had nothing to do with belated remorse at the elimination of an enemy – he would have said simply that it was not a pleasant thing to see a man shot at point-blank range. The two captives were terrorists and he had orders to eliminate them.[1]

After the second shot, Coetzee looked back again at the two men lying dead on the ground. Captain Koos Vermeulen lifted his foot from a dead man's neck and walked back towards his colleagues.

The events surrounding the fate of the two captured ANC activists had started two weeks earlier when Coetzee was summoned to Brigadier Willem Schoon's office. "There is a man in the Brits police cells with the name of Mavuso. He is stubborn and uncooperative. We must get rid of him, we can't let him go free."

In January 1981, the South African Defence Force had launched an attack on the Mozambican capital of Maputo, killing at least 13 people. During the attack, known as the Matola raid, the invaders captured suspected ANC guerrillas and brought them back to South Africa. One of the suspects was Vuyani "Vusi" Mavuso, whom the South Africans believed to be a highly trained and dangerous terrorist. The captives were secretly held at an army base just outside Pretoria.

After an international uproar about the raid and the South African government's kidnapping of ANC members, the captives were handed over to the police, transferred to Pretoria's Central Prison and detained under the Terrorism Act.

Under security police interrogation, Mavuso admitted that he was a senior member of Umkhonto we Sizwe, and that he had undergone intensive military training in foreign countries. He also admitted involvement in the bombing of municipal offices in Lamontville near Durban. His statement was sent to Brigadier Willem Schoon, Coetzee's superior, head of the ANC-PAC desk at Security Branch headquarters.[2]

The police could not find enough evidence to charge the captive and bring him to justice, however. Moreover Mavuso refused to co-operate with his captors, making him an unlikely candidate for the security police's counter-insurgency unit at Vlakplaas. "Charge me or shoot me," he challenged his interrogaters. They took him at his word.

When Schoon instructed Coetzee to kill Mavuso, he told him to use the opportunity to get rid of "poor Peter" as well. Nkosinathi Peter Dlamini, who was a member of the Vlakplaas unit, was a frail, timid and pathetic guy who was always late and could do nothing right.

Dlamini had left South Africa in 1978 and joined the ANC, which sent him to study and train in Bulgaria. In April 1981, he defected to the South African Embassy in Greece and told officials that he wanted to return to South Africa. On arrival he was met by security police and detained for questioning. Dlamini decided to co-operate with his captors and became an askari at Vlakplaas.[3]

Peter's fellow askaris loathed him and frequently assaulted him. The general consensus was that he was not "all there", which seemed to be confirmed when he wrote a letter to police headquarters complaining about the conditions at Vlakplaas.

Schoon and Coetzee decided that they would officially release Mavuso from the detention cells at Brits where he was now detained. They would pretend that he was going to join the Vlakplaas unit but instead they would abduct him, kill him and dispose of his body. They decided that the best method of execution would be poison. Coetzee, lacking the stomach to shoot the two men, had heard that General Lothar Neethling, chief of the police's forensic laboratory, had in the past provided poison to security policemen. Schoon called Neethling to make the arrangements.

That same day, Coetzee went to fetch the poison at the forensic laboratory in downtown Pretoria. He walked through the double wooden doors and found the general, a formidable and feared officer in the force, in his small, crowded office. While the general opened his big police safe to take out the poison, Coetzee looked around. His attention was drawn by two picture frames against the wall. There was a certificate from British Airways stating that "Dr LP Neethling" had flown on board Concorde from London to Washington, and a photograph of the Oostelikes rugby team with the general sitting in the second row.

Years later, Coetzee's remarkable memory of the certificate and the rugby photo would prove that he did visit the general's office on that day in October 1981. It was as good as a fingerprint left behind in the office, a judge found.[4]

Neethling took some "knock-out drops" from his safe, telling Coetzee that about four drops of the colourless, odourless and tasteless substance should be enough to put an average-sized man to sleep. He warned Coetzee that an overdose could be fatal. He also handed over two dosages of a lethal powdered poison, each wrapped in a tiny piece of tin foil. According to

Neethling, the poison had been tested with excellent results on sheep, bringing about a heart attack within 15 minutes. Before Coetzee left, Neethling asked him to take precise notes on the effects of the knock-out drops as he was not sure how long they would take to have the desired effect.

It was probably on that same day that Neethling gave his two office telephone numbers to Coetzee, in case he needed further advice. One of the numbers was a special extension to Neethling's office that did not appear in the official police telephone directory. Coetzee wrote the numbers down in a little police pocket book in which he scribbled the names, addresses and telephone numbers of people he had come into contact with during his 18 months as commander at Vlakplaas.

Nine years later, the little pocket book, by then well worn and showing signs of age, would be a vital piece of evidence to prove that Coetzee did meet Neethling and that this highly decorated police officer and distinguished forensic scientist did supply poison to Coetzee.

When Coetzee arrived at the Brits police station, he fetched Mavuso from the cells, handcuffed him and put him in the back of the police car. One of the askaris guarded him as they left for Zeerust in the Western Transvaal. Coetzee's first stop was at the municipal waste dump on the eastern side of the town, to fetch some old motor car tyres. The captured guerrilla, who had been told at Brits that he would be released but now watched Coetzee load the tyres, was quiet and never spoke a word.

The group then travelled to a police farm near the border between South Africa and Botswana to meet up with Coetzee's friend and colleague Koos Vermeulen, who had brought Peter Dlamini from Vlakplaas with him. Dlamini, who was under the impression that he was there to guard the captive, was handcuffed to Mavuso.

Coetzee gave Mavuso three blank police pay slips to sign with two different pens. He wanted to know why, but Coetzee told him: "Just sign and don't ask any questions." If the activist's family were to inquire about his whereabouts, the police could produce the signed pay slips as proof that Mavuso had been released from custody and gone to Vlakplaas to become an askari. The police could say that he had escaped from the farm and gone back to join his former comrades in exile.

Cans of cold drink and beer were opened. Koos Vermeulen slipped the powdered poison into Mavuso's cold drink and Dlamini's beer. The men watched as their captives swallowed the poison and waited for the heart attack to occur. Minutes went by, but nothing happened. The poison didn't work.

By now the sun had set and the braaivleis fire was lit. Coetzee opened another cold drink, and this time put knock-out drops into the can and gave it to Mavuso to drink. Fifteen minutes later, he started talking incoherently and fell over, scrabbling at the ground. He carried on like that for much of the night, but by morning seemed normal again. Coetzee made accurate notes of the effect of the drops.

The next day, Vermeulen went back to Pretoria to report to Neethling that his poison had had no effect on the men. When he returned, he said the general could simply not believe it and had doubled the dosages to 120 milligrams each. Again they administered the poison to the two men; still it failed to work.

Joe Mamasela, the "rehabilitated" ANC guerrilla, a feared killer, decided to teach Mavuso how to pray before he met his Creator. Mavuso had to kneel on two bricks and recite the Lord's Prayer, to the great amusement of the other squad members. Every time he faltered, Mamasela would kick him. After a few hours of this gross entertainment Mavuso's face was bleeding and swollen. Coetzee didn't interfere; Mavuso was going to die anyway, he thought.

The following day, Coetzee and his men were instructed to go to the Groblersdal area for surveillance work. They stayed on a smallholding outside the town. A few days after the squad had arrived in Groblersdal, Vermeulen and Coetzee decided to go and see the general again. The askaris were left behind to guard the two captives.

It was a Sunday morning, and they found Neethling still dressed in his pyjamas at his Pretoria home. He had returned the previous day from a visit to West Germany. They waited in the porch for the general to get dressed. As the general walked to the front door Coetzee could sense that the house had a wooden floor, although it was covered with wall-to-wall carpets. Coetzee's memory of Neethling's house would also give vital substance to his allegations years later that the general had provided him with poison.

They accompanied Neethling, wearing shorts and slippers, to the laboratory where he took a chemistry text from the bookshelf and paged around in it. He said the poison should definitely work and had no explanation for its failure. He tripled the dose to 180 milligrams for each victim. He dissolved the poison in a liquid and drew the potion into two of Coetzee's disposable insulin syringes, wrapping them in tin foil.

Coetzee and Vermeulen went back to Groblersdal, where Vermeulen squirted the contents of the syringes into Mavuso's and Dlamini's drinks. Again, nothing happened. The two security police officers decided that the poison would never work and that they would have to resort to bullets, dosing the men with the remaining knock-out drops before killing them.

Coetzee suggested that they take the two captives to the Komatipoort area to dispose of them. He had a close relationship with the security police in the area. Next morning they were received by the head of the Security Branch at Komatipoort, Major Archie Flemington. The group travelled from

34

Komatipoort to a secluded spot a short distance from the Mozambique border, on the banks of the Komati River.

Vuyani Mavuso must have known by then that he was going to die at the hands of his captors. Yet he never spoke or pleaded for mercy. Peter Dlamini, too, must have realised that he was not there as Mavuso's guard.

Two years later, Coetzee, who had by then been transferred to head office recruitment, was summoned to Willem Schoon's office, where the brigadier told him that Mavuso's attorney was still enquiring about his client's whereabouts. He was becoming a nuisance and they would have to silence his suspicions. Coetzee made a statement that Mavuso had been released from police custody, worked at Vlakplaas for three months and then completely disappeared. As proof, they produced the three pay slips signed by Mavuso.

In his 1985 police trial, Coetzee declared that Mavuso and Dlamini had defected back to the ANC. Naturally, he could not say that they had been killed by a Vlakplaas death squad. He might have ended up in court with criminal charges against him.

By the time Mavuso and Dlamini were killed, Dirk Coetzee had become a hardened killer and skilled criminal – a gangster of practically Olympic achievements. Not until he had fled South Africa could he admit his crimes or hope for redemption.

Dirk Coetzee was born in April 1945 in Pokwani, the son of a post office worker. He had a happy childhood in a very traditional, loving and caring Afrikaans family. At school, the young Coetzee was only interested in sport, failing standard nine at the first attempt and initially passing only four matric subjects. In 1963, he was selected as winger for the final trials to select a Northern Transvaal school rugby team, but was sidelined by a broken arm. He was captain of his school's athletics and swimming teams.

His rebellious nature and quick temper caused considerable friction between him and his teachers. He objected strongly to corporal punishment and during his last two years at school refused to subject himself to it. The fact that he was not at all interested in school work only aggravated the situation. Later in his adult life, corporal punishment to his two boys prompted him on three occasions to write to the Minister of Education and he managed to stop malpractices at various Pretoria schools. Until his departure from South Africa, he was a member of a society fighting corporal punishment in schools.

After a short stint as a post office worker, he joined the South African Police in April 1970. In July that year Student Constable Coetzee had his training at the Police College in Pretoria and graduated as the best student. He received his trophy on the famous Loftus Versfeld rugby field from the Minister of Police. Soon afterwards, he passed four matric legal subjects first class and only six months after completion of his training, he became a sergeant. Just three years later, in July 1973, Coetzee passed his warrant officer's examination with a first class. In the meantime, he had qualified as a dog handler and a scuba diver.

His considerable achievements and exemplary service in the Uniformed Branch contrasted sharply with the criminal career that was to follow later on in the security police.

In March 1974, Dirk Coetzee was introduced into that secret world when he was sent to Rhodesia to serve as a dog handler with Prime Minister Ian Smith's security forces in their bitter bush war against the guerrilla forces of Robert Mugabe and Joshua Nkomo. Coetzee was stationed at a police base near Mount Darwin and although he was not directly involved in military operations, this was where he had his first lesson in how to dispose of a body. On this occasion, a senior officer of the Rhodesian Special Branch required assistance to dispose of the bodies of guerrillas killed earlier that day. The bodies were loaded into a Land Rover and transported to a clearing in the bush. Shallow graves were dug and lined with plastic. The bodies, as many as seven at a time, were put in the graves, covered with branches, doused with petrol and set alight. As soon as the bodies were burnt beyond recognition, the graves were covered with soil. Coetzee had to accompany the officer several times.

Later on, he witnessed the mutilated bodies of landmine victims and massacred villagers. These barbarous killings made a deep impression on him and he took photographs of the bodies to show the people back home what was really going on in the Rhodesian bush.

Although Coetzee was never told why the bodies had to be made unrecognisable, he suspected that the victims were captured guerrillas killed by the Special Branch. After the new state of Zimbabwe was born, the government found the mass graves of hundreds of guerrillas whose bodies had been mutilated in the manner Coetzee described.

The Rhodesian bush war experience was a tremendous adventure to Coetzee, and it created in him the desire to serve in the security branch of his own country. It also showed him how serious the dreaded "communist threat" really was.

In a recently published book, *The Rhodesian Front War*, a former Rhodesian special branch officer, Henry Ellert, wrote that, in the worst tradition of Nazi Germany, the Selous Scouts may have used humans as guinea pigs to try out their poisons. In 1975, he says, a group of young Africans were arrested in Salisbury and taken to a camp near Mount Darwin where army doctors were present to receive the captives. A few days later the bodies were taken out of the camp for disposal.[5]

A few months after returning from Rhodesia, Coetzee was transferred to Sibasa in Venda, where he wrote and passed his examinations for lieutenant with a first class. It was here that he met David Tshikalange and Koos

Vermeulen, who were later to become members of his death squad at Vlakplaas.

Coetzee had to attend an officer's course at the Police College in Pretoria, and it was there that he received his first formal lectures on the ANC and met eye to eye with the legendary "Sagmoedige Neelsie" (Sweet Neelsie), Brigadier Neels du Plooy of security headquarters. He describes Du Plooy as a kind-hearted, soft-spoken and humble Christian who opened and closed his lectures with scripture reading and prayer. He was a man with a formidable knowledge of the enemy – the African National Congress, the South African Communist Party and the Pan Africanist Congress. He knew everything about the communist onslaught and the Soviet Union's real intention behind the wars in Angola, Rhodesia and South-West Africa. Du Plooy was a sought-after speaker at women's clubs and public societies. He was always accompanied by a "rehabilitated" ANC guerrilla, Silumami Gladstone Mose, whose ties with the security police brought him notoriety. In later years, Mose was involved in various shooting incidents and atrocities where ANC infiltrators were killed. Even today, he is still feared and loathed.

Coetzee said from the moment Neelsie and Mose entered the lecture room the young policemen were spellbound. When Neelsie spoke, you could hear a pin drop. He entered the room with an arsenal of enemy armoury that gave an ominous and impressive weight to his words. Neelsie's lectures consisted of cycles of emotion. He would start in a calm and collected manner and gradually work himself into a frenzy that left the audience in a trance. He supported his claims with a display of subversive and banned literature that ordinary citizens could never see.

The ANC was made out to be the most despicable threat imaginable to Christianity in South Africa. They were the heathens – callous, heartless and cruel killers of innocent people like nuns and children. In fact, Coetzee thought, looking back at the lectures, many of Neelsie's descriptions would fit elements of the South African security police remarkably well.

After becoming a police officer, Coetzee was promoted to the Police College as a lecturer. The students had to do late-night preparation for inspections and Coetzee received a tired and unresponsive class. He therefore gave his students permission to sleep in his lesson, provided they put up their hands first and informed him of their intention.

With the Soweto uprising of June 1976, Coetzee was in charge of a group of policemen guarding certain key points in Johannesburg. They also had to assist at the mortuary, where Coetzee controlled the milling crowds of parents and relatives looking for the bodies of the children killed in the uprising. He was extremely annoyed by the grieved people who threw "tantrums" and packed every room and space that could be found. What did they expect to happen if their children burned down their schools and threw stones at the police? Anarchy and revolt could not be tolerated.

Later that year, Coetzee was transferred to the southeastern Transvaal town of Volksrust as station commander. The town was experiencing an unprecedented wave of housebreaking and theft. He immediately assigned three policemen to permanent night patrol to concentrate on housebreaking. That year in December, when housebreaking is supposed to be at its worst, not a single case was reported. After he left, however, theft soared again and the business community lodged a complaint at high level.

In 1977, Coetzee's dream came true when he was recruited by the security police. He was interviewed by two men who later played a significant role in his life – Brigadier Jan van der Hoven, then chief of the Security Branch in the Eastern Transvaal, and Captain Nick van Rensburg, Ermelo Security Branch commander. They gave him a choice between Oshakati in SouthWest Africa or the Oshoek border post between South Africa and Swaziland.

Throughout his police career, Dirk Coetzee had been nurtured and groomed to one day join the ranks of the Security Branch. He was a brilliant police student, a dedicated policeman, full of ambition. He swapped his blue uniform for civilian clothes and started what he called his "apprenticeship" in the Security Branch. Although Coetzee was still officially a member of the Uniformed Branch, the position of border post commander fell directly under the Security Branch. He had to take an oath under the Official Secrets Act that he would never reveal any information about his work.

When Coetzee arrived at Oshoek, he set about upgrading conditions at the border post and improving relations with the Swazis. There was an air of mistrust between the South Africans manning the border post and the Swazi customs officials. The appearance of the post was unsatisfactory and the spirit generally unhealthy. He drastically reformed his staff's working conditions, arranging for additional posts so that the wives of the border personnel could also be employed and re-organising shifts so that husbands and wives could work together.

The Swazis gave the South Africans name plates for their offices, stickers to mark passport control properly, fixed the toilets and provided paint for the inside of the building. Coetzee got RSA emblems from a government department to enhance the post's image as a gateway to South Africa, he obtained photographs of all the South African prime ministers and police commissioners, installed electrically controlled locks and persuaded a mining company in the area to provide floodlights to light up the public and parking areas properly.

Coetzee converted an old ruin, once used to accommodate pigs and sheep, into a clubhouse with a thatched roof, wall-to-wall carpets, a huge bar and well-stocked fridge. This unlicensed police shebeen was supplied with free electricity via a clandestine connection installed by a Swazi friend.

Relations with the Swazis improved overnight. Coetzee was eventually a guest of honour at Swaziland's tenth independence anniversary and the eightieth birthday of His Royal Highness, King Sobhuza II. The King had four special deputies, called "the eyes and the ears of the nation", and the most senior of the four, Malaza, was Dirk and Karin Coetzee's special escort at both these functions.

He enjoyed special recognition from the King and the royal family. At the start and end of each hunting season, the King's secretary, Martin Mdsiniso, brought the border post a gift of a blue wildebeest and four impala. Later on when his superiors learned about these gifts, they begged Coetzee to arrange some venison for them as well. This led to some poaching of the benevolent King's game.

To the Security Branch, the improved relations offered an ideal opportunity for more covert operations into Swaziland. They began grossly exploiting the unusual goodwill and involved an eager Coetzee in their operations. Nick van Rensburg asked Coetzee to use a friend in Swaziland to get more information on the movements of ANC guerrillas from there to Mozambique.

Coetzee became friends with Rall Mattheus, a Portuguese citizen who managed the Mozambican Deta Air agency in Swaziland. Refugees from South Africa meeting up with the ANC in Swaziland would eventually be flown to Mozambique by Deta Air. Mattheus supplied all the passenger lists to Coetzee, enabling Nick van Rensburg to keep his files up to date. Rall was caught by the Swazi authorities, locked up and released on bail. He was smuggled across the border in the boot of Coetzee's official car.

During the same period, Portuguese from Mozambique had a racket in which they bought escudos with dollars on the black market in Maputo at very favourable exchange rates. They then brought the money to South Africa where they again exchanged it for rands with Mozambican citizens working on the South African mines. The mine workers got escudos that they could take to Mozambique without having to declare the money at the border post and pay tax on it. The Portuguese would then use the rands to buy dollars, and the whole business would start all over again.

Coetzee apprehended a Portuguese citizen bringing 15 million escudos into the country and detained him. The man was frightened and begged Coetzee to let him go back to Swaziland. Van Rensburg told him to release the man and keep the money. A few days later, another Portuguese tried to bring seven million escudos into South Africa; he too was kept in custody for a few hours and sent back over the border without his money. A member of the Security Branch exchanged the money on the mines and the proceeds were deposited into a secret security fund to be used for clandestine operations.

Swaziland had a strong opposition party under the leadership of Dr A Zwane, who was strongly pro-ANC and anti-South Africa. The Security Branch had pamphlets made in the name of Zwane, inciting the Swazi people against the King. Coetzee and members of the Ermelo Security Branch distributed the pamphlets at public places around the capital of Mbabane. Zwane spent long periods in detention as a result.

The ANC had always maintained a low profile in Swaziland, prevented from operating actively by the government's fear of reprisals by South Africa. Despite this, ANC guerrillas had used Swaziland as a springboard for attacks against South Africa and infiltrators from Mozambique entered South Africa through Swaziland.

Coetzee said that he could sense by that time that Security Branch operations, at least in the Swaziland border area, entailed much more than just guarding the fence and passport control. It was also important to the safety of the country to disrupt and harass the enemy. Van Rensburg and the Security Branch members at Ermelo were drawing Coetzee more and more into their inner circle, entrusting him with their security secrets, among other things that they were stealing the enemy's cars in Swaziland and giving them to the Rhodesian Special Branch.

Coetzee made friends with the owner of a garage in Mbabane where the ANC took their Peugeots and Toyota Land Cruisers for servicing. The idea was to obtain duplicate keys. After a lot of eating, drinking, promises and threats, the garage owner, Jose Rollo Noivo, was persuaded to give him a duplicate key to the car of Stanley Mabusela, then chief representative of the ANC in Swaziland and today deputy head of the foreign affairs section.

As Coetzee and his men attempted to steal the car, the alarm went off and they had to run away. Noivo showed them how to stick pliers through a slot near the bottom of the engine and cut the hooter wire. A few nights later, Stanley lost his car. After Coetzee had fled South Africa and joined the ANC, he met Mabusela in Lusaka and they had a good laugh about his stolen car.

The car theft operation was eventually extended to include vehicles from so-called "hostile embassies". One night, Coetzee and members of the Ermelo Security Branch saw seven brand-new Land Rovers that the United Nations had bought standing at a local garage. They decided to steal the lot. They gained entrance to the workshop, but as they attempted to push out the first Land Rover, it fell into the service pit and blocked the entrance.

There were several other thefts and attempted thefts. One evening, after a drinking spree at the Portuguese Club in Manzini, one of the policemen noticed an old Volkswagen Beetle with the keys in the ignition. He and some of his colleagues got into the car and drove off. After struggling up a hill, they realised that the old wreck would never reach the border post. They shoved the car over the side of a steep slope into the bushes and continued the journey in a police car.

But bigger and better things were yet to come. Van Rensburg instructed Coetzee to break into the offices of the United Nations High Commissioner for Refugees and steal the refugee files, which contained vital information on exiles in Mozambique and Swaziland.

One Friday night in December 1978, a group of Security Branch men entered the house on the northwestem comer of Gilfillan Street in Mbabane in which they thought the Commissioner's offices were situated. Once inside, they discovered that it was the offices of a Swazi government department. After leaving the premises, Coetzee had an inkling that the Commissioner's offices might be in the outbuildings.

The next day he contacted Charlie Bell, the Swazi police's detective chief, who had become a good friend, and asked him whether any reports of a break-in to a government department the previous night had been reported. Bell said no and asked Coetzee why he wanted to know, but Coetzee told him not to worry.

That night the same team returned to Swaziland and entered the outbuildings through a window. Coetzee tore the filing cabinets open with a crowbar and they removed all the files, several telex tapes, letterheads, envelopes, UN vehicle door stickers, some books and a paper shredder. After the men had ransacked the whole place, they took all the petty cash and left, stuffing the loot into Coetzee's car. They drove to the Royal Swazi Spa Hotel, where they treated themselves to food and liquor with the money they had stolen.

A United Nations spokesperson said the following Monday that the offices had been virtually destroyed and that all the files on refugees were taken. He said he suspected the South African government of being involved in the burglary.[6]

And indeed, nearly four years later, the letter bomb that killed Ruth First in Maputo was concealed in a parcel covered with United Nations stickers stolen that night. (First, who was professor in African Studies at the Eduardo Mondlane University in Maputo and wife of South African Communist Party leader Joe Slovo, had been the first woman to be detained in the 1960s under the infamous "90-Day Act".)

Late one night, Coetzee had to meet Van Rensburg and his men at a nightclub in Swaziland. "Dirk, we have just planted a bomb. You must look at tomorrow's newspaper. It's going to be a big bang."

An hour earlier, the Ermelo Security Branch had planted the bomb, fitted with a time device and a tilt switch, in the post box of a Manzini law firm. The target was an ANC member, Bafana Duma, who worked at the firm and collected the post every morning. The post box was also used by the ANC.

The timing device worked on two circuits. The first was in a small pocketwatch of Russian origin, with the minute-hand removed, giving the operative up to twelve hours to make up the parcel bomb, close it, transport it and plant it without risking detonation in that period.

The contact point was at 12 on the watch face, and the other wire went to the middle of the watch on the centre shaft of the hour-hand. The second circuit was a glass tube at a 45-degree angle with a drop of mercury at the bottom of the tube, and two contact points at the top of the tube. As soon as the parcel tilted, the drop of mercury rolled forward into the contact point, closed the circuit and the bomb would go off.

Early the next morning, the bomb went off as Duma opened the door of the post box. When Coetzee arrived at the scene an hour or two later, Duma's spectacles were still lying where he fell on the pavement, his arm severed from his body.[7]

Looking at the scene, Coetzee said, he felt extremely proud to be associated with the Security Branch. A terrorist had been given the hiding of his life, one he would never forget and always regret. When he saw the Ermelo police later, they celebrated the success of the operation. Swaziland was their playground, and they thoroughly relished the games they were playing.

But one of their war games turned into disaster. One day a security policeman ran into Coetzee's office to make an urgent phone call. He dialled an informer in Swaziland and told him to leave the country as soon as possible as his cover might have been blown. Hours before, an elaborate operation in Swaziland had gone wrong and an ANC guerrilla had shot two security policemen.

In an operation combining various Security Branches in Natal and Eastern Transvaal, they had planned to ambush a Land Cruiser carrying insurgents from Mozambique to the South African-Swazi border. Two Security Branch men posed as land surveyors on the road near the Namaacha border post inside Swaziland waiting for the vehicle with its load of trained terrorists. The site selected for the ambush was in a dip on the dirt road. The farm next to the road belonged to a friendly farmer, Deneys de Bruin. The squad of policemen entered Swaziland through his farm, which borders South Africa.

The policemen decided to chase some of De Bruin's cattle into the road to force the vehicle to stop. A squad of security policemen hid in the veld ready to ambush and kill the insurgents. There were no passengers in the back of the Land Cruiser as it stopped for the cattle in the road. One of the policemen posing as a surveyor ran forward with a baseball bat in his hands to smash the windscreen. The driver started shooting and both policemen fell to the ground, seriously wounded. The rest of the police squad opened fire and wounded the driver, but the single passenger jumped out and escaped to Manzini where he reported the incident to the Swazi police. The Land Cruiser was covered in petrol and set alight.

The policemen were taken to Nelspruit, where emergency operations were performed on them. The next day, the Swazi government accused South Africa of violating its territory for attacks against the ANC. South Africa rejected the allegation and blamed PAC guerrillas. Coetzee said that the wounded driver, later identified as an ANC member called Kehla, was brought back to South Africa, but mysteriously disappeared.[8]

While at Oshoek, Coetzee had his first serious hiccup with his superiors when he gave a false alibi to one of his informers that eventually backfired on him. Rika Lourens-Botes had an agency in Johannesburg that organised visas, work permits and temporary and permanent residence permits for Portuguese immigrants.

One day, while she was having visas stamped into the passports of immigrants whom she had come to collect at the border post, she asked Coetzee to provide her with a back-dated entry-and-exit stamp in her own passport, which he did. Coetzee also arranged for her to get the necessary stamps on the Swazi side of the border.

Lourens-Botes phoned Coetzee a few days later to tell him that she had been caught in a diamond trap and had used the stamps as an alibi. The police could prove, however, that she was in Johannesburg at the time. The investigating officer informed Brigadier Johan Coetzee of Security Branch headquarters in Pretoria, who ordered the CID chief for Eastern Transvaal to investigate the matter.

Jan van der Hoven intervened and came to Coetzee's rescue, but in the end Coetzee had to make an affidavit admitting that he had provided Lourens-Botes with the stamps. Although Coetzee never heard about the matter again, in later years it became clear that Johan Coetzee had not forgotten the bad conduct and irresponsibility of his border post commander.

Coetzee also landed himself in trouble when he assisted a friend and fellow police officer to smuggle a pornographic movie from Swaziland into South Africa. Coetzee and his police friend went to Mbabane one Sunday night to visit a cinema owner who had a good selection of pornographic movies. The two sat in Cineland in Mbabane as the owner showed a movie just for them. As they left, he gave one to Coetzee's friend.

Back home in Pretoria, Coetzee's story continues, the policeman showed the movie over and over to his police friends until he could replay it in its entirety with his eyes closed. The movie was eventually passed on to a colleague at the Security Branch's technical division and from there to a Pretoria attorney who circulated the pornography among his circle of acquaintances.

Next, when it seemed that all of adult Pretoria's morals had been duly undermined, the attorney passed it on to his brother-in-law, whose wife caught him red-handed. Raging with anger, she there and then phoned the police, who arrested the unlucky man and wanted to know where he got the movie from. It was traced all the way back to Dirk Coetzee and the information was passed on to the head of the narcotics bureau, Colonel Basie Smit (today General Smit, chief of the Security Branch), who informed Johan Coetzee. This was another incident that Johan Coetzee would use years later to try to discredit the rogue cop who joined the ANC.

Just before Dirk Coetzee was transferred from Oshoek border post, he was invited by Nick van Rensburg to accompany the Ermelo Security Branch on a mission to blow up a Swazi railway line. This venture turned out to be a highly successful operation in the most unusual way, further improving the already good relations between South Africa and Swaziland.

The Waverly border post was deserted but Van Rensburg had a key and opened the gate. The squad went through with their bomb and drove to the Mpaka railway station where they left Coetzee behind with a shotgun to guard the car. When the bomb was in place on the track the group left, arriving home just before dawn.

Around nine o'clock the squad was back at Oshoek, telling Coetzee that the bomb did not go off and was discovered by railway workers who informed the Swazi police. They did not have a bomb disposal expert and called the Ermelo Security Branch for help. The squad used fishing tackle to haul the bomb off the railway line and then proceeded to detonate the device. They were heroes in the eyes of the Swazi police and received a standing ovation for their brave effort.[9]

A former chief of the Security Branch, General Ferdi Zietsman, visited the border post in November 1979 and was so impressed by what he saw that the story of the clubhouse and how it fostered good relations between South Africa and Swaziland was published in the May 1980 edition of *Servamus*, under the headings "The house that Dirk built" and "Oshoek, symbol of good relations with black states".[10]

At the end of 1979, Coetzee was transferred from Oshoek to Middelburg, where he was second-in-command of the Security Branch. The first five months were a peaceful period that was cruelly interrupted by an unusual divorce action and a bombing mission he had to lead into Swaziland.

Coetzee was handed 12 files on suspected ANC members who had left the country and instructed to do follow-up visits on their families and friends to try to find out what had happened to them.

The area he had to cover included two tribal areas and he frequently visited witch doctors and tribal chiefs. To obtain the goodwill of the witch doctors, he visited the Kruger National Park and obtained animal material that they needed for their medicine. It was most useful to have their support because of their importance to the local communities. Criminals would visit the witch doctors for medicine for protection.

A typical daily routine out in the veld was to pry around during the day, get to a bottle store before closing time, buy 12 beers and a two-litre can of wine, find a peaceful place in the great outdoors, have a braai, fall over and sleep. Coetzee's little band of roaming Security Branch men included his Venda friend David Tshikalange, another black policeman and often his four-year-old son, Dirk.

Domestic problems shattered Coetzee's carefree existence, though. Just after the family arrived in Middelburg, his son Kalla became ill and his condition deteriorated. While Coetzee was working and drinking in the veld, happier than ever, Karin had to make so many trips to doctors in Pretoria that she decided to move in with her mother. Shortly afterwards, the child fell into a coma and doctors diagnosed diabetes.

Coetzee continued to spend most of his time in the bush, driving to Pretoria to visit his family over weekends. Karin started to threaten her husband with divorce and eventually issued him with a summons, which he ignored. She issued a second summons, which he ignored again. One morning in June, Karin left home and did not return. He discovered later that day that he was Case Number 30 on the court roll for that day and was by now no longer married.

He took a few days' leave and went on a legal crusade to try and save what was his marriage. Karin agreed to take him back, and within three weeks the divorce order was set aside. The case became a reported case in the marital law of South Africa.

Because of the "apprenticeship" he had so dutifully served at the Oshoek border post, Coetzee was ready to be used for bigger, more dangerous operations. In the early days of June 1980, the Sasol petroleum plant at Secunda in the Eastern Transvaal was rocked by a bomb blast that caused serious damage and ignited a major petroleum fire. It was seen as one of Umkhonto we Sizwe's most successful military operations and an important morale booster for the ANC.

The police suspected that the ANC bombers had infiltrated South Africa through Swaziland. Coetzee was instructed to report to Major Nick van Rensburg in Ermelo to lead a revenge bombing mission aimed at two houses in Manzini.

At last, they trust me enough to assign this sensitive and vital mission to me, he thought as he left for Swaziland on his first assassination mission. I will not disappoint my superiors, but further foster their trust in me.

Shortly before the mission, Coetzee had to collect two Russian pocket watch timing devices prepared by the Security Branch's technical division and a box of explosives from Military Intelligence. When he arrived in Ermelo, the rest of the mission members were already waiting for him. They were to blow up an ANC transit house and the house of a Swazi citizen whom the police suspected to have built false panels into the vehicles that were used to smuggle the explosives into South Africa.

Under a bridge just before entering Swaziland, they stopped to prepare the two 20-kilogram bombs. They kneaded the PE4 explosive until it was like dough, put yellow cordite in the middle of the two bundles, folding each up into a ball and placing it in a plastic bag. They then stuck in the detonators and the pocket watches, and all that remained was for the batteries to be connected. They also filled two big bags with sand, to be placed on the bombs to concentrate the blast. They loaded the bombs into the car, found a convenient spot to light the braaivleis fire and opened the beer and brandy while waiting for midnight.

Later, Paul van Dyk, who knew the border area intimately, guided the team along a dirt road to a spot where they could flatten the fence and drive across. They made their way through young wattle brush to a road and proceeded to Manzini. They had their service pistols, two machine guns, two pump-action shotguns and two hand grenades in the car in case there was a road block and they had to fight their way back to South Africa.

They stopped close to the first house, set the pocket watch for a quarter of an hour and placed the bomb against a bedroom wall with a sandbag on top of it. At the transit house, the bomb was set in a similar place before they drove off to a spot just outside Manzini where they opened some more beers and waited for the bombs to detonate. A few minutes later, a bright white mushroom shot into the air, followed by a huge explosion. Less than a minute later, the second bomb exploded as well. The rowdy team, drinking as always, rushed back to South Africa to report the success of the operation to their superiors.

The two bombs exploded on 4 June 1980. The first house, which was made of wood, was totally demolished and planks were strewn all over the area. The only person in the house that night was a small boy, who was instantly killed. In the other house, one ANC infiltrator was killed and three more wounded. Fifty-three houses over an area of three kilometres were damaged by the explosion.[11] Coetzee heard afterwards that there was discontent at security headquarters because of the child being killed.

Coetzee went back to Swaziland a few days later to assess the destruction their bombs had caused. Standing at the demolished house, he thought about the young boy blown to pieces. Back home, his own two boys were waiting for their father to return from Swaziland. His colleagues told him not to worry too much about the death of the boy: sooner or later he would have become a terrorist himself.

During this time, Coetzee was promoted to the rank of captain. Because of his nearly failed marriage and his youngest son's diabetes, he asked for a transfer to Pretoria. He was told by Brigadier Jan van der Hoven, who in the meantime had become chief of the Security Branch in the Eastern Transvaal, to report to Brigadier Jan Viktor, head of Section C (the ANC-PAC desk) at Security Branch head office in Pretoria. He was appointed commander of the Vlakplaas counter-insurgency unit. Dirk Coetzee was creeping deeper and deeper into the heart of the whore.

CHAPTER FOUR

In the heart of the whore

VLAKPLAAS is a 44-hectare police farm alongside the Hennops River on the border of Pretoria's western suburbs. When Dirk Coetzee arrived there as commander of the unit in August 1980, it was used as nothing more than a place to accommodate "rehabilitated terrorists". The smallholding included an old farmhouse with some outbuildings, a vegetable garden and a scattering of livestock. A storeroom in the farmhouse was stocked with supplies that Johan Viktor, in charge of Vlakplaas until the end of 1980, had received from his Rhodesian police friends after the bush war had ended – canned food, shoes, shirts, trousers, blankets, beds and mattresses.[1]

During Coetzee's command at Vlakplaas, there were altogether 17 askaris. Most of them had been "turned" by their security police interrogators, but there were also a few who had gone over to the police of their own accord. The askaris were registered as head office informants and received a monthly allowance of R200. Eventually, of these 17 "rehabilitated terrorists" at Vlakplaas, two were killed and one allegedly killed by Coetzee and his men, three deserted back to the ANC and two landed up in prison for murder. The remaining askaris are still serving in the SAP. In Coetzee's time most of them smoked dagga and drank heavily. There were also three former Zapu guerrillas brought from Zimbabwe to work as labourers on the farm, while five Renamo fighters from Mozambique occasionally spent some time on Vlakplaas. A black warrant officer was in charge of the askaris when Coetzee arrived.

Viktor decided that the askaris should be used in a surveillance capacity. They were to mix with the population at public places such as shebeens, bus stops, railway stations and taxi ranks, spot their former comrades and point them out to qualified policemen who would arrest them. Whenever the askaris were needed for a task, the required numbers would be fetched by the different Security Branches country-wide and returned when they had finished their mission.

The rations for the askaris came out of a secret security fund and from Viktor's connections in the Rhodesian Special Branch. Through the police quartermaster, Coetzee requisitioned a supply of daily essentials – bread and milk, meat, fruit and vegetables. He arranged a generator for an electrical power supply, exchanged some of the Rhodesian loot for a deep freeze and obtained a television set out of the police facilities fund.

To further improve the living standards of the askaris, Coetzee had them appointed as policemen, which gave them a better salary, free police medical benefits and a clothing allowance. It also meant that they could get pistols to protect themselves, though two askaris chose to shoot their girlfriends and others used their weapons to solve personal problems at shebeens. Coetzee got them pass books and travel documents and gave them driving lessons. The askaris received no police training, as they had already had a military training from the ANC or the PAC.

Almond Nofemela and other fully qualified policemen arrived at Vlakplaas a few months after Coetzee. They were to accompany the askaris on their missions, working under the white security policemen of the various branches that needed them. Although the black policemen were not askaris, they soon adopted the name as their own.

Coetzee suggested that white policemen be appointed at Vlakplaas to take charge of the different askari squads. The proposal was accepted and in August 1981, three white security policemen arrived at Vlakplaas. Coetzee renewed his acquaintance with Captain Koos Vermeulen from Sibasa and Warrant Officer Paul van Dyk from Oshoek. It was only with the arrival of the white officers that Vlakplaas was finally established as a counter-insurgency unit. Four squads were formed, each consisting of black policemen and "rehabilitated terrorists" operating under the command of a white officer. While the policemen and askaris mixed with the local population, the whites would remain in the vicinity, out of sight. Often the blacks would be found mingling all too well at the shebeens, while the whites had similar haunts of their own.

Looking back at the formation of these squads, it may seem that they were planned as forerunners of organised death squads. Coetzee believes that this was definitely not the case. From beginning to end, the primary function of the Vlakplaas squads was surveillance and the detection of infiltrators.

It was inevitable, however, that Vlakplaas would become involved in the secret and unconventional war against the enemy. Because of the unit's secretive nature, it was the ideal base for operations and people who were not to be seen. Some of the askaris were highly effective soldiers who were simply also employed to perform hit operations.

Coetzee was present at various conversations where former members of the Rhodesian Special Branch told how they had booby-trapped arms caches by removing the delay fuses of hand grenades, and poisoned food supplies, clothes and water holes used by the guerrillas.

There was never one specific death squad in the security establishment. Murders and atrocities were committed before and after Coetzee's period in the security police. The Vlakplaas units operated in response to requests from branches and received their instructions from the various branch commanders and from Viktor or his successor, Brigadier Willem Schoon. If they were instructed to perform an atrocity, they asked no questions. It was part of their function.

Coetzee's squad of askaris consisted of Almond Nofemela, David Tshikalange, Brian Ngqulunga and at times Joe Mamasela.

Nofemela left school after passing standard nine and worked as a bricklayer before joining the police in 1980. After he completed his six months' police training at the "black" college near Hammanskraal, he was recruited by the security police. He was one of the few squad members who did not drink or smoke. Nofemela denied that he murdered the Brits farmer, but the presiding judge found him guilty and sentenced him to death. He is still on death row.[2]

Mamasela 'became a police informant in 1979 while in jail awaiting trial for housebreaking and theft. He was released shortly after a security policeman visisted him and persuaded him to "combat terrorism". He infiltrated the ANC in Botswana, undergoing intelligence training with them. In the winter of 1981 his cover was blown and he was kidnapped and taken to an ANC base in Botswana. A fellow police informer was allegedly tortured and killed, but Mamasela escaped and joined the Vlakplaas unit. He is still in the security police and today holds the rank of sergeant.[3]

Ngqulunga joined the ANC in 1977 but later became disaffected and was detained in Maputo. He drank insecticide in an attempt to commit suicide and escaped shortly afterwards, only to be caught and detained again. He was held in a maximum security prison for nearly two years before being deported back to South Africa by the Mozambican authorities. When he was debriefed by the security police, he volunteered to assist them in tracking down insurgents. While at Vlakplaas, he had to be hospitalised after a fist fight with Nofemela and twice used his service pistol in violent acts while off duty. He was one of a number of askaris who were eventually appointed as police constables without ever attending police college. He was charged with attempted murder, but was found not guilty. His bullet-ridden body was found in 1990 in the veld near a black township north of Pretoria. AK-47 cartridges were found nearby.[4]

The trusted Tshikalange, who had followed Coetzee from Sibasa to Yolksrust and from there to Oshoek, Middelburg and eventually to Vlakplaas, was first appointed as a guard, later as an informant and eventually became a police constable. He was forced to resign from the police force in 1985 after two drunken driving convictions and an accident with a police car. He was found guilty of assault in 1984 when he shot a man through the hand in a Pretoria bar. After Coetzee left Vlakplaas, he became his successor's driver. He suffers from epilepsy and frequently consults witch doctors to try to find a cure for his condition.[5]

Dirkie Coetzee accompanied his father and the askaris on many of the surveillance missions and stayed for up to two weeks in the field. He was allowed to clean his father's weapons and could dismantle the hand machine guns. One night in the Eastern Transvaal, the squad came across an ANC arms cache and decided to lay an ambush for the infiltrators. Tshikalange was instructed to take the child away and wait for the squad at the camp site three kilometres away. Dirkie heard shots as fighting broke out. One day, his father told him about the attorney they had killed in Durban, but warned him not to tell his mother about the incident.

Although the primary task of the Vlakplaas squads was to identify and arrest former comrades, they failed miserably in achieving this. Coetzee says that in his 18 months as commander, no ANC or PAC infiltrators were apprehended. Nofemela identified and arrested only one infiltrator in his seven years at Vlakplaas, while Ngqulunga later admitted that during his nine years on the farm not one arrest had arisen from his work, as he had failed to identify anybody.

Coetzee drove around with enough firepower in the boot of his car to start a small war. There was a 40-kilogram case of explosives, a case of offensive and defensive Russian hand grenades, five hand machine guns, Makarov and Tokarev pistols with silencers, a shotgun, fuses, igniters and Russian pocket watches. He also had corpse bags and strychnine in his car in case of need.

His official car's registration number was DJC 036 T – his initials and his age at that stage. Security police headquarters had their own printing press and provided Vlakplaas with false registration plates, third party and licence discs and most of the askaris had false travel documents.

The first important mission Coetzee undertook at Vlakplaas caused an international diplomatic incident when his team of askaris kidnapped a teacher – a former ANC activist – from Swaziland. In February 1981, Coetzee was instructed to lead his squad into Swaziland to scout for suitable ANC targets and to hit as many as possible in one night before getting out again. An explosives expert was sent with the group to manufacture bombs for ANC transit houses.

The askaris made slow progress and found it difficult to identify any ANC targets. Willem Schoon called Coetzee back to Pretoria to explain the lack of progress. While he was there, the askaris stumbled upon Joe Pillay, known to them as a senior member of Umkhonto we Sizwe in Natal. Coetzee received a message that the askaris had kidnapped Pillay and brought him to the Oshoek border post, where he was detained. Inspired by their success, the roaming band of askaris had returned to Swaziland to search for more victims.

The next day Ermelo security policemen brought Pillay to Vlakplaas, where he was detained while they waited for police officers from the Security

Branch in Durban to interrogate him. On their arrival he was blindfolded and taken to an underground military interrogation centre near Pretoria where he was questioned for two days by the Durban policemen and a member of Military Intelligence. Pillay had been badly beaten up by the askaris and "truth serum" was intravenously administered during the interrogation. It became obvious that he was no longer actively involved with the ANC, however; the police had no use for him. Tshikalange – cuffed to Pillay and armed with a knobkierie – was given the task of guarding the prisoner.

The kidnapping of Pillay had been a noisy affair. Eyewitnesses had noticed the registration number of the car into which the struggling and screaming teacher was bundled and reported the incident to the Swazi police. The askari car was spotted the next morning and a high-speed chase ensued. The askaris fled into a house and tried to hide in cupboards, but the police teargassed them out of their shelters and arrested them. They were later released on bail and smuggled back to South Africa.

The kidnapping caused an international uproar. General Johan Coetzee and an official from the Department of Foreign Affairs had to meet Swazi officials and undertook to release Pillay immediately. They assured the Swazi government that the police had acted without official consent and tendered their apologies.[6] Johan Coetzee fumed with rage over the embarrassment the incident had caused the Security Branch – not the first time Coetzee had put him in a spot. Dirk Coetzee remarked afterwards: "Success has many fathers: failures are orphans."

But it later turned out that Johan Coetzee's anger and embarrassment were not only the result of an illegal kidnapping and a diplomatic incident. One of the askaris who participated in the kidnapping of Joe Pillay dropped his passport, and Mozambican intelligence files identified him as a member of the Renamo rebel movement. His presence among the South African security policemen caused considerable embarrassment to Pretoria.

Amaro Silva was one of the Renamo soldiers who spent some time at Vlakplaas. He worked for South Africa in at least five countries. The former school teacher had fled the civil war in Mozambique and handed himself over to the South African Police. They sent him to Rhodesia where he was trained and put into Renamo, which was originally created by Rhodesian intelligence. He was sent back to Mozambique to assassinate President Samora Machel, but instead bombed a cafe in downtown Maputo, injuring 50 people. Silva was caught in 1980 but escaped the following year and returned to South Africa, where he spent some time at Vlakplaas and participated in the kidnapping of Pillay. By now a highly trained and battle-hardened soldier, he was sent on anti-Swapo missions in Namiba, then returned to Mozambique in June 1982, but was caught and executed.[7]

During the planning of the South African attack on Mozambique in January 1981, which became known as the Matola raid, two of Coetzee's askaris were instructed to join in the raid. Both of them had stayed in the target house in Maputo while they were still members of Umkhonto we Sizwe.

One of the askaris was Steven Mashamba, who – before being arrested and "turned" – had been the political commissar of a structure known as the Natal Urban Missionary, with the task of creating military cells. Just before the Matola raid, Mashamba went back to Mozambique to stay in a house called the "Castle", where exiles from Natal were housed. As the attackers stormed into the house, Mashamba showed them around and took sensitive documents with him.[8]

Various other attacks into neighbouring countries were planned at Vlakplaas. A Lesotho police informer, Ernest Ramatlala, had to stay on the farm for a few months after a failed attempt to blow up the military leader of the ANC in Lesotho, Chris Hani (later the organisation's military chief of staff).

Ramatlala was a senior member of the Lesotho Youth Organisation and Hani's close confidant. The plan was to plant a bomb, triggered by a wheel mechanism prepared by the technical division of the security police, in Hani's car. His dogs knew Ramatlala well enough not to raise the alarm as he planted the bomb. However, the would-be assassin accidentally triggered the mechanism as he was planting the bomb. He was seriously injured by the blast and further assaulted by a raging and cursing Hani, who stormed out of his house. Ramatlala spent months under guard in hospital recovering from his wounds. When he eventually appeared in court, bail was arranged and he escaped into South Africa, where he was harboured at Vlakplaas.[9]

The South African Police will always be haunted by the death of Steve Biko, the founder of the South African Black Consciousness Movement. On 12 September 1977, Biko died in detention after being left for two days mortally injured on a mat in chains. An inquest magistrate exonerated the police, but even four years later, they dreaded being caught with a detainee's blood on their hands again.

That is exactly what happened when a young Eastern Cape activist, Goinisizwe Kwezilomso Kondile, his hands cuffed behind his back, dived through the window of an interrogation room and fell head-first onto the cement outside. Although he did not seem to be seriously injured at first, his behaviour became peculiar and the interrogators asked a doctor they could trust to examine him. As they heard his warning that the man had sustained head injuries, the ghost of Steve Biko rose amongst them.

Kondile had been detained by security police in June 1981 when he tried to enter South Africa from Lesotho with a false travel document. The car he was driving at the time, a two-door Datsun Stanza, later turned out to belong to Chris Hani. He was being interrogated at various police stations in the Eastern Cape when the accident happened.[10]

Kondile had had his first run-in with the police the previous year while completing a law degree at the University of Fort Hare. During demonstrations at the university he was picked up and taken to the Alice Police Station, where he was charged with taking part in an illegal gathering. Lawyers made a bail application and the case was postponed. Kondile jumped bail and fled to Lesotho, where he hoped to continue his studies, but where he also made contact with the ANC.[11]

Coetzee's involvement in the saga of Goinisizwe Kondile started in September 1981 when he visited the Eastern Cape with his team of askaris. Nick van Rensburg had in the meantime been promoted to the rank of colonel and was now the head of the Security Branch in Port Elizabeth.

The visit to the Eastern Cape started off on a fun note when Coetzee helped Van Rensburg to harass a labour union by chasing up their telephone bill. The union's lines were tapped. Through an intricate system, two of the telephones in the union's office were connected via the recording room at security head office in Port Elizabeth to two phones in Van Rensburg's office. By phoning two people, one from each telephone, and then connecting the instruments, they could talk at the union's expense.

When Coetzee got there that night, everything was set up. He phoned all over South Africa, to Namibia and the United States. He phoned a friend in America and connected her with her daughter in Johannesburg. He put his friend in Windhoek in contact with his brother in Pietermaritzburg. The game continued throughout the night, and the next morning, the security policemen tapping the conversations of the union wanted to know what the hell had been happening on the phones the previous night. Van Rensburg spluttered and shook with merriment.

Van Rensburg gave Coetzee a key to an Audi motor car belonging to the local organiser of the National Automobile and Allied Workers' Union in the Eastern Cape, Edward Maepi. Coetzee, Almond Nofemela and David Tshikalange went to a black township where they found the car parked in front of its garage. There were people in the sitting room of the house, so Tshikalange held the front door handle tight while Coetzee started the car and reversed it out of the driveway. When he was out in the street he threw the passenger door open and Tshikalange ran for the car amidst chaos and pandemonium that broke loose in the house.[12]

The squad drove to a spot near the coastal town of Jeffrey's Bay, where they planned to burn the car. One of the Port Elizabeth security policemen who had accompanied them asked Coetzee if he could have the car's brand-new tyres before they burnt the vehicle. Coetzee agreed, but told the policeman he would have to get rid of the car himself.

As they parked the stolen car, Coetzee saw a light-coloured two-door Datsun Stanza in one of the garages at the Jeffrey's Bay Police Station. Eight years later, the former police captain's incredible memory of the car he saw that night proved vital yet again, solving the bizarre murder and dis-appearance of Goinisizwe Kondile.

Nick van Rensburg was waiting for the squad as they walked into the police station. Coetzee followed him into the "white" unmarried quarters where Van Rensburg entered a bedroom. Handcuffed to a bed was a slender, bearded black man, guarded by a black policeman. Van Rensburg asked if everything was in order and they left again.

On their way back home, Van Rensburg explained that the captive was one Sizwe Kondile, who had been arrested as he tried to enter South Africa from Lesotho. Van Rensburg said the detainee had sustained a head injury and that they could not afford another Steve Biko case in the Eastern Cape. They would have to make a plan to get rid of the injured man.

"Why don't you bring him to Komatipoort where we can safely kill him and burn his body to ashes? I'll drive Kondile's car to Swaziland and park it at a local hotel and everyone will believe the terrorist fled to Swaziland," Coetzee offered.

At that time, Kondile had already been officially released. On 10 August 1981 Captain Hermanus "Doep" du Plessis of the security police in Port Elizabeth had sent a message to Security Branch headquarters in Pretoria informing them that the interrogation of the "subject" was completed, that there was no case against him but that he was willing to become a police informer. According to the message, he was then released.[13]

Sizwe's father, Port Elizabeth attorney Dumile Kondile, was told by Du Plessis that on 10 August he personally took the detainee back to Bloem-fontein where his car was standing. His son was allowed to proceed to wherever he wanted to go and he was not seen again by any member of the South African Police. However, nine years later a police document would show that more than a month after Kondile's official release he was still in police custody in the Eastern Cape.[14]

A few weeks after Coetzee had returned to Vlakplaas, he was summoned to Willem Schoon's office and instructed to report to Archie Flemington at Komatipoort, where Nick van Rensburg would join them with a prisoner. Coetzee told Schoon that they would need knock-out drops for the operation and that he should make the necessary arrangements to obtain the drug from General Lothar Neethling.

Coetzee and Paul van Dyk fetched the drops at the forensic laboratory and proceeded to Komatipoort, where they were met by Flemington and two of his men. The group went to a secret police farm in the area, where Van Rensburg and Doep du Plessis arrived with a handcuffed prisoner with a balaclava over his head. After it was removed, Coetzee recognised him as the same bearded, slender prisoner who had been cuffed to the bed at the Jeffrey's Bay Police Station.

A cold drink was spiked with Neethling's drops and given to Kondile to drink. As he fell over, one of Flemington's men stepped forward, pushed the barrel of the Makarov against the back of his head and pulled the trigger. Half an hour later, the dead man's body was burning on the pyre of bushveld wood and tyres and seven hours later, he was cremated.

After the beer and brandy had been opened and the meat was sizzling on the grill, Van Rensburg told the group of security policemen that members of the Security Branch at Ermelo had taken Kondile's car to Swaziland and left it at a hotel. He also told them that Kondile had indeed been officially released and taken back to Bloemfontein, but was afterwards kidnapped and detained at the police station where Coetzee saw him.

The following morning, Kondile's ashes were raked level with the ground. As the men left for their various units, they were convinced that Biko's ghost had been exorcised.

In the last months of 1981, Coetzee was involved in the murders of Peter Dlamini and Vuyani Mavuso, Griffiths Mxenge, Sizwe Kondile and a Lesotho diamond dealer. In the same period, he participated in a raid into Botswana in which a woman was shot.

Before the Vlakplaas team entered Botswana that night, the white members blackened their faces and pulled special caps over their hair and ears. Joe Mamasela and Almond Nofemela were armed with Russian-made pistols, Koos Vermeulen had a submachine gun and a hand grenade and Coetzee a submachine gun. Their target was the house of Joyce Dipale in Gaborone, which the security police believed was used as an ANC transit house.

Earlier on the afternoon of 26 November the squad had assembled on a police farm near Zeerust where they planned the operation. Mamasela and Nofemela entered Botswana through the Kopfontein border post to do surveillance on the house. After they returned, Coetzee took the same vehicle into Botswana to familiarise himself with the surroundings. Years later, the records of the Botswana customs authorities would provide corroboration of their movements.[15]

The squad crossed the fence south of the border post into Botswana, where Mamasela, who had gone into Botswana again, picked them up. About two blocks from Dipale's house they left Tshikalange and Paul van Dyk to guard the vehicle and proceeded on foot. Coetzee decided to wait for a thunderstorm that was building up to break, in order to give them better cover.

Vermeulen took up position near a bedroom window while Coetzee, Nofemela and Mamasela were at the back door deciding how they were going to enter the house. The next moment, however, the key turned on the inside and a woman opened the door. Mamasela grabbed her, covered her mouth and shot her point-blank. She collapsed on the stoep. Another woman screamed and retreated further inside the house.

Coetzee pushed Nofemela and Mamasela aside and ran into the kitchen spraying bullets down the passage. Vermeulen fired through the bedroom window but later found that he had forgotten to throw the hand grenade.

Coetzee ran out of the house again and shouted to the others to get the hell out of there. They raced towards the border and reached their base cold, tired and wet.

The woman who was shot, Joyce Dipale, miraculously survived the attack with only a flesh wound in her neck. She made an affidavit saying that she recognised her attacker as Joe Mamasela, whom she had met while he was with the ANC in Botswana.[16]

Peter Dlamini and Vuyani Mavuso were not the only activists who had to be eliminated because they became a nuisance or refused to co-operate with the security police. Isaac "Ace" Moema, a trained and "turned" ANC guerrilla who came to Vlakplaas in 1981, suffered the same fate. Askaris complained that his heart was not with Vlakplaas, but still with the enemy in exile. Coetzee instructed Nofemela to keep an eye on Moema, but Vermeulen insisted that they get rid of him before he could sell them out to the enemy.[17]

Schoon said that they should do what they thought best. Soon Koos Vermeulen went on a surveillance mission to the Western Transvaal, taking Moema with him. He returned a few days later without the askari and reported to Coetzee and Schoon that he had been taken care of.

Shortly after that another askari, Chris Mnisi, escaped from Vlakplaas and went back to the ANC. He told the ANC that he had been a member of Vermeulen's squad on that fateful mission to the Western Transvaal and that Vermeulen, Moema and a member of the Nelspruit Security Branch had left the group for a whole night. When Vermeulen returned alone the next day, he was tired and dirty and his arms, eyelashes, brows and hair were scorched. The group immediately knew that Moema had been executed and cremated.

Coetzee's register of terror also explains the disappearance of a young anti-apartheid activist and student leader from Port Elizabeth, Siphiwo Maxwell Mtimkulu. Mtimkulu, 21 years old and leading a resurgence of student militancy in the Eastern Cape, became an obvious candidate for the attention of the security police during the turbulence of 1981.

Out to crush the Congress of South African Students, the police swooped on 31 May during anti-Republic Day festival demonstrations in Port Elizabeth. Mtimkulu was shot and arrested and treated for for his gunshot wound at the Livingstone Hospital.[18]

He was in perfect health when the security police incarcerated him, but when he emerged five months later from the Algoa Park Police Station, he was a shadow of his former self. On the day he was released, he began complaining of pains in his feet and stomach. Two days later he was unable to walk. He was admitted to Livingstone Hospital and transferred to the Groote Schuur Hospital in Cape Town for fuller examination in November. Medical tests at the hospital showed he had been poisoned with thallium, a rat poison outlawed in South Africa and most Western countries. This lethal poison has been called a homicide's dream: it is tasteless, colourless and odourless.[19]

Mtimkulu's parents insisted that no one had been allowed to visit him while he was in detention and that the only people who had access to him were his security police interrogators. The security policeman in charge of his interrogation was Doep du Plessis of the security police in Port Elizabeth, who was also implicated in the murder of Sizwe Kondile.

Before Mtimkulu's release, Dirk Coetzee had been warned that he would have to assist in the disappearance of an activist then in detention. He might have been killed and disposed of in the same way as Sizwe Kondile, but the security police were reluctant to arrange another disappearance so soon after that of Kondile and Coetzee was told that they were going to poison the activist instead. The case became known among security policemen as "the chap in the wheelchair".

Mtimkulu told doctors at Groote Schuur and Livingstone hospitals that Doep du Plessis had given him three different types of tablets during his last month in detention, saying they were to treat the pain he had started experiencing in his feet.

He had been beaten on the feet with electric heater cords. Doctors also noticed scars on his back. In addition, Mtimkulu claimed to have been beaten with wet towels and fists, electrocuted through his feet, submerged in water and forced to stand for nine days without any rest.

The seriously ill Mtimkulu had to spend 10 months in hospital recovering from thallium poisoning. He brought two actions against the police: the first was a R40 000 claim against the Minister of Law and Order for being assaulted in detention; the second, brought on 2 April 1982, was a claim of R140 000 in which he accused the police of poisoning him during his months in jail.[20]

Nearly two weeks later, Mtimkulu was given a lift to Livingstone Hospital by a friend, Topsy Madaka. At the time Mtimkulu was still not able to wear shoes and had to use a walking stick. Mtimkulu and Madaka disappeared that day and were never seen again. Mtimkulu's wheelchair was later found with Mdaka's car near the Lesotho border. The Commissioner of Police, General Johan Coetzee, said he believed that Mtimkulu had left South Africa.[21]

Dirk Coetzee, who had already left Vlakplaas by the time Mtimkulu disappeared, said that Brigadier Jan du Preez told him later that the security police had decided to kidnap Mtimkulu, kill him and dispose of his body. Du Preez said the police had decided to leave his friend's car near the Lesotho border to create the impression that Mtimkulu had for some reason decided to leave the country.

Mtimkulu's mother, Joyce Mtimkulu, has searched for the past nine years for her son. Likewise, the parents and friends of Peter Dlamini, Vuyani Mavuso, Ace Moema and Sizwe Kondile – together with the ANC, human rights lawyers and even the United Nations have made extensive inquiries to establish their whereabouts or whether they are still alive. In its efforts to refute Coetzee's allegations, the South African Police have also searched for the missing men. In not a single case could anybody produce a shred of evidence that they were still alive.

Coetzee's skills and expertise as a car thief were put to good use at Vlakplaas when he stole two more motor vehicles and burnt another three. The vehicles that were set ablaze belonged to a "hippie community" – a communist sanctuary, according to the police – at Rhodes village in the Eastern Cape. Robert Sacco, whose truck was burnt out that night, went to see Coetzee in exile in 1990 to meet the arsonist. He told Coetzee that three months later his house had been fire-bombed and he lost all his possessions.[22]

In another case, a group of Eastern Cape unionists were to be prevented reaching their destination in Zimbabwe where they had to attend a conference. The police first tried to stop their journey by planting dagga cigarettes in the microbus's airvents, but when they were stopped in a road block, the police could not find the drug and had to allow the unionists to continue their journey. Coetzee and his men eventually stole the microbus from a Johannesburg hotel. Coetzee said that, a few days later, the police made an anonymous phone call to the union's insurance company to prevent insurance money from being paid out.

Nine years later, it was discovered that the National Automobile and Allied Workers' Union left Port Elizabeth in August 1981 to attend a conference in Harare and that they were stopped by the police at Cradock and searched extensively. The insurance company also confirmed that they had received two anonymous phone calls saying that the theft of the microbus had been contrived.[23]

But Dirk Coetzee was not only involved in death squad related crimes while stationed at Vlakplaas. In October 1981, Joe Mamasela, Almond Nofemela, David Tshikalange and Ernest Ramatlala asked for a loan of R5 000. They wanted to buy diamonds in Lesotho, sell them at a profit and become rich. It sounded like a good investment to Coetzee and he decided to assist them in their small business enterprise. He borrowed R5 000 from his mother-in-law and offered to help them sell the diamonds should they experience any problems.[24]

A few days later, the entrepreneurs arrived at Coetzee's home with five tiny uncut diamonds. Coetzee took one look and instructed them to return to Lesotho and get his money back: they had been taken for a ride.

They returned with a grey Datsun Laurel with Lesotho registration plates – and the diamonds. The askaris had tricked the dealer into leaving Lesotho with them, and after passing through the border post, demanded their money back. When he refused, they shot him dead and left his body in a eucalyptus plantation.

Coetzee put false number plates on the diamond dealer's car and left to fetch the dead man. Nofemela and Tshikalange dragged the body out of the bushes, put it into a plastic corpse bag and left for Durban, where the askaris were needed for surveillance work. Coetzee reported to Brigadier Jan van der Hoven and told him about the unfortunate incident. They decided to dispose of the body in Swaziland.

That same night, they burnt the diamond dealer at an old farm ruin just inside the Swaziland border. The next day, Coetzee sold the stolen car for R5 000 – so as to repay his mother-in-law – to an Indian businessman. Before the car was delivered to the buyer in Swaziland, the radio was taken out and installed in Willem Schoon's car.

All of Coetzee's murder victims were black activists, but shortly before he left Vlakplaas, an excited Willem Schoon told him that he was going on a very special mission to Botswana to eliminate a prominent white ANC activist, Marius Schoon. For his mission, Coetzee would have used a black briefcase fitted with a nine-millimetre machine pistol with a silencer.

The briefcase was prepared by the technical division of the security police. The pistol was cocked inside the briefcase before it was closed and then carried in the normal manner. To fire the machine pistol, the briefcase had to be clutched under one's arm with one hand on an extended trigger mechanism underneath the case.

Coetzee was ready to depart for Botswana when Willem Schoon called him in and told him that the mission had been cancelled by the highest authority in the security police. Marius Schoon later made a statement to the ANC saying that he had been warned by the British High Commissioner in Botswana that they had received information from their intelligence services of a South African Police plan to assassinate him.[25]

Marius Schoon escaped death, but his wife and young daughter, Jeanette and Katryn, were killed in June 1984 by a parcel bomb sent to them in exile in Lubango in southern Angola. Coetzee says that shortly after the murder, his friend and confidant, Major Craig Williamson, asked: "Did you see what happened to Jeanette Schoon?"

Coetzee met Craig Williamson, South Africa's superspy and later National Party politician and member of the President's Council, shortly after arriving at Vlakplaas. Williamson had become a police informant while studying at the University of the Witwatersrand and achieved notoriety when he infiltrated the International University Exchange Fund (IUEF) in Geneva, becoming its assistant director. In that time, he made contact with senior Umkhonto we Sizwe officers in Europe and, according to the police, provided the South African security services with invaluable information about the organisation. According to the IUEF, Williamson took nearly R50 000 with him to South Africa when he left Europe in 1979 after discovering that his cover was about to be blown.[26]

Back in South Africa, Williamson was appointed second-in-command of the foreign section (Section A) of the security police. The section head was the infamous Brigadier Piet "Biko" Goosen, the security police officer in charge of Steve Biko's interrogation, promoted just after the activist's death. Section A bought their own secret police farm with the money that Williamson had brought back from Europe.

Coetzee was introduced to one of Willamson's secret agents, Peter Casselton, a British national who came to South Africa to be trained in surveillance and counter-surveillance. After his training, Casselton was sent back to Europe to set up a network of agents. He had an account on the Isle of Man through which police funds were channelled to him. A close friendship developed between Williamson, Coetzee and Casselton. This allowed Coetzee access to some of Section C's innermost secrets.

One day in 1982, after Coetzee had left Vlakplaas, Casselton came back to South Africa for a short holiday and during a meeting the two discussed the possibility of starting a diamond smuggling venture. Coetzee had a contact in Swaziland who had shares in a diamond mine in the Free State. Casselton told Coetzee that they could smuggle the diamonds to him in London in the South African diplomatic bag. This bag, he said, was used to smuggle explosives to him, as they were planning to blow up the ANC's offices in the British capital.

In April 1982, a huge explosion rocked the London offices of the ANC. After Coetzee saw the news on television he visited Williamson, who told him that an explosives expert had been sent to Europe to assemble the bomb for Casselton. Other security police officers had been standing by at various strategic places to assist if something should go wrong.

A few nights after the explosion, Casselton phoned Coetzee and wanted to know when the first consignment of diamonds would arrive at the South African Embassy in London. However, he was arrested by the British police a few days later and charged with sabotage. He admitted in court that he had burgled the ANC offices but denied any knowledge of the bomb. He was convicted of housebreaking and sentenced to four years' imprisonment, but released after two years in jail.[27]

The London operation was regarded as an enormous success and a private medal parade was held in General Johan Coetzee's office, where he awarded decorations to the men involved. While Casselton was in jail, he was promoted to the rank of lieutenant and his salary was paid into his bank account every month.

A few months after Coetzee's allegations were published, he was questioned by Scotland Yard in London and a warrant for Casselton's arrest was issued. Interpol confiscated a luxurious yacht in the Mediterranean that was co-owned by Williamson and Casselton.

Coetzee performed his last death squad operation at Vlakplaas in December 1981 when Willem Schoon instructed him to kidnap an ANC member with the Umkhonto codename "General" from Swaziland. The plan was to bring him to South Africa, interrogate him about ANC activities in Swaziland and dispose of him afterwards. They obtained knock-out drops from the forensic laboratory for the kidnapping.

Coetzee and Almond Nofemela sneaked into General's house and waited for him in his bedroom. When their target suddenly walked into the room, however, pandemonium broke out. General was a small man, but as strong as a lion. Nofemela tried to smother General's screams for help while Coetzee tried to choke him. General sank his teeth into Nofemela's forearm, who in turn got his teeth into the struggling man's scalp. General let go of Nofemela's forearm and the two intruders scrambled for the open window and escaped into the night.

That month Dirk Coetzee was informed that his name was on the list of transfers of security police officers and that he was to report to the Krugersdorp Security Branch on 1 January the next year. He wrote a long letter to Johan Coetzee saying that he could not leave Pretoria because of his youngest son's diabetes. The Commissioner of Police responded: "Transferred to headquarters (fire-arm section)."

Coetzee's behaviour in the security police had become unacceptable to his superiors. Johan Coetzee clearly disliked his Vlakplaas commander, who had not only embarrassed him with a pornographic film and a false alibi, but had also caused a diplomatic row with Swaziland.

Coetzee had come to the end of his career in the security police. The commissioner's decision was not only a demotion in status, it was a deliberate insult. Coetzee felt as though he had been thrown to the wolves.

CHAPTER FIVE

Outcast

A S members of the Security Branch, performing illegal operations inside and outside the borders of the Republic of South Africa, Dirk Coetzee and his colleagues enjoyed special protection. This enabled them to operate above the laws of the country and above the rules and regulations of the South African Police. However, this protection is not statutory and is difficult to define. It is vested in a culture belonging to the close-knit family that the Security Branch really is. The culture is a syndrome of arrogant exclusiveness, secrecy, loyalty to one another, mutual trust and understanding and a very special relationship between superiors and subordinates.[1]

The security police's culture, their techniques, skills and methods had much in common with those of a gang of ordinary thugs. What distinguished them from common criminals was that they believed themselves to be fighting a secret twilight war against an evil enemy. Any method that could lead to the destruction and disruption of the enemy was permitted and tacitly condoned. Dirk Coetzee and his colleagues were not bound by legal niceties – for them the country's borders were just fences and laws and regulations nothing more than words. They saw themselves as being involved in a kind of jihad – a holy war against the total onslaught.

In committing these atrocities, there was one golden rule: Never get caught. In the security police they refer to it as "the eleventh commandment".

Unfortunately, their illegalities in the course of duty often gave rise to illegalities outside the call of duty. Many of the askaris who found their way to Vlakplaas were nothing more than misfits whose criminal skills were employed to further the aims of the security police and, ultimately, the state.

Many askaris were appointed as South African policemen without any training or orientation. The skills they had acquired in the military training camps of the ANC and the PAC were regarded as adequate for the perfor- mance of their duties at Vlakplaas. In the guerrilla camps, they were trained in terror, and when they came to Vlakplaas, they were used as terrorists.

In an article published in October 1981 in the police magazine *Servamus*, Craig Williamson wrote: "Law enforcement officers, such as members of the SAP and other organs of the security forces, understand that the RSA is faced with a revolutionary onslaught which, if it is ever allowed to succeed, will plunge the southern tip of Africa into chaos. Therefore the only real answer is secret operations against the enemy, using many of the secret operational methods devised by the communist revolutionaries themselves."[2]

Many askaris had no choice but to join the Vlakplaas units. The techniques that were used to "turn and rehabilitate" them were similar to those used by many regimes all over the world. The South African Police, and particularly the security police, have a fearsome reputation for interrogation and torture. In June 1990, Daniel Madisha became the seventy-third detainee since 1963 to die in police detention. A study at the University of Cape Town claimed that 83 per cent of its samples of detainees had experienced some torture at the hands of the security police.[3]

After days of constant interrogation, torture, no sleep and no food or water most people break down. Sometimes detainees are exposed to loud continuous noise for 24 hours non-stop. They become disorientated, losing their conception of space, time and place, and their contact with reality. In moments like these, people very easily change their loyalties and swear allegiance to new masters. Vlakplaas was often a more acceptable choice than a South African jail or even execution by a death squad.

There is something ironic and sad about these disaffected guerrillas who turned against their former comrades. Having grown up in a South Africa of violence and repression, many left the country to join the struggle for liberation. But now they were inflicting that same violence and repression on their people again. The police view was that they were giving those who had seen the light a "second chance".

In their own communities, they are regarded as traitors and *impimpis* and to the police they will always remain "rehabilitated terrorists", not completely trustworthy.

The behaviour of the askaris proves – at least in Coetzee's and Nofemela's time on the farm – that they were ill-disciplined, badly trained and not always motivated. They drank a lot, smoked dagga, frequently assaulted each other and became involved in shebeen brawls. Their violent behaviour was by no means limited to the atrocities they committed in the line of duty. Moreover, their record shows that as an insurgent-detection unit they were a disaster. In the total history of Vlakplaas from 1981 to 1990, there is no evidence that more than two infiltrators per year on average were apprehended by the various squads.[4]

Why then were the Vlakplaas units allowed to survive? If they were so ineffective, badly disciplined and poorly trained, why did Vlakplaas grow from a small beginning in 1980 to a large police unit that still operates today?

Dirk Coetzee and his squad covered up to 10 000 kilometres every month as they raced around the country looking for infiltrators and suspected ANC guerrillas. Although they never apprehended any suspects, they were so invaluable in performing "clandestine operations" that what would otherwise have looked like inexcusable inefficiency was easy to condone.

Coetzee's superiors knew they could trust him with special assignments. If they needed his services, he was a phone call to Willem Schoon away.

It was safe to use the Vlakplaas units all over the country. They were not known to the local populations and could return to Vlakplaas and lie low for a while after an operation. Their security masters never thought that three members of the unit would one day stand up and admit their part in the death squads. They were all too deeply incriminated.

Dirk Coetzee was never officially appointed death squad commander at Vlakplaas. His main function had always been counter-surveillance but because he was trusted by many Security Branch commanders, certain projects were entrusted to him. Because of his desire to please his superiors and his blind ideological commitment, he never questioned any command. During his stay at Vlakplaas, Coetzee was awarded the police medal for faithful service.

The Vlakplaas units were especially effective where South African security legislation, harsh as it was, had failed the authorities. Griffiths Mxenge had to die because there was a lack of evidence to charge and convict him. Had the police discovered incriminating evidence, Mxenge would still have been alive today.

Vuyani Mavuso had to be eliminated because he could not be convicted either, but was too much of a danger to release. Peter Dlamini and Ace Moema had displeased their new masters and were executed. Sizwe Kondile posed a potential political embarrassment and the young Swazi boy simply had a father who happened to be an activist. With the possible exception of the infiltrator who died in the bomb explosion in Swaziland, not one of the people whose murder Coetzee was involved in posed any direct military threat to the security police or the welfare of the state.

If you were engaged in ANC activities and the police could prove it, you would probably have been prosecuted and sent to jail. If the police believed that you were engaged in ANC activities but could not prove it, they might well have called in the Vlakplaas counter-insurgency unit and, according to their norms, justifiably sentenced you to extra-judicial execution.

As will be seen in Chapter 7, in which the genesis of death squads will be explained, the formulation of the "total onslaught" doctrine presumed that the enemy was not merely in military camps and on the battlefield preparing for war; he was everywhere, in the legal and medical professions, universities, trade unions and every other sphere of life.

It is no accident that during the past few decades, as the apartheid order matured and as the struggle against white supremacy grew in scope and force, the number of political deaths sharply increased. Dirk Coetzee was a small but very important link in this chain of state-sponsored lawlessness. Although he had only been at Vlakplaas for 18 months, he painted a sordid picture of a dark and evil period from apartheid's history.

From 1982 to 1985 Coetzee's position in the police force would further deteriorate to the level where he faced seven internal charges ranging from disrespect towards a superior to a proposed money-smuggling scheme.

Coetzee's transfer from the security police back to the Uniformed Branch was a devastating blow to his self-esteem – in his words, "as bad as making the Pope a Dutch Reformed minister at Putsonderwater" (a dusty village whose name means empty well).

Before he could report to the police firearms section, he was transferred again to the South African Narcotics Bureau (Sanab) where he had to concentrate on liquor, gambling and immorality offences. He found it difficult to function as an ordinary detective. For years his main priority had been state security, with common criminals as his principal allies. Now he was supposed to persecute former underworld friends who had been his main source of information. He was disillusioned and demotivated.

It made no sense to him that the same police force could have such diverse attitudes towards crime. At Vlakplaas he had a bag of dagga in his car that the askaris had found at a shebeen. When they had finished their daily task, he would let them help themselves to a smoke. Now he had to hunt down people smoking and trading in the drug. After some half-hearted uncovering of the odd shebeen here, a dagga joint or a few mandrax pills there, he was called in by the head of Sanab, Colonel Basie Smit (today General Smit, chief of security police), who wanted to know why he was not delivering the goods. Coetzee explained that he would rather co-ordinate the detective work and avoid showing his face to the underworld. He might get the opportunity one day to return to the security police and did not want to blow his good contacts.

A young detective sent to Coetzee was introduced to an underworld contact in Swaziland. The detective, under cover, infiltrated a huge mandrax and stolen vehicle network whose operations extended into South Africa. Coetzee stayed in the background, co-ordinating the project. The Swaziland investigation led the team to Botswana, where another drug ring was exposed. The leaders were arrested and large quantities of mandrax seized.

Coetzee thought he was back in favour again. But while his superior officer was away on leave, he transferred one of the unit's men, regarded as lazy and incompetent, to another section. Basie Smit was unhappy and in August 1982 decided that there was not enough work for Coetzee in the narcotics bureau. He was transferred to head office recruitment, where he was in charge of recruiting white members. Already demotivated, Coetzee could not get along with his superior officer. After sitting for a year and four months writing letters, he could not take it anymore.

He arranged an appointment for himself and his superior to go and see the brigadier. When they entered, he tauntingly told his superior that he was looking for grave trouble and should put up his fists and defend himself because he was going to get the beating of his life. Coetzee was transferred to the divisional commissioner for Northern Transvaal.

He stayed in the commissioner's office until May 1984, when he was transferred to the Flying Squad. Coetzee had ended up where he started his promising police career. When he started with the Flying Squad in 1972 as an aspiring young constable he at least had a dog, but now he was just an officer who had to play policeman over policemen. He had to attend to police accidents, prepare reports and visit patrol cars and police stations.

In June 1984 Coetzee applied for study leave to complete his second-year legal studies at the University of South Africa. He had passed his first year with distinctions in Afrikaans and Latin. It was during this period of leave that he decided that it was time to leave the force altogether. He also decided to quit his legal studies. He went to see his house doctor, who declared him medically unfit for continued police duty as a result of an uncontrolled diabetic condition.

Coetzee's final and decisive battle with the police's top echelon started in 1984 when he befriended Frans Whelpton, who was private secretary to former Minister of Manpower and Mineral and Energy Affairs, Fanie Botha. When Coetzee met Whelpton, he had already resigned as Botha's secretary and was in business partnership with Brigadier Jan Blaauw, legendary South African Air Force fighter pilot and Korean war hero. The police were investigating charges of extortion and corruption against Whelpton and Blaauw that eventually led to the downfall of Fanie Botha, at one stage the most senior cabinet minister.[5]

Coetzee heard from a friend in the Security Branch that a colleague had been assigned to a very special project. The friend casually remarked that the project concerned the investigation against Blaauw and Whelpton with regard to certain oil and diamond concessions. He knew that the investigation involved the tapping of Blaauw's and Whelpton's telephones.

Coetzee spoke to the divisional commander of the Northern Transvaal security police, who told him in the strictest confidence that he had led the original investigation against Whelpton and Blaauw. The investigation was ordered personally by the Minister of Law and Order, Louis le Grange, and the Commissioner of Police, General Johan Coetzee, after a visit by Fanie Botha. The investigation involved allegations by Botha that Whelpton and Blaauw had tried to blackmail him in order to obtain valuable diamond concessions. The divisional commander confirmed that the suspects' telephones were tapped and advised Coetzee to cool his relationship with Whelpton.

Coetzee received further information that the investigating team had called in the help of Brigadier Hannes Erasmus, head of the gold and diamond branch, to set a diamond trap for Whelpton. Coetzee immediately relayed the warning to Whelpton, who told him that he had already been approached by illicit diamond dealers.

The police were furious when Whelpton suddenly declined to buy their diamonds. It also became clear that Whelpton knew his telephone was tapped. They made enquiries about Coetzee's knowledge of the investigation and started tapping his telephone as well. A friend was questioned about his sex life, drinking habits and personal life. Craig Williamson also warned Coetzee to lie low for a few months and not to continue his private investigation.

By now Coetzee was being followed almost daily by the CID chief, General Jan Grobler, and investigating officer Brigadier Jaap Joubert. In one encounter, Grobler, a small man, had to jump up and down in a parking lot to keep track of the renegade policeman while Coetzee, to the amazement of bystanders, shouted at a cringing Joubert in a car some metres away to stop harassing him.

At the end of 1984, police raided Frans Whelpton's attorney and found a statement signed by Coetzee in which he gave a detailed description of how the police were illegally tapping the telephones of Whelpton and Blaauw. The document was addressed to the Minister of Postal Affairs to warn him that the police did not have his permission to tap these telephones.[6]

Colonel Basie Smit came to see Coetzee in December 1984 to tell him that General Johan Coetzee wanted to see him. Coetzee told Smit that he was on sick leave and that if the general wanted to see him, he could come and do so at his house: he had nothing to say. Coetzee had dared to defy the commissioner; a day later he was suspended from duty.

Coetzee was becoming desperate and it was clear to him that his police career had come to an end. He drew up a document explaining the details of the telephone tapping and what he saw as a vendetta against him. Along with Whelpton, he went to see the National Party Member of Parliament for Randburg, Wynand Malan, to whom he not only explained the illegal telephone tapping, but also spoke in detail about Vlakplaas and his involvement in security police death squads. A prominent former Afrikaans newspaper editor, Harald Pakendorf, was present, but Coetzee told him that the death squad information was not for publication.

When nothing happened, Coetzee went to see the Conservative Party politician Koos van der Merwe, who gave the report to his party leader, Dr Andries Treurnicht. Again nothing happened and in January 1985 he wrote a letter to the leader of the official opposition, Dr Frederik van Zyl Slabbert. Slabbert responded immediately and sent his spokesman on Law and Order, Tian van der Merwe, to see Coetzee. Coetzee briefed Van der Merwe for two days, and also told him about the death squads.[7]

Coetzee was an angry man. He clearly hated Johan Coetzee and Basie Smit with a vengeance. For him, it was nothing less than a war the police were waging against him, and he was hitting back with everything he had. His lurid telephone vendetta against the higher echelon's adulterous escapades and their "hanky pankies" on the side became a daily institution.

Coetzee did not only tell politicians about death squads, he was prepared to tell virtually anybody that would ask him. At Whelpton's birthday party, where there were Pretoria professors, business people and lawyers, Coetzee told his story to some guests in detail. Whelpton would call him away to a group of people and say: "Dirk, quickly tell them what thugs the police really are."[8]

It is difficult to say whether Whelpton's guests believed Coetzee or not. Nobody seemed shocked; neither did anybody say they disbelieved him. It is probable that Whelpton's party guests shared Coetzee's values and took it for granted that the police killed anti-apartheid activists. During the party one of Coetzee's sons called him to come and look at a little mouse he had found in the garden. Coetzee strode out and crushed the mouse under his foot. Whelpton's guests told him the next day that they could swallow the murders and burnings, but what he did to the little animal was unforgivable.

Coetzee was travelling on his motorcycle on the freeway one day when he noticed something was wrong and coasted to a stop. A crucial bolt in his front braking and suspension mechanism was gone. Had he applied the brakes hard the front wheel would have locked. He took the bike to cycle agents who assured him that the bolt was fixed with a lock nut and that it was impossible for it to work loose and fall out. While he was visiting his attorney some time later to prepare for his trial, his motorcycle – parked close to police headquarters in Pretoria – was spray painted. He reported both incidents to the police.

Coetzee's motorcycle had always been his pride and joy. He wanted my colleague, Martin Welz, to write a story about the harassment and the damage to his cycle. Welz jokingly said to him: "I won't. I like the new colour of your cycle."

Veering between extreme anger and horror, Coetzee decided that he was going to kill Welz by unscrewing the bolts of a front wheel on his car. This plan was aborted when he realised that Welz took his children to school every morning: he did not want to hurt the kids.[9]

Coetzee's telephone tapping allegations caused an uproar and were published on the front pages of most newspapers. Louis le Grange denied the allegations that the police were illegally listening to telephone conversations. He said that the investigation against Whelpton and Blaauw concerned state security and that the police had obtained the necessary permission.

Coetzee was informed that the police were investigating seven charges of misconduct against him: in March 1985, Le Grange signed a letter appointing the president of the Pretoria regional court to preside as chairman over Coetzee's internal police trial. A general was appointed to assist the chairman and a law professor acted as prosecutor. Jaap Joubert was authorised to join the prosecutor's team. The chairman ruled that the case was to be heard *in camera*.[10]

During Coetzee's police trial Brigadier Jan du Preez described him as follows: "The opinion I formed of him is of a reasonably intelligent person. He was a very enthusiastic and energetic worker, but frequently unorthodox. He was hard-working with a lot of initiative. Hours did not matter to him but I know he is not well [referring to his diabetes]."

Asked about Coetzee's unorthodox methods, the brigadier replied: "The general rule is that the security police or the Security Branch should adhere to all rules of the legislator . . . Now it is unfortunately so that the rules of the game of security work do not always permit this and there can be deviations at times depending on the particular circumstances, so there can be deviations from the rules. The disciplinary rules have nothing to do with the execution of the policeman's duties as a member of the Security Branch, but in the execution of his statutory work there can at time be deviations."

The first charge Coetzee was found guilty of was that in July 1984 he had asked Craig Williamson to help him bring $150 000 into South Africa illegally. Coetzee was approached by a wealthy Johannesburg surgeon to import the money at a commission. Coetzee knew that Williamson had access to the South African diplomatic bag and asked him if he could help. Unbeknown to Coetzee, his friend and ally recorded the conversation and reported it to Basie Smit and Jaap Joubert. Coetzee, who felt utterly betrayed when Williamson testified against him, wryly remarked that for a man whose profession it was to betray his allies and live a life of lies and deceit, it couldn't have been too difficult.

Coetzee was also found guilty of obtaining information he was not entitled to. Needing official confirmation of security police telephone tapping, he persuaded a friend to make him a photocopy of the police register containing the names and numbers of people they listen to. He was also convicted of disclosing official information, a false accusation of adultery and absence without leave.

Coetzee was charged for his "contemptuous, rebellious or cheeky" attitude to Basie Smit when he was visited by him in December 1984. According to the charge sheet, he said to Smit: "You cannot take me away from my environment and trample on me at head office. I will batter Kleinjan Grobler to death. Lord Jesus! Is there no justice?" This charge was eventually dropped.

The false accusation of adultery referred to the confiscated statement Coetzee had given to Whelpton's attorney, in which he also alleged that a senior policeman's wife was having an affair with another security policeman. He repeated the remark over his tapped telephone because the senior policemen whose wife was having the alleged affair was the officer listening to his calls. Just before the police trial started, the two policemen instituted civil proceedings against Coetzee suing for damages of R10 000 each.

While he was awaiting the outcome of the chief magistrate's findings, Coetzee used his tapped telephone to good effect as he told his colleagues what a farce he thought the whole case was, that the commissioner was pursuing an ugly vendetta against him and that he intended to appeal against the verdict. He was informed that 35 new charges of using vulgar language over the phone had been prepared against him. He used this language, Coetzee protested, because he felt exasperated, and swearing at the commissioner and his men was an escape valve for his emotions and frustrations.

The chairman recommended to Louis le Grange that Coetzee was no longer fit to stay in the police force and as a gesture of mercy and in view of mitigating circumstances, his salary be reduced by two notches and he be allowed to retire on pension as medically unfit.

While awaiting Le Grange's decision on his future, the defamation case proceeded in the Pretoria Supreme Court. Coetzee could not afford legal representation and applied to the Legal Aid Board for assistance. The Board provided Coetzee with an attorney and advocate, but after they received a phone call informing them that he was doing free-lance jobs and therefore did not qualify for aid, it was withdrawn.

At the hearing Coetzee informed the judge that he was handling his own case. When he began to tell his story to the court, he was informed that he had not complied with certain pre-trial technicalities and could not proceed. On the third day of the hearing, Coetzee threw in the towel. He signed a document admitting that the accusations of adultery had been false and undertook to pay each of the plaintiffs R100 and their legal costs, which amounted to R20 000. He did not have the money and was sequestrated a month or two later.

Louis le Grange approved the recommendations of the chairman and Coetzee had to appear before a medical board of inquiry. Coetzee lied to the physician examining him, exaggerating his diabetic condition in order to ensure that the board would declare him medically unfit, which it did, recommending that Coetzee be put on early medical retirement. On 31 January 1986 Dirk Coetzee left the South African Police.

In the years that followed, Coetzee's efforts to get on his feet again were continually frustrated. He was offered a job as a specialised investigator at an insurance company solving cases the police could not crack, with a good salary, a car and housing subsidy. Coetzee accepted the job, but received a phone call informing him that they could not employ him.

This happened again and again. He was told by the chief security officer at one of the companies that they had received a phone call from the police asking them not to employ him. Coetzee reflected bitterly that a criminal discharged from jail gets assistance to find a job and start a new life, but he lacked a criminal record and therefore did not qualify for such consideration. In the end, the police had in a way created this monster now in their midst.

For the next three years, Coetzee lived off charity and goodwill from friends and family. He was a casual labourer at the Kyalami race track outside Johannesburg, where he put up posters to advertise racing events.

Just before Coetzee left the country, he approached the South African Insurance Association with a proposal for a venture to trace the owners of recovered stolen vehicles for insurance companies. The police sell large numbers of recovered stolen vehicles in cases where the owners cannot be traced. Coetzee was convinced that each vehicle, like a human being, is unique and that it must be possible to identify it and trace the owner. A week after he had fled South Africa, the scheme was approved.

The life of Dirk Coetzee, I believe, is one of wasted talents and missed opportunities. He can certainly never be presented as a shining example of a crusader for what is right and proper, but he has always been honest, open and loyal to me.

One of the people closest to him is his brother Ben, a computer scientist. Ben has also been a victim of the vendetta between Coetzee and the police, often failing to get the security clearance necessary for his work. A Defence Force officer refused to give reasons, but assured him that decisions about security clearance are taken by very responsible people.[11]

Dirk has always confided in his brother. In fact, Ben Coetzee was present one day when Coetzee and Brigadier Jan du Preez discussed the murder of Mxenge. The two of them visited the brigadier to ask him whether he could help Ben to get security clearance to enable him to work on a sensitive computer project. It was Ben who had to tell his parents that their youngest son had left the country to join the ANC and that a terrible story about his wrongdoings in the police force would be published soon. He remembers how proud Coetzee was to be a member of the security police. At that time, he said, his brother was a staunch patriot, telling him about how dirty the war really was and how difficult it had become to combat terrorism.

Coetzee's discharge from the police force was a devastating blow to his self-esteem. His former police friends shunned him and he became an outcast, lonely and disillusioned. The irony is that he has always seen himself as a policeman, plain and simple. He hopes that one day, in a new South Africa with an ANC-dominated government, he may get the opportunity to serve in a newly constituted police force.

When I met Coetzee, he was involved in the underworld looking for contacts to import oil to South Africa. I know he approached Frans Whelpton and Jan Blaauw and told them that he would find out exactly where oil can be bought, at what price and at what risk. As far as I know, he collected an enormous amount of information.

During this time Coetzee was asked by a friend of Whelpton's whether he could get rid of a poacher on his game farm in the Northern Transvaal. Coetzee started making plans, asking the farmer whether there was enough good firewood and a river flowing through the farm. He planned to use his own trusted recipe once again. I don't know how serious Coetzee was about killing and burning the poacher, but the plan was aborted, anyway.

I think the fact that he was needed again played an important role in Coetzee's decision to leave South Africa. After years of leading a useless existence, people needed his help – the ANC needed him, *Vrye Weekblad* needed him, and human rights lawyers needed him to prove the death squad allegations. There was suddenly a renewed purpose and meaning to his life.

Life in exile has not been easy. After he was debriefed in Europe, Coetzee was brought to Bulawayo where he met up with David Tshikalange. They were moved from house to house, cut off from the rest of the world.

As Coetzee went into hiding in Zimbabwe, a massive campaign to discredit him started back home. Police said he was embittered at having been dishonourably discharged from the police force, and was ill with diabetes. Further allegations were that he had been involved in crimes ranging from the illegal importation of pornography to alcohol smuggling. Craig Williamson told the media that Coetzee's mental equilibrium was upset as a result of his diabetes and that this was supported by psychiatric evidence.

The Sunday newspaper *Rapport* published a sourceless article saying that Coetzee had in fact never left South Africa and was hiding somewhere on a farm outside Pretoria. He was sick, without his medicine and in a semi-conscious state, stumbling around on the farm. Although Coetzee released a statement from Europe, the newspaper never published a correction.[12]

Coetzee phoned the *Sunday Times* one day and gave them a tip-off about a death squad member they should approach for information, they published an article saying that Coetzee had phoned them and that they had immediately informed the security police about the call.

In the weeks and months that followed, Coetzee, now a self-confessed murderer, poisoner, arsonist, bomber and thief, was also branded a liar, perjurer, traitor, gangster and psychopath. For others, however, he became a hero, a martyr and even a freedom fighter.

The Christmas of 1989 was a sad and lonely affair as Coetzee and Tshikalange spent the day in a sparsely furnished house in Bulawayo. They were not allowed to phone their families for fear that the telephones in South Africa were tapped. Their only contact with the outer world was a small transistor radio. Domestic problems made matters worse: Coetzee heard that Karin had started an affair with a young Pretoria student who had moved into his house. The ANC later became convinced that the student was a police spy because he knew the names of Coetzee's ANC contacts back in South Africa and asked Karin to record their conversations. Dirk and Karin were separated, but later reunited.

After Coetzee was transported to Lusaka, he lived in a hotel outside the Zambian capital. Although he became a member of the ANC, he was never fully trusted by certain members of the organisation and was for security reasons not allowed to visit the intelligence offices. He sat for days on end in his hotel room without contact with anybody.

The inefficiency that plagues Zambia led to enormous frustrations and confrontations with the people around him. He could not bear the slow service, the poor telephone lines and the bad food. He would jump over a counter to show the attendant what quality of service he really expected or would bitterly swear at waiters and civil servants. In fact his short temper saved his life in Zambia when a bomb concealed in a walkman tape player was sent to him from South Africa. He refused to pay the high import duty on the item and after a heated exchange of words with the post office worker, stormed out of the building empty-handed. The parcel was sent back to South Africa and later exploded in an attorney's face, killing him instantly (see Chapter 14).

Conditions improved when his two sons joined him in Lusaka and the three of them were later taken to Livingstone near the Victoria Falls. Eventually he persuaded the ANC to transfer him again, and he and the two boys now live in a small flat in central London. They live a simple life, but are a happy and dose-knit family. Coetzee has been forced into the role of school teacher to help the two boys through the correspondence school courses they follow.

The ANC has had a tremendous impact on Coetzee. It has changed his outlook on life, his political convictions and even his vocabulary. Terrorists have become freedom fighters, the enemy is now the movement, the once brutal savages are his comrades and the communist onslaught is actually a liberation struggle. In a piece he wrote about four months after he joined the ANC, he said: "Working with the ANC is a spiritually rewarding experience. Every member radiates an advanced and mature culture. The ANC want a new and just South Africa where the interests and culture of every reasonable person will be respected as a matter of grave principle. Freedom of expression and democracy are held in the highest regard. Members in exile conduct their daily affairs by this creed. They belong to diverse cultures and live harmoniously by their serious and tested blueprint for a new South Africa.

"Members in exile live in the most modest conditions where they proudly apply themselves to their tasks. Most have suffered gross injustices, physical abuse and humiliation under the system of apartheid. Many have dear ones who are still suffering and dying in this manner and many have lost their lives in the armed struggle. Despite these hardships and sacrifices, there is an amazing lack of bitterness and a firm tradition of forgiveness that augur well for the future of our country."

The ANC and its members have forgiven Coetzee for what he did. In fact, many of them admire him. I went with him to the ANC's offices in London one day and as we entered the building, the woman behind the counter jumped up and shouted: "But this is Comrade Dirk!" She embraced him and told him what a wonderful experience and honour it was to meet him. She called her other colleagues and the whole emotional process was repeated.

Archbishop Desmond Tutu visited Coetzee in London and told him that the people of South Africa forgave him because he had expressed his sorrow.

People who meet Coetzee usually like him, although sometimes a bit reluctantly, as happened when *Vrye Weekblad*'s legal team travelled to Lusaka in September last year to consult with Coetzee about our forthcoming defamation case against General Lothar Neethling. Visiting Lusaka was a traumatic experience for our senior counsel, Bobby Levin. The dirty streets, the empty shops and the total wreck of a taxi that took us from the hotel to the city centre were a far cry from his double-storey house in Johannesburg's nothern suburbs and his Mercedes sports car. To aggravate the situation, his main witness in the trial was branded a lunatic and a psychopath.

Just after Levin had met Coetzee, the former policeman went into a rage about "that afterbirth" who was still courting his wife. He continued for five minutes with a string of words and expressions that Levin had never heard before. I think that by then our senior counsel was a devastated man. During the following consultation, he kept his distance from Coetzee, politely calling him "Captain".

After Coetzee's evidence in London a month later, however, Levin confessed to Max du Preez: "You know, I actually like Dirk." After the court case, Levin told me that he had already believed Dirk Coetzee during their first consultation in Lusaka.

People often ask me if Coetzee really regrets his death squad deeds. Does he genuinely feel sorry for the Mxenge orphans or for the activists he killed in cold blood? It is a difficult question, and I really do not know. People who have listened to his story have always been struck by his clinical and unemotional descriptions of the various atrocities and murders. One never really detects any remorse.

He was at most times an eager participant in the atrocities and even when the activists were to be shot and burnt, he felt no pity and had no mercy on them. When he told me years later about the Mxenge murder, and even when we conducted the interviews in Mauritius, no repentance was evident.

"What do you expect from me? To start weeping and snivelling every time I talk about the killings and the burnings? There would be nothing left of me. I have met many people who suffered deeply at the hands of the security police and their death squads. I have to look each and every one in the eye, and I can assure you that I don't feel proud about my past," he told me.

I do believe that his contact with the ANC has made a difference. There were very emotional periods during his debriefing when the ANC told him about the victims and their families and showed him photographs. He certainly believes today that what he did was wrong, and that having told the truth and admitted his guilt in the atrocities, he deserves a new life and a new future.

Coetzee faces an uncertain future. The ANC has fully complied with its undertaking and Coetzee and his sons are well looked after. He has expressed willingness to return to South Africa and stand trial for his crimes. His only condition is that those who were with him around the fires and waiting for a report back at security police headquarters should be prosecuted with him.

At the time of writing there were intense negotiations between the South African Police and the ANC regarding Coetzee's fate and his possible return to South Africa. In the new political climate of 1991 it is just possible that Coetzee may qualify for a criminal indemnity which will enable him to return to his country of birth.

It is difficult to imagine what life would be for Coetzee back home in South Africa. His life would certainly be in danger. He had turned against his kin and would in many circles never be forgiven. At the time of writing he was in hiding after a man tried to break down the door of his London flat with a crowbar. The man fled, but Coetzee believes it was yet another attempt on his life. The ANC in London was so concerned for his safety that it moved him out of the city. The incident happened only two weeks after the bomb that was intended for him killed the Johannesburg attorney.

The house that the Coetzee family had lived in for many years has been sold, there are no work prospects for the former policeman and he has lost his police medical benefits because he had left the country without the approval of the Commissioner of Police. He gets a meagre police pension.

Coetzee has suffered great hardship since he left the country in November 1989. When I phoned him on a Friday afternoon in January 1991 to tell him that at last a judge had believed his story, he replied: "So, after all, everything was not in vain."

I have often pondered over the real value of Coetzee's revelations and *Vrye Weekblad*'s exposure of state-sanctioned death squads. I often hear: "So what's the big deal all about?"

Because of Coetzee's willingness to talk we now know about a very important moral and political evil that existed in apartheid South Africa. In a future political dispensation, we can guard against the occurrence of a similar situation and prevent our future leaders from abusing their entrusted political power. Many of the people of Nazi Germany would later say: "Wir haben es nicht gewusst" (We did not know). South Africans will have no such excuse. Dirk Coetzee has warned us all.

CHAPTER SIX

A licence to kill

NEEDLESS to say, Vlakplaas did not cease to exist with the departure of Dirk Coetzee. But the man who soon emerged at the centre of the complex web of death squad operations is surrounded by an aura of mystery and fear.

Eugene de Kock received his counter-insurgency training between 1968 and 1972 with the Special Air Service in Rhodesia. In 1981 he attended an instructor's course in explosives. He was transferred from the notorious Koevoet unit in Namibia to take over the police counter-insurgency unit in 1983. He has been linked to a number of deaths, including the point-blank shooting of a man to prevent him from identifying Almond Nofemela.[1]

Krugersdorp security guard Japie Maponya had committed no crime, but his brother Odirile was a trained member of Umkhonto we Sizwe, sought on a charge of killing a policeman. (In 1988 Odirile blew himself up while attempting to plant a bomb in Pretoria.)

Nofemela arrested the guard as instructed on a fraud charge and took him to Vlakplaas, where Eugene de Kock was waiting for him. In Nofemela's words: "We were kicking him and punching him and slapping him . . . [De Kock] ordered us to put him in the kombi and we closed the door. De Kock tear-gassed inside that particular kombi for a while. Maponya was inside there alone, struggling to exhale and inhaling. De Kock took him out again. We were talking now about the people that he knows, his relatives . . . De Kock asked me whether the man can recognise me in future, then I said yes, then he said he must get rid of him. I saw him taking his pistol with silencer and the man was blindfolded . . . then he shot him in the head. From there he took a plastic out of his car and I assisted him in wrapping the body . . . we put it in the boot of the car, then he ordered me to leave, then I drive for my home."[2]

De Kock has also been implicated in various ambushes of alleged ANC infiltrators and activists and a number of assassinations and kidnappings in Swaziland. Information about him is sketchy and he seldom appears in public. He does not grant interviews and in several court cases the magistrate or judge has prohibited the taking of photographs of him. In the witness box

De Kock, a short and stocky man, is confident and self-assured. Nicknamed "Brille" (Afrikaans for spectacles) by his friends, he is loathed and feared by the askaris who worked under him.

He occupies one of the most responsible and prestigious positions in the security police, acting on his own initiative and responsibility. We know, however, on his own evidence, that some of his operations went wrong, obliging him to kill people in "acts of self-defence".

It was a macabre ritual in the Piet Retief police mortuary: four security policemen walking gloatingly around the bloodied bodies of four infiltrators they had shot an hour earlier, passing a bottle of Old Brown sherry from one to the other and taking deep gulps as they congratulated each other on the magnificent blow they had dealt the enemy. One of them turned to James Stevens and Marthinus Grobler, pointing at a body: "You see this one here. He's mine."[3]

For the young constables watching the exhibition, it was just too much to stomach. Grobler and Stevens, appalled by what they saw, retreated back into the police station where Grobler was on charge office duty.

Earlier that night, Grobler had booked out weapons to the security policemen on their way to a spot outside the small Eastern Transvaal town to lay an ambush for ANC members who were expected to infiltrate South Africa from Swaziland. They told Grobler they were going off on "special duties". Around midnight they returned with four bodies — three female and one male, ripped to pieces by high-velocity bullets – in the back of a police van.

The bodies were moved into the adjoining mortuary where a woman constable was called to perform internal searches on the women. Later that night, one of the security policemen told Grobler that after the shooting had stopped, the door of the vehicle in which the infiltrators had been travelling fell open and a wounded woman started pleading for mercy as the policemen approached the vehicle. One of them shot her point-blank. Grobler's informer also confessed that the wrong people had been killed. The intelligence on which the police had acted had been inaccurate. However, four days later, another four bodies were delivered to the mortuary. This time they were supposedly the "right people".

A few days later Minister of Law and Order Adriaan Vlok announced that ANC infiltrators en route from Swaziland to Durban had been killed when their cars, packed with Russian arms and ammunition, tried to evade a road block. Nine people had died in the Piet Retief district in three different incidents between 8 and 12 June 1988.[4]

The police claimed that the infiltrators had shot at them first. It was the stock explanation: ANC infiltrators were frequently mown down by the police in acts of "self-defence". In the two years preceding the two Piet Retief incidents, another eight people – four in the Eastern Transvaal and four near Durban – had died in similar mysterious circumstances. In three of the four cases, the "counter-insurgency" squads from Vlakplaas were involved in the operations.

According to the court records, while the police were "defending" themselves against the four infiltrators on a deserted road outside Piet Retief, Major Eugene de Kock prayed that the people into whom he was emptying his Uzi sub-machine gun would not die. In his evidence at the inquest into the death of the four ANC members De Kock assured the court that it was never his intention to kill anybody. Intending the infiltrators to be arrested, interrogated and convicted, he had planned the entire operation to avoid death and injury at all cost.[5]

De Kock said he had received information from an ANC informant in Swaziland about the infiltration the day before the shoot-out. The informant told him that a party of two people was going to cross over the border at a particular point and that a vehicle was to meet them there. De Kock decided to send an askari, Lieutenant Silumami Gladstone Mose, along to meet the group of infiltrators. He was to meet them at a certain spot and, using the code name of Amos, lead them into De Kock's ambush.

In his evidence, Mose said that when he approached the pick-up point, a person by the name of Martin arrived and apologised for handing over four people instead of two. The people got into his car and they drove back in the direction of Piet Retief. When they approached the spot where he had left Eugene de Kock the lights of a police vehicle blocking the road were switched on and Warrant Officer Frederik Pienaar – also present in court – indicated with a torch that they should stop.

Mose said he heard an Indian man say in English: "It's only two." Stopping the car, he heard a sound behind him and when he looked around, the Indian man had a pistol in his hand. "I jumped out and ran to the front of the motor vehicle in the direction of the trees. Lots of shots rang out, then I heard Major De Kock tell his people to stop firing."

De Kock said in his evidence that he had hailed the occupants of the vehicle: "This is now the South African Police and get out." The next moment, the back window of the car was opened and one of the infiltrators started firing at him. After the infiltrator fired a shot, said De Kock, his men hiding in the bushes opened fire. He himself had an Uzi machine gun while some of his men had R-1 assault rifles.

The plan, said the major, had been to arrest Mose with the group of infiltrators in order to protect his cover. He had suspected that the people might be armed and had prepared his men for a shoot-out. It was a tragedy that the people were killed, he said. If he had wounded them, he would have applied first-aid and taken them to hospital.

Counsel for the families of the dead, Zac Yacoob, accused De Kock: "You did nothing, you planned nothing to minimise injury or loss of life if the people in the car used weapons against you?"

"I only had my weapon," De Kock responded. "One would not use it injudiciously and kill people on purpose . . . If that Indian man did not fire, nobody would have been injured."

It appeared from an affidavit from a person in Swaziland stating that when the deceased left for South Africa, they were not armed, that the killers might have "planted " the pistol that they alleged had been found on one of the infiltrators to substantiate their claim that they had fired in self-defence. This was coolly denied by De Kock, but a number of highly irregular acts committed by the police in what seemed like an attempt to cover up their actions that night were less easy to explain. Incredible as it may seem, a police officer who participated in the shootings appointed himself as the investigating officer in the case.

Frederik Pienaar said he was the investigating officer in the case as he investigated all security matters in the Piet Retief district. He had not investigated the case in depth because it was a simple case of a group of policemen defending themselves, nor had he checked the medical report.

It was established in court that the motor car in which the infiltrators had travelled was repaired before any ballistic examination was done, no photographs of the inside of the car were taken and the Makarov pistol allegedly found next to the body of one of the infiltrators was not sent for fingerprint analysis. There were at least 62 entry wounds in the four bodies – many more than the number of shots the police claimed they fired, and notification of the next of kin was delayed until decomposition of the bodies was sufficiently far advanced to cover up possible evidence of torture. Their clothes were burnt without any investigation having been conducted.

Pienaar had a bizarre explanation for why he burnt the clothes. Asked whether he had followed police standing orders and made an entry into a register that the clothes were destroyed, he answered: "Not tatters of clothes like this, particularly not now in a time any sickness can be brought into the country by blood. That is why I burnt all the clothes."

Under great pressure the magistrate dismissed Pienaar as the investigating officer and appointed a senior officer to continue the investigation. At the time of writing, judgement in the Piet Retief inquest has not yet been delivered and the inquest into the second shooting has not started. The four people who died in a microbus four days later were killed in exactly the same circumstances – according to the police, in self-defence.

Marthinus Grobler and James Stevens were never called to give evidence in the Piet Retief inquest. While a string of security policemen testified that they shot the infiltrators in self-defence, the two constables were sitting in the charge office guarding their secret about what really happened on that night in June 1988. It was only after Dirk Coetzee's testimony that they came forward and told me what they knew about the incident. Shortly afterwards, they fled to Lusaka to join the ANC.[6]

They said that for some strange reason the date of the attack had been falsified. Both men were absolutely sure that the incident did not occur on 8 June. They stole the firearms register from the Piet Retief Police Station and showed that the policemen involved did not draw weapons on the day the incident supposedly took place.

Grobler said that the bodies and the vehicle in which the infiltrators had been travelling were riddled with lead- and steelpoint bullets. (Lead points are illegal in terms of police standing orders.) Moreover, he said there were powder burns on the clothes of one of the women, indicating that shots had been fired at point-blank range.

The police had claimed that, besides a Makarov pistol, two hand grenades were discovered in the car, but according to Grobler no weapons found on the deceased were booked in at the charge office after the killings.

During the course of the evening, Grobler and Stevens had inspected the Toyota Corolla in which the infiltrators travelled. Grobler said it was remarkable how little blood there was in the car. All he noticed was a mess of brains splattered on the roof of the car. This was in line with a theory held by the families of the deceased that the infiltrators were taken out of the car and executed before their bodies were returned and further shots fired into the car in order to tie the evidence in with the police version of events.

After *Vrye Weekblad* published the allegations made by Grobler and Stevens, they had to live on the run in small, dingy hotels in Johannesburg while waiting for clearance from the ANC to go to Lusaka. Officials of the United Democratic Front cared for them for a while and a foreign newspaper paid their airfare to Lusaka. They were too scared to return home to collect clothes or money.

Marthinus Grobler comes from a police family: ironically, Eugene de Kock is his father's second cousin. When Grobler decided to blow the whistle, his family disowned him. He lost his new job and his flat.

Piet Retief is a conservative community, a place in which one can expect incidents of racial prejudice and discrimination. Grobler and Stevens found the town's police force to be no different. In December 1988, for example, a man held at Piet Retief Police Station was so severely tortured that he spent two weeks in the intensive care unit of the local hospital. On being discharged, he laid a charge of assault againt his interrogator.

The case came to nothing: the policeman had a friend whose mother was a senior state prosecutor. A few telephone calls later the case was dismissed for lack of evidence. The case was never investigated and nobody ever tried to find out what kind of evidence there was. James Stevens said he had watched as the interrogator lifted the handcuffed man into the air and threw him down on the concrete floor. In another incident, the same policeman allegedly beat a man to death in the township outside Piet Retief. Again his friendship saved him from prosecution.

A portrait that should be placed alongside the sketchy image of Eugene de Kock is that of Silumami Mose, the ANC defector who assisted at Brigadier Neels du Plooy's riveting Police College lectures while Dirk Coetzee was a student. His name had been cropping up in connection with death squad activities long before the Piet Retief shootings. He joined the ANC in his youth, but was one of the first trained guerrillas to return to South Africa and become a member of the security police.

In an incident in 1985 in the rural district of Calla in the Transkei, a young man by the name of Bathandwa Ndondo was arrested by four members of the police force – three men and a woman. Ndondo, a co-ordinator of a rural project, had gained prominence in the nominally independent homeland when he was elected student vice-president at the University of Transkei. He was a staunch opponent of the dictatorial Mantanzima regime and was branded an "enemy of the state".

Ndondo's captors were known to the people of Calla as the "death squad". Aware of their reputation, Ndondo asked a friend to follow the white panel-van in which they took him away. The friend lost track of the van, but what happened was witnessed later by villagers.

When the van came to a standstill near the outskirts of Calla, Ndondo managed to escape through the window. He ran around the nearest house, only to be felled as he tried to gain entry. The killers fired several more bullets into him as he lay on the ground. He was shot eight times, at least six bullets entering his body at point-blank range. A villager asked the policemen why Ndondo had been shot down "like a dog". They replied that he was a terrorist and did not deserve any better.[7]

One of the men who killed Ndondo in cold blood was Silumami Mose, who shot the young activist three times. Transkei's CID chief admitted that policemen from both South Africa and Transkei had been involved in the shooting, and a year after Ndondo's death two policemen were charged with murder. People were outraged that Mose and the woman who accompanied them, Xolelwa Sosha, were not also brought to justice.

In the meantime, however, six more people – friends and relatives of the murdered man or witnesses in the pending trial – were detained and then banished. Moreover, when the two constables charged with the murder did not turn up for two hearings they were neither reprimanded nor arrested, and Transkei authorities allowed the trial to peter out, the charges finally being dropped after one of the men jumped bail.

Xolelwa Sosha was recruited into the ANC in 1980 and underwent military training at Gamalunde training camp in eastern Angola. She was appointed a commissar for the women's unit and received further training in East Germany and Libya. In 1984 she was sent back to South Africa on a military mission but was arrested and detained under Section 29 of the Internal Security Act, and ended up a member of the Vlakplaas contingent.[8]

Nine months after the Ndondo killing, Sosha was involved in an incident in which four young activists were killed. From his cell on death row, Almond Nofemela described a Vlakplaas operation in the middle eighties that involved infiltrating the United Democratic Front in Lamontville near Durban. The Vlakplaas squad had been doing routine patrols in the Durban area under the command of Major Eugene de Kock.

Nofemela and another askari, Jeffrey Bosigo, were ordered to stay behind as the rest of the squad – issued with an AK-47 – moved into the township to infiltrate the "enemy". Half an hour later, Nofemela recalled, he heard firing, identifying it as shots from an AK-47.[9]

When the men returned to the CR Swart Police Station in Durban, they reported to De Kock that the mission had been successful. A murder docket was opened, but they were assured by a security police officer that they had nothing to fear, he would sort out the problem.

The incident that Nofemela referred to was in June 1986, when four members of the Chesterville Youth Organisation, a UDF affiliate, were killed in a shootout with the police. A unit of seven policemen lured six youths into a small backyard room and fired at least 68 shots at them. An activist who survived the incident claimed that they were tricked and murdered by the dreaded police death squad.

According to the survivor, 14-year-old Tibello Mbatha, he was awoken on the night of 19 June by friends who told him that they had received information that the "A-Team" – a gang of vigilantes – was about to attack them. They asked him to join them to collect people to avert the danger.[10]

They went to the shack of his friend Chwepheshe Mlambo, where Mbatha was introduced to a man and woman who told them that they had come to help them in their struggle against the "A-Team". The unknown man opened his jacket and produced an AK-47 assault rifle. Demonstrating how to disassemble and reassemble the weapon, he said they had been trained in foreign countries and had brought some weapons for the activists as well.

The unknown man later turned out to be Thabo Makgage, a highly skilled and well-trained soldier. He had in fact left South Africa in 1976 to join the armed struggle of the ANC, receiving training in a military camp in Angola. But on that fateful night, Makgage was not there to assist the Chesterville Youth Organisation in their battle against the vigilantes. He had surrendered himself to the South African Police in 1979 and become a security policeman. His female companion was Xolelwa Sosha.

Outside in the cold night, five more security policemen had surrounded the shack. "Go and fetch some hand grenades," Makgage told Sosha. That was a sign for her to go outside and inform Sergeant Simon Radebe that they had made contact with the activists.

According to Tibello Mbatha, when Makgage also left the room a shot was suddenly fired and the light went off. A barrage of bullets hit the shack and the 14-year-old was felled by bullets in his left thigh, left hip, right leg, right thigh and back.

Four of the activists died instantly. A total of between 68 and 88 rounds of bullets were fired. All seven policemen were armed and participated in the shooting, with one firing as many as 21 bullets.

Tibello Mbatha is now confined to a wheelchair, paralysed from the waist down and still fearful for his life. The sixth activist, also wounded, disappeared after the incident. The Commissioner of Police banned a single funeral for the Chesterville Four, as they had become known, allowing two funerals each attended by a maximum of 400 people. The media were banned from Chesterville for the duration of the funerals.

Constable Thabo Makgage said in his evidence that the activists had told him they needed hand grenades and rifles to attack the police station. He was called out of the room by Sosha, and Radebe whispered to him that they should arrest the group, but suddenly they heard a shot being fired. Believing it was the activists shooting at them, they shot back in self-defence. Makgage pushed the barrel of his AK-47 through the window and sprayed his bullets across the small room. The police left the scene immediately, fearing an attack by other activists in the area.

The investigating officer, Major Marthinus Pretorius, said that he had examined the interior of the shack and found a bullet hole that appeared to have been made by someone firing a shot from inside. However, ballistic tests conducted by the police could not prove that any shots were fired from the inside. No weapons were found on the activists or inside the shack.

Eugene de Kock had an explanation for this. Referring to the activist who disappeared, he said that his experience in counter-insurgency investigations had taught him that "terrorists" remove their weapons and their injured from the scene of a shooting to prevent the police from investigating the incident.

Pretorius said that due to the state of emergency, the number of killings by "necklace" in the area and reckless firing at police patrols, the Vlakplaas squad could easily have thought that they had been led into an ambush.

Constable André Cilliers said in his affidavit that he was on patrol duty that night. At around ten o'clock he received instructions to return to the police station as a special operation was in progress by other members of the security forces. It seemed that Eugene de Kock and his men had cleared the "regular" police out of the area before attempting to "arrest" the suspects.

Brigadier Willem Schoon, De Kock and Captain Paul van Dyk testified that the unit was in Durban to help counter the increase in "terrorist" activity. Its aim was to infiltrate suspect organisations and apprehend their members. They had given permission for the unit to carry an AK-47 to enhance its credibility as a pro-ANC team.

The inquest magistrate's verdict, delivered in May 1990, outraged the parents of the dead activists and the community as a whole. Magistrate BJ

Olivier found that the police had fired in "reasonable defence". He acknowledged that the single shot which led to the police burst had not come from the house occupied by the youths, but accepted the police's testimony that they thought the shots had come from the shack.

Olivier found that the police witnesses had corroborated one another in their evidence on what had happened. He did not accept the argument that they had acted as a death squad, saying that if they had been such a squad they would not have reported the incident to the police.

Eugene De Kock was involved in a similar incident in August 1986 in which five alleged members of the ANC were shot near the Swazi border at Amsterdam in the Eastern Transvaal. Seven members of the Vlakplaas squad, including Almond Nofemela and Paul van Dyk, were present. Warrant Officer Frederik Pienaar of the Piet Retief Security Branch also participated in the operation.[11]

De Kock told his men that he had received information that ANC cadres would be entering South Africa from Swaziland. A group waited in a plantation for the "terrorists" to arrive. After a while they saw four men – some of them armed – walking towards them with bags on their backs. The men passed them and walked to a car, into which they loaded the bags. The car drove off towards Amsterdam, and three men walked back towards the Swazi border.

"Major de Kock said the targets had come to fight against us and we therefore had to eliminate them before they could accomplish their plan. He also said that he had no time for all the questioning which would arise if the matter had come to court and that was why we had to kill the enemy," Nofemela said in his affidavit.

As soon as the three men appeared again, Nofemela said, the group started shooting. Two infiltrators were mown down, the survivor escaped across the border.

In the meantime a roadblock had been set up by De Kock and Pienaar. According to police claims, when the car was stopped the driver jumped out holding an AK-47; a passenger had a Makarov pistol in his hand. The police had to shoot in self-defence, killing the driver and two passengers, one of whom had two hand grenades. Twenty-five hand grenades, ten kilograms of plastic explosives and two limpet mines were found in the car, Paul van Dyk said in an affidavit after the incident.

The man who had escaped across the border was arrested a few days later, brought to trial and sentenced to ten years' imprisonment.

To Dirk Coetzee and his fellow death squad operators, Swaziland was a playground in which they could operate freely and virtually without interference from the peaceful Swazis.

In more than a decade of cross-border violations into Swaziland, the Vlakplaas death squads were never challenged by the Swazi authorities. Like most of its other neighbours, Swaziland was powerless to act against the South Africans transgressing its borders. One of the reasons for this was that the border, virtually unpatrolled and badly fenced, was as easy to cross as centuries ago before colonialism drew political lines across the African map.

Swaziland never suffered the degree of destabilisation that was inflicted on Zimbabwe or Mozambique. Under tremendous pressure from South Africa, the Swazi government restricted the ANC by not allowing them to use the country as a springboard for attacks on South Africa.

But powerless as the Swazi authorities were to stop South African death squads from operating in the country, they were also powerless to stop ANC members infiltrating South Africa from Mozambique through Swaziland. Inevitably, Swaziland became embroiled in the struggle between the ANC and the death squads. Since 1980, at least 22 alleged ANC members have been assassinated in Swaziland.[12]

Almond Nofemela himself was involved in two attacks on ANC transit houses in Swaziland. In the first incident, which happened in 1983, Eugene de Kock led a death squad of seven security policemen. Nofemela said in his affidavit that De Kock kicked the door open and flung a hand grenade into the house. After the grenade had exploded, the whole squad burst in and sprayed their victims with gunfire, leaving 22 bullet holes in the walls. Zakhele Nyanda, a former medical student who fled South Africa in 1976, and Keith McFadden, a Swazi national, died instantly. A third man managed to escape though a window.[13]

The second raid into Swaziland took place in June 1986, when Nofemela was a member of a death squad that attacked a transit house in Mbabane. In this raid, three people were shot with pistols equipped with silencers.

A former Commissioner of Police, General Mike Geldenhuys, denied in the Johannesburg Supreme Court in November 1990 that the South African Police had ever been involved in any operations in neighbouring states. He denied any knowledge of the bombing of transit houses or railway lines, letter bombs or assassinations in neighbouring states.[14]

Geldenhuys, who was Commissioner of Police between 1978 and 1983, said the only time the police were involved in neighbouring states was when they conducted investigations. But then, he added, their presence always had the permission of that state's government.

The incidents mentioned by Coetzee and Nofemela constitute only a handful of the South African operations in Swaziland. In each and every case the South African government denied any involvement, maintaining their allegation that the Pan Africanist Congress was responsible for the attacks.

There is a long history of kidnappings of activists from neighbouring states. The most famous is Rivonia trialist Wilton Mkwayi, who spent more than a quarter of a century in jail after being abducted from his hiding place in Botswana and brought to South Africa. Another that made the news, happened in Pine Valley, a secluded piece of paradise in the cool and moist Swaziland mountains. On 15 December 1986 senior ANC member Ebrahim Ismael Ebrahim, who was responsible for organising the political under-ground in the Transvaal and Natal, had just finished his supper and was watching television when there was a knock on the door that changed his life into a nightmare for the next four and a half years.[15]

As he opened the door, guns were held to his head. The gunmen threatened to shoot him if he resisted "arrest" or tried to escape. They tied him up and searched the house, taking documents which they put into a steel container. They also took about R4 500 in cash, a suitcase full of clothing and a walkman radio.

Ebrahim was blindfolded and put in the back seat of a car. Later, he was made to walk a small incline at what he believed to be the border between South Africa and Swaziland. His blindfold was removed and he was told to jump over the fence. He was put into leg-irons and his hands were cuffed together before he was bundled into a car again. On their way to Pretoria his captors questioned him about bombs they alleged he had planted around the country and the presence of ANC members in Maputo. He refused to speak to them and was threatened with torture and death.

He was taken to Security Branch headquarters, where he was introduced to Brigadier Willem Schoon. To Ebrahim's complaint that he had been abducted, Schoon replied: "How you arrived here is of mere academic interest. Now that you are here, you are going to give us information about the ANC."

One of his interrogators was a former ANC member with the code-name of "September", who had been kidnapped in Swaziland four months before Ebrahim and "turned" by the police. Almond Nofemela said in his affidavit that he had been a member of the Vlakplaas squad that kidnapped September from a Swaziland jail on 12 August 1986.

September, whose real name is Glory Lephosa Sidebe, was detained at that time by the Swazi authorities because of his ANC activities. Nofemela said he accompanied Eugene de Kock and Paul van Dyk into Swaziland and that September was kidnapped from the Manzini prison with the aid of the Swazi police.

"Major de Kock had told us that this was organised with the Commissioner of Police in Swaziland and that no police at the police station at the time would be armed. This is when we were to effect the kidnapping. We then brought him to Piet Retief. He was interrogated and he was sent to Piet Retief prison and thereafter I met him in 1987 working with the Vlakplaas squad."[16]

In the Ebrahim case September testified *in camera* that he had left the country in 1977 when he became a member of the ANC in order to further his studies. He went to Mozambique, Angola and East Germany, where he received military training. He reached a high position in Umkhonto we Sizwe and was head of Transvaal Military Intelligence. He also visited the Soviet Union and Zambia. After the Nkomati Accord in 1984 the Mozambicans limited the number of ANC members in their country and September was deported to Zambia. Shortly after, he infiltrated Swaziland again and remained there until his arrest by the Swazi authorities in August 1986 for being in possession of false documents.[17]

In his testimony, September claimed he was freed by his own ANC comrades, who arranged for him to cross the border into South Africa. When he entered South Africa, he thought: "The only thing I ever wanted to go and do was study, I have landed up being a member of the ANC, the Swazis want to kill me, the boers [South African Police] want to kill me, I am walking through the bushes here and all I want to do is be a peaceful man, I want to go on with my studies."

He there and then decided to go and hand himself over to the South African authorities. He walked through the night to Piet Retief, where he handed himself over to Warrant Officer Pienaar.

It was an absurd story. September decided to desert the ANC in order to proceed with his studies but instead became an informer. Claiming to have been tired of life with the ANC because of having to live under cover, he chose to become an informer and still lives under cover. If his key aim was to study and his defection was not caused by some political rebirth he certainly could have studied while with the ANC. Instead, he left his wife and child in Mozambique and gave up his senior position in the ANC for that of a constable in the SAP.

According to the intelligence files of the ANC, September was involved in most of the attacks into Swaziland during 1986 and 1987 – a period in which, according to the ANC, eleven of its members were assassinated. Within 12 hours of his kidnapping, the homes of several ANC members were attacked. One of the homes was that of Peter Motau, whose wife identified Sidebe as one of the attackers.[18]

Ebrahim was transferred to John Vorster Square in Johannesburg, where he was mentally tortured. He was exposed to loud continuous noises for up to 24 hours. He said he thought he was going off his mind and at one stage could not sit or sleep. He paced up and down the cell.[19]

He managed to smuggle a letter to his lawyers, stating that he had been kidnapped and tortured. His lawyers brought an urgent application for his release but before judgement he was formally charged with treason.

Ebrahim told the judge that his captors had spoken to soldiers at a road block and their car had not been searched, that they had passed unchallenged through strict security checks at the entrance to security police headquarters and that the security police had held the keys to his handcuffs and leg-irons.

The judge rejected his plea that he had been illegally abducted and therefore could not be charged by a South African court. He was sentenced to 20 years' imprisonment. It was Ebrahim's second term of imprisonment on Robben Island, as he had served 15 years between 1964 and 1979 for sabotage.

In a landmark decision, a full bench of the Appeal Court in Bloemfontein found in March 1991 that Ebrahim had been illegally kidnapped and that the South African Supreme Court had had no jurisdiction to try him. The court found that he had been kidnapped by people acting on instructions from a state institution.

According to Dirk Coetzee's passport, he visited Swaziland early in September 1987. During this visit, he said, he met some of his old colleagues from the Ermelo Security Branch and a night of heavy drinking ensued. At one stage, one of the security policemen asked him: "Dirk, how did you like that job when we pulled the taxi from the road?"[20]

Coetzee's story provided unexpected confirmation of evidence given in a sensational 1988 murder trial. In the Rand Supreme Court, a former member of the Brixton Murder and Robbery Unit told how he had overheard security policemen planning an attack in Swaziland. Sergeant Robert van der Merwe, who was to be found guilty of murdering three drug dealers, testified that he had been instructed to kill the men because two were allegedly ANC members smuggling drugs and the third had ANC connections. He said that at the time he believed what he did was in the interest of national security.[21]

Asked whether he would have acted as unquestioningly if ordered to shoot a common criminal, Van der Merwe said he would not. "I believed these were ANC supporters, and that's why I did it . . . I feel open hatred towards the ANC." Van der Merwe told the court that he thought that clandestine operations against the ANC were justified. While he was doing duty at the Oshoek border post in June and July 1987, he met four security policemen who were on their way to Swaziland. The four were intoxicated, and when he asked them what they were going to do in Swaziland, they replied that they were on a clandestine operation. One of the men told him that he would read about the operation in the newspapers.[22]

He later overheard them say: "The BMW and the weapons are already on the other side and we must see the informer tomorrow night. The targets are awaiting us."

On 10 July 1987 he read in a newspaper that three members of the ANC – two men and a woman – had been shot dead the day before on the road between the airport at Matsapa and Mbabane by three white men. The victims were on their way to Mbabane by taxi when they were stopped by the three men travelling in a BMW. The three men jumped out of the car and started shooting at the passengers.The two men sitting at the back were killed instantly and the woman was shot as she tried to run away.[23]

One of the people killed was a member of the ANC National Executive Committee (NEC) and a senior military official, Cassius Make. The others were ANC official Paul Dikelede and Eliza Tsinini. Make is believed to have been the most senior ANC official to be assassinated since the killing in 1981 of Joe Gqabi, ANC representative in Zimbabwe.

Make was the youngest member of the NEC, ranking about fourth in Umkhonto we Sizwe. He was among the ANC's most outstanding young guerrilla commanders and had earned considerable respect within its ranks for his achievements in the armed struggle.[24]

According to ANC intelligence received from an askari who escaped from Vlakplaas and returned to Lusaka, Major Eugene de Kock exchanged his official white BMW for a dark blue one after he returned from a mission in Swaziland in 1987. Glory "September" Sidebe was positively identified by the taxi driver as one of the killers.[25]

At the same time I met Marthinus Grobler and James Stevens, a former policeman, Detective Sergeant Barend Horn, decided to make a confession about his experiences in the police's riot squad before leaving the country to seek political asylum in Europe.

Horn entered the police force at the tender age of 17. Three months after completing his training, he shot his first man as he fired on a suspect running away. He was severely reprimanded by his seniors but was not not charged. He soon came into contact with detainees being tortured.

"The suspect, middle-aged with a stubble beard, was sitting in an ordinary office chair with his hands handcuffed behind his back. [The policeman] stood directly behind him, holding a wide piece of an inner tube from a tyre, slit open and two feet long. Every time the suspect . . . was unable to answer his questions, [the policeman] would put the tube over his face and pull very tight. The suspect was not able to breathe," Horn said in an affidavit.

"Policemen talk all the time about the shock machine, how well it works, it's efficient. It's common knowledge. Every policeman knows about it . . . I heard someone screaming and shouting at the top of his voice. I went to have a look . . . There was a canvas bag over his head . . . One wire was connected to the guy's neck muscles just below his hairline at the back. Another wire was connected to tender flesh underneath the upper arm.

"The black suspect said he didn't know anything about a car radio being stolen. The policeman was smiling as he turned the handle [of the shock machine]. It looked like the guy was having a convulsive fit. He was shaking, his muscles were contracting. He was screaming and his bladder released."

Horn said the shock machine was affectionately known as "Sophie". At another police station where he served it was called "Doctor Groenewald". Horn later began to torture suspects himself and would appear in court afterwards to deny everything. With tedious regularity magistrates rejected the victims' torture allegations.

In June 1984, as South Africa was brought to the brink of civil war, Horn was transferred to the Eastern Cape for riot control. For weeks he drove

89

around townships in an armoured vehicle together with other policemen armed with shotguns and R-1 assault rifles, tearsmoke and rubber bullets.

It was a mad, bizarre period in Horn's life, chasing and shooting rioters as the townships around them exploded in an orgy of violence. The policemen were ill-trained, scared and mentally unprepared for the rioting they encountered. They eventually looted a liquor store and found some reassurance and confidence in the brandy and whisky they stole.

"It was war. It was a period of my life that I will never forget. We had acid bombs thrown at us, petrol bombs, we were shot at, we were attacked. I felt we had a free rein. It was up to us to use our discretion."

The death toll in the Eastern Cape became so high that the riot police were told to use their sharppoint ammunition with discretion and concentrate on rubber bullets instead. The policemen countered by inserting torch batteries into the rubber bullets. They were also shown how to make a slug from a shotgun round. Horn described the shooting of a woman with a rubber bullet – which had a battery inserted in the front: ". . . the whole skin on top of her head sort of peeled open. She was hit on the temple. She was just an innocent bystander. She was definitely not the person who threw the brick. No medical attention was given to her. She was just left there."

In 1985 the Kannemeyer Commission of Inquiry into the massacre of 21 people shot dead by police in the Eastern Cape heard evidence by a police colonel of top-level orders for the elimination of activists who threw petrol bombs.

Colonel Adolf van Rooyen said the order to shoot petrol bombers had come in a telex message from the Senior Deputy Commissioner of Police, General Hennie de Witt (later Commissioner of Police).The general had also ordered that R-1 rifles be issued to all police members patrolling riot areas and that the policemen should not hesitate to use the weapons when danger to lives and property was involved.[27]

The policeman who gave the order to shoot at the crowd of funeral-goers at Uitenhage, Lieutenant John Fouché, said in his evidence: "I was under great shock. I could not handle it. I couldn't think rationally and even went to the doctor to get tranquillisers."

Judge Donald Kannemeyer criticised the police severely for their handling of the events leading up to the shooting and for their "deliberate " policy of not using standard riot control equipment. They used buckshot rather than birdshot and had not been issued with either teargas or rubber bullets. Fifteen of the people who died had been shot by the police in the back while they were running away. Kannemeyer found however that no individual was responsible for their death.[28]

Horn was eventually transferred to the East Rand near Johannesburg, again for riot control. There was an extra dimension to the job, however. The policemen were shown photographs of certain activists and instructed to kill them. They were specifically looking for a young man by the name of David

Maswai. Horn and his men had no luck, but when they returned to the police station that afternoon, two members of the East Rand security police told them not to worry, Maswai was no longer a problem. Horn saw Maswai in the boot of their car. He was lying in a foetal position, covered in blood, and his eyes were closed.

The two policemen discussed the idea of disposing of him down one of the disused mine shafts in the area. They got into their vehicle and left, returning without Maswai. "I wanted no part of their action so I kept quiet," said Horn. "I didn't want to become involved. I didn't bother asking them what happened to Maswai."

Horn took his discharge from the police force in October 1989. After he left, he had to undergo psychiatric counselling and was hospitalised with severe depression. He said he became a committed Christian and confessed his experiences to his preacher, deciding to tell all and start a new life. He left South Africa in January 1990 and was granted political asylum in Holland.

What is important about the testimony of the three young policemen is not only what they witnessed and experienced, but what it tells us about the police culture in which death squads originated, functioned and flourished. What we have learnt is that a brotherhood has formed of policemen: they stick together, they lie for each other, they cover up for each other. Those who break these unspoken rules become outcasts and are regarded as traitors.

I am not suggesting that all South African policemen torture suspects or shoot activists. The South African Police is a force of 70 000 policemen of whom only 4 000 are members of the Security Branch. There are many honest and dedicated policemen who have committed themselves to the proper maintenance of law and order. South Africa must be one of the worst countries in the world in which to be a policeman. Under the rule of apartheid, the police force was never allowed to be neutral.

Many policemen know about death squads. Grobler said their existence was common knowledge in the force. In Piet Retief they accepted that Frederik Pienaar and his men were part of a special unit that killed the enemy, a necessary part of the war against the ANC.

Marthinus Grobler might have been sincere when he said that his fate was directed by his own conscience and that he wanted the truth to come out. James Stevens was another story; he was persuaded to undertake the "Lusaka Safari" by a sense of adventure and the threat of prosecution.

Stevens was evading a number of criminal investigations arising out of the use of excessive force while carrying out his duties as a policeman. These charges included assault and illegal discharge of a firearm. In all cases the violence was directed against black people. He constantly made racist remarks and gleefully described the torture of black suspects by his police friends.

Having travelled to Lusaka, Grobler and Stevens were detained for a short while and debriefed by the ANC. They were eventually allowed to join the organisation. Stevens, however, disillusioned by the conditions and lack of adventure in Zambia, returned to South Africa. Before he left, Dirk Coetzee asked him to steal old police petrol books at Piet Retief that he believed could help him prove some of his allegations. He also gave Stevens letters for family members.

Stevens betrayed Coetzee when he handed himself – and the letters – over to the police. In a lengthy statement about Coetzee and the ANC he told them that Coetzee had masterminded a sinister plot for the ANC to blow up Security Branch headquarters in Pretoria.[29]

The police had remained defiant after Coetzee's exposures and Nofemela's confessions, claiming that death squads had never existed and that the whole story was a figment of the two former security policemen's imagination. In fact, even though Nofemela had been on death row since September 1987 and was never visited by Coetzee, I know that there was an attempt by the police to show that the whole story was a conspiracy between Nofemela and Coetzee.

Nofemela said in his affidavit from death row: "I complained about the attitude of Brigadier [Krappies] Engelbrecht, he was questioning me aggressively. The Brigadier was trying to cover for the other people saying that some of my allegations were unbelievable. He was putting the blame on Captain Coetzee as he repeatedly questioned me whether Captain Coetzee came to visit me."

It could never be expected that other policemen would come forward and confess their part in the death squads. Coetzee and Nofemela were both exceptional cases. Other policemen had too much to lose: they all had houses, jobs and families which they could not put at risk. They knew that the police would protect them to the bitter end. There was nothing else they could do but deny all death squad allegations and call Coetzee and Nofemela liars.

After independence in Zimbabwe in 1980 a flood of former Rhodesian security force members confessed their part in bush war atrocities. Some wrote books and others granted interviews to newspapers and magazines. Perhaps the same will one day happen in South Africa.

There are signs, however, that many agents fear the future and the possibility of retribution by a new South African government. In the first days of 1990 we traced the London bomber, Peter Casselton – frightened and on the run.

Casselton, who has a pilot's licence, was working as a crop-spraying pilot in Mozambique when Coetzee made his allegations. He hastily returned to South Africa for fear of being extradited to the United Kingdom. Interpol issued a warrant for his arrest shortly after it became known that he had been involved in the London bomb explosion. Casselton was trapped in South Africa.[30]

The former agent phoned Karin Coetzee and arranged a meeting with her at a Pretoria restaurant. When she arrived at the shopping centre, the place was swarming with security policemen in plain clothes. Casselton told her that he was no longer working for the security police and that he wanted to establish contact with her husband. He feared for his life and had to find a way to leave the country. 'I'm stuffed," he lamented, 'I'm stuffed. Why did Dirk do it to me? I'll rot away in jail for 25 years. I was in jail before: I do not want to go back."

Three security police vehicles full of policemen were waiting for Casselton to leave the shopping centre. One of the vehicles was a microbus filled with black policemen who just had to be askaris from Vlakplaas. While Max du Preez and I were monitoring the meeting between Casselton and Karin Coetzee, we were called by a black security guard who told us that some men in a pick-up van had tried to break into our car.

We walked to the van parked some distance away. Inside were two bearded, safari-suited men. One had a walkie-talkie on his lap and the other held a file. They didn't see us coming until Du Preez roared at them: "Were you trying to break into our car?"

The one with the file threw it on the floor, the other tried desperately to hide the two-way radio under the seat. "Negative," the one with the radio answered.

Du Preez: "Were you never near our car?"

Policeman: "Negative. Was something stolen? Do you have any witnesses? Have you found any fingerprints?"

Du Preez: "Sir, what is your name?"

Policeman: "Gert Prinsloo."

Du Preez: "Are you a policeman?"

Policeman: "Negative."

Du Preez: "You talk like one."

Policeman: "Negative. I don't know what you're talking about."

After Karin Coetzee left, we found Casselton still sitting in the restaurant and asked if we could talk to him. He denied that he was Peter Casselton and asked us to leave. We told him that the building was surrounded by policemen waiting for him.

As he stood up and walked into the parking garage, we followed him. He turned around and approached us. He was sweating and looked confused as he told us: "Leave me alone. Just leave me alone. I'm very nervous. I'm an old hand at this. Just turn around and walk away. Don't talk to me. You'll have to get up much earlier in the morning if you're dealing with me."

Casselton sat in his car for an hour, then roared out of the parking garage. He was followed by the three vehicles in a high-speed chase through Pretoria. We lost them. A few days later, a man approached us saying that Casselton had asked him to arrange a meeting with us. The go-between, a giant of a man who introduced himself as "Twiggy", said Casselton wanted to talk about the bomb explosion, weapons he had hidden in bushes just outside London and his falling-out with Craig Williamson. We arranged a meeting with Casselton, but he never turned up.

I sensed the real anguish of a security police agent's fear for the future when I was approached one day by a man who had operated against the ANC in neighbouring states. I cannot reveal this agent's name as I gave an undertaking to protect him and his family.

We met in a Johannesburg bar where he told me that he could no longer go on with his double life and wanted to meet with the ANC to discuss his future in a South Africa under black majority rule. He was a respectable man with a good job and a stable family life who had been drawn into the secretive world of the security police and participated in various operations abroad.

I put him into contact with Andre Zaaiman and in the weeks that followed he had various meetings with officials of the ANC, including Chief of Intelligence Jacob Zuma. For various reasons I did not attend the meetings. However, from what I gathered from Zaaiman, his chief concern was to obtain an assurance that he and his family would be safe from prosecution in a future South Africa. He gave the ANC a detailed description of what he was involved in and whatever knowledge he had about the security police, and handed over the weapons that had been issued to him by the security police. As far as I know, they have been cached in a neighbouring state, but before they left South Africa, I had an opportunity to photograph some of them and judge what the agent had been up to.

Among the weapons were a modified R-1 assault rifle, a throwing knife and a very special plastic assassination revolver. The .44 calibre assassination revolver is called a "Super Blackhawk" and is designed to resemble a toy, right down to the "Made in Korea" inscription. It is fitted with a plastic telescope. The revolver's appearance, as intended, belies its lethal purpose. It has six built-in bullets and the plastic barrel is screwed off and replaced with a conventional steel barrel. It is manufactured in such a way that it can be taken through customs without being detected. After firing six shots, the revolver is thrown away, leaving no traces.

The agent had never fired the plastic revolver and had never received any instruction to assassinate an opponent with it. It was given to him just in case.

Dirk Coetzee described the technical division of the security police as a "bomb factory" where security policemen could obtain an array of "dirty tricks" devices for internal and cross-border operations. The genius behind the division is Colonel Wal du Toit, who prepared the bombs that blew up Bafana Duma and the infiltrator and young boy in Swaziland. It was Wal du

Toit who prepared the briefcase-cum-machinegun for Coetzee's aborted assassination attempt on Marius Schoon.[31]

According to his teenage brother, Charles, Almond Nofemela often came home with an arsenal of weapons, including what is believed to have been an AK-47 assault rifle, Makarov and Tokarev pistols and a rifle fitted with a telescope. Nofemela's best friend was "Sipho", an AK-47 he used to carry around in a black briefcase.

"Although he carried other smaller weapons, he would never go anywhere without Sipho. At the time of his arrest, when he was on leave, he had taken Sipho to Pretoria for repairs. My brother would at times allow me to handle the guns and I once asked him if I could also do the job he was doing. He told me it was possible, but only when I was grown up. He said the type of job he was doing required one to be brave and ruthless," said Charles.[32]

It is difficult to tell if any of the anguish of the anonymous security police agent is expressed among the various motives revealed by Nofemela in a consultation with his lawyer: "I am a born-again Christian and realising that I was going to be killed. I consider it unreasonable that I should conceal my sins and I decided to confess. Another reason is that the police had deceived me that they will help me. They said that they were talking to the minister to get a reprieve. I was told that I will be taken out of prison to rejoin the death squad. I felt used and unfairly betrayed.

"I have no history of mental illness or disorder. I was never examined by a psychiatrist or psychologist. The only thing is that when I worked with the death squad I could think of nothing else but to kill. There was not a year that went past since 1981 that I did not kill. I suffered a lot of nightmares of the killings until I became used to my work."

In 1981, when Dirk Coetzee was at Vlakplaas, there were less than 20 askaris and the farm's entire clandestine arsenal fitted into the boot of his official police car. The nature of Vlakplaas has changed enormously since then. In the last few years there has been a dramatic build-up of arms, staff and facilities.[33]

At the beginning of 1990 a 26-year-old Zimbabwean national fled from Vlakplaas and joined the ANC in Zimbabwe. All his life Godfrey Ndaowana had been trapped in the conflicts and bloodshed of southern Africa.

Ndaowana started school in 1970 at Manunura primary school in Zimbabwe, but his education was interrupted five years later when the entire population of the Manica province was forcibly removed by the Rhodesian government of Prime Minister Ian Smith to a concentration camp called "Kiep".[34]

He was only 13 when he became a member of the Zimbabwean National Liberation Army (Zanla) in 1976; shortly afterwards he was captured by members of the Rhodesian police and sent to the Ruda camp where he was interrogated and assaulted. Freed by members of the guerrilla forces, he became involved in various military operations against the Rhodesian forces.

Ndaowana was captured again in 1978 and detained for six months before being taken to a camp called Lusape, a place similar to Vlakplaas, where guerrillas were "turned" and integrated into the Rhodesian forces. As Rhodesia approached independence, Ndaowana was brought to South Africa under mysterious circumstances. While working as a gardener at a Salisbury police station, he was informed that he had been transferred to Bulawayo, where he would be employed on a local farm. He was, however, taken to the Beit Bridge border post, where he was handed over to members of the South African Police. They took him to Messina Police Station, where he stayed for a night before being transported to Vlakplaas. The only explanation for his transfer is that Vlakplaas was then in the process of being established and that Brigadier Jan Viktor needed labourers to work on the farm. He used his contacts in the Rhodesian Special Branch to obtain the services of former guerrillas.

Ndaowana met Viktor, Dirk Coetzee and David Tshikalange when he arrived at Vlakplaas, where he was told that his chores on the farm would entail general maintenance work, cleaning, assisting with the construction of various buildings and attending to the livestock. He remained there as a labourer until 1990, when he fled to his country of birth.

The Zimbabwean was just a labourer and not a member of any squad, but being one of the "old-timers" on the farm, he was privy to a great deal of information related to him by other members, and could corroborate many details of Coetzee's and Nofemela's testimonies. He was able to give the ANC the names of 45 policemen, 70 askaris and 11 labourers whom he could remember in his nine years at Vlakplaas. At the time of his departure there were 70 askaris – with Silumami Mose in charge – based on the farm, among them names like "Ninja", "Vietnam", "Confusion", "Ghost", "Stalwart" and "Stretcher". In many instances the askaris seemed to have chosen to retain their Umkhonto we Sizwe codenames.

When Dirk Coetzee left Vlakplaas, there were four squads. When Ndaowana left, there were nine, each comprising four to six askaris as well as one or two white policemen, each team working for about 20 days per month and taking the rest of the month off. A full-time black officer was responsible for solving the administrative, salary and employment problems of the askaris, who now lived in the Lethlabile township near Brits and in Soshanguve near Pretoria.

New facilities on the farm included upgrading of old buildings, new offices, new living quarters, garages, a clubhouse, a shooting range, security fencing, a soccer stadium and a braai area next to the river.

According to Ndaowana six Aids cases had been identified at Vlakplaas. Most of the askaris had come from countries such as Angola, Mozambique, Zambia and Tanzania, where the virus has reached epidemic proportions.

Two of the confirmed cases had been identified among former PAC members and three among ANC members. One carrier is an ordinary black policeman.

Where askaris received only informal training in the first half of the eighties, they now receive formal training in marksmanship and in various combat and other tactics. Some of the askaris have even attended a two-month parachuting course at Phalaborwa in the Eastern Transvaal.

The armoury section at Vlakplaas is under the command of a warrant officer who is in charge of three armouries at Vlakplaas and two armouries at Daisy a few kilometres away. A large range of weaponry is available at Vlakplaas, including a range of 60 millimetre and 81 millimetre mortars, Russian-made RPG rocket launchers, light machine guns, approximately 30 AK-47 assault rifles, Tokarev pistols, anti-tank landmines, a range of limpet mines, hand grenades and explosives.

The Russian weapons were brought from Namibia to Vlakplaas in 1989 as that country approached independence. Eugene de Kock and three security policemen left for Oshakati in northern Namibia and returned a week later in a convoy of vehicles loaded with Russian arms.

After Coetzee exposed police death squads, Ndaowana was one of the labourers on the farm who had to get rid of the Russian arms to create the impression that Vlakplaas was just another police unit. Big trucks were used to transport the death squad arsenal to Daisy. Official police weapons were all that remained in the strongrooms at Vlakplaas for the world to see.

There seems to be no good reason, in the present political climate, for the continued existence of a squad of "rehabilitated terrorists" roaming about looking for their former comrades. Yet, even now, there are no indications that the Vlakplaas teams are to be disbanded.

CHAPTER SEVEN

The Genesis of death squads

If a man sins because of darkness, the guilty one is not he who sins, but he who causes who the darkness. Victor Hugo

THE brutal murder of anti-apartheid activists testifies to the crisis in which South African society found itself. It had become necessary to do increasingly terrible things to defend the apartheid order.

Death squads cannot be seen in isolation from the apartheid government's full arsenal of repressive methods, ranging from formal and legal means such as detentions, bannings and the use of the courts to criminalise political opponents, to extra-legal and informal repression such as the use of "dirty tricks" squads, vigilantes, death squads and surrogate forces.[1]

Anthropologist and anti-detention campaigner David Webster said just before he was assassinated himself that death squads had the effect of controlling opposition when all other repressive methods, such as detention or intimidation, had failed. In the end the death squads became apartheid's ultimate and most secret weapon.[2]

This chapter will trace the origin of death squads, which I believe goes back as far as the previous century, when the foundations of state lawlessness were laid. I want to look at the factors and dynamics in South African society that allowed death squads to roam the political arena assassinating opponents of the state. Then there are certain structures and a culture existing within the police force that make it possible for death squads to exist and function. First, there was security legislation that encouraged some policemen to think they were above the law and led to a breakdown in public accountability that was abetted by compliant courts. Second, the culture within the police force – the so-called "cop culture" – created a particular set of norms and values. Third, the militarisation of South Africa and the effect of the "total onslaught" ideology created an atmosphere in which policemen believed that they were involved in a "total war" which had to be countered by a "total strategy".

Finally, as South Africa moved towards a government dominated by securocrats and Defence Force officers, under the leadership of PW Botha, the security forces were placed in a position of tremendous power. As internal resistance to the apartheid system grew in magnitude, the Defence Force became involved in the counter-insurgency warfare and increasingly played a policing role. Of the various specialist military units operating in the battlefields of Angola and Namibia and attacking South Africa's neighbours, one eventually emerged as a death squad operating against anti-apartheid activists inside and outside South Africa.

Death squads are not an anomalous outcome of the apartheid state in its dying stages, they are its natural and inevitable product.[3] By the same token, their roots are one with the foundations of state lawlessness, laid long before 1948 when the National Party came to power and formally introduced the system of apartheid. And each of the infamous Acts passed to uphold the willed inequality of South African society carried within it the seeds of the violent measures that would eventually have to be taken to defend it. Despite the repressive measures introduced by successive governments, the resistance of the disenfranchised majority increased in momenturn. And as the resistance increased, so did the violence to which the state had to resort to maintain the status quo.

A watershed day in South African history – and an important step on the road to death squads – was 21 March 1960. Sixty-nine people were shot dead and 180 wounded as police opened fire on a crowd of 5 000 people engaged in a peaceful protest against the Pass Laws. Nearly all the Sharpeville victims were shot in the back.[4]

Prime Minister Hendrik Verwoerd reacted with repression. He introduced laws to declare the ANC and the PAC illegal and under new Emergency regulations 18 000 people were detained. In July 1961 he made John Vorster Minister of Justice. Vorster later recalled the meeting at which Verwoerd appointed him: "I remember saying to Dr Verwoerd that he should let me deal with the threat of subversion and revolution in my own way. I told him that you could not fight communism with the Queensberry rules, because if you did then you would lose. He agreed with me and said that he would leave me free to do what I had to do – within reason."[5]

This was the beginning of the era of informal repression – torture, death in detention, "dirty tricks" against anti-apartheid activists and, ultimately, death squads. It was during this era that the ANC launched its armed struggle, arguing that if non-violent protest, external pressure and economic collapse had failed to move the government, then the only remaining option was violence.

Vorster did as he had promised. He further strengthened the security laws and gave the police increased freedom to ignore civil liberties. In 1963 he introduced legislation providing for detention without trial. The so-called "90-day Act" empowered a commissioned police officer to arrest without warrant and detain any person he suspected upon reasonable grounds of having committed or having intended to commit sabotage or an offence under the Suppression of Communism Act or the Unlawful Organisations

Act. A detainee could be held in custody for interrogation for 90 days or until, in the opinion of the Commissioner of Police, satisfactory replies had been given to all questions. A person could be redetained for an additional 90 days.[6]

John Vorster justified detention without trial when he told Parliament: "There is no spontaneous rebellion in South Africa. It is an organised rebellion by a group of people inside and outside South Africa, a group which knows all the tricks to stay out of the hands of the law and has at its disposal the best possible advice."[7]

The "90-day Act" elevated police officers above the law and put detainees at the mercy of their captors. It created a sub-culture in the police force that encouraged policemen to act mercilessly in their struggle against communism and in the protection of Volk and Vaderland.

The 90-day Act was repealed in 1965 and replaced by a 180-day detention law. A new provision in the Criminal Procedure Act authorised the Attorney General to order the detention of persons likely to give material evidence for the state in any criminal proceedings relating to certain political or common law offences. Ostensibly its purpose was the detention of potential witnesses; in practice, however, some ended up as accused rather than witnesses.[8]

On 5 September 1963, detainee Solwandle "Looksmart" Ngudle was found hanging in his cell. In the same month B Mampe also died in detention. These two were the first of many arrested under the new security laws to die in detention; they were also the first of many for whose deaths magistrates found nobody could be held responsible. For the next quarter of a century this verdict was heard in inquest courts all over South Africa. Vorster's laws eventually led to the deaths of at least 74 detainees.[9]

It is important to look at deaths and torture in detention because the step from torture to assassination is a small one. Three independent research surveys conducted in the eighties showed that the vast majority of political and security detainees were tortured by their interrogators.

In April 1982, the Detainees' Parents Support Committee published a memorandum on torture in detention to support its claim that the security police were abusing detainees during interrogation. Eighty-three per cent of the sample of 175 detainees claimed some form of physical torture. In a study by the Medical and Dental Association conducted on detainees seen by its members between December 1985 and June 1986, a very high level of physical abuse was also recorded – 72 per cent of a sample of 131 detainees. The study went further in examining the detainees for injuries consistent with the alleged forms of assault and found that in 97 per cent of cases where injuries were present, the claims were substantiated by the nature of the injuries.[10]

The most comprehensive study on torture was done by the Department of Psychology of the University of Cape Town, which found that 145 of the 175 people in their sample (83 per cent) had suffered some form of torture.[11] When their preliminary report was released in the latter half of 1985, it occasioned a major political storm.

The most frequent form of torture (75 per cent) was beating, while the next three most frequently reported forms were forced standing (50 per cent), holding a position as if sitting in an imaginary chair (34 per cent) and forced exercises (28 per cent). In addition 25 per cent reported having been subjected to electrical shocks, 18 per cent to strangulation and 14 per cent to suspension in various forms. There were also incidents of constant manacling (15 per cent), pulling out or burning of hair (5 per cent), genital abuse (3 per cent) and sticking pins or needles into feet or the body (3 per cent). There were also incidents of being wrapped in canvas, having burning matchsticks placed under nails, being thrown into the air and allowed to fall, having hands cut with a knife, fingernails crushed by a brick, petrol poured over the body and set alight and scrubbed on face and body with a hard brush. While only 31 per cent of whites claimed they were tortured, 93 per cent of black people in the sample suffered torture.

Several months after a State of Emergency was declared in July 1985, a young district surgeon, Dr Wendy Orr, made an urgent appeal to the Supreme Court to stop the police ill-treating hundreds of detainees under her care in the Port Elizabeth prisons. She told the court that in August and September 1985 she had examined hundreds of detainees bearing numerous injuries, including weals, bruising and blisters on their backs, arms and palms, freshly perforated eardrums, bruising and swelling around the eyes and split skin over their cheekbones. Orr's testimony was supplemented by 270 pages of additional testimony from 42 other applicants in the suit, including former detainees, relatives of those still detained, prominent trade unionists, clergy and community leaders. In December 1985 the applicants filed 93 more affidavits containing allegations of "horrific assaults". The torture included electric shocks, being forced to drink petrol, being throttled or nearly suffocated with a wet towel, being slapped, kicked, whipped, punched and beaten all over the body and face. The case was remanded for trial in June 1986, but the temporary lifting of the State of Emergency altered the situation as all the detainees protected by the original injunction were released from detention. Just prior to the hearing date, the Minister of Law and Order agreed to pay costs in the case.[12]

The International Commission of Jurists (1978) and Amnesty International (1978) have charged South Africa's security forces with the widespread use of torture and violence as part of their repressive strategy. The International Commission of Jurists stated in a 160-page report in May 1988 that the government was faced with the dilemma of how to reconcile "a repressive strategy to contain the disenfranchised majority" with their "pretentions to legitimacy within the western liberal tradition."[13]

Even children have not escaped abuse in detention. At a recent symposium on children in detention, it was revealed that 34 per cent of the children in a study had been detained in solitary confinement, 25 per cent had experienced attempted suffocation and 14 per cent had received electric shocks. At least five children are known to have died in detention.[14]

Fifty thousand people were held by the state during the three-year period January 1985 to December 1987. The number of detentions during these three years equals the total number of detentions during the preceding quarter of a century. Between 1960, when this form of repression was first introduced, and 1990 a total of 100 000 were detained.[15]

Given the numbers of detainees and the obstacles in the path of those organisations that tried to keep track of them, it is hardly surprising that "disappearances" from detention were easily engineered. A notable case was that of the former secretary-general of the Mamelodi Civic Action, Stanza Bopape, who disappeared from police custody in October 1988. Police claimed that Bopape, who was held under security legislation, escaped from custody while being transported to another police station. They claimed that he had obtained the keys to his handcuffs while his three escorts were changing a flat tyre. There are, however, a number of factors to support the family's claim that Bopape is dead. He has failed to reappear in South Africa or anywhere else and has not tried to contact his family. It took the police three weeks to inform the family that he had escaped and they never searched for him at his parents' home.

Bopape's father, Matome Bopape, was told during a meeting with the Minister of Law and Order that his son, who had been handcuffed, had picked up a policeman's jacket, taken out the keys to his handcuffs, unlocked them, climbed out of the car and walked into the veld. The police did not see or hear him escape.[16]

The South African courts must bear some responsibility for the extent of torture and death in detention. According to Professor Tony Matthews, dean of the faculty of law at the University of Natal, the courts failed to denounce torture by the police in unequivocal terms. He says: "It is the steady and progressive breakdown of public accountability which explains the modern phenomenon of death squads."[17]

On 3 February 1982, the Minister of Police assured Parliament that "every possible measure was taken to ensure that detainees could not injure themselves and commit suicide". Yet, two days later, Dr Neil Aggett died in detention at John Vorster Square. Human rights lawyer George Bizos coined the term "induced suicide" during the inquest. Aggett had received no medical attention during nearly three months of detention, despite injuries sustained during interrogation. In a statement, he had described being kept awake and interrogated continuously for 62 hours during which he was given electric shocks. The police sergeant who had recorded Aggett's statement did not request that he be medically examined, later stating in an affidavit: "The security police were busy with him." On the day following the sergeant's visit, Aggett's body was found hanging in his cell.[18]

Criticising the magistrate's findings that nobody could be held responsible for Aggett's death, human rights campaigner Helen Suzman said that detainees found themselves in a totally helpless situation and could not expect to find relief in the courts. She said that the magistrate had dismissed all the evidence given by detainees and accepted all the evidence given by the security police. "He totally ignored the effects of solitary confinement and the fact that detainees faced retribution if they made complaints and these complaints were ignored. Does the minister realise that the magistrate's findings went further than the counsel for the police requested?"[19]

Suicide has been the most commonly claimed cause of death. Many believe that the high incidence of findings of suicide by hanging may be attributed in part to strangulation techniques of torture being used during interrogation. The history of deaths in detention is riddled with magistrates who found that detainees had committed suicide while their bodies were covered with bruises and signs of physical torture.

In 1971 Ahmed Timol died after falling from a tenth-floor window at police headquarters at John Vorster Square. The post-mortem revealed abrasions and bruises all over his body, and pathologists testified that these had been inflicted during the period of his arrest. The magistrate found that Timol committed suicide rather than betray his comrades.[20]

The best-known death in detention is without doubt that of Black Consciousness leader Steve Biko, who died on 12 September 1977 in police custody in Pretoria, the forty-sixth detainee to die in detention. Evidence given at his inquest by police, doctors and warders revealed that he had been kept naked and manacled for 20 days, during which time he was not allowed out of his cell even for air or exercise. He received various blows to his head, some of which caused brain damage. The day before he died, he had been driven from Port Elizabeth to Pretoria naked in the back of a Land Rover.[21]

It is important to stop for a moment at the death of Steve Biko because it so clearly indicated the rot that had spread among the higher echelons of the police, the state and even the doctors who had to treat Biko for the injuries he sustained during his interrogation. Biko's death was no worse than several others; it merely attracted world attention. He was never found guilty of any crime, never arrested for inciting violence and never accused of it in an open court.

The head of the Eastern Cape Security Branch and the officer in charge of Biko's interrogation, Colonel Piet Goosen, said the police regarded their captive as a dangerous "terrorist" leader.

Counsel for the Biko family, the celebrated Sydney Kentridge, asked Goosen: "Show me a piece of paper that gives you the right to keep a man in chains – or are you people above the law?"

Goosen: "We have full authority. It is left to my sound discretion."

Kentridge: "Under what statutory authority?"

Goosen: "We don't work under statutory authority."

Kentridge: "You don't work under statutory authority? Thank you very much, Colonel, that's what we have always suspected."[22]

A Port Elizabeth district surgeon, Dr Ivor Lang, examined Biko in Goosen's presence. The detainee was lying on a mat, manacled to a metal grille. During his examination, Lang found a swollen laceration on the patient's upper lip, a bruise over the sternum, a ring mark around each wrist, and oedema of both hands, feet and ankles. His movements were uncoordinated and his speech slurred. And yet Lang wrote in his report: "I have found no evidence of any abnormality or pathology on the patient."[23]

The next day Lang was summoned again. This time he examined Biko, lying on a mat now soaked in urine, in the company of his superior, Dr Benjamin Tucker. Biko was taken to hospital for a lumbar puncture, the results of which revealed bloodstaining in the cerebrospinal fluid. Lang wrote in his report: "No change in condition ... no pathology ... lumbar puncture was normal ... returning him to the police cells."[24]

The next day, a warden found Biko collapsed, glassy-eyed, hyperventilating and frothing at the mouth. Yet, incredibly, Tucker gave his permission to the police for the patient to be transferred by motor vehicle 1 200 kilometres to Pretoria. Biko was unaccompanied by any medical personnel and no medical records on his condition were sent with him.

The verdict of magistrate MJ Prins angered the world: "The available evidence does not prove that the death was brought about by any act or admission involving or amounting to an offence on the part of any person."

Exiled editor Donald Woods wrote: "Judicial officers are supposed at all times to bear in mind the principles of natural justice. Magistrate Prins had no moral right to outrage these principles when he offered no word of censure against the horrifying picture that emerged at the inquest. It is a picture of unbridled political police power over life and death – a power which, condoned by the State, descended to a level of brutality and callousness unmatched in any society that still clings to at least some vestiges of legality."

But the rot was not only in the security police and the courts. Both the South African Medical and Dental Council and the Medical Association of South Africa announced after the inquest that they had found no evidence of improper conduct by Tucker or Lang and that a charge of unethical conduct could not be sustained. The complainants – mainly concerned doctors from the medical faculties of the Universities of Cape Town and the Witwatersrand – were forced to seek Supreme Court review of the matter and in January 1985, more than seven years after Biko's death, the court ruled that there was evidence of improper or disgraceful conduct on the part of the two doctors.[28]

Shortly after the Biko inquest, Piet Goosen was promoted to the rank of brigadier and transferred to Pretoria where he commanded the foreign section (Section A) at security police headquarters. It was an act of pure defiance to promote Goosen, but it also showed the state's utter indifference to the death of Steve Biko, an indifference that can be measured in the infamous words of the Minister of Justice, Jimmy Kruger, when he told a congress of the National Party: "I am not glad and I am not sorry about Mr Biko. It leaves me cold . . . Incidentally, I can just tell the congress, the day before yesterday one of my own lieutenants in the prison service also committed suicide and we have not yet accused a single prisoner."[29]

Woods's comment on Kruger's statement: "But precisely who struck the fatal blows is relatively unimportant. [The ten security policemen who interrogated Biko] are petty offenders in the scale of outrage. The real killer is the System – and all its representatives involved in this tragedy. Two members of the South African cabinet are most responsible for the circumstances under which Steve Biko died: Police Minister JT Kruger and Premier BJ Vorster."[30]

There can be little doubt that words like those of Jimmy Kruger, the failure of magistrates to speak out and the harsh security laws introduced by Vorster created the conditions, the climate and the state of mind that led to deaths in detention and ultimately to death squads. As Sydney Kentridge said during the Biko inquest: "Any verdict which can be seen as an exoneration of the Port Elizabeth security police will unfortunately be widely interpreted as a licence to abuse helpless people with impunity."[31] A year after Biko died, the spate of death squad assassinations started with the killing of Durban academic Rick Turner.

Very few policemen have ever been convicted of torturing or killing detainees. The first policeman to be charged and convicted after the death of a detainee was Sergeant Harms van As, who was sentenced to ten years' imprisonment for shooting Paris Malatji through the head at point-blank range during interrogation. The death of Malatji, who was the sixtieth detainee to die, could hardly be concealed by the police. Van As served only six years of his sentence.[32]

Political detainees are not the only victims of torture in detention. In 1989 four policemen of the firearms unit in Port Shepstone were convicted of culpable homicide after a suspect died with a plastic bag over his head. They each received a fine and a suspended sentence. Mr Justice Shearer said in his judgement that the only reason they had not been sent to prison for their crime was that the practice of placing a plastic bag over a suspect's head during interrogation appeared to be standard practice in their unit.

In November 1990 a Free State policeman was sentenced to seven years' imprisonment and two other policemen received suspended sentences when they dumped the body of a dead suspect on a highway after he had been kicked, hit and stamped on. The policemen tried to create the impression that the man had died in a hit-and-run accident. The testimony of their commanding officer, Colonel WN Visser, was remarkable. According to him, the policemen were "decent boys" who ran into trouble when their "unorthodox" investigation went out of control. "Some policemen often assault suspects," he said.[34]

One of the most glaring features of the police disciplinary record is its failure to discipline or expel those of its members who have been found guilty of assault or torture. Official figures indicate that only about ten per cent of those police convicted of violent crimes are eventually discharged from the police force. Far from facing disciplinary action, several members of the security forces who have been identified over the years as having participated in assault or torture have been promoted. This is in contrast to the various ministers' assertions that firm action would be taken against police who committed abuses against detainees.[35]

How can human beings inflict such awful treatment on others without any remorse or alteration of psychological states or values? To answer this question, it is necessary to look at the culture in the police force.

Donald Woods described the security policemen testifying at the Biko inquest as follows: "We at the inquest could see their faces, could watch their demeanour under cross-examination, and could hear their words – their version of the story. For the first time, these men, products and inheritors of the Afrikaner Nationalist tradition, were flushed out of their police stations and their little interrogating rooms. For once they were in the position of having to account for themselves. These men displayed symptoms of extreme insularity. They are people whose upbringing has impressed upon them the divine right to retain power, and in that sense they are innocent men – incapable of thinking or acting differently. On top of that they have gravitated to an occupation that has given them all the scope they need to express their rigid personalities. They have been protected for years by the laws of the country. They have been able to carry out all their imaginative torture practices quite undisturbed in cells and rooms all over the country, with tacit official sanction, and they have been given tremendous status by the government as the men 'protect the State from subversion'."[36]

It is important to remember that the SAP has for decades been misused as a political instrument by National Party governments to maintain and uphold the apartheid system. As John Vorster, then Minister of Police, explained: "Had our country been inhabited by a homogeneous population subscribing to a uniform political philosophy with a traditional appreciation of the norms of civilised white society and a thorough knowledge of and strict adherence to the laws of the country, the task of the Police would probably have been far more pleasant. However, as we do not live in such a country, the task of the Police is more difficult. The multiracial composition of our population should be borne in mind. This results in the Police having to persuade people who fundamentally differ from the white man and even

106

from each other and who respect their own distinct norms, to obey laws they do not understand and maintain a kind of order which is foreign to their nature."[37]

South African policemen live in a society where violence begets more violence. Jacklyn Cock, professor of sociology at the University of the Witwatersrand, explains: "In this spiralling process, violence comes to be accepted as a legitimate solution to conflict. This acceptance threatens to destroy our humanity; to erode our capacity for human/humane responses. In South Africa, at present, the normalisation of violence and atrocity threatens to blunt our human sensibilities."[38]

The Chief of the South African Defence Force, General Constand Viljoen, warned South Africans in 1984: "South Africans must be prepared to accept certain levels of discomfort, disruption and even violence in their everyday lives."[39]

South African policemen – white and black – of the last three decades have lived under tremendous stress in countering what they were led to believe was a revolutionary onslaught. In the five years between 1985 and 1990 nearly 400 policemen died in the execution of their duties, while between January and July 1990 there were 275 attacks on the homes of black policemen and 985 attacks on policemen. In the period February 1990 – when the State President introduced his historical reforms – to July 1990, 180 people were killed and 1 633 injured in police action.[40]

It is important to look at the SAP's rank and file, as they contributed greatly to the character of "cop culture". After the National Party election victory in 1948, the police force was "Afrikanerised". Even today, white policemen and women in the regular force are almost exclusively Afrikaans. The police have low status and reward, attracting mostly working-class Afrikaners, many with an insular rural background.[41]

There have been recent attempts to upgrade the police force academically, place it on a more professional basis and improve its public image. The former Commissioner of Police, General Hennie de Witt, said in his annual report for 1988 that of 7 800 people who had joined the SAP in that year, 101 had degrees and/or diplomas.[42] This, Minister of Law and Order Adriaan Vlok said recently, "should provide a conclusive answer to persons who may be inclined to regard the South African Police as a source of livelihood for pupils who are mentally retarded or backward and who lack the intellectual ability to study."[43]

There have also been attempts to improve the working conditions and remuneration packages of the force. According to a *Sunday Times* investigation at the end of 1989 an average of 12 policemen were leaving the force every day. Some of the reasons given for the resignations were poor salaries, excessive and unpaid overtime and virtually non-existent housing facilities.

Commissioner of Police General Johan van der Merwe said in January 1990 that in a confidential meeting State President FW de Klerk had acknowledged that the SAP was in a "critical position" and had said that the government would urgently look to solving grievances over salaries and working conditions. New salary structures and fringe benefits were introduced later in the year, but on the whole the average policeman remains terribly underpaid.[44]

Since the government made it possible for young men eligible for national service to serve three years in the SAP instead of two years in the Defence Force, the numbers of English-speaking police have increased. The majority, however, remain Afrikaans-speaking and tend to be loyal to Afrikaner hegemony and to the political interests of the Afrikaners.

The history of the police force is full of allegations of racism within the force itself. The Landsdowne Commission of 1937 had "no doubt" that an attitude of "mutual distrust, suspicion and dislike" existed. The hostility was in turn a function of discriminatory laws and of the "harshness, lack of sympathy and even violence" with which such laws were enforced. The commission noted that the most important interaction between the police and the black community was the "constant raiding" of locations to enforce pass, tax and liquor laws, and expressed concern at the force's abuse of power and image of brutality in the black community. The commission pointed to the disastrous effect that a system based on racial discrimination was to have on its police force.

After 1948, the police became the most immediate symbol of oppressive rule, a label they carry up to this very day. There is a strong suspicion that the majority of white policemen support political parties to the right of the National Party – the Conservative Party, Herstigte Nasionale Party (HNP) and even the Afrikaner Weerstandsbeweging (AWB). The Conservative Party itself has claimed in Parliament that the majority of white policemen support their policies, while the AWB also claims wide support.

Many former members of the SAP are in leadership positions in rightwing organisations. Eugene Terre'Blanche, leader of the AWB, was a warrant officer and guarded Prime Minister John Vorster before he resigned in the late 1960s. Servaas de Wet was a divisional commander in the SAP and held the rank of colonel before he became the commandant-general of the AWB commandos. Theuns Swanepoel, a former SAP brigadier, was the chief interrogator in the Rivonia Trial and was involved in suppressing the 1976 uprising before he became commander of the AWB's Aquila security guards. In the last general election, several former police officers came out of retirement to stand as candidates for the Conservative Party. Among them was the former chief of the Bureau for State Security, General Hendrik van den Bergh.

Lower echelons of the police tend to come from that part of the Afrikaans social structure most threatened by the reforms implemented by the National Party and from which the Conservative Party drew its traditional electoral support. In the September 1989 general election the majority of Afrikaans speakers supported the Conservative Party and it can therefore be inferred that the majority of white policemen support the CP.

It is thus fair to say that the average policeman is conservative, poorly educated, and comes from an environment where he has gained little or no knowledge about South Africa's realities. He has been heavily indoctrinated by the ideology of the total onslaught – which I will discuss later – and finds himself in a position where he has to uphold unjust laws and policies that are rejected by the majority of South Africans.

A notion close to the hearts of conservative white South Africans is that of a biblical justification for apartheid. The Afrikaans churches must carry part of the blame for the apartheid state's justification of its apartheid policies and the subsequent dilemma the policeman found himself in. The policies of the powerful Dutch Reformed Church (DRC) on racial and political matters had until the eighties read like a blueprint of the policies of the National Party government. For many years the cliche "The Dutch Reformed Church is the National Party at Prayer " was probably justified.

It was the policies of the Dutch Reformed Church that enabled Prime Minister PW Botha to say in 1981: "Who has done more to spread Christianity in southern Africa than the Afrikaner people and its churches? . . . A false image of the National Party is being created by people misusing Christianity for their own ends. It is not true that we are worse than other people. We are not perfect but we have nothing to be ashamed of."[49]

Minister of Law and Order Adriaan Vlok is cited in a police commemorative album as saying: ". . . the Force has, in the principles on which its duty has been performed, always maintained Christian norms and civilised standards. The Force has ensured the acknowledgement and maintenance of individual freedom of faith and worship and has ensured the inviolability of freedom in our country. The Force has at all times ensured the independence of the judiciary and equality in the eyes of the law as well as maintaining law and order and promoted the spiritual and material prosperity of all its people."

Where were the Afrikaans churches when 74 people died in detention or complained of torture and when innocent people were assassinated or disappeared? In fact, in the hearts and minds of those very people who committed the atrocities, the silence of the church – added to the silent approval of the government – justified their deeds.

It is important to look at the way the South African Police perceives itself. The Commissioner of Police commissioned a former senior police officer, Marius Dippenaar, to write a commemorative album in celebration of the seventy-fifth anniversary of the SAP. The 883-page treatise can best be described as a police history of the police and provides a crucial insight into the state's perception of the police. University of Stellenbosch sociologist Elrena van der Spuy describes Dippenaar's *The History of the South African Police, 1913-1988* as having been "written from the belly of the beast itself".

It is striking how little Dippenaar has to say about the importance of crime control in relation to other police duties. The long and bloody history of public-order policing is interspersed briefly with sensational reports on the exploits of "real hard criminals", of "daring robbers" and "psychopathic murderers".

It is rather a history of the policing of large "collectives" of black people, such as black industrial strikers, tribal groups at war, factions on the mines, and "fanatical" crowds of black "uprisers", demonstrators and protestors.[51]

The forces of law and order are juxtaposed sharply with the forces of anarchy. Protestors, demonstrators and rioters are all given to "vandalism" and to "orgies of violence". Dippenaar makes extensive use of catch-phrases like the "unjustified allegations", "blatant lies and flagrant distortions of facts" espoused by the "forces of anarchy".

Apart from referring to the amorphous "mob", Dippenaar also indulges in more specific descriptions of "trouble makers" who are in possession of "diabolical plans". A wide range of groups – ANC, UDF, PAC, the English press and clerics – are lumped together as subverters of the "lawful, democratic and constitutional order".[52]

Reflecting on the conduct of students involved in a campaign by the National Union of South African Students (NUSAS) for free and fair education in 1972, Dippenaar writes: "The Police Force nevertheless took careful note of the slovenly, badly clothed and foul-mouthed student whose appearance and filthy colloquial usage imbued the concept of 'academic freedom' with a totally new meaning. The expletives used by English-speaking students shocked the Afrikaans-speaking policemen who had generally grown up in homes where swearing and discourtesy was not tolerated."

He provides a running commentary on the "liberalistic" leanings of the English press which he accuses of publishing a continuous stream of "unjustified criticism and verbal attacks" on the police and of grossly inaccurate, one-sided and biased . . . reportage on the uprisings". Clerics are accused of spreading the "grossest of allegations against the Police". He further warns against the political manoeuvres of "white leftist liberal radicals".[53]

Van der Spuy notes in her analysis that it is against this background of hysterical protest politics that Dippenaar then presents a sanitised view of police action. The police, Dippenaar says, have an "unblemished image and excellent record" and are responsible for the "complicated and delicate task" of maintaining law and order in a "calm, disciplined" manner, with a policy of "firm but non-violent" action.

The police are never the aggressive provocateurs, but act as benign catalysts. They restore order where disorder once prevailed. During the Soweto uprising of 1976, Dippenaar says, the police were "obliged" to fire, and in order to bring the situation under control, "people [had to] be shot dead".

Swapo in Namibia is described as "murdering defenceless civilians in cold blood" by means of "cowardly tactics" while the notorious Koevoet was "obliged" to employ "unorthodox methods".

According to Van der Spuy, Dippenaar's history is proof of the obsessive preoccupation with communism among the "political elite of the racist state". In the eyes of the police black resistance is always inspired by communism and never by an unjust political system.

Dippenaar concludes that the combating of terrorism "proved to be a prolonged and enduring police duty". He applauds the power bestowed upon the police by the Terrorism Act, describing it as "a very handy lever for the South African Police . . . allowing them to . . . act as if the country were in a state of war, that is to say, to eliminate armed infiltrators". It is important to equate Dippenaar's statement to Dirk Coetzee's state of mind during his period of "combating terrorism" on the Swaziland border, at Middelburg and later as commander at Vlakplaas. Coetzee stated that the police thought they were in a state of war, a "twilight war" where "everything went".

By the late seventies, South Africa was described as being subjected to a "total communist onslaught". Van der Spuy describes this onslaught as a closed world view in terms of which South Africa is besieged by a multi-dimensional onslaught, orchestrated by communist imperialist powers and enacted by terrorist front organisations. The aim of this onslaught is the violent overthrow of the South African democratic state, and the destruction of Christian values and capitalist society.

"The Government of the Republic which had been democratically elected by the inhabitants of the country, decided to stand by its decision [regarding the declared national State of Emergency], despite the fact that this would inevitably lead to international isolation, a weakened economy and inevitable car bomb attacks. The South African Police understood and supported the views of the Government," Dippenaar writes.

There are isolated glimpses of police violence in Dippenaar's history that give an insight into a militarised policing function: "To rub salt in the wounds of the ANC the Police cracked down on a shack in the Soweto township of Port Elizabeth, where a terrorist was reputedly hiding . . . One policeman drove a Casspir vehicle right into the tin shack, or what remained of it . . . the bodies of a trained terrorist and two sympathisers were found . . . The incident in Soweto, Port Elizabeth, should have served to demonstrate to the terrorist organization that policemen are not without initiative when it comes to the elimination of terrorists."

It is a remarkable and frank admission from an official police historian that the police do not always "follow the book". How then, Van der Spuy rightly asked, is one to interpret the absence of police misconduct and abuse of power in the stories told by Dippenaar? Perhaps the answer is what

Coetzee described as the sacred brotherhood among security policemen. They protect each other, lie for each other and are sworn to absolute secrecy.[54]

Research has shown that some policemen tend to be "trigger-happy". University of Cape Town criminologist and Chairperson of the Social Justice Resource Project, Desirée Hansson, investigated fatal police shootings in the Cape Town area from 1984 and 1986 and concluded: "The most striking finding in this study is that the police used deadly force with a marked lack of restraint. For, irrespective of their purpose or situation, this sample of the SAP implemented disturbingly few of the internationally-accepted controls when using firearms with deadly effect. Notably, it was 'Blacks' who fell victim to fatal shootings by predominantly 'White' police officers. Surely the SAP must have responded to similar incidents involving 'Whites', yet no 'Whites' were killed."[55]

From 1 September 1984 to 31 December 1988 the SAP killed 1 113 township residents. During 1985 alone, the police killed 763 people as a result of the "unrest". The Security Emergency Regulations gave all security force members the power to use force against anyone whom they perceived as a danger to public safety. The only control required was that of an oral warning. Regulation 15 indemnified the security forces against criminal prosecution and civil liability for actions taken "in good faith".[56]

According to Hansson the consciousness of the total onslaught ideology had produced "a readiness to kill" on the part of the SAP. ". . . this lack of restraint is in part a product of a police consciousness based on a siege mentality and the dehumanisation of 'Black' political opponents. It would seem, however, that the effects of this consciousness have permeated police practice in general. For in this example, police officers of all ranks, ranging from special constable to captain, exhibited a readiness to kill which was not limited to incidents of unrest. If this is so, the police as a force do appear to be treating 'Blacks' as the enemy," Hansson concluded.

Johannesburg human rights lawyer Nicholas Haysom concluded in his study of the SAP's use of deadly force: ". . . the unnecessary or reckless use of firearms by the police is not the result of 'rogue policemen' or reckless individuals. It is a widespread systematic use of lethal and violent weapons principally on South Africa's black citizens."[57]

According to University of the Western Cape law professor Nico Steytler the concept of cop culture forms a valuable part of any explanation of the existence of state-sponsored death squads. Its central feature is a sense of mission or purpose – a feeling among policemen that policing is not just a job but a way of life with a worthwhile purpose. This mission is easily identifiable among the norms that underlie the existence of death squads in South Africa. Moreover, the state's policy of militarising the SAP to counter military insurgency by the ANC and the PAC has made it possible to imbue cop culture with military techniques and methods and the norms that support these methods.[58]

The link between military regimes and death squads lies in the "very absoluteness" of military action.[59] The aim of the military is the total and final destruction of the enemy, which is in stark contrast to the basic principle of policing, which is the minimum use of violence. The military is a killing machine, while the police force is a preserver of life. Where political problems can no longer be dealt with using normal police practices, the military method becomes an alternative option and the militarisation of the police the consequence.

Since the early sixties the SAP has adopted a highly militarised form of crime control. Because of the many threats to public order, the SAP's strong paramilitary character has been increased and therefore police training has included military skills which are put into practice during periods of obligatory service by the police in the operational military areas. In the blending of military and police operations in the townships, traditional distinctions have become obsolete.

The militarisation of the South African police force has to be seen in the context of the arms its members carry. All members of the SAP, irrespective of race and gender, carry a sidearm and are issued with a semi-automatic rifle, which is usually kept in a strongroom at the police station. In "riotous circumstances" they can also be issued with submachine guns and shotguns.[60]

Police training has included a strong military component in response to guerrilla incursions in Namibia and Zimbabwe, and later terror attacks in the urban areas in which the police were indentified as a particular target. Counter-insurgency training has for many years been built into the making of a South African policeman. From 1967 to 1975 the SAP did active military service in Rhodesia, and from 1967 to 1985 fought in the bush war in Namibia. During this time, paramilitary units were formed in or under the direction of the SAP.

In Namibia, Koevoet was established in 1976 and concentrated on "offensive action in the tracking and eradicating of terrorists". In 1984 Koevoet was described by Lieutenant-General Verster as a "cold, calculated, effective and ruthless unit and the major thorn in the flesh of the Swapo terrorists". Countering the claims of brutality levelled against Koevoet, the police claimed that controversy over this unit had arisen "for the simple reason that it was obliged to employ unorthodox methods". The death squad commanders Brigadier Willem Schoon and Eugene De Kock have both held positions in Koevoet.[61]

The Human Rights Commission has recorded more than 400 instances of death squad activity between 1985 and 1990. According to the Board of Inquiry into Informal Repression, about 165 buildings were targets of petrol and chemical bombs, arson and thunderflashes from May 1985 to September 1989. As a result three people died and four were injured. There were 15 cases of bombing. The Board also listed 47 cases of vandalism against activists, nine homes were the targets of unknown gunmen and there were 37 break-ins at political institutions.[62]

Evidence of state complicity in the murder of anti-apartheid activists had been emerging for many years before the revelations of October 1989. In fact, when Nofemela spoke from death row and Coetzee followed him a few weeks later, they merely confirmed the suspicions of most South Africans.

The language used by powerful people was sometimes revealing. In 1988, the Minister of Defence, Magnus Malan, visiting the scene of a land mine explosion in the Northern Transvaal, said: "Wherever the ANC is, we will eliminate it."[63] In a speech to the Institute for Strategic Studies at the University of Pretoria in the same year, Malan said that like other countries, South Africa sometimes used "unconventional methods" to achieve its policy objectives. "Like others, we do not talk about them," he added.[64]

Major Craig Williamson echoed the minister's words in a British television programme in 1990 when he said: "It is going to be silly to argue that all the ANC people of this world who have ever started their cars and then been blown into the hereafter would have nothing to do with the South African security forces. I mean, nobody is going to believe you. But it is a fact that there has been a war and they have been blowing us up and killing us, and we have been blowing them up and killing them. And obviously some of the actions are admitted and some of them are not admitted."

Rumours of official death squad units within the South African intelligence establishment were fuelled in the late seventies by a remark from the head of the Bureau for State Security (BOSS), General Hendrik van den Bergh, probably the second most powerful man in the country at the time, when he said before the Erasmus Commission of Inquiry into Information Department irregularities: "I can tell you here today, not for your records, but I can tell you I have enough men to commit murder if I tell them to kill . . . Those are the kind of men I have. And if I wanted to do something like that to protect the security of the State nobody would stop me. I would stop at nothing."[66]

The police brigadier credited with quelling the 1976 student rebellion, Theuns "Rooi Rus" Swanepoel, talked publicly of "ANC and Swapo bastards" and bragged of his ability to "kill terrorists", criticising his successors for being too soft during the violence of the middle eighties.[67]

The language used by security officials, especially by Law and Order Minister Adriaan Vlok, when referring to internal extra-parliamentary opponents of the government is an echo of Malan's comments on the ANC. Vlok spoke in 1987 of the need to "eliminate" and "annihilate" those whom he calls "revolutionaries". At a National Party election meeting in the southern surburbs of Johannesburg in 1989, he said it was government policy to "take out" activists. Vlok denied on being questioned by a member of the audience that it was state policy to kill activists. He said they should be "removed from society".[68]

The first hard evidence of the existence of "askari" death squads organised and led by police officers was revealed in an ANC terrorism trial in Cape

Town early in 1989 when detainee Bongani Jonas told the court that police had attempted to recruit him into an askari group.

The reference to the group surfaced during an inquiry into Jonas's refusal after his second day in the witness box to testify for the state in the marathon Yengeni trial. Jonas told the court he had been shot in the hip by an askari when he was arrested in September 1987. Another askari later stood on the wound. He had been chained to his hospital bed for about six months and agreed to join a unit that was due to be established in Cape Town as a survival tactic. He said he was released in February or March 1988 and held in solitary confinement at a Cape Town police station where he was regularly interrogated. In May 1988, when the 14 accused appeared in court for the first time, he was taken to security police headquarters in Cape Town where he was told by a Major Du Toit to co-operate and be a state witness or "face the hangman's noose or go to the shallow pit".[69]

Jonas said the askari unit was composed of defectors from the ANC led by the South African Police. He was promised a house, security and the opportunity to marry, "but I was told that my wife will have to stay in the base because I must understand that my life will never be the same again. In order to be protected by the state, you have got to work in a team. During the course of my detention I got to know two units. One, based in Pretoria, is led by Sergeant Bellingham and uses a Mitsubishi kombi."[70] Another operated from the Eastern Cape and was known as the Gestapo.

Asked what the work of an askari was, Jonas said: "It is to go around the townships acting on information the security police have, to seek out and kill their former colleagues. Some of them said that I am fortunate to be alive." Describing his recruitment, he explained: "This Gestapo group told me if I was found by them, my head would be moved in the opposite direction. They said that if we leave these people to survive, then we'll be known and we won't be safe."[71]

Jonas was shot by a member of the Pretoria unit, Sergeant David Musimeke, a policeman who also gave evidence in court and admitted that he was attached to the counter-insurgency unit. Musimeke denied calling himself an askari. He said the name was used "mostly by terrorists". He conceded the existence of a team of "rehabilitated" former ANC and PAC members who worked in a unit for the police. The size of the unit was "top secret", he said, and their identities were "a secret of the state".[72]

He denied that the unit's role was to eliminate members of the ANC, saying the intention was to bring them to court. He did, however, say: "If possible we can eliminate them" and conceded that he never fired warning shots as a matter of policy, as this would be "a waste of Government money".[73]

In the 1988 murder trial of police sergeant Robert van der Merwe (described in the previous chapter) evidence was heard of how police accepted the activities of death squads. Van der Merwe said he had not hesitated to kill two men he believed had ANC links "because I knew it had happened before".[74]

Evidence of direct state sanction for death squad activities emerged for the first time in 1981 when a former BOSS agent, Gordon Winter, blew the whistle on his former masters in his book *Inside Boss* (banned in South Africa until recently). Winter, a former arms smuggler, was recruited by Military Intelligence in 1963 after befriending John Vorster, then Minister of Justice. He became a dose confidant of the arch-conservative head of BOSS, Hendrik van den Bergh.

According to Winter, the five-member BOSS killer squad, known as the "Z-Squad", was formed in the late 1960s after a fire-bomb was thrown into the Soweto home of a black agent who had given evidence against two members of the ANC. Van den Bergh frequently discussed the existence of the Z-squad with Winter, once saying: "They kill our chaps, so why shouldn't we kill theirs?" Winter said the Z-Squad was responsible for the death of activist Abraham Tiro, who received a parcel bomb in February 1974. Tiro had left South Africa in 1973 just before the issue of a warrant for his arrest and was involved in the training of Umkhonto we Sizwe members in Botswana. According to Winter, a BOSS agent operating in Switzerland had taken the wrapping from an old parcel posted in Geneva by the International University Exchange Fund and this was carefully sealed around the parcel bomb sent to Tiro.

Eleven days after the killing of Tiro, another activist, John Dube, received a parcel at his office in Lusaka and suffered the same fate. Dube (his real name was Boy Mvemve) was thought to be the mastermind behind the planting of two bombs outside two Johannesburg post offices. Van den Bergh could not resist cracking a joke: "I think it is poetic justice that we got this mad post-office bomber with a bomb sent through the mail," he said to Winter.

In 1976 two of the Z-Squad killers were seriously injured while making some kind of midnight attack. According to Winter, Van den Bergh decided to recruit a new team from the ranks of the Defence Force's reconnaissance commando. The two best recruits were then drafted into the Z-Squad to do "part-time work".[75]

The killings of Tiro and Dube are recognised as the first death squad killings. The counter-insurgency unit of the security police was only formed in 1980, although we know that individual branches had been conducting death squad missions, especially in the neighbouring states, before that time. If the Z-Squad did exist, it would probably have been disbanded in 1978 when Van den Bergh retired. Shortly afterwards, PW Botha became Prime Minister and replaced BOSS with the National Intelligence Service (NIS).

According to human rights lawyer Nicholas Haysom, by October 1988 over 90 per cent of "unrest-related" deaths were caused by vigilante and counter-vigilante violence.[76]

But what exactly are vigilantes, and what is their nexus with death squads? In 1985, two thirds of people who died in township unrest were killed by police. However, over the next 18 months, a new pattern evolved as the overwhelming majority of deaths were due to what government commentators referred to as "black-on-black violence" – in other words blacks were killing blacks, creating the impression that the security forces were playing a peace-keeping role, and that the black community was tearing itself apart.[77]

What was in fact happening, was a major change in police tactics. The police became more proactive, banning meetings, rallies and funerals rather than breaking them up while in progress. Secondly, they began to dictate the numbers that could attend and to lay down restrictions on conduct for the occasions, and thirdly, free rein was allowed to vigilantes who performed the same divisive and disruptive work formerly undertaken by the police.

Why did the state decide to sub-contract its dirty work? Vigilantes are capable of destabilising communities far more effectively than official organs of the state and a far more chilling level of violence can be used than that which the state could ever bring to bear without suffering immense damage, both locally and internationally. The state is of course able to capitalise on this violence by depicting it as "black-on-black violence".[78]

Vigilante terror is best illustrated by the events in January 1986 in the squatter camps of Crossroads and KTC in the Cape Peninsula. For several years these communities, comprising nearly 70 000 people, had been engaged in a struggle with the authorities over their right to live in these squatter settlements. Despite being threatened and detained without trial, they had persisted in their campaign. In May and June 1986 the "Witdoeke" vigilante group tore through the camps, demolishing and burning houses and driving out inhabitants. Throughout the burnout, as it became known, the police role seemed to involve taking no steps against the Witdoeke.[79]

Instead, the police gave them back-up support by dispersing counter-attacks from the besieged communities with teargas, shotgun and rifle fire, and when necessary, giving Witdoek marauders into the squatter communities the protection of their armoured vehicles. The Witdoeke also took people prisoner and tortured them without police intervention. Fifty-three people were killed and 7 000 homes were destroyed in the attacks.

Over 3 000 former KTC residents have sued the Minister of Law and Order for police complicity in the events. Without accepting any liability, the state agreed to pay the squatters nearly R2 million compensation. From the evidence it was clear that the systematic destruction of the squatter camps took place in two separate but related operations which were carefully planned and executed with military precision.

Major Dolf Odendaal, second in command of the Peninsula Riot Squad, explained the police conduct at Crossroads and KTC in the Cape Supreme Court: "If black people decide to fight, there is nothing I can do. You do not know black people when they decide to fight." Odendaal told the court that he believed it would be a solution if, in unrest situations, police were by law allowed to shoot anyone holding a stone.[80]

In the words of a booklet on counter-revolutionary war distributed to state officials through the National Security Management System (NSMS), the state must first "cripple the revolutionary attempt to mobilise the masses", then itself mobilise the masses. In certain instances, the booklet states, "Government forces must use the same destructive and constructive strategy as the guerrilla." This may involve the development of a "counter revolutionary guerrilla force which . . . must be supported by security forces . . . and which is employed according to guerrilla tactics to annihilate the revolutionary guerrillas and take over the population."[81]

During a conference on death squads and vigilantes held by the Catholic Institute for International Relations (CIIR) in London 1988, it was said: "Vigilantes [and] death squads can also be viewed as the creatures – or, at any rate, the proxies – of states which fall back on systematic terror as a means of shoring up the security of dominant interests and social policies . . . the death squads/vigilantes/bandits are a logical consequence of the crisis of the oppressor."[82]

The existence of death squads is suggested, more than anything else, by the failure of the South African Police to apprehend the killers. In addition, although the murder of only one anti-apartheid activist has been admitted – that of Eric Mtonga, who was murdered by members of the Ciskei police – there is evidence in the murders themselves that points to police complicity.

The use of poison by the security police was exposed for the first time in 1977 when five-year-old Mary Woods, daughter of Donald Woods, put on a T-shirt that the family had received as a gift in the post. At that time, Woods was being persecuted by the security police for his close ties with Steve Biko and the family was finalising plans to leave the country. As Mary pulled the T-shirt on, Woods heard high-pitched screams. She shouted: "My eyes are burning." The family rushed to assist her and Woods picked up the T-shirt, noticing as he did so that it had been impregnated with a powder that stung the hand on contact.[83]

Woods called his confidant and friend Donald Card, a former security police officer who later became the mayor of East London. When he smelt the shirt, he said: "Those bastards at Security have done this. I know this stuff. I've worked with it myself. It's used by security police – it's like mace." It was later established that the substance, Ninhydrin, was a Swedish-invented acid-based powder supplied to police forces all over the world to trace fingerprints on paper.

Card launched an investigation into the incident and before long a postal worker confessed to Woods that two security policemen, Warrant Officers Marais and Van Schalkwyk, had taken the parcel with the T-shirt from the post office and returned it the next day. For the next few days, Card watched the two policemen as they arrived for their daily visits to the post office. All the facts of the investigation were communicated to the police, but Jimmy Kruger later said in Parliament that police investigations of the incident had cleared the security police.[84]

No comment is even necessary on the police's apparent willingness to poison a five-year-old child because her father befriended a black activist. The poisoning of Siphiwo Mtimkulu (see Chapter 4) with thallium just before his release in October 1981 further illustrates the police's readiness to use poison as a weapon against anti-apartheid activists. It is important to note that thallium is not readily available to the average person. It is, however, kept in the police forensic laboratory.[85]

The poisoning of the secretary-general of the South African Council of Churches, Frank Chikane, in 1989 also points to security force complicity. Chikane was hospitalised on four occasions after having been overcome by a sudden and mysterious illness. The first episode occurred in Namibia and the second when Chikane had left for the United States as part of a team of church leaders which was due to meet various members of the US Congress and Senate as well as President George Bush. During this period Chikane spent some time in an intensive care unit before it was established that he had been poisoned by a highly toxic compound used in pesticides and chemical weapons.[86]

The police appointed its top investigator, General Jaap Joubert, to investigate the poisoning but, predictably, no breakthrough or arrests were made. The suspicion that the South African armed security forces poisoned Chikane was strengthened when in 1990 members of a Defence Force death squad admitted they had monitored his movements and one of them told police brigadier Floris Mostert that poison had been put on Chikane's toilet seat.[87]

The state has of course vehemently denied that it has ever used poison in its fight against apartheid. The carpet was pulled out from under this innocent posture in Januray 1991 when a Supreme Court judge ruled that the police's forensic expert, General Lothar Neethling, had indeed supplied poison to kill anti-apartheid activists (see Chapter 13). The same judge also found that a Defence Force member had in all probability poisoned an ANC activist in Maputo. A few months before, a judicial commission of inquiry heard about a Defence Force plot to assassinate a Durban attorney by poisoning his shaving blades (see Chapter 10).

Although it is highly unlikely that anybody will ever be charged for the poisoning of Siphiwo Mtimkulu and Frank Chikane, and the police remain adamant that they have thoroughly investigated both cases and cannot trace the culprits, evidence has shown that the South African state did not hesitate to poison those regarded as threats to state security, irrespective of their age, status or legal innocence. In many cases, solving one murder leads one to the culprits of the other, although there is not always enough evidence for a conviction to succeed in court.

Human Rights Commission spokesman Dr Max Coleman pointed out that if the Minister of Law and Order wanted to find out who was responsible for the attack on Frank Chikane, he should "begin by looking in the ranks of his own police force".

A particular combination of circumstances brought about the increasing involvement of the SADF in the war against the liberation movements. The chief enabling factor was the formulation of the "total onslaught" ideology. This provided the impetus and the moral justification for state-sanctioned death squads to operate both inside and outside South Africa's borders against people perceived to be threats to state security.

The emergence of death squads tends to coincide closely with the rise to dominance of the military in national politics. In Central and South America this trend has been particularly pronounced where death squads within the security forces have served to obscure military regimes' responsibility for the elimination of political opponents.

From the middle seventies, South Africans were told that South Africa was facing a massive and unprecedented communist onslaught. In the words of General Magnus Malan: "The dark clouds rolling towards South Africa pose a threat that makes essential the transition from a prosperous society to one that is geared for survival."[88]

South Africa became a militarised society in which the SADF was no longer simply an instrument for policy implementation but an active participant in policy making, not merely in military matters, but in wider security issues, both domestic and external. The policy was predicated on a belief that South Africa was a besieged state. There was an increasing overlapping and interlinking between the functions of the SAP and the SADF. By the middle eighties, there were thousands of soldiers in the townships combating the revolutionary onslaught shoulder to shoulder with their comrades in the police force.

Central to an understanding of the rise of the security establishment in South African society is an appreciation that South Africa's government officials and policy makers lived in a world they perceived to be hostile to South Africa, a world whose attitude could be encapsulated under the rubric "total onslaught". As General Magnus Malan, then chief of the SADF, said in 1977: "South Africa has for a long time been subjected to a total and protracted revolutionary onslaught."[89] ". . . The enemy uses all possible means at his disposal. The onslaught is not just military: it is political, diplomatic, religious, psychological, cultural, economic and social."

The answer to the total onslaught was a total strategy. PW Botha explained in his 1977 White Paper on Defence: "Total strategy coordinates all aspects of national life – the military, economic, political, sociological, technological, ideological, psychological and cultural – in an integrated defence of the nation."[91] Just before he became Prime Minister in 1978, he said: "South Africa is experiencing unprecedented intervention on the part of the superpowers ... The Republic of South Africa is experiencing the full onslaught of Marxism and it must not be doubted that the Republic enjoys a high priority in the onslaught by Moscow."[92]

According to the goverment's White Paper on Defence and Armaments Supply, 1982, "the ultimate aim of the Soviet Union and its allies is to overthrow the present body politic in the RSA and to replace it with a Marxist-orientated form of government to further the objectives of the USSR, therefore all possible methods and means are used to attain this objective. This includes instigating social and labour unrest, civilian resistance, terrorist attacks against the infrastructure of the RSA and the intimidation of Black leaders and members of the security forces."

The government created a perception in white minds that the onslaught was inspired from abroad and co-ordinated by the communist powers. The Soviet Union was regarded as the root cause for the discontent in South Africa; never apartheid itself. Because of this onslaught the misconception was also created that South Africa was a keystone in the defence of Western freedom and values.

The ideology of the total onslaught had a tremendous impact on white South Africans. When I was in standard ten a senior Defence Force officer came to address the school on the total onslaught and the new commitment required from us. We sat in awe as the officer showed us maps with red arrows pointing towards South Africa, reading from communist literature and explaining the new military conscription system of four years' compulsory service for all young white men. We went away instilled with a sense of fear and duty.

It must have had a tremendous impact on the minds and attitudes of white security force members when their Prime Minister said: "It is a struggle between the powers of chaos, Marxism and destruction on the one hand and the powers of order, Christian civilisation and the upliftment of people on the other."[94]

The rise of the military can be traced back to 1978 when PW Botha, former Minister of Defence, became Prime Minister. Vorster was ardently supported by BOSS head Hendrik van den Bergh, while Botha was the patron of the military. The security forces were polarised; the Bureau for State Security sided with Vorster and the military sided with Botha. As Botha emerged the victor from that bitter political battle, the military rose in prominence. However, because the police remained loyal to Vorster, the new Prime Minister began to use the military to fulfil functions which in normal circumstances should have been a police preserve.[95] Moreover, the growing influence of the military was reflected in the numbers of SADF personnel now in positions of power as public decision-makers. South Africa was now to be governed largely by "securocrats".

In 1979 a parallel system of government was established in the National Security Management System (NSMS). First set up to eliminate competition between departments of state and as an answer to the total onslaught, the NSMS acts as an alternative to parliamentary and cabinet government. The main advisory and planning body of the state's total strategy became the State Security Council (SSC), which meets twice a week and includes key ministers and military and police chiefs. At local level, a network of some 500 Joint Management Committees provides a civilian political base for the security forces and formulates strategies to combat opposition based on detailed local information. At the regional level of administration there are 12 Joint Management Centres located conveniently at the 12 SADF command headquarters throughout South Africa.[96]

The full membership of the SSC has never been publicly disclosed, but it includes at least the following members: the State President, the ministers of foreign affairs, defence, law and order, justice and the most senior cabinet minister. Other cabinet members who regularly attend include the ministers of finance, education and development aid and constitutional development and planning. The SSC also includes the top-ranking civil servants in each of those key departments. Thus the directors-general of foreign affairs and justice, the director-general of the Office of the State President, the chief of the SADF, the commissioner of police and the director-general of the National Intelligence Service (NIS) participate.[97]

In 1979/80 a highly secret document was presented to the SSC which gave details of the establishment and function of police and military "special units". The document, entitled "Institutions and Functions of the Special Forces", is believed to outline the structures in which the death squads operate. The document became the subject of an *in camera* court case after it was stolen from the psychological unit of Military Intelligence by a soldier who passed it on to a friend. The soldier, Corporal Gerhard van der Werff, who worked for this unit, was tried and convicted of the theft of this document. The state argued that the document's contents were so secret that possession was illegal and not even the defence lawyers were allowed to see it.[98]

The *Weekly Mail* reconstructed the contents of the document after interviewing one of the ex-servicemen involved and concluded that it contained information about the secret funding of the "special forces" so that they would not need to answer to Parliament, but only to the SSC, regarding their secret operations. Normal state funding channels were not to be used in the case of special operations and secret funds were set up for these purposes. This also provided for the recruitment of operatives from the ranks of the

SADF, the SAP and other branches of the civil service. Recruits were to be subjected to stringent testing at state-run psychological units. The document also described destabilisation techniques and the running of secret operations in neighbouring states.

The secretary of the SSC, General Charles Lloyd, confirmed the suspicions of many when he said in 1988: "Sometimes you have to take out the revolutionaries if they are controlling the people."[99]

During 1984-6, violence escalated in many of South Africa's black townships. According to Jacklyn Cock, the immediate trigger event was the implementation of the tricameral parliamentary system, which came into force in September 1984. The SADF was sent into a number of townships, ostensibly to contain the violence. During 1985 alone, 35 000 troops were used in townshps throughout the country. In October 1984, army units joined the police in patrolling Soweto. This was followed by Operation Palmiet, when 7 000 soldiers sealed off the township of Sebokeng, carrying out house-to-house searches and making at least 350 arrests.[100]

This represented a shift away from a reliance on the police force alone to maintain what the state called "law and order". Since that time, the SADF has been used extensively in internal repression in diverse areas of black experience such as housing, health, labour and education. The army has evicted rent defaulters in an effort to break the rent boycott and occupied classrooms in an effort to break the schools boycott. It has been deployed to guard polling booths, invade health clinics to identify the injured, maintain beach apartheid, conduct forced removals, monitor demonstrations and suppress resistance to homeland independence.

The Detainees' Parents Support Committee (DPSC) reported a pattern which involved soldiers picking children off the street and holding them for several hours in military vehicles or in remote areas of veld. The children have described being beaten with fists and rifle butts and even being subjected to electric shocks. During this period, the SADF often acted together with the SAP. Their activities were indistinguishable to many township residents as they fused in a pattern of indiscriminate violence.[101]

If one looks at the way in which the SADF was drawn into the political battle arena in South Africa, it comes as no surprise that the military eventually formed its own special squad to disrupt the enemies of the republic to the maximum possible extent. It could be anything from breaking a window to murder.

Since the middle seventies, the SADF has been involved in counter-insurgency wars in Rhodesia, Namibia and Angola. At intervals the war in Angola developed into a semi-conventional battle between Cuba and Angola on the one hand and the SADF on the other. More than a thousand South African soldiers lost their lives in these battles.

Since 1981 the SADF has been involved in cross-border raids into neighbouring states, so that southern Africa witnessed more cross-border violence than any other region of the world in the 1980s.[102] South Africa has also destabilised its neighbours by invading no less than three capitals, crossed four other borders and tried to assassinate two prime ministers. SADF commandos, in the words of their Minister of Defence, tried to eliminate the ANC wherever it was.

The increasing counter-insurgency role that the SADF played during the eighties is clearly illustrated by the military's campaign against the End Conscription Campaign (ECC). In 1988 the ECC applied for an order restraining the SADF from harassing the organisation, listing 64 acts of intimidation against it, beginning in November 1985. The campaign included the ECC's front door being broken down and anti-UDF pamphlets strewn around, a petrol bomb being thrown at the building, documentation being stolen and a constant stream of abusive telephone calls to the ECC office and individual members' homes. The order was granted and the judge found the campaign to have gone "beyond lawful opposition".[103]

The campaign was exposed with the court martial of three servicemen alleged to have conspired to disseminate information to the ECC. The opposing affidavit by General Jan van Loggerenberg, who was the Chief of Staff, Operations, when the actions against the ECC commenced, admitted that the SADF was engaged in secret projects aimed at discrediting the ECC. The SADF admitted that it had manufactured postcards, pamphlets and T-shirts discrediting the ECC and that pamphlets had been dropped over Cape Town suburbs from a commercial helicopter. The court also heard claims that the SADF had published posters reading "ECC does it from behind" and "ECC members are yellow" as well as T-shirts bearing the slogan "End Communism Campaign".[104]

The SADF members who were involved in the implementation of the Defence Minister's policy of aggression against civilians whom he thought threatened the security of the state must have believed that no harm would befall them if they were caught. This was substantiated in 1987 when six soldiers were charged with the murder of the Namibian nationalist and former Robben Island prisoner, Immanuel Shifidi. PW Botha used the Defence Act to intervene in the trial and indemnify them.[105]

As the combat between the SADF and its enemies was largely unconventional, military units specifically trained to deal with unconventional combat were created. The Rhodesian war was a valuable source of manpower for the SADF's special units, especially after Zimbabwe's independence in 1980, when large numbers of Selous Scouts joined the SADF. It was out of this realm that specialised military units were born to deal with the revolutionary onslaught against South Africa. Highly trained commandos hunted down the enemy, blew up strategic installations and assassinated ANC members. Targets, aside from military, included civilians and members of the administrative and political structures of the ANC, PAC and Swapo. As the military began to play an increasingly aggressive role, the traditional divide between the military and the police became blurred around dealings with ANC activities.

As we will see in the next chapters, by the mid-1980s the SADF had identified the ANC, PAC, SACP and various white activists as targets – inside and outside the borders of South Africa – for harassment and elimination.

CHAPTER EIGHT

Apartheid's ultimate weapon

IN the spring of 1969 David Webster lived as a peasant in the south of the Portuguese colony of Mozambique. Here the once conservative South African student worked in people's fields and helped them build huts, went fishing and hunting, made pots and attended court cases. Describing this time, he said: "The system was so fascinating, and I began to realise that these people had intelligence, and a grasp of the subtleties of politics, and the ability to sum up someone's character. This was something quite out of my ordinary experience. I began to realise then that having an education and being literate has nothing to do with intelligence."[1]

This was one of a series of personal experiences that changed the young anthropologist into a tireless human rights activist in South Africa. Although Webster never became a prominent public figure, he was a passionate anti-detentions campaigner. He played an important role in the founding of the Detainees' Parents Support Committee and the Detainees Support Committee – in his words: ". . . we started to broaden out to monitor the police, to make their life as difficult as possible, to make each detention a high political price to pay. And then taking on the state itself, because it becomes clear that apartheid is undemocratic, that the only way you can maintain such an undemocratic and illegitimate stature is by repression. So if you really want to end detentions, you have to end apartheid . . ."[2]

Webster became famous among ex-detainees and detainees' parents for intervening on their behalf and arranging gatherings at which people could sing, pray and be comforted. But these gatherings enraged the South African authorities. In April 1989 one was held at St George's Church in Johannesburg. Fifteen minutes after it began, people started singing Nkosi Sikelel' iAfrika. In response, a Captain van Huyssteen announced through a bullhorn that the meeting was being suspended because it posed a threat to law and order under the Emergency Regulations. A few months earlier, the same policeman had told Webster: "You will not have any more tea parties."

During this time, Webster had written a report for the Human Rights Commission on repression in South Africa. It contained chilling details of harassment, abduction, disappearance and assassination, noting how rare it was for such assassinations to be solved.

There was an element of tragic prescience here, just as when Victoria Mxenge uttered her prophetic words at the funeral of the Cradock Four, saying she was prepared to die for Africa.

At ten o'clock on May Day, 1989, assassins fired 16 coarse-grain shotgun pellets into Webster's body as he was opening the back door of his van outside his Johannesburg home. He died soon afterwards.

The killing of the 44-year-old Webster is to an alarming degree reminiscent of the assassination more than a decade previously of Dr Rick Turner, political science lecturer at the University of Natal. In fact, the slaying of Turner at his Durban home on 8 January 1978 was one of the things that inspired Webster to become involved in resistance politics.

Webster and Turner had a lot in common. They were both prominent leftwing academics, shared a commitment to ending injustice in South Africa and were outspoken critics of the apartheid system. They were both shot at their homes by deliberate, efficient and ruthless professional killers. Both killings bore the hallmarks of political assassinations.

Rick Turner, who for six years before his brutal death was a restricted person, was a tower of strength in anti-apartheid politics in Natal and initiated a groundswell of resistance against the State. He was killed three weeks before his restriction order was due to expire. An unknown gunman fired a single shot through the front window as Turner answered a midnight knock on his door. He was shot in front of his two daughters, Jann, then 13, and Kim, then nine. I met Jann Turner in New York in 1990, twelve years later – and a year after the death of David Webster. The anthropologist's assassination brought back the memory of that day when she cradled her dying father's head in her lap.

Jann said that she could never permanently return to her country of birth unless her father's killers were apprehended. When I met her, she desperately wanted to know whether we had any leads on his assassins. I could not help her.

Turner's mother, Jane Turner, has never stopped looking for the killers. Her search has taken her around South Africa and to the Seychelles islands where she spent weeks in 1982 trying to arrange an interview with a former South African agent and mercenary. The man she wanted so desperately to question was Martin Dolinchek, who was then awaiting trial for his part in the abortive Seychelles coup led by Colonel Mike Hoare. Dolinchek had been Turner's case supervisor in Durban, but had later joined the ANC. Jane Turner was eventually allowed to speak to him, but he could not help her.[3]

Jane Turner was strongly critical of the police investigation in the wake of her son's murder. She claimed that they never interviewed neighbours and did not use tracker dogs, despite the fact that there were strong indications that the killer had walked through a neighbour's garden to get to Turner's home.

Later a group of friends and university colleagues hired a private detective to try and find some clues. They did so in protest against the constant failure of the police to find and prosecute people responsible for rightwing terrorism. An inquest court found that Turner had been murdered by "persons unknown". It was a phrase which was to be repeated regularly over the next twelve years.

The police reacted with unusual speed and vigour to David Webster's death. Shortly after the ambulance had taken him away, the deputy chief of the CID, General Jaap Joubert, was on the scene and personally supervising an intense police hunt. The head of the Brixton Murder and Robbery Unit, Brigadier Floris Mostert, was instructed to investigate the killing.

Law and Order Minister Adriaan Vlok expressed "shock and total disgust" at the murder. In a statement, Vlok said the government strongly condemned the killing and, in the light of media reports of it being "politically motivated", no stone would be left unturned in the hunt for the murderers. He added that the police were offering a R10 000 reward for any information leading to the arrest and prosecution of the murderers.[4]

Within 48 hours of the killing the police issued identikits of three suspects on descriptions from an anonymous witness. Mostert said it was possible that the murder had not been political at all as no one had claimed responsibility for the gruesome act.

Opposition organisations expressed surprise that police came up with such detailed identikit portraits of the suspects so soon after the event, when it was alleged that the shots had been fired from a moving car. Some of Webster's friends and colleagues claimed that the police were trying to create the impression that they were hunting down the killers while actually doing very little.

Webster's close friend and Human Rights Commissioner, Dr Max Coleman, said it was clear that Webster had been assassinated by a highly professional death squad. "I find it hard to believe that the authorities are unaware of the existence of these crack death squads. Instead of offering rewards and releasing identikits after the event they should be conducting intensive investigations into the activities of these squads. The killers were professional, well-informed and expert. There may be no more profitable place to start searching than within the ranks of the police themselves."[5]

Webster's address was not in the telephone directory and the killers must have had him and his house under surveillance for some time in order to know his movements. The assassins had used a shotgun, an ideal weapon as it is deadly accurate at close range and its pellets cannot be traced back to the murder weapon.

A mood of open defiance of Emergency laws emerged in the wake of Webster's death. Scenes of mass open-air protest of the sort not seen since the declaration of the State of Emergency three years earlier were witnessed in Johannesburg and around the country. At Webster's funeral, attended by about 10 000 people, the black, green and gold flag of the still-banned African National Congress was carried by mourners, while thousands of copies of a pamphlet by the South African Communist Party were freely distributed inside and outside St Mary's Cathedral. A wide spectrum of anti-apartheid figures were among the mourners, including several activists who defied emergency restriction orders and others who emerged from long periods in hiding.

Unprecedented pressure was applied on the police and the government to bring Webster's killers to book. On several occasions the police seemed to be on the verge of a breakthrough, but each time hopes were dashed.

There was an overwhelming public response to the original identikits distributed by the police and six days after the murder, Floris Mostert said breakthroughs had been made and details would be announced soon. Two days later, he admitted that no suspects had been positively identified and accused the press of "dangerous speculation". Three weeks after the murder, the police announced that they had traced another eyewitness and that they had improved identikits, but refused to release them. In August, Jaap Joubert said the investigation had reached a cul-de-sac. In September, the reward for information leading to the arrest and conviction of the murderers had reached R100 000.

Five months after Webster was killed, his killer's trail had run dead cold. The apparent reluctance of the police to investigate with sufficient vigour once again fuelled speculation that the killers might have close links to the South African security forces.

There was speculation that Webster was assassinated because members of the South African Defence Force believed that he had uncovered evidence of a Renamo support network in the Kosi Bay area of northern Natal where he worked as an anthropologist. Webster had been told by a KwaZulu agricultural officer that he had seen three mobile Renamo bases in the area more than two years ago. The *Weekly Mail* were informed that, nearly a year after Webster's death, there was still an insurgents' base located at Lake Sibaya, south of Kosi Bay. The possible involvement of Military Intelligence in Webster's murder was mentioned for the first time.[6]

In the months to follow, this possibility grew in stature as a series of unusual events gushed forth more evidence of state complicity in the harassment and death of opponents of the apartheid system.

Calla Botha is a big and burly man with a 52-centimetre neck and a child's button nose. A provincial rugby forward whose massive figure makes him stand out in a crowd, he was a security policeman until he joined the Brixton

Murder and Robbery Unit in 1987. Botha had a fearsome reputation among activists. One of them was Boetie van der Merwe: "When we were in detention in 1985 they brought in Calla Botha . . . They said: Do you see how big this fellow is? He will break your bones if you don't talk. Then Botha assaulted me – punching, kicking and sjambokking me. He assaulted one of the other guys so badly they had to hospitalise him."[7]

In 1988, Sergeant Calla Botha was one of a group of Brixton policemen who suddenly resigned from the unit and left the South African Police. Among them was one of South Africa's best known and most famous policemen, Lieutenant-Colonel Daniel Ferdinand du Toit "Staal" Burger, whose nickname, which literally means "steel", was taken from a popular radio comedy series about an invincible cop. Like Botha, he has a Springbok rugby forward's frame. During his 24 years in the South African Police, Burger gained a reputation as a fearless and ruthless detective who always got his man. He was attached to the Brixton Murder and Robbery Unit for 14 years and his surprising resignation came just 10 months after his promotion to head of the unit that had gained a notorious reputation for its high "death rate" and the torturing of detainees.[8]

Burger's shock departure from the SAP was followed by two more resignations at Brixton Murder and Robbery, those of Lieutenant Abram "Slang" van Zyl and Warrant Officer Chappie Maree. Van Zyl, once a rising star in the SAP, got his nickname from fellow police force officers who thought his eyes looked snake-like.

The resignation of the four policemen followed shortly after a controversial court case during which two of their colleagues, Sergeant Robert van der Merwe and Captain Jack la Grange, were convicted of murder and sentenced to death. The media speculated that the resignation of Burger and his men was connected to the court case, but it turned out later that there was a much more sinister reason.

Within days of David Webster's murder, a founder member of the End Conscription Campaign, Roland Bruce White, had been tipped off that two men were trying to find out about his movements. The security personnel at his work spotted them on a couple of occasions in and around the parking garage.

White did not want to take any risks. He informed his employer, who phoned the police. Police inquiries indicated that the two men responsible were not from the police, and a squad car was put on hold with instructions to move quickly if they were spotted again.

The two men were spotted in early June and were immediately detained for questioning. They turned out to be Calla Botha and a former West Rand Narcotics Bureau detective and convicted criminal, Ferdi Barnard, who had received a nine-year sentence in December 1984 for murdering two drug addicts after leading them into a trap, attempting to murder a third addict and stealing three cars. He was released in December 1988 on parole from the Pretoria Central prison. They told the police that they were debt collectors and were after a white car "and not a Mr White".[9]

Botha and Barnard were released after their details had been taken. White said that their operation appeared to be amateurish. They spent some time hanging around the garage of his office and were very noticeable, both being large men. At first glance, the event seemed to be nothing more than two former policemen turned debt collectors looking for a debtor.

Shortly after this incident, a notorious and ruthless assassin known in the underworld as "The Cleaner" was introduced to Calla Botha. His name was Donald Acheson, an Irish national and former Rhodesian soldier. This man with the weary, hangdog look came from Belfast but left Ireland nearly 20 years ago to hitch-hike through Africa, doing odd jobs, until he came to Rhodesia in 1974 where he joined the Grey Scouts, a counter-insurgency unit fighting the black nationalists.[10]

Like many specialist soldiers who left Rhodesia when the country became independent, Acheson joined the South African Defence Force and was based at 5 Reconnaissance Unit near Phalaborwa in the northern Transvaal. He left the Defence Force in the middle eighties and worked part-time for an international trading company, telling friends he was involved in sensitive business deals "north of the Limpopo". In May 1988, he was convicted of shoplifting in Johannesburg and fined R400.

A year later Acheson was arrested again on a charge of shoplifting. He became friends with the investigating officer, Detective Sergeant William Knox, who introduced him to Ferdi Barnard. Apparently the two criminals immediately formed a close rapport, although Barnard later claimed that he only knew Acheson by the name of "Donald Dolan". The Irish criminal told him that he had worked as a mercenary in the Congo and as a bounty hunter in America, and that he had contacts with the Irish Republican Army and the Rhodesian Special Forces. Barnard, who also used a false name, told Acheson that he worked for a very special South African security force unit that could certainly use his services. Acheson, who agreed to work for Barnard, thought his new employer was a member of the so-called "Z-squad".[11]

Barnard introduced Acheson to "Deon" and "Stefan", who would act as his handlers. "Deon" was Calla Botha and "Stefan" was Chappie Maree. Acheson did not know who his handlers were, but he knew he was working for some kind of South African death squad. He said that shortly after meeting the three, they offered him $200 000 to kill a prominent liberal newspaper editor and Swapo supporter in Namibia, Gwen Lister.[12]

According to the plan, Acheson had to put poison either in Lister's personal sanitary belongings or in her toothpaste. The Irishman thought it was an utterly ridiculous plan and that it would be much easier to assassinate her with an AK-47 assault rifle, but his handlers insisted that he do it their way. He was also told to get a car, hire a flat and keep an AK-47 handy in case he should need it.

Johannesburg, 1 September 1989. A group of former South African policemen, among them Staal Burger and Chappie Maree, secretly met at a plush Johannesburg hotel to discuss a special project. The meeting was conducted according to the strict military "need-to-know" principle and two of their former colleagues, Slang van Zyl and Calla Botha, were asked to leave the room as they were not directly involved in the project.[13]

The project the two men were discussing concerned the well-known foe of apartheid and Swapo's so-called "white son", Namibian advocate Anton Lubowski. Six days days before the meeting took place, Van Zyl had done surveillance on Lubowski who had just returned from an overseas visit. He was not told why he had to monitor the Swapo leader.

Around this time, Acheson and Maree met each other three times in Swaziland. After each meeting, Maree handed R5 000 to Acheson, who would fly back to Windhoek where he stayed at a R70-a-day flat rented from a German landlady.

Acheson's last trip to Namibia took place on 10 September 1989. On September 11 he hired a white Volkswagen Fox in Windhoek. On the same day, Acheson's handler, Chappie Maree, flew into Windhoek. The next morning, Acheson returned the car and complained of faulty brakes. He said he did not want a white car and swopped the vehicle for a red Toyota Conquest. In the meantime, Staal Burger, who was unknown to Acheson, had flown into Windhoek under the pseudonym of "Gagiano".[14]

On the night of 12 September Acheson's German landlady watched him get into his hired car carrying something that appeared to be a motor car jack hidden inside a sack. By the time he returned to his flat, Anton Lubowski had been slain in front of his Windhoek home.

On the night of 11 September Anton Lubowski had been seen on South African television as he greeted Swapo exiles at the Windhoek airport. He was six inches taller than anybody else around him as he embraced Swapo leader Andimba Toivo ja Toivo, welcoming him back on Namibian soil. Two days later, Lubowski appeared on the front page of *The Star* as policeman put his corpse into a body bag. He had died the previous night in a hail of bullets fired from an AK-47 rifle.

For many, it was difficult to believe that the likeable and flamboyant "white Swapo" who had fought so hard for the freedom and liberation of Namibia had been killed on the eve of independence. In a tribute to him, Max du Preez wrote: "My friend Lubof . . . of all the people I knew, he was the one who adored and loved life the most.

"Five years ago Anton and I were drinking beer in the garden of the old Kaiser Krone hotel when a couple of rough boys at the table shouted out at him: white kaffir!

"I remember as if it were yesterday the way his face lit up. It's true, he said to me, I am a white kaffir.

"He was too.

"... Anton was no revolutionary. Unless there is such a thing as a humanitarian revolutionary who can party until the early hours of the morning, who is partial to tailor-made trousers, silk shirts and fast cars, who cries openly when he speaks about his children who no longer live with him and who has a sense of humour."[15]

In April 1984 Anton Lubowski had received a letter from State President PW Botha. You are discharged from any further service in the South African Defence Force and your officer's commission is withdrawn, he was told. Your military services are no longer needed.

Weeks before, in March 1984, Lubowski had become the first prominent white person to declare his allegiance to Swapo, saying that he would fight for its military wing, the People's Liberation Army of Namibia (PLAN), if his services were required. This led to Botha's letter, telling him that he had become a disgrace to the Defence Force and that because of his membership of an "enemy organisation" could no longer serve his country. Lubowski, who held the rank of lieutenant in the SADF's citizen force, was at that time still eligible for military camps.[16]

His membership of Swapo started a five-year campaign of terror and harassment which ended brutally in his death on September 12. He received countless death threats and survived an attempt on his life when his car was sprayed with bullets one evening while returning to Windhoek from the Katatura township. Poison letters arrived daily, his advocate's practice was boycotted and there were smear campaigns in the Afrikaans newspapers. He was detained six times by the South African authorities and the last time was locked up in solitary confinement.

He was hated even more because of his background. He was an army officer, went to school at the elite Paul Roos Gymnasium and attended the University of Stellenbosch. He was an excellent rugby player and excelled academically. His mother, Johanna Jacoba van der Merwe, was of good Afrikaner stock and his father, Wilfried Lubowski, was a respected German Namibian. What Anton did, many thought, was an act of treason against his own kin.[17]

Lubowski described his own involvement with Swapo in 1985 in a literary magazine: "Swapo shoots, and takes weapons from wherever it can get it, because we simply want to get rid of South Africa's despicable system of apartheid and military occupation of Namibia. Swapo doesn't fight against the whites; it fights against a system. For the past 24 years, Swapo has stated time and time again that it is prepared to negotiate with South Africa about a suspension of armed activities and an internationally acceptable process towards independence."[18]

Lubowski usually parked his car inside an electronically controlled security area when he returned home. He knew he was a target for assassination by death squad: he had mentioned the possibility to his father.

Because of this, he always drove his car into the security area leading into his garage. On the night of 12 September, however, he had made two crucial telephone calls to his girl-friend, human rights lawyer Michaela Clayton. They had an appointment that night, and Anton phoned to tell her that he was going to be 15 minutes late and would stop outside the house, without entering the security gates, to pick her up.

Whoever killed him, must have listened to that call. It was the perfect opportunity: they knew he was changing his schedule and that for once he would be a target outside his home. The street lights in Sanderburg Road were put off, giving perfect cover. When the police arrived after the killing, they were able simply to phone the electricity department and have the lights switched on again.[19]

Lubowski arrived home at 20 past eight that night. He pushed the buzzer at the security gate to call Clayton. She heard a sharp crackle and thought somebody had thrown fire-crackers into the garden. Instead, Lubowski lay dead outside the gate. His murderers were seen speeding away in a red car.

Lubowski's neighbour, a former West German policeman, found his body shortly after hearing the shots. He immediately described the killing as a most professional assassination. The job must have been done by more than one person and carried all the hallmarks of professionals. To fire 11 high-velocity bullets from an AK-47 into a small target area requires skill and experience. The police were convinced that more than one person had driven off in the killer's car, and there were two pairs of footprints around the garden path leading to the gate, one of them Acheson's.

The morning after the killing, Donald Acheson's landlady called the police and informed them that a man staying in one of her flats had acted suspiciously the previous morning. In the politically charged atmosphere of Nambia the police were under immense pressure to get their man. Later that day police detained Acheson under immigration laws and he was told that he was also being held on suspicion of murder.

Acheson told the Namibian investigating officer, Colonel Jan "Jumbo" Smith, that he was in Windhoek on a "secret mission". He said he worked for a shoplifting syndicate in South Africa and intended to set one up in Windhoek. He identified Ferdi Barnard from a photograph as the man who had recruited him and whom he knew under another name. A radio page number in Acheson's possession was also traced back to Barnard.[20]

The murder trail led Smith to South Africa where he exchanged his information with Floris Mostert, who was investigating the murder of David Webster. Mostert's knowledge of Barnard was traced back to the Roland White incident, and it soon emerged that the actions of the two "debt collectors" were less innocent than the pair had claimed. In due course, the liaison revealed a link between the murders of Lubowski and Webster. On 31 October Floris Mostert pounced on Ferdi Barnard and detained him under

134

Section 29 of the Internal Security Act. Shortly afterwards, he detained Calla Botha as well.[21]

Barnard provided Mostert with invaluable information. He claimed that he was a member of a secret organisation committed to a strategy of violently intimidating the radical left. Mostert also soon established that Barnard had been in contact with Donald Acheson on at least two occasions before Lubowski was killed. Furthermore, he suspected that there was a link between Barnard and Military Intelligence.

The clue acquired new significance towards the end of January 1990 when Barnard's father, a retired police colonel, launched an urgent application in the Rand Supreme Court to have his son released. The application, which was opposed by Mostert, was later withdrawn. However, Mostert spoke in his affidavit of a "secret organisation" that terrorised "leftwing radicals". He said he believed that the group was responsible for murdering both Webster and Lubowski and said that Barnard and Botha had monitored the movements of a "leftwing radical" (Roland White) whose name could not be released because the person's life could be endangered.[22]

Mostert said that Barnard was still withholding important information about the secret organisation. In his judgement Mr Justice HJ Preiss said enough facts had been revealed for the court to reasonably judge the police's suspicion that Barnard was withholding vital information in connection with a rightwing organisation responsible for the murders of Webster and Lubowski.

On 7 February 1990 Mostert detained Slang van Zyl as well. A few days later, his wife, Brenda van Zyl, launched another court application. She said that Van Zyl had worked for the South African Defence Force from May 1988 to the last quarter of 1989. She said that the police had known more than a month before they detained him that he worked for the Defence Force.

These claims came in the wake of a confession by Ferdi Barnard, who confirmed Mostert's suspicions when he told his father that he had been acting under the command of Military Intelligence. A statement by his father said that Barnard did not wish to proceed with the original application for his release, fearing that he would be killed by "interested parties". Mostert was forced to furnish further details. In another affidavit, he linked the secret organisation directly to the South African Defence Force. "I established that the aforesaid secret organisation was responsible for different incidents of murder, arson, bomb explosions at buildings, assaults and intimidation. From questioning Barnard and Botha I established that the mentioned secret organisation was actually a unit of the South African Defence Force that was known as the Civil Co-operation Bureau (CCB)."[23]

Mostert revealed that the organisation was organised in cells, and that Botha, Van Zyl and Chappie Maree were all members of the same cell but, according to his information, Barnard was not. Staal Burger, the cell's leader, was being sought by the South African Police, but until then had eluded them.

The Star revealed that the CCB was a section of the SADF's Special Forces, was commanded by a general, had at least 16 cells across the country and used prominent companies as fronts for its activities. The newspaper claimed that the secret squad's activities had been sanctioned at the highest level and at a cost of millions of rands to taxpayers.[24]

Following the revelations of Mostert, Namibian Prosecutor-General Hans Heyman informed the South African Department of Justice that Burger and Maree were wanted as co-accused with Donald Acheson, while Barnard, William Knox, Botha and Van Zyl were sought as witnesses. Burger and Maree disappeared after Namibian warrants for their arrest were issued. The warrants were issued before Namibia's independence and were thus temporarily valid in South Africa.

After Mostert's affidavits, the Civil Co-operation Bureau was blown wide open. Not only was an official Defence Force death squad exposed, it was also linked to the assassination of two of apartheid's most vigorous opponents.

Burger and his men had bungled. Had they followed all the regulations and security instructions of the CCB, Acheson, who was not supposed to know who his handler was, would never have been able to identify Barnard or lead the police back to him. In the end, all the built-in security precautions were of no avail. The CCB, so secretive that Magnus Malan could later claim that he had not known of its existence, was exposed.

A bizarre situation had developed: one security arm of the government was mercilessly hunting down another. But not only was the SAP the hunter and the SADF the prey; Floris Mostert was hunting down his former colleagues at Brixton Murder and Robbery. Mostert's disclosures came less than three months after the revelations of Dirk Coetzee and Almond Nofemela and the exposure of the CCB threatened to explode in the government's face. The Minister of Defence, General Magnus Malan, was embroiled in a battle for his political life: both the left and the right of the political spectrum demanded his immediate resignation.

In a desperate bid to save his political career, Malan made an astounding disclosure in Parliament on 26 February 1990. He stood up and said under protection of parliamentary privilege: "I want to disclose today that Lubowski was a paid agent of Military Intelligence. I am assured that he did good work for the SADF. The Chief of Staff Intelligence, General Witkop Badenhorst, would therefore never have approved actions against Lubowksi." Malan denied that he ever gave orders or authorised any offences that the Defence Force might have committed. A witchhunt was being waged against the Defence Force and he had no intention of yielding to the campaign against him. Neither would he allow the Defence Force to be thrown on the pyre of "untested hearings and private enquiries".[25]

Malan's claim was met with shock and outrage. Even known adversaries of Anton Lubowski expressed disbelief. Here was a member of Swapo's politburo, a South African agent planted in the bosom of the organisation. Malan's statement came amid mounting evidence that the CCB had murdered Lubowski: in fact, both the Namibian and South African police said that they had good reason to believe this. It was seen as a desperate move by Malan to save his dwindling political stature.

"You have besmirched a hero. Not a single black person in South Africa or Namibia believes you," Democratic Party co-leader Denis Worrall told Malan. Swapo's Theo-Ben Gurirab, who became Namibia's Minister of Foreign Affairs after independence, said: "Malan's allegations were a cheap shot by a drowning man clutching at the smallest straw. You know as well as I do that Anton was harassed over the years by these people. If De Klerk is to succeed in his attempts to reform society, then the unmasking of security force death squads will have to be the first order of business."[26]

Malan admitted in a parliamentary debate that the CCB was an integral part of Special Forces and performed assignments like intelligence and infiltration "in the interests of the country and about which no army readily talks". He said that an internal investigation had already been instituted in connection with the CCB. He repeated his denial that he had ever given any orders to anyone to commit murder. No orders had been given to eliminate either Anton Lubowski or David Webster. "I trust the National Executive Committee of the ANC can say the same about deeds which have been performed by them, for example the Church Street bomb and many other examples."[27]

The national chairman of the Democratic Party, Tian van der Merwe, responded: "General Malan has consistently covered up the existence of the CCB and its activities, something that was a gross infringement of all standards of democracy and decency. He sat here silently in Parliament and watched while the public was brutally misled about SADF actions . . . He has denied that he gave orders to commit murder, but did he know about any of these murders or crimes before or after they were committed?"[28]

In his reply Malan did not answer to a single question put in debate and referred indirectly to the need for secrecy in security by quoting a previous speech in which he said: "Southern Africa is a marshland of international agents of Western and communist secret services. It is a grey world of which John Public often only hears. It is a world with its own rules and morality. South Africa is, because of its safety needs, also necessarily involved in this grey matter . . . we can't talk about these matters in public."[29]

The disclosures of Dirk Coetzee and Almond Nofemela had already put immense pressure on State President FW de Klerk to appoint a judicial commission of inquiry. At first De Klerk had deflected demands for a judicial and public inquiry by appointing Natal Attorney-General Tim McNally and the CID Chief, General Alwyn Conradie, to investigate Nofemela's claims.

After the McNally report was handed to De Klerk in late November 1989, De Klerk turned a deaf ear to the demands for a judicial commission, saying that an inquiry would take a long time. "Justice delayed is justice denied," the State President said; the law would be allowed to take its course and people alleged to be assassins would be prosecuted. Nofemela was charged with the murder of Griffiths Mxenge and a short while later, the Attorney-General of Natal issued a warrant for the arrest of Dirk Coetzee and David Tshikalange.[30]

Legal experts, politicians and civil rights activists angrily accused De Klerk of a cover-up. They claimed that he was trying to conceal the chain of command directing the death squads by his refusal to appoint an independent judicial inquiry. The director of the Centre for Applied Legal Studies at the University of the Witwatersrand, Prof John Dugard, said he feared prosecutions would be used to contain the issue by suggesting that only a limited number of rogue policemen operating on their own without higher orders were involved. "I believe that the chain of command stretches very high into the upper echelons of the Government. The refusal to release the McNally report is a concerted attempt to try to conceal the fact that orders came from higher up. Junior officers will take the blame as scapegoats," Dugard said.[31]

Denis Worrall insisted that "President de Klerk has to take personal responsibility. He should understand that the issue will not go away. Coetzee will continue to give his newspaper incriminating information. There will be criminal and civil trials, and newspapers will continue to dig. It would also not help anybody for there to be witchhunts when the new South Africa comes into being. De Klerk's record is flawed by his failure to appoint a judicial or other independent inquiry into the allegations of a death squad operating within the state mechanism."[32]

Within the ranks of the National Party tremendous pressure was brought to bear on De Klerk to act. The government-supporting newspaper *Beeld* said that the time had come for the appointment of a judicial commission of inquiry. The explanation that a judicial commission would take too long was no longer relevant. Even the *Citizen*, normally a strong supporter of the security establishment, stated that there was *prima facie* evidence to suggest that a death squad may well have existed. A strong voice of concern also came from the Dutch Reformed Church when respected clergyman Willem Nicol said there had long been suspicion that the police might have been involved in the ugliest form of violence in the country.[33]

In a desperate effort to divert attention away from state-sanctioned death squads, the police uncovered another "death squad" – five rightwing extremists calling themselves "The Order of Death" were arrested. In a deluge of publicity and media hype, they announced that an arms cache had been uncovered and that there was a "hit-list" containing the names of, among others, De Klerk and Adriaan Vlok themselves. Most observers were unimpressed: the sensational revelation smacked of disinformation. "That would have created chaos in the country," General Jaap Joubert told a briefing for journalists.[34]

De Klerk's promised statement in response to the McNally report was inexplicably made several days after it had been promised and coincided with the exposure of "The Order of Death". The government refused to release the report. A defiant Adriaan Vlok told a National Party meeting in the Free State that the police had once again become the target of revolutionaries who were doing everything in their power to destroy the morale of the security forces. "There is now a new attempt to break down the morale of the police. The South African Communist Party-ANC alliance and its colleagues are directing all their attention to the police. The ANC has been engaged in conflict with the police for years but the security forces have always stood in their way. The police force will remain steadfast and not allow itself to be brought down by what is being directed at it. We have withstood many onslaughts against us in the past 76 years and have survived. Our cause is right. We are fighting for South Africa's interests," Vlok said.[35]

The death squad row had doubtless widened the gap between the De Klerk administration and the security community – which, under PW Botha, had ruled the country virtually on its own. De Klerk, in one of his first steps to return South Africa to civilian rule, scrapped the National Security Management System (NSMS) with its network of joint management committees and replaced it with a "needs-orientated" system to co-ordinate joint state actions.

De Klerk outlined new ground rules for the police when he warned 500 officers at a meeting behind closed doors in Pretoria not to become embroiled in politics. He told the officers that the force had a proud reputation but warned them that they risked public discreditation if it continued to be dragged into politics. "Matters that have been dealt with in the past with strong-arm tactics will in future be handled differently," he stated.[36]

The Government bowed to demands for an inquiry into death squads when on 31 January 1990 the Minister of Justice, Kobie Coetsee, announced that the State President had appointed a one-man judicial commission of inquiry into "murders and deeds of violence allegedly committed with political motives". Mr Justice Louis Harms was appointed as chairman of the commission.

The announcement came the night before Dirk Coetzee was due to address his first international press conference in Harare and a planned illegal protest march to Tuynhuis organised by Afrikaner clerics and academics to call for a judicial inquiry into death squads. Lawyers and politicians immediately welcomed the appointment, but criticised it for having terms of reference so broad that it could take years for the investigation to be completed. On the other hand, the commission could only investigate atrocities and acts of violence that were committed inside the borders of South Africa.

The President's decision not to investigate external operations was immediately seen as approval of the elimination of all ANC members outside the country. Newspapers quoting informed sources in the government said that the cabinet had decided that all security force actions against ANC "terrorists" outside South Africa were authorised actions in the war against the ANC. The *Sunday Star* reacted in an editorial: "The Government either condones murder or it does not. Once it turns a blind eye to killing in its name outside the country, it gets on to a very slippery slope of dubious logic. The Government's point is that it is acceptable to approve the killing of 'terrorists' abroad. But it would be criminal to try to blur the stark difference between a hot-pursuit action, involving two armed forces in combat, and a cold-blooded assassination across the border. There have been too many cases in neighbouring states of innocent victims of poor military or other intelligence. There are too many cases of civilians, including children, who were murdered simply because they happened to be in the wrong place at the wrong time."[37] Peter Harris, legal adviser and member of the Independent Board of Inquiry into Informal Repression, said De Klerk should have acted in November when allegations of alleged police death squads first surfaced. "Who knows what steps have been taken in the meantime by any of those implicated to cover their tracks and ensure the truth does not come to light?"[38]

As pressure mounted on Magnus Malan to furnish evidence to prove his allegation that Lubowski was a paid agent, De Klerk came to his rescue, broadening the terms of reference of the Harms Commission and instructing the judge to investigate whether or not Lubowski was an agent of Military Intelligence. He did not, however, authorise Harms to find the murderers. South African courts have no jurisdiction over crimes committed in Namibia, he explained. At that time, this was not true. Namibia was still under the control of a South African Administrator-General and the South African Appeal Court was still the highest court in the territory.

If Malan's allegation about Lubowski was correct, there were only two possibilities behind the assassination. The first is that Lubowski was murdered by Swapo because he turned against his former masters or was about to reveal important information about them. The second is that he was killed by the CCB, who did not know that he was a South African agent. There are sources that claim that Lubowski was not popular among certain Swapo factions. He rose to fame rapidly and was president-designate Sam Nujoma's favourite son. He might have been killed by Swapo guerrillas who knew he was an SADF agent. However, to date, neither the Police nor the Defence Force has come up with a single shred of evidence to show that it may have been an "inside job". If Lubowski was a paid agent, his death must have been the biggest bungle in South African espionage history. Later evidence before the Harms Commission showed that the CCB had in all probability become embroiled in a terrible mix-up.

Eight years ago, walls in Johannesburg and Durban were sprayed with brightly coloured grafitti: "Who killed Griffiths Mxenge?"

It was a mystery that had haunted South Africa for many years. After decades of people slipping on soap in police cell showers, during which a long list was made of unsolved political murders and anti-apartheid activists who disappeared from the face of the earth, many thought the day of reckoning had finally arrived. The Harms Commission, they hoped, would give South Africans the opportunity to publicly scrutinise the actions of the Security Branch and the CCB and cross-examine the perpetrators on their reign of terror. A warning was sounded by the Independent Board of Inquiry into Informal Repression that failure to take vigorous action against the perpetrators of acts might well lead to the belief that perpetrators of these acts were indeed beyond the reach of the law.

Publc confidence in the integrity of the government had been badly shaken by reports and allegations that implied high-level condonation of political murder. Promises from the State President that the death squad saga would be "cut to the bone" fuelled the public's hopes that this festering sore in South African society would be excised.

Louis Harms was dubbed "The Prince of Probes" and "Commissioner Supremo". As an investigator, he had acquired the aura of a white knight set to solve a deep and sordid mystery.[39]

Harms first rose to prominence when he headed a judicial commission of inquiry into fraud and corruption in the Transkei. He was credited with exposing fraud involving 600 investors and R150 million and forced an admission from flamboyant hotelier Sol Kerzner that he had bribed a homeland leader with R2 million. The influential *Business Day* said in an article after the release of his corruption report: "According to members of the legal profession, a hallmark of Louis Harms' career has been his incisiveness. He is authoritative, goes for the jugular and does not fear anyone, they say. He doesn't waste time getting sidetracked on technicalities. He gets to the core of the matter very quickly. Another member describes him as fearless and not afraid to make decisions and stand by them."[40]

Harms, De Klerk's chosen instrument to dissect and expose alleged death squads, had a brilliant legal career and was appointed as a Supreme Court judge at the tender age of 46. He had graduated *cum laude* from the University of Pretoria and been offered a professorship at the age of 28. In the late seventies he led the battle to open the Pretoria Bar to all races and succeeded after more than two years of intensive lobbying. Harms is an expert in patent and copyright law and was much sought after as counsel on these matters.

I had only seen Harms in action once before the start of his inquiry into death squads and that was when he was the presiding judge in the sensational trial of the fanatical mass-murderer, Barend Strydom. This former policeman drew his gun in downtown Pretoria in November 1988 and shot and killed seven innocent black people in cold blood. He laughed as he pulled the trigger. Days earlier Strydom had killed another black woman in what was descrbed as a "trial run." I was immensely impressed with Harms as he handled the emotionally laden proceedings with sensitivity and firmness. He showed extreme patience towards the unrepentant Strydom as he dug into the evidence seeking extenuating circumstances to save the young man from the gallows. In the end, a clearly upset Louis Harms found that he had no choice but to sentence Strydom to death eight times.

In an interview shortly before the start of proceedings, Harms said: "The expectations raised about my commission are unreasonable. I'll solve certain things, but you can only solve things when you have witnesses." Unfortunately, the commission's shortcomings were not only the lack of witnesses willing to come forward and testify. The terms of reference of the commission, whereby operations conducted and atrocities committed outside the boundaries of South Africa were excluded from investigation, were far too narrow. They prevented many questions from being asked and answered, and prevented the commission from investigating some of the most controversial and sinister aspects of the scandal. In the end, Harms could only investigate a small portion of the death squad activities.

Death squads operated far beyond South Africa's borders. A murder committed in South Africa was often preceded or followed by a raid across the border. In the end, it was established that the CCB operated as far abroad as Europe and was divided into at least ten different "regions". Harms was only allowed to investigate the conduct of one region. Time and time again, as the death squads were poised at South Africa's borders, the story of their strike and raid were cut short by Louis Harms.

Although the commission was chaired by a judge, he did not have the powers a judge would have had in a criminal trial. This meant he could not provide indemnity to witnesses, many of whom simply refused to answer vital questions on the grounds that their answers might incriminate them. An amendment to the Commissions Act might have been considered whereby witnesses could have been forced to answer incriminating questions subject to the proviso that the evidence was led *in camera* and was not used against them in criminal trials. The commission could also have subpoenaed witnesses under Section 205 of the Criminal Procedure Act, compelling them to testify or face imprisonment. But perhaps the biggest shortcoming of the Harms Commission was the fact that a team consisting of an attorney-general and senior police officers was appointed to investigate the allegations and present the evidence to the commission. Once again, one organ of the state was directed to investigate itself and another sister organ.

The internal investigation by Tim McNally in the end proved to be nothing more than a police cover-up. De Klerk only released the McNally report in November 1990 – nearly a year after it was handed to him. In his report, McNally found that there was no evidence to suggest that either Coetzee or Nofemela had been telling the truth: Nofemela was probably trying to save his life and Coetzee seemed to be unreliable and had a grudge against the police. Yet the same Tim McNally, who had already made up his mind that police death squads did not exist, accepted an assignment to lead evidence to the Harms Commission. In a court of law such prejudice as to the conclusion of the commission could be used as grounds for demanding a recusal, or even to invalidate the findings of the court as a whole.

Following publication of the McNally report, John Dugard said that McNally should have recused himself or never have been allowed to lead evidence to the Harms Commission because he had already decided that death squads did not exist. "Without reflecting on the Harms Commission at all, I will find it hard to accept any finding on police death squads. I would give my eye teeth to cross-examine him on this issue."[41]

Brigadier Krappies Engelbrecht, the former Brixton Murder and Robbery commander was one of the policemen who had to assist in the investigation into the allegations. Nofemela also accused Engelbrecht of being hostile towards him. Colonel Hermanus du Plessis, implicated by Coetzee in the murder of Sizwe Kondile and the interrogator of Siphiwo Mtimkulu, also assisted in the investigations. It was inconceivable that policemen could objectively investigate allegations of police death squads. McNally was further empowered to evaluate documentation and evidence before presenting it to the commission.

As South Africa entered the nineties, there were no less than five judicial commissions of inquiry engaged in an unprecedented search for the truth. Early in 1990, *The Star* published a series of articles about a spy network in the Johannesburg City Council that used ratepayers' money to spy on "radical leftist organisations". Judge Victor Hiemstra was appointed to investigate the allegations.

Evidence before the Harms and Hiemstra Commissions overlapped, but the two inquiries had markedly different styles. While Louis Harms repeatedly allowed CCB members to refuse to divulge details regarding intelligence operations, Victor Hiemstra ruled that the Defence Act could not be used to shield Military Intelligence from the inquiry. Hiemstra said that given the nature of the city council spy operation, questions regarding the SADF were unavoidable and accepted argument that such revelations would not affect the capacity of South Africa to defend itself as the Defence Act requires.[42]

While the Harms Commission had an attorney-general leading and preparing evidence, the Hiemstra Commission had an independent senior advocate to assist the chairman. It was the kind of independent expertise that the Harms Commission desperately needed.

Of course the various members of the police force and CCB who testified before the commission would not willingly admit that they had committed or had any knowledge of atrocities. They knew beforehand that in most cases there would be no hard evidence against them. The Government should have equipped the commission with all possible aid and expertise to enable Louis Harms to uncover the truth.

The Minister of Justice compiled a list of 71 unsolved murders for the

Harms Commission to investigate. It was a peculiar compilation as it also included the names of scores of northern border farmers killed in landmine attacks, together with still-born twins whose mother was injured during a bomb-blast in an entertainment centre in Johannesburg. There was even a mistake in the list: one Oupa Masuku was named with his wife as having been murdered in 1986. His wife Esther was murdered, but Oupa is still alive and well. People who had gone missing or were mysteriously abducted were conspicuously absent from the list.

The public's initial perception that Harms and his team of investigators would unearth the full story of the death squads soon proved to be sorely misplaced. It was months of utter frustration as files went missing, witnesses appeared in clown-like disguises, documents were never produced and state witnesses bluntly denied any knowledge of death squads.

Louis Harms, in the words of former Supreme Court judge Laurie Ackermann, wielded a blunted scapel. He could not cut through the tissue of lies.[43]

CHAPTER NINE

The brotherhood of silence

IT was towards the end of 1988 that a small group of South Africa's best-trained and most feared soldiers joined hands to work out a masterplan for a very special South African Defence Force unit. The group of soldiers studied the structures of the CIA, KGB and Mossad in order to structure their organisation in such a way that it could function and survive completely independently of the SADF. It had to have the ability to generate its own funds, buy its own weapons and gather its own intelligence. It had to be so secretive that it could never be exposed. No member should know the identity of any other; even the top echelons should not know all the members who worked for them. There also had to be members who did not know who they were working for.[1]

The unit had to consist of the very best the South African armed forces could offer: brave and fearless men, who had earned their decorations and promotions not by being mere "pen pushers"; battle-hardened men who could destroy, disrupt or intimidate the enemy at any place or time, using any method. It was an organisation that took it upon itself to charge, try, condemn and even execute people regarded as enemies of the state. The enemy was not only the ANC and PAC in their military camps in southern Africa or armed cadres trying to infiltrate South Africa, it was also those people inside the Republic who supported "leftist" organisations, fought against apartheid and struggled for a non-racial society.

There was only one rule for members to follow in conducting their operations: never should their tracks be traced back to the South African Defence Force. Therefore a bizarre organisation with a civilian facade was formed. It was established on the lines of a private company, in which the government was called the "Controlling Trust", the overall commander the "Chairman" and the commanding officer the "Managing Director", with "shareholders", "clients" and "suppliers". The managing director had to submit a budget to a "Board of Directors". This organisation was eventually called the Civil Co-operation Bureau, a sinister-sounding name for a deadly group of men, acting as if with complete immunity from the law. Although it formed part of the SADF's Special Forces, there was no indication that it was part and parcel of the military. At Special Forces it functioned under the codename "Triplane".[2]

This covert unit, part of the SADF's Special Forces, started life in the early eighties under the name D40 (D stands for Delta and 40 for the number of people who first joined the organisation) and consisted of "operators" and former members of the Rhodesian security forces. D40 transmuted, in turn, into Barnacle, 3 Reconnaissance Regiment and eventually into the Civil Co-operation Bureau (CCB). The first phase of the CCB was commenced during April 1986 and in 1988 it became a "civilian organisation".

In its final form the CCB's tentacles stretched from South Africa all over southern Africa to Europe. It spent millions of rands of taxpayers' money on establishing a network of agents who spied on anti-apartheid activists, acquired Russian and foreign manufactured weaponry on the black market, bribed African businessmen and government officials, established a resort for political refugees "sympathetic towards their cause", hired professional assassins to execute enemies, tried to buy an island off the Mozambican coast and sponsored agents and operatives who had fled South Africa to avoid persecution or extradtion for their atrocities.

While the military had previously only operated outside South Africa, the emphasis had now clearly shifted to the situation within its borders, where the South African government was embroiled in a "total war" against the "total onslaught".

As mentioned in Chapter 7, the government's doctrine of the "total onslaught" spawned a "total strategy" that combined formal and informal repression of any organisation or movement that threatened the existence of the apartheid state. Formal repression was conducted through police and army action and the implementation of harsh security laws. Informal repression took many forms from harassment to murder. The reason for the existence of the CCB could be found in the style of rule of the PW Botha regime. The military became a government within a government, so that the CCB could covertly operate under the protection of the Defence Act, sustained by secret funds and accountable only to its military leaders. Awkward questions could always be deflected by an assertion that operations were "secret".

From 1979 onwards the Defence Force adopted a proactive stance against extra-territorial bases of organisations such as the ANC and the PAC. Hand in hand with this development went increasing involvement in the Namibian war. Pre-emptive strikes into neighbouring countries became commonplace. As the combat was largely unconventional, military units were trained specifically for this kind of warfare.

But why did the Defence Force start to perform functions that were normally reserved for the police? There had long been conflict between the police and the Defence Force, the roots of the dispute were in the conflict between former Prime Minister John Vorster, and his successor, PW Botha.

Vorster, as a former Minister of Police, favoured the police force, while Botha, a former Minister of Defence, was a patron of the military. As the conflict between the two personalities grew, the security forces became polarised. The police remained loyal to Vorster, while the military sided with Botha. When the latter became the head of government in 1978, the military gained in influence. During Botha's reign, the military became a multi-functional security organisation.[3]

In the middle eighties the distinction between the function of the security police and certain sections of the military, like the CCB and Military Intelligence, lost its clarity. The CCB and the security police were both harassing, intimidating and assassinating opponents of the apartheid system inside and outside South Africa. There had been some attempt to demarcate certain geographical areas to allow the security forces to operate at parallel levels. The military for example never interfered in the security police's operations and activities in Swaziland. That country remained the police's "playground". The military was mainly involved in Zimbabwe and Mozambique, while they both operated in Botswana and Lesotho.

The CCB became a sinister monster, the creation of securocrats obsessed with retaining power and blinded by the delusion of a communist plot to expel the white man from South Africa. But after years of dirty tricks against activists – skinned cats on doorsteps, slashed tyres and severed brake cables, poisoned clothes and newspapers, bizarre death threats and menacing grafitti – after years of death and destruction, the truth was emerging.

Abram "Slang" van Zyl, a tall and soft-spoken man with a wild quiff, decided in March 1990 to break ranks and blow the lid off the activities of the CCB. Van Zyl appears to have awoken from his delusions while on holiday and decided that working for the CCB was not for him. He told the Harms Commission that since President FW de Klerk had assumed office, organisations such as the CCB were not needed in the new South Africa.

Yet when he was recruited in 1988 for the internal region of the CCB by his former Brixton commander, Staal Burger, Van Zyl regarded it as a great honour to be invited to join an elite unit of the South African Defence Force. They were the first internal cell of the CCB in South Africa. He was introduced to the managing director of the CCB, Joe Verster, who told him that the unit would disrupt the enemies of the Republic of South Africa. His cell was part of the CCB's internal wing, known as Region Six.

"I was of the view that the security forces of the Republic of South Africa were involved in a clandestine war with the enemy. It became clear to me that the conventional war outside the borders of the country was not effective and that action in a clandestine manner was required against the enemy. We were advised that the disruption of the enemy could, for instance, be anything from the breaking of a window to the killing of a person and that this depended on the target's priority classification. The chairman would determine the priority classification for action allocated within these classes, namely the breaking of a window to the killing of a person . . . the managing director told us that we would be indemnified against prosecution for acts of violence that we committed during the execution of authorised projects," Van Zyl said in an affidavit to the Harms Commission.

Operative Calla Botha echoed Van Zyl's patriotism and said that he understood and believed there was a war raging inside South Africa and that it was about the survival of moderate South Africans. He saw it as a struggle involving South Africans and believed that the State President knew about the activities of the CCB.

Working for the CCB gave both Van Zyl and Botha the opportunity to combine patriotism with profit. During an interview Botha was told that he would earn a higher salary than his police salary. In May 1988 he was appointed a full-time member with a salary of R3 500 a month, a housing subsidy, a telephone subsidy, a pension scheme, a travel allowance and he was given R30 000 to buy a car.

Van Zyl told the commission that he had a soft spot for rightwingers: "Personally, I must say, I preferred leftists as targets rather than rightists." However, he conceded, the decision to murder people had never been easy. It had to be avoided at all costs, but unfortunately circumstances demanded that in order to survive such action had to be undertaken. The action of the CCB, he said, was "for me, for you, I'm talking about the whole of South Africa."

Van Zyl, according to his own account, did not actually commit murder, but he admitted involvement in conspiracy to murder and attempted murders. His testimony before the Harms Commission about the operations he conducted for the CCB revealed a mind full of a mixture of absurdity and misinformation, all taken in with unbelievable gullibility. It was difficult to believe that Van Zyl was once a rising star in the Brixton Murder and Robbery Unit.

In October 1988, acting under the codename "Andries Rossouw", Van Zyl recruited "unconscious" agent Edward "Peaches" Gordon, who had just been released after three months' imprisonment for assault. When Van Zyl left the CCB a year later, Peaches had taken well over R15 000 from the CCB and delivered nothing but lies and confidence tricks in return. The gangster soon discovered that secret agents were lucrative targets.

On one occasion, Van Zyl ordered Peaches to steal heart pills from Cape lawyer Dullah Omar – legal representative for African National Congress leader Nelson Mandela – so that they could be substituted with poison pills. The project was discussed and approved by Staal Burger and Joe Verster. At first the CCB had meant to shoot Omar with a silenced Makarov pistol. The gun and R15 000 for the assassins were handed over to Van Zyl, who passed them down the line to Peaches. When this plan was succeeded by the poison idea Peaches simply took two pills from his sister-in-law, who also had a heart condition, and handed them over to Van Zyl. This time, his handler returned bearing a small glass bottle filled with a white powder and instructed the convict to put the poison into Omar's food. "On the way from the airport, I opened the glass bottle and threw the powder out of the window," Peaches admitted. It later turned out that he admired Omar too much to kill him.

Asked to monitor the movements of the Congress of South African Trade Unions general secretary Jay Naidoo in Cape Town, Peaches reported that Naidoo was driving a Volkswagen kombi and produced the registration number. "This was false information. The registration number belonged to a stationary kombi on a vacant lot in Athlone, Cape Town," Peaches later admitted. Van Zyl said in his testimony that the CCB discovered that the microbus was used to transport ANC and UDF supporters to a terrorist trial in Cape Town. He drew up a report and presented it to the CCB's management who decided that the vehicle should be burnt to disrupt the "enemy". Answering a question on how the attendance of a court case could have constituted a threat to the country, Van Zyl answered: "It would have disrupted them . . . For the accused it would have meant that their loyal supporters could not be there to encourage them to stand strong during the trial."

Days later Peaches was instructed to see that the kombi was burnt. Burning vehicles was, along with breaking people's windows, a famous method for fighting the battle for a secure South Africa, according to Van Zyl. Peaches contacted an accomplice called Ismael with instructions not to burn out the kombi, but merely pretend he had. Ismael was paid R4 000 for his effort.

When Peaches was requested to monitor Archbishop Desmond Tutu and the Reverend Allan Boesak, he simply looked their addresses up in the telephone directory. This was one of the very few instances where he supplied correct information. Peaches claimed in his affidavit that Van Zyl told him to find out when Desmond Tutu or Allan Boesak were going overseas as the CCB wanted to kill them abroad. Another scheme that failed was when Peaches was brought from Cape Town to Johannesburg to assassinate journalist and End Conscription Campaign member Gavin Evans. In a plan reminiscent of the assassination of Griffiths Mxenge, Peaches was instructed to use a knife and to make the crime look like a robbery. The project was cancelled when they discovered that they had the wrong address for Evans.

During the year of his association with the CCB, Peaches seems to have done nothing of any value for the organisation. One of the criminal's cronies, according to Van Zyl's testimony, took part in the bombing of the Early Learning Centre in Athlone, but this was only when Van Zyl himself took charge of the operation after his superiors had expressed dissatisfaction with the way the project was progressing.

Peaches himself is blunt about the relationship between himself and Van Zyl: "I cheated them . . . They were fucking dumb," he declared in his sworn affidavit.

After his testimony, Peaches Gordon came face to face with the man he was told to kill when he met Dullah Omar in Cape Town. Peaches said: "It is so good to meet him at last. Since my youth I have admired him for what he has done for the community and for what he had stood for, and now I am honoured to finally meet him." Omar said: "My wish is for Edward to settle down and live a normal life. Because of his experiences, I am sure he can make a contribution to building this new South Africa." However, in January 1991 Cape Town the body of Peaches Gordon was found on a highway near Cape Town.[4]

In 1988, the CCB decided that a monkey foetus should be hung up at Archbishop Desmond Tutu's official residence in Cape Town. "I just received an instruction from the managing director who told me that the foetus of an ape would be made available to me and that he would accompany me to Cape Town to hang the ape there . . . It was a very sensitive case and there was no discussion about the reason for placing the foetus. We live in a military environment where you receive a command which you have to obey," Van Zyl said.

Van Zyl climbed over the wall of Tutu's residence and hung the foetus in a tree. The foetus was inside a bottle and it had to be hung in such a way that although not too conspicuous, it would eventually be found. The nails had first been treated by a witchdoctor to ensure the success of the operation. Joe Verster was asked in his evidence whether the CCB had a plan to intimidate Desmond Tutu. He said: "No, one or two jokes were made in regard to his superstitions."

For the rest, Van Zyl seemed quite happy to simply abandon projects, such as the planned assassination of Dullah Omar. The projects he was involved in, code-named Goldie, cost R97 742 during the course of 1989.

A Cape Town man claimed in an affidavit before the Harms Commission that he was used by Slang van Zyl (known to him as Theuns de Wet) to help blow up a hall in Athlone in Cape Town. Isak Hardien said that on various occasions Van Zyl paid him large sums of money.

On one occasion he was flown to Johannesburg and handed R3 000 as "spending money". In September 1989 Hardien gave Van Zyl information on meeting times of the United Democratic Front at the Early Learning Centre in Athlone, where Hardien coached a children's soccer team and supervised their studies.

Several weeks later he was asked to meet Van Zyl at DF Malan Airport, where he was handed two bags. "He told me I must take the heavy bag and place it in the Early Learning Centre. I asked him what it was and he said it was a bomb. I asked him to open the bag. He told me he was joking and that no one would get hurt or die."

Hardien took the bag to the Early Learning Centre and placed it on a table in a box. Later that evening he collected Van Zyl and another person and took them to the Centre, where people were holding a meeting. "After we had made sure that everyone had left the building . . . the person in the back pressed four numbers into a calculator and there was a loud bang. I asked De Wet [Slang van Zyl] what it was. He told me not to worry and that I should drop them at the airport . . . The following week, Van Zyl handed me R18 000 . . ."

Van Zyl said in his evidence that they had done everything in their power to prevent any injury or loss of life: "There was no intention to kill any people during the explosion . . . We waited until all the people were out. We waited until each and every car had left the parking area and until we were satisfied that there was nobody in the hall . . . There could have been people inside the building, but there was nobody in the hall in which the limpet mine was placed."

According to the evidence before the Harms Commission, the CCB consisted of nearly 300 members and operatives and was involved in more than 200 projects. Each of the CCB's ten regions was run by a regional manager and a co-ordinator, while in each region cells of between six and 29 operatives made up the basic task force. There were more than 40 CCB cells.

The CCB operated as a system of independent cells all managed by the various co-ordinators who reported to Joe Verster, the managing director. There is no doubt that the CCB was politically inspired. Members did not receive formal political instruction, but the organisation was obviously right wing. Although it professed to act against all enemies of the State, both to the left and the right of the political spectrum, no evidence of a single instance of action against the right wing has emerged.

The CCB worked on the so-called need-to-know principle, with operatives and controllers being given only enough information to carry out specific tasks. This meant that Joe Verster directed the flow of information and instructions to those above and below himself. Often CCB operatives had to carry out a task without an idea of its purpose. Individuals only knew those people with whom it was absolutely essential to co-operate, and normally communicated with one another under the guise of assumed names. Ideally, an operative's knowledge was restricted to the people and activities of his own cell.

The CCB operated in nine active regions: South Africa, Swaziland and Mozambique, Namibia, Botswana, Zimbabwe, Lesotho, Angola, Zambia and Europe. Each region had an area manager and a co-ordinator who reported to the managing director. There were also sections that handled logistics and administration. The South African or internal region, Region Six, was not activated until 1988. Joe Verster claimed that this region only gathered specialist information but Slang van Zyl and Calla Botha testified that they were told that the CCB's primary task was "maximum disruption of the enemy". The nucleus of Region Six was formed in June 1988 when Verster hired Staal Burger, Slang van Zyl, Chappie Maree and Calla Botha.

By means of the "Blue Plan" CCB members would lead ordinary civilian lives through businesses that would be set up to provide civilian cover for a cell member or his cell. This enabled the CCB to infiltrate industry, local government and the private sector at various levels.[5]

The CCB assigned a priority classification to its enemies, among them the SACP, ANC and other banned restricted and legal organisations and their members inside and outside South Africa. The "Red Plan" targeted victims and detailed action to be taken against them. According to the scenario, a person or a target would be identified as "an enemy of the state". A cell member would then be instructed to monitor the target, whereafter a project, which could entail elimination, intimidation or harassment, would be registered with the co-ordinator. The co-ordinator would then have the project authorised by the regional manager and the managing director. A CCB operative would then do a reconnaissance to study the target's movements in order to establish the most effective method of eliminating or harassing him. If the managing director felt this method was efficient, he would sign the proposal at what was called an in-house meeting. Adjustments could be made to the plan before it was approved. The budget would be considered and finance would be made available for the project. A co-ordinator would be requested to make available the necessary arms and ammunition, limpet mines, poison and other logistical support such as transport, false passports and registration numbers and accommodation. Finally, the project would be carried out and the target would be eliminated or harassed. To do this, the cell member could engage the assistance of so-called "unconscious members". These were essentially underworld criminals who would, for money, kill as instructed. The unconscious members were never told of the SADF connection and a false motive was usually supplied.

The structure of the CCB consisted of an inner circle and an outer circle. The inner circle, which formed the nucleus of a cell, was made up of full-time members of the CCB who were aware of the fact that they were employed and paid by the SADF. The "unconscious" members formed the outer circle. Many of them believed that they were working for a business cartel, the police or another unit of the security forces. The name CCB was never mentioned to them. The managing director was the head of all the regions and was in fact in charge of the CCB. The chairman was a member of the general staff of the SADF and also the head of Special Forces. When the managing director authorised a project, he would submit it to the chairman who would have a second in-house meeting with the managing director and the co-ordinator for final approval. It thus seemed that the chairman of the CCB was the man who made the final decisions. Although the CCB had civilian cover, all instructions were military orders and had to be obeyed.[6]

It was apparent from the evidence before the Harms Commission that the CCB faced major problems when it started to operate under civilian cover. It was removed from the information gathering fraternity of Military

Intelligence, National Intelligence and the Security Branch because it did not wish to divulge any facts about its existence or activities. There could no longer be frequent exchanges of information between the CCB and these security fraternities and the managing director became the only channel to the agencies. This meant that members were not able to verify information which, in many circumstances, had been obtained from unreliable sources.

Neither Van Zyl nor Botha was capable of giving any substantial information about intended victims or the reasons for their elimination. One of the reasons for the decision that Dullah Omar should be killed, for example, was that he defended "terrorists" and was a member of Lawyers for Human Rights. Van Zyl did not know why Gavin Evans should have been murdered, claiming to have inherited the project from someone else and never bothered to enquire. At no stage were any of the CCB members able to provide a comprehensive profile of any of their victims despite the fact that some operatives claimed the CCB was only a data gathering organisation.

The CCB operatives could not provide profiles of any of the leftwing organisations targeted for attention, or the reasons why they had become targets. They confined themselves to allegations that these organisations were ANC fronts, which clearly shows how inadequate the CCB's own data gathering processes were. The fact that organisations such as the End Conscription Campaign and the Five Freedoms Forum were targeted is an indication that the CCB was more concerned with the political agenda than with so-called security risks.

It appeared from the evidence before the Harms Commission that the CCB had a sad history of waste and unauthorised spending. Thousands of rands were spent on criminals for unsuccessful investigations of CCB targets. The CCB was claimed to be accountable, but there was no evidence whatsoever that any checks and balances had been applied to its internal activities. The CCB's books were audited by a retired SADF accountant who could merely perform a "mechanical audit". Brigadier Hein Pfeil testified that he had no access to CCB files during his audit and that there was no real way the expenditure on projects could be compared with the amount approved. All he had to do was to issue a certificate to the effect that funds had been appropriated in terms of policy and to say he had assured himself that proper control had been exercised to prevent possible fraud or other irregularities. Sensitive documents were destroyed with the authority of the chairman after they had been audited.

Opposition politicians slammed the funding of the CCB after revelations that it had snowballed into a free-for-all spending spree. The splurge got so out of hand that a top-level military inquiry was launched to investigate allegations of corruption. The annual budget of the CCB was R28 million, while agents of Region Six spent more than R14 million infiltrating African states and on local projects. Agents were paid in cash, sometimes in brown paper wrappers which escaped the Receiver of Revenue. The CCB paid its full-time agents incentive bonuses of up to R2 000 for a job well done. The

CCB budget could be increased at the stroke of a pen for unexpected expenses that could run into millions.

The Chief of the Defence Force, General Jannie Geldenhuys, said expenditure for the CCB was not allowed to run rampant. "The fact that there is no reference to the CCB in the printed budget is not unusual. Expenditure on the CCB was 0,28 per cent of the Defence budget. No country in the world provides information about covert operations in a public document like the budget."[7]

If Parliament had controlled the funds available to the SADF, it is unlikely that the CCB could ever have existed. Unfortunately, the Botha era left South Africa with a Defence Force which had become a law unto itself – a state within a state, owing accountability to nobody and wasting millions of rands. The starting point in the CCB's money chain was the Reserve Bank, which transferred a portion of the CCB's budget directly to CCB accounts overseas. The rest of the CCB budget was sent through normal channels to SADF headquarters in Pretoria from where it was transferred to CCB headquarters in amounts of between R500 000 and R1 million in cash. The money transfer was handled by CCB bookkeeper and convicted murderer Theuns Kruger. From CCB headquarters the money was distributed in cash to various regional bases where agents handled amounts as large as R100 000 at a time.

According to an article in *The Star* the gambling habits of a secret agent rebounded on his spymasters when he lost R480 000 of CCB funds on the roulette wheels of a Swazi casino. The agent, codenamed Louw van Wyk, had been given the cash by the CCB in 1986 to undertake clandestine operations in Swaziland. After the incident the CCB's accounting procedures were tightened. Applications for money, receipts and statements of expenditure had to be countersigned by senior CCB operatives. Before the changes, agents handled huge amounts of money purely on the basis of trust.[8]

The report of the Auditor-General on the CCB described a tangled web of unauthorised payments on internal projects, untraceable files, cash vouchers cut up and a running battle between his office and the SADF over access to files of the CCB. He eventually found that R12,5 million of CCB inland and ultra-sensitive projects between 1988 and 1990 had been unauthorised. He said that the Chief of the Defence Force had sent him a certificate signed by two CCB commanders saying that they had approved all projects verbally and that written approvals of budgets had been given in advance. He expressed great reservations about this verbal and "ex post facto" certification, but said that since he did not wish to question the integrity of the Chief of the Defence Force and his CCB commanders, he was prepared to withdraw his opinion that the money spent on ultra-sensitive projects had been unauthorised. ". . . I have a strong suspicion that virtually everything my audit team sought was/is, in fact, available in writing somewhere but that the archives have been selectively and purposely withheld or destroyed," the Auditor-General found.

The South African Defence Force's most secret man came in from the cold as the third week of the inquiry opened. A tall, heavily built man who looked like a modern-day Voortrekker entered Commission Room 3 before the start of proceedings. If it was indeed Joe Verster behind the long, false grey beard down to his chest and the equally wild wig, nobody really knew. Everybody agreed that he looked like an amateur theatrical character straight from the props department. Earlier, Louis Harms had ruled that under no circumstances was Verster to be identified either by being photographed or having his address revealed as his life could be endangered. But Verster was not the only CCB operative to be protected by the commission. Operative after operative appeared in comic disguise. In most cases, they were allowed to use pseudonyms.

Before the exposure and official disbanding of the CCB, top spy Joe Verster, 45, was one of the most powerful military leaders in South Africa. As managing director of the CCB, he had in practice the power to charge, try and recommend the elimination of political opponents of the state. Verster received a general's salary and his military status and power were far superior to the rank of colonel he held when he officially resigned from the Defence Force. A battle-hardened and decorated soldier, Verster started his path to military power as a parachute instructor at 1 Parachute Battalion in Bloemfontein before undergoing specialised training as a reconnaissance soldier. He also attended a warfare school in the Republic of China and received further training with the Rhodesian Selous Scouts. Before joining the CCB in 1985, he attended military courses in Beirut and Israel. Verster had been a founder commander of 5 Reconnaissance Regiment and gained extensive battle experience in Namibia and Angola. He is described in an article in the *Sunday Times* as "an honest and an upright man . . . A dedicated soldier who would follow orders down to the last comma."

When State President FW de Klerk ordered that the CCB be investigated Joe Verster put a CCB emergency plan into operation to make the project files disappear. Verster said he instructed his men to activate the emergency plan after it had become clear that their identities could be revealed and their safety jeopardised.

Verster, who was detained by Floris Mostert for a short period in March 1990, said he had been "contaminated " and branded as a terrorist. As a result, his own underlings did not trust him any more and refused to reveal to him where the project files were. "People got a fright and we don't know which way this thing is going. We don't know whether people's identities are going to be revealed and nobody wants to talk to me . . . There are people who from that time [October 1989] have not slept at their houses at all. At the moment we have cases where wives with little kids go to their husbands to introduce the kids to them and then go away again at night . . . If it was possible for me to get the files, I would have done so. But at this stage I cannot."

Harms, who was clearly upset by Verster's attitude towards his commission, responded: "... I don't believe you have an emergency plan. The second problem I have with your emergency plan is that if the emergency situation comes to an end you are not in a position to get the stuff back ... Do you want to tell me that the emergency plan has been so inadequately devised that it may be impossible to get your files back? ... Well, then it is a hopeless emergency plan ..."

One of the investigators of the commission, Colonel Johan Wright, said in an affidavit that he visited the headquarters of the CCB in February 1990 to confiscate the project files. The building was surrounded by high walls and there was a television camera at the gate. The investigators pushed a button to announce their presence and told the CCB members that they were from the Harms Commission and that they had a warrant to take the files into their possession. They refused to open, so Wright jumped over the eight-foot wall and knocked at the door. When the personnel opened after five minutes Wright entered the building and told everybody to stay where they were. Two women locked themselves in an office. Wright confiscated a suitcase full of financial statements, but could not find the key to the safe. After two hours, a CCB member brought the key and opened the safe, which was empty. By then the emergency plan had already been implemented.

Without the project files of the CCB, there were no hard facts to link the organisation to any acts besides those that were admitted by Slang van Zyl. While a number of CCB projects were uncovered, it was clear that the commission had only seen the tip of the iceberg.The police were at least partly responsible for the lack of evidence. It emerged during cross-examination of Floris Mostert that they had known about the existence of the CCB as early as December 1989 – two months before the activation of the emergency plan – but no attempt had been made until 28 February to raid the CCB headquarters to confiscate documentation which could have a bearing on the Webster killing.

Counsel for the Independent Board of Inquiry into Informal Repression, Paul Pretorius, labelled the delay "inexplicable" and said the CCB must have been alerted to the suspicions by then because at least three of its members had been detained.Either Mostert or his superior officers in the police were reluctant to act against the CCB, Pretorius said.

Senior counsel for the Defence Force, Willem Burger, argued that the public had no real right to know about the activities of organisations such as the CCB. He said the commission had already had co-operation from all parties involved and it was not necessary for other documents to be made available. He said discretion had to be taken into consideration.

Harms said he had personally seen the Minister of Defence and the Chief of the SADF regarding the missing documents. At one stage, the judge threatened to order a court martial if orders were not obeyed. "The commission has, since its inception, tried to obtain documentation through subpoenas, threats of dire consequences and consultation . . . Unless we call witnesses one by one, we will not be able to ascertain where those documents may be . . . What should I do, have them shot? . . . We have been hampered by delay, delay, delay. My patience is wearing thin." The only conclusion that could be drawn from the CCB's failure to produce its project files was that its members did not want to testify about the organisation's many internal projects. The CCB was in fact refusing to obey a command from the State President and the Minister of Defence to co-operate with the commission.

Witness after witness told Harms that they had had access to CCB files until mid-January 1990, when they had disappeared. The organisation's administrative manager, Braam Cilliers – a codename – was told outright by Harms that he lied when he said that he did not know where the files were. "I am not that dense," Harms exploded. "If Joe Verster did not know where the documents were, you had to know . . . It was an absolute lie. You are speaking absolute [sentence incomplete] . . . You are trying to mislead the commission." In the end the search for the documents and the cross-examination of witnesses were of no avail. The documents were never produced and the one man who could order his officers to tell the full truth and produce the missing documents, Magnus Malan, was never subpoenaed to testify what he had done to find them.

It remains one of the puzzles of the commission that CCB members were allowed to get away with an alleged activation of an emergency plan. The question that begs an answer is why it was so difficult to seize these files and why the commission did not take steps to force CCB men to hand them over. The Independent Board of Inquiry into Informal Repression said the CCB had embarked on a cover-up with regard to giving evidence to the commission,in all probability with the blessing of Magnus Malan. There was no evidence that Malan had attempted to establish the whereabouts of the documents.

Louis Harms said in April 1990 that Magnus Malan had told him that he was willing to give evidence before the commission. Tim McNally indicated that Malan would testify after certain CCB members had done so. As the minister in charge of the SADF, Malan is clearly politically responsible for the CCB's actions. The human rights lawyers wanted to investigate his personal knowledge of the CCB and its activities because there was evidence before the commission that ministerial approval was required before a covert organisation such as the CCB could be established.

Malan was one of a host of witnesses whom the lawyers believed could have shed light on the murders that were never called to testify. He escaped the whole scandal, at least as far as the Harms Commission was concerned, unscathed. Besides Harms's refusal to call Malan, the human rights lawyers were refused an opportunity to cross-examine three senior generals who testified before the commission.

With the exception of Slang van Zyl, the testimony of CCB members revealed very little. It took one of three directions: a flat denial of CCB involvement in any atrocity, the right to silence to avoid self-incrimination and a description in the broadest of generalities. Key witnesses, amongst them Eddie Webb and Joe Verster, simply refused to answer questions on the basis of self-incrimination. Webb said he had only become aware of the CCB's actions inside South Africa eight months after his appointment as head of Special Forces and chairman of the CCB. He denied responsibility for their internal actions and refused to answer two questions because he might have incriminated himself.

Eddie Webb has been described as "a man of integrity who had inherited a can of worms for which he now must take responsibility". Like Verster, Webb was trained at 1 Parachute Battalion in Bloemfontein. In the seventies he served as officer commanding the Caprivi Strip in northern Namibia, Chief of Staff Operations in Windhoek and officer commanding 7 SA Infantry Battalion at Bourke's Luck in the Eastern Transvaal. He was the commander of the Army Battle School in Lohatla in the northern Cape before being appointed Commander of Special Forces. He was one of a small, elite group of South African soldiers who underwent the rigorous Special Service training of the Rhodesian Army.[10]

Joe Verster admitted that a CCB member could have murdered David Webster but denied that the CCB had been officially responsible for the murder. Webster had never been a CCB project and the organisation did not have a file on him. He denied that the CCB had had any plans to murder Gavin Evans or Dullah Omar and said they were merely monitored. He declined to answer questions about the monkey foetus or the bomb explosion at the Early Learning Centre as it might have incriminated him. He also stated that CCB members viewed current political reforms with a great deal of suspicion, and hinted that the CCB's political agenda differed from that of the government. He said the security of the CCB was threatened by the unbanning of the ANC and the changes in the political situation.

Staal Burger refused to answer questions about surveillance work and the monkey foetus, also on the grounds that he might incriminate himself. He denied knowledge of the whereabouts of vital project files missing from CCB headquarters and said that he had last seen them in a Johannesburg hotel room when he had given the files to someone codenamed Christo Brits for safekeeping.

The appearance of Burger on the witness stand followed the lapse of a warrant for his arrest for the murder of Anton Lubowski issued by the Namibian police. On 21 March Namibia attained its independence from South Africa, and a week later, Burger declared his willingness to co-operate with the commission. Former CCB operative Willie van Deventer refused no less than nine times to answer questions in his testimony. He had claimed in an interview with *Vrye Weekblad* that he had information about the killing of

Mamelodi doctor Fabian Ribeiro and his wife Florence, but then refused to give information to the commission.

In none of these cases was the commission able to force an answer, threaten a witness with jail or offer indemnity to get to the truth. Although both FW de Klerk and Magnus Malan had promised to get to the bottom of the death squad saga, the contemptuous attitude of CCB members made a mockery of their undertaking.

Disappointed families of alleged victims were calling the commission toothless and asking why important figures in the CCB were allowed to appear in ludicrous disguises while the names and personal details of victims and targets were available to all. "Quite frankly," said the national director for Lawyers for Human Rights, Brian Currin, "after months of tiring and expensive commission work, we know very little more. Except we now know that security forces have been involved in political assassinations, something that was only suspected before." Currin expressed fear that after the failure of the Harms Commission, the CCB could roam the country with impunity and become a major rightwing threat, making it difficult for ANC exiles to return to the country.

Of the long list of political murders submitted to the commission, mention had been made of only three. As the commission wound up its hearings on the CCB, South Africa had learnt the real names of less than ten of its operatives. The three months of hearing evidence had raised more questions than answers although it appeared that 11 organisations, of which four were banned, and 25 individuals living in South Africa were considered by the CCB as enemies of the state. Clear evidence emerged that five activists were projects for elimination.

Criminal charges including treason, sabotage and murder should be brought against the men behind the CCB. Among those who could be prosecuted were Magnus Malan and senior officers in the SADF, the David Webster Trust submitted in argument to the Harms Commission. The Trust said that Malan used the military to commit acts of aggression against law-abiding, peaceful citizens under the guise of military necessity. Instead of protecting the integrity of South Africa and guarding all its people, the SADF was turned into an instrument of political harassment. A situation was created which was fraught with the potential of escalating into violence and death.

The David Webster Trust were forced to withdraw an accusation against Louis Harms of creating the impression of bias in his conduct of the inquiry. "An allegation that the impression has been created that a judge . . . is biased is an extremely painful subject to broach, but those whom we represent are of the view that the Honourable Commissioner has created the impression of favouring the organs of State."

The evidence at the Harms Commission shed very little light on the murder of David Webster. Slang van Zyl testified that the manner of

Webster's assassination bore all the hallmarks of a CCB killing and that the anthropologist was the type of person who could have been monitored by the CCB and against whom action could have been taken as a result of his leftwing activities.

In disguise and giving evidence under the codename of Christo Brits, the co-ordinator of Region Six testified that ammunition was issued to CCB agents three days before the murder of David Webster. In his diary, confiscated by the commission, the pages for 31 August and 1 May were missing. The first missing diary page is the date on which the Early Learning Centre in Cape Town was bombed, while the second is the date on which David Webster was murdered. The page for 12 September – the date on which Anton Lubowski was gunned down – was also missing. Legal counsel for Lubowski and Webster called the missing pages "conspicuously coincidental".

During the raid on the CCB offices outside Pretoria a police officer assisting the commission took possession of a file marked "Region 6 and 9" that contained more than a hundred names. Under the heading "Five Freedoms Forum" the name of David Webster appeared as a member of the executive committee. His home and office telephone numbers were recorded next to his name. A sinister diagonal arrow was scratched next to his name with the letters DREK next to the arrow. Next to another name appeared the name DEREK. Derrick was a codename for Chappie Maree, implicated by both the Namibian and South African Police in the assassination of Anton Lubowski. When "Christo Brits" was asked about the arrow, he said the list had been obtained from another CCB member who could not be traced to get a statement.

It thus seemed that Maree, who never testified before the Commission, had been assigned to monitor David Webster. It is not known what efforts the commission made to trace Maree, who disappeared after the Namibian warrant for his arrest, to obtain an explanation of the ominous appearance of his codename next to David Webster's name.

In a dramatic turn-around from his affidavit before the Supreme Court in February, Floris Mostert said in his evidence before the commission that he was reasonably certain that the three CCB members held by the police had not been involved in the killing of Webster. He also admitted that identikits issued shortly after the death of Webster had proved inaccurate. Although the brigadier still believed that the CCB killed Anton Lubowski, it transpired that his suspicion that the CCB was involved in Webster's murder was based on a report that it was "whispered in the corridors of the CCB".

Evidence before the Hiemstra Commission of Inquiry into the Johannesburg City Council spy ring revealed that council agents with close ties with Military Intelligence had spied on David Webster. Webster's name was recorded in a number of council documents marked "top secret" which detailed his activities in the Five Freedoms Forum. The council also spied on Gavin Evans, the Johannesburg jounalist who was an assassination target of the CCB. Photocopies of the reports were sent to Military Intelligence and the police but the City Council file on Webster had mysteriously disappeared from the security department's records by the time the commission wanted to see it. Hiemstra found in his report that the spy ring had spied on more than 100 individuals and illegally infiltrated at least 20 anti-apartheid organisations over a period of four years.[12]

Although the killing of David Webster had all the hallmarks of a CCB killing, there was a lack of evidence to link the murder to one of Staal Burger's men. In the case of Anton Lubowski, however, the killer's tracks clearly pointed to the CCB, although Louis Harms did not allow any evidence to be led on his death.

Slang van Zyl admitted in his evidence that the CCB considered Swapo a hostile organisation, that he had to monitor the human rights lawyer less than three weeks before his death and that Staal Burger and Chappie Maree discussed the Lubowski project in a Johannesburg hotel twelve days before he was murdered.

Van Zyl started monitoring Lubowski on 25 August. "I was monitoring Mr Lubowski and the people he contacted, but I was not advised why he was being monitored," he said, adding that he was not aware that Lubowski was an agent of Military Intelligence. He revealed that at a CCB meeting at the Rosebank Hotel in Johannesburg on 1 September, the project on Lubowksi was discussed. "... there was talk about co-ordinator Chappie Maree; I believe it was over Anton Lubowski," Van Zyl testified, but said he and operative Calla Botha had been asked to leave the meeting as they were not directly involved.

It was further established that Staal Burger arrived in Windhoek on 12 September in a seat booked in the name of "Gagiano". Burger left Windhoek again on 13 September, the day after the murder. Van Zyl admitted that he knew that Burger and operative Chappie Maree had been in Windhoek around the time that Lubowski was killed.

Louis Harms stopped the advocates for the Lubowski family dead in their tracks every time they tried to obtain more information about the killing. Eberhard Bertelsmann, senior counsel for the family, presented argument to Harms about why he should hear the evidence: "From the evidence which has been led so far by the present witness it has appeared that certain Swapo members in the Republic of South Africa were kept under surveillance by the CCB, including Mr Lubowski. It is also quite clear from the evidence given by Mr Van Zyl that murder was one of the weapons employed by the CCB in the fight against the so-called enemies ... there exists at least the possibility if not a likelihood, that the CCB was involved directly or indirectly in the planning, preparation and execution of Mr Lubowski's murder."

Bertelsmann argued that the conspiracy against Lubowski and other acts of violence had been initiated in South Africa. Aiding and abetting such a conspiracy could be heard in South African courts. A co-conspirator who remained in South Africa after having provided the eventual killer with logistical or practical assistance would commit the crime of murder on his common purpose within South Africa if he was within the borders of the Republic when the crime he had promoted was committed. Therefore a conspiracy to commit murder or another crime of violence must fall within the terms of reference of the commission.

The judge said he had fully considered the question."If I can assist, I shall assist. If the commission stumbles upon evidence, it shall provide that evidence to the relevant authorities. I'm afraid I cannot change my decision."

It thus remained that the only evidence that could be heard about the death of Anton Lubowski was whether he was a paid agent of the state. The Chief of Staff Intelligence of the SADF, General Rudolf "Witkop" Badenhorst, persuaded Harms that the hearing about whether Lubowski was a spy could jeopardise the lives of certain people and the security of the state. The judge ordered an *in camera* hearing. The legal team for the Lubowski family protested in vain. They could not be present, the judge ruled. The protection of lives weighed heavier than other interests, he said. The Defence Force issued a decree under Section 118 of the Defence Act that prevented Lubowski's legal team from investigating his bank account.

With only the judge and one official of the commission present, the SADF presented evidence supporting Malan's claim. On 22 March Harms issued a statement that Lubowski was a paid agent and that he had delivered certain "counter-performances". The judge found that two cheques, one for R40 000 and another for R20 000, were paid into the Paradiso Trust bank account in Cape Town in June 1989. Lubowski had sole signing powers on the account. A third payment of R40 000 was paid through an intermediary into Lubowski's personal bank account during the same time. All the payments were made through this intermediary, who in turn received three cheques from the South African Defence Force. According to original documents, the payments were intended as an advance for an agent whose bank account number corresponded with that of Paradiso Trust. Other original deposit slips and microfiches displaying deposits were handed to the commission.

Harms was accused of convicting and sentencing Lubowski on one-sided and untested evidence as his lawyers were denied the right to cross-examine. Brian Currin said in a statement: "Surely the commission should accept nothing it hears or receives from SADF Special Forces or Military Intelligence on face value. Agents are taught to lie, deceive and forge. Often the success of their work and their very lives depend on those vices."[13]

In April, the Lubowski family withdrew from the Harms Commission. Bertelsmann explained: "Their decision to do so is motivated . . . by the fact that the Commission's present terms of reference do not include an inquiry into the murder of Mr Anton Lubowski. Regarding the allegation that Mr Lubowski was a paid agent of the South African Defence Force, the evidence presented to the commission must remain untested. As this impedes our clients' ability to clear Anton Lubowski's name, they have decided to withdraw from further participation in the Commission. Nothing is intended as a slight upon you or the Commission."

In his final report to the State President, Harms explained that the fact that Lubowski was paid by Military Intelligence was undeniable. "Cross-examination would have made no difference," he said. He was recruited, Harms said, in the first half of 1989 while "desperately seeking funds to keep his overdrawn bank account below the limit allowed by the bank". The recruitment had taken place because Lubowski had access to Swapo "and because he was particularly vulnerable through having lived far above his income."

Harms said Lubowksi was so desperate for money that in June 1989 Military Intelligence paid him R100 000 in advance, contrary to normal procedure. The judge said he could not reveal the counter-performance Lubowski delivered, but that his death was a serious setback for Military Intelligence.

Harms said the fact that Lubowski was a paid agent did not mean that the CCB had not been responsible for his death. The CCB operated independently from Military Intelligence and had no direct access to its operations or intelligence, he concluded. "Without suggesting that the CCB was responsible, the facts do not show that the CCB was not responsible for the act."

The Lubowski family reacted with anger and bitterness to Harms's findings. "We reject with repugnance the Commission's finding that Anton received R100 000 as an agent of Military Intelligence. The Commission's decision to hear evidence *in camera* resulted in a secret, one-sided character assassination of Anton. On the other hand, the security establishment, who we have no doubt is responsible for his murder, was protected."[14]

By all accounts and according to evidence, Lubowski did receive three payments from Military Intelligence. We know an amount of R100 000 was paid into his bank accounts and that the payments were authorised by the SADF. But does this necessarily mean that Lubowski was a spy and that he revealed sensitive information about Swapo to his new masters at Military Intelligence? The money was paid through an intermediary into the various accounts. That intermediary was a civilian company called Global Investments, a front for Military Intelligence.

Like the CCB, Military Intelligence recruited agents by using innocent-looking middlemen and civilian front companies to give the appearance of ordinary business transactions. The middleman pays the person for work being done, the latter not knowing that he is indeed a "spy". In fact, intelligence establishments all over the world operate according to this principle. Those who moved in the same circles as Lubowski feel that his willingness to talk to anybody, as well as the fact that he was politically naive, could have made him an unwitting source of information for agents. People close to him said he was a generous and open person who would speak to even bitter political enemies to try and convince them of his convictions. This very attitude could have made it easy for Lubowski to be "set up" by a genuine spy who could get close enough to him to extract sensitive information.

There are many aspects of Lubowski's private and public life that need closer scrutiny to establish the truth. According to some of his friends, his life was an open book; others would say there were some aspects shrouded in a veil of secrecy. For example: some weeks before his assassination Anton Lubowski made a secret trip to Europe to arrange a Namibian residence permit for Sicilian banker Vito Roberto Palazzolo, who was then in a Swiss prison cell.

In April 1991 I met a former Military Intelligence agent who operated in Namibia in 1989 doing propaganda work for the SADF. Major Nico Basson, who was a permanent force officer before he resigned to become an undercover agent, met Lubowski frequently during 1989 on his own initiative in attempts to persuade the Swapo leader to change his political allegiance and join the more moderate Democratic Turnhalle Alliance (DTA). Basson offered Lubowski an amount of R250 000 to join the DTA, but Lubowski refused the offer and said that he could never leave or betray Swapo. There were certain aspects of Swapo with which he was dissatisfied – among others the scandal surrounding the torturing of detainees – but according to Basson never to the extent that he would have considered working for Military Intelligence.

However, Lubowski might have been vulnerable at another level. Basson gave me a Namibian security police document drawn up by an agent who had had close ties with Lubowski and monitored the Swapo leader. The document reads: "Although Lubowski had personal financial problems, he said that rumours that he might have taken Swapo funds for his personal use were devoid of any truth. Lubowski said he did get financial support from some friends who helped him out of his financial predicament . . . On Thursday, 17 August 1989 Lubowski travelled from Johannesburg to Frankfurt in West Germany, from where he went to Lugano in Switzerland. He probably stayed in Lugano on 21 and 22 August. Lubowski went to Lugano after an attorney phoned him and asked him to come to the city to advise/defend/testify for a drug dealer who was under arrest. From Lugano Lubowski went to Zurich, Brussels, Frankfurt and back to Johannesburg. It is unknown whether any fee was paid to Lubowski and if so, where it was paid. Lubowski did not have an account abroad, but had friends in Luxembourg who could have helped him with the handling of funds."

Basson received this information shortly before Lubowski was killed. Its significance was pieced together by my former colleague Martin Welz who revealed that Lubowski visited Lugano to arrange a Namibian residence permit for Palazzolo. As a result of Lubowski's efforts, instead of being deported to Italy, Palazzolo came to southern Africa when his Swiss prison term ended. A Cape Town attorney confirmed that he knew that Lubowski had gone to Switzerland to see Palazzolo; he himself had gone to Windhoek

164

to consult Lubowski about the Italian's property interests in Namibia in June 1989, accompanied by Palazzolo's son, Christian.[15]

According to Welz, Lubowski himself told a close friend and associate that he was undertaking the mysterious mission to see Palazzolo in jail in Switzerland in order to earn a quick but "enormous" fee. No trace has been found of the fee Palazzolo is supposed to have paid Lubowski. The only known unusual payment that Lubowski received around this time is the R100 000 that was mysteriously paid into his bank account by Global Capital Investments. What is significant is that Palazzolo also used a National Party Member of Parliament, Peet de Pontes, to arrange permanent residence for him in South Africa. For the same service as that rendered by Lubowski in Namibia, De Pontes received R130 000.

The mystery surrounding the three payments to Lubowski seems to be much more complex than Louis Harms – who only heard the SADF behind closed doors – found. There is no proof that Lubowski was in such a financial predicament that he could have been persuaded to reveal sensitive information about Swapo to Military Intelligence. From the untested evidence before Harms, it appears that the money was paid in advance in order to compromise Lubowski. Harms said Lubowski lived way above his monthly income and had a huge overdraft. It thus seems that when the money was paid into the Paradiso account in June, he had not yet done any work for Military Intelligence. What Harms ignored was that the two amounts paid into the Paradiso account were never paid over into Lubowski's personal bank account. If he had such financial difficulties and such a huge overdraft, why did he not use the money? This aspect, and others like the so-called "counter-performances", was never fully explored at the commission. Justice was not seen to be done.

Because of Namibian independence on 21 March 1990, the murder trial of Donald Acheson never got under way. The Namibian government formally requested his extradition together with the CCB men, but the South African Department of Justice declined to help, saying that the Namibian authorities had not followed the correct procedures. They also claimed that there was not enough evidence against Burger and Maree. On 7 May, after only one brief appearance in court, Acheson was released after eight months of incarceration in a Namibian jail. Unknown sources paid his legal costs, amounting to R40 000.

Why did Lubowski have to die? His murder has produced more riddles than answers. He would certainly have constituted a prime target for a death squad. He was a white activist, prominently involved in an organisation that the CCB admitted they regarded as an enemy, he defended accused involved in security trials and he was a human rights lawyer. It only appeared later that Lubowski might have been the victim of a CCB campaign to disrupt the independent elections in Namibia before the former colony gained full statehood in March 1990. A prominent Swapo leader had to die to sow dissent in the organisation. That target might have been Anton Lubowski.

Although the search for Lubowski's killers has run into a cul-de-sac, valuable information has been obtained. All hopes that the three CCB members accused of his death will stand trial in Windhoek have been dashed. However, the SADF is suspected of either the deliberate murder of an opponent or the assassination of one of its own agents.

Although the Harms Commission left one with a sense of deep dissatisfaction and frustration because of its failure to unearth the death squad secrets, the commission did achieve one very significant breakthrough: it solved the assassination of Dr Fabian Ribeiro and his wife Florence, who were gunned down in the courtyard of their Mamelodi home on 1 December 1986.

Fabian Ribeiro, who was affectionately referred to in Mamelodi as the "people's doctor", became a security force target in the sixties when security policemen started visiting his home and surgery. After the Soweto riots of 1976, the couple were taken to Security Branch headquarters on a number of occasions and interrogated. Ribeiro and his son, Chris, were often accused by the police of assisting youngsters to leave South Africa to receive military training and join the armed struggle. It came as no surprise when Ribeiro was detained in 1979 in terms of the security laws. He used to smuggle notes out of prison, written on toilet paper, in which he gave details about torture and interrogation. He was detained until he was charged in 1980 with terrorism, but the state's case against Ribeiro collapsed and he was acquitted.[16]

After the trial Ribeiro took a firm decision to get out of the public eye but as a medical practitioner he could not avoid being involved at grassroots level as South Africa entered the period of open resistance that erupted in civil war and gave rise to the State of Emergency in 1986. Ribeiro examined youths injured or assaulted by the police, took photographs, prepared medical reports and eventually testified as an expert witness in court.

The Ribeiros' house in Mamelodi was extensively damaged in 1986 when petrol bombs were thrown through the windows during the early hours of the morning. When the Ribeiros ran outside, members of the SADF were already on the scene, standing on the pavement watching the fire. Until their assassination nine months later, they received numerous anonymous death threats and feared for their lives. Their lawyer at that time, Brian Currin, said that Ribeiro phoned him on at least two occasions late at night to tell him that plainclothes members of the security forces were with him in his surgery, abusing and threatening him.

On 1 December 1986, the couple was shot dead by two men wearing balaclavas. There was confusion at first as to whether the assailants were white or black. Chris Ribeiro, who was shot at twice, grappled with the men as they got into their car and noticed that the driver's hand was white. Other witnesses said one of the men spoke Afrikaans. The assailants were followed to the outskirts of Mamelodi where they swapped their car for a white Land Rover. The two vehicles then drove off in the direction of Pretoria. After confusion over the correct registration number of the vehicles was resolved, a former member of the Rhodesian Selous Scouts, Noel Robey, was traced as the owner of the Land Rover and arrested for the murders.[17]

Hopes were raised that a political murder of an anti-apartheid activist would at last be solved, but apart from linking Robey to the murder through the registration number, there was no other evidence against him. He had an alibi that he was having a barbeque with friends and he was cleared of all allegations against him. The police alleged during the examination that the Ribeiro couple might have died at the hands of black political opponents. Riot policeman Brigadier Daantjie van Wyk said as far as he knew, Fabian Ribeiro supported the UDF, which was at the time fiercely opposed by Azapo.

Another mystery in the circumstances surrounding the murders was an incident on the day of the couple's funeral, when a key witness to the murders, Joseph Mampuru, went to investigate sounds coming from the deserted Ribeiro home and encountered two men wearing balaclavas. Mampuru was shot in the stomach and had to be hospitalised. It transpired later that one of the men, Graham William Cook, was a member of the Defence Force. Charged with attempted murder, he told a Pretoria magistrate that he and another soldier had been monitoring the dead couple's home when an "aggressive mob of blacks" approached them and shouted: "Chase them. Get the bastards. Get them. Kill them." The magistrate found that Cook shot in self-defence and acquitted him.[18]

Speculation was rife in Mamelodi in the days following the shooting of Mampuru that the men had come to look for a piece of key evidence left behind by the killers. However, under the Emergency Regulations the police refused permission to newspapers to publish any version of events at the Ribeiro home but its own. After that, police failed to come up with any new leads and the Ribeiro case was shrouded in mystery until one day in April 1990, when a former member of the CCB came forward and claimed that he had information on the brutal slaying of the Mamelodi couple.

I met Tony Adams in a London pub where he told me that he had been a CCB operative for four years until he resigned from the organisation in 1987. He claimed that he had been involved in various operations inside and outside South Africa and that he had information about two murders that the CCB committed inside South Africa and various assassinations outside the country. He claimed he was a former corporal in a reconnaissance unit and that he joined an organisation codenamed Barnacle in 1983. He said he left the CCB four years later after a quarrel with Joe Verster.

Adams was in a desperate financial predicament: his housing business in Bophuthatswana was on the verge of bankruptcy, he feared for his life and he needed money to make a new beginning elsewhere. He said his jacket with all his money had been stolen in the British capital. He asked me whether I could arrange a meeting with the ANC as he had invaluable information about the training of Inkatha soldiers by the Defence Force. He said his information would implicate Inkatha leader Gatsha Buthelezi in atrocities committed in Natal and was so important that it might swing the negotiations between the government and the ANC. He wanted R250 000 for his information.

After some more meetings, he admitted that his name was Willie van Deventer and not Tony Adams. He said he had not been involved in the murder of the Ribeiro couple, but was present when agents of the CCB planned the assassination. He said he had left a tape recording with all the information with an attorney in Pretoria and that he was in possession of documents that would prove his allegations.

Van Deventer had two meetings with a senior representative of the ANC in London and also tried to sell his story to various British newspapers and television networks. When he failed, he had to return to South Africa and after *Vrye Weekblad* had published his allegations, he was subpoenaed to testify before the Harms Commission.

Despite having pledged his co-operation, Van Deventer eventually retreated behind a curtain of secrecy and refused nine times to answer questions on the grounds that he could incriminate himself. He also claimed to have lost his memory between the time he made the claims in London and giving testimony before the commission.

The Harms Commission launched its own investigation into the Ribeiro murders and evidence was led in August 1990, after the legal teams had already presented argument to the judge. It turned out that the CCB was deeply implicated. According to the evidence before the commission, Noel Robey was a member of the CCB. It was also established that the Defence Force had paid R33 700 towards legal costs after his arrest in 1987 and that there had been an attempt by Robey to conceal his identity at the identification parade after the Ribeiro murder. He shaved off his beard, resulting in the witnesses pointing out two men with beards.

Noel Robey was not available for questioning by the commission, having suddenly left South Africa when its investigators started making enquiries. An amount of R30 000 in cash was deposited into his bank account before he left the country.

The former chairman of the CCB, General Joep Joubert, admitted that Robey was a full-time member of the CCB and operated in Region Four under the pseudonym of Lionel Kirby. Joubert said the CCB had decided to pay his legal costs to protect him as a member of the Defence Force. The legal costs were concealed in a file used for furniture transactions and Joubert admitted that he had no authorisation to pay for them. According to SADF regulations, the state can only pay for an employee's legal defence if the offence was committed in the line of duty. Louis Harms remarked that it seemed as though Robey's legal fees were paid because he acted in his official capacity. Joubert admitted that Fabian Ribeiro was considered to be a "leftist radical" and was probably monitored, but denied that the CCB was in any way involved in the murder.

There was a further hitch when the commission was informed that the police murder dossiers had mysteriously been stolen. A senior detective, Colonel Karel "Suiker" (Sugar) Brits said in an affidavit that his car, with three attaché cases full of documents in the boot, had been stolen. Brits had tried to trace two black members of the CCB who might have had further information about the murder, but the one was dead and the other was in Botswana.

In its final report the Harms Commission found that Noel Robey and the CCB were probably involved in the murders of Fabian and Florence Ribeiro. The judge further said that Noel Robey might have been involved "in an official capacity" along with two black operatives, and that top officials of the covert organisation authorised the payment of Robey's legal expenses.

CHAPTER TEN

Blunders, failures and wrong targets

MAPUTO, 7 April 1988. It was a warm, sunny morning in the Mozambican capital as Albie Sachs, the ANC lawyer, writer and academic, made his way to the Costa Do Sol beach for a run.[1]

It was a public holiday – Women's Day – and there were many people strolling the streets of the capital as a cheerful Sachs, dressed in bathing trunks, walked out of his Polana apartment towards his red Honda car. He had packed a frosty beer for after his run.

Earlier that morning, a bomber had attached a five-litre tin, filled with plastic explosives and connected to a tilt switch, underneath the Honda. The bomb, powerful enough to blow up a small house, was supposed to detonate as soon as somebody started the car and drove away. But as Sachs opened the door, the Avenida Julio Vinti Quatro was engulfed in an inferno. For many seconds after the blast, the only sound audible was that of burning metal. Then people started screaming. All that remained of the car was a heap of crumpled metal with two beach chairs protruding from the back.

For Sachs, everything went abruptly dark. He said he felt arms coming from behind him, pulling at him under the shoulders. That bright sunny day in Maputo, Albie Sachs refused to die. His book, *The Soft Vengeance of a Freedom Fighter*,[2] is the testimony of a survivor.

"Oh shit ... I am feeling strange and cannot see anything. I must have banged my head. The darkness is not clearing, this is something serious, a terrible thing is happening to me, I am swirling, I cannot steady myself as I wait for consciousness to return and light to return ... I am being kidnapped, they have come from Pretoria to drag me over the border and interrogate me and lock me up. This is the moment we have all be waiting for, the few ANC members still working in Mozambique.

"I feel a sudden surge of elation and strength as I struggle, making an immense muscular effort to pull myself free. I might be an intellectual but at this critical moment without time to plan or think I am fighting bravely and with the courage of the youth of Soweto even though the only physical violence I have personally known in my life was as a schoolboy being tackled carrying a rugby ball . . . But I am unable to struggle any more, I just have to go along and accept what happens, my will has gone."

As doctors started fighting for Sachs's life in the Maputo Central Hospital, the bomber made a phone call to Pretoria to tell his handler that the ANC academic had been blown up. The fact that Sachs did not die, but was in a critical condition in hospital, did not matter, the bomber told his handler. There was panic and chaos in the streets of Maputo as people realised that South Africa had struck yet again. According to the first reports, Sachs would probably not survive the blast.

But Sachs did not die. Apart from his mutilated right arm, he had four broken ribs, a fractured right heel and a severed nerve in his left leg, a lacerated liver, lots of shrapnel wounds and ruptured eardrums.

"I am wrapped in complete darkness and tranquillity," he described his ordeal. "If I am dead, I am not aware of it. If I am alive, I am not aware of it, I have no awareness at all, not of myself, not of my surroundings, not of anyone or anything."

Sachs remembered a friend, surgeon Ivo Garrido, speaking to him: "Albie . . . you are in the Maputo Central Hospital. Your arm is a lamentable . . . we are going to operate and you must face the future with courage." The operation lasted seven hours as a team of Soviet doctors took out scores of pieces of shrapnel from all over his body and head. He described the discovery that his right arm was missing: "Watch . . . my hand creeps over my shoulder and slides down my upper arm, and suddenly there is nothing there . . . so I have lost an arm . . . that's all, they tried to kill me, to extinguish me completely, but I have only lost an arm. I came close to death and survived."

For this ANC stalwart, today a law professor at the University of the Witwatersrand in Johannesburg, recounting what happened is one way to heal his own scars and the psychological damage that has been inflicted on generations of South Africans by the system of apartheid. Sachs remains adamant that although an active supporter of the ANC, he was never involved in military work for Umkhonto we Sizwe. What he will never forget, is that a Mozambican passer-by was killed and a young boy injured.

The South African government dismissed allegations that its agents were responsible for the attack on Sachs. Foreign Affairs Minister Pik Botha suggested that the bomb attack in Maputo was the result of a power struggle within the ANC. Botha was quoted as saying: "The South African Government cannot accept responsibility for the conflict in Mozambique and definitely not for the acts of violence flowing from it."[3]

There are two things that Pieter Botes loves to boast about. The one is how he "stuffed up the enemy" in Mozambique; the other is the "gravy" he made out of Albie Sachs's right arm.

On the surface, the chubby and ruddy-faced Petrus Jacobus "Pieter" Botes seems like a gentle and mild-mannered person, not the highly trained reconnaissance soldier he really is. Seemingly an everyday family man, he used to own a personnel agency in an upper-class suburb of Pretoria and lived on a smallholding outside the capital where he also farmed sheep. But one Friday afternoon in April 1990 this 35-year-old farmer employee of the CCB became the first spy to break ranks and tell how this secretive organisation went about its nasty business. He called me and introduced himself as Marius, a former CCB operative. The name Marius was by then known to me, as it had been mentioned at the Harms Commission in connection with a bomb explosion at business premises in Pretoria.

I met Botes at a coffee shop where he told me that Marius was his "administrative name" in the CCB. "I will tell you my real name when I trust you. The only thing you need to know now, is that for the past two years I was a co-ordinator in the CCB. I left the organisation a few months ago after Joe Verster blew up my office and tried to kill me. I want to get back at them; I am going to stir them."

Botes was extremely nervous and spoke softly, glancing around him. "I think I am being watched." He kept quiet for long periods as he fidgeted and fiddled with his pen. I asked him in what section of the CCB he operated. "Region Two. Mozambique and Swaziland. They were our playground where we took what we wanted."

Botes said he had handled many CCB operatives fighting against the ANC in Mozambique, but refused to divulge any more information about his operations. He did mention, however, that shortly before he left the CCB, he had been involved in a project in Namibia to disrupt Swapo before the November 1989 independence elections. "Verster told us to put cholera germs in the drinking water of a Swapo refugee camp. There were many other projects I will tell you about, like Anton Lubowski who should never have died. The murder was a terrible mistake."

Botes said because of his dispute with Verster, 18 of his operatives had gone without pay for many months. If the SADF did not pay him and his men within the next two weeks, he promised me he would give a complete breakdown of the structure of the organisation, the operations he had been involved in, and would break a vital rule in the cloak-and-dagger game of spying: reveal the real names of agents in the field.

I asked Botes how many eliminations he had been involved in. "Six," came the matter-of-fact reply. The look on his face was positively cherubic as he added: "They were good, clean operations." Just before we parted, he asked me: "You know Albie Sachs, that ANC person who used to live in Maputo? . . . Well, I was the man who made gravy out of Albie's right arm."

Pieter Botes remains extremely proud that he was the man who planned and executed the attack which ripped Sachs's right arm from his body and left him close to death. "It was a huge success. It was a professional job by a group of highly skilled and dedicated soldiers. I have never met Albie and have nothing personal against him, but we knew he was working for Umkhonto. It was war and soldiers shouldn't cry."

I met Botes many times after our first encounter at the coffee bar. He constantly referred to the Sachs operation in his smugly macabre way: "We made gravy out of Albie's arm", using the Afrikaans diminutive "sousie".

I asked Botes how he could be proud of maiming Sachs, an internationally respected constitutional expert who, although a member of the ANC, could never have posed any significant threat to South African security.

"I was a soldier and Albie was a soldier, no matter what he said. The psychological impact of the explosion delivered a tremendous blow to the enemy. It set them back for months. Other ANC members got the scare of their lives and left Mozambique. In the end, it was fortunate for us that Sachs did not die. You know, in a war it is sometimes better to maim than to kill the enemy. We knew that everywhere Sachs went in Maputo, people would see the stump of his arm and say: 'Look, the Boers blew it off,' knowing that we can do the same to anybody we choose."

Botes said that the instruction to kill Sachs had come from a senior member of the CCB and was signed by Joe Verster. As co-ordinator for Region Two, he was responsible for carrying out the operation.

There were South African and Mozambican operatives – both "conscious" and "unconscious" – in the three teams of six each that infiltrated Mozambique through the Namaacha border post between Swaziland and Mozambique. They used false passports and cars with false registration papers and number plates. To maintain security, none of the teams knew each other or why they were doing the work. Botes was in Swaziland to monitor the whole operation, using a phone box to communicate with his men in the field.

This CCB operation went by the book. Each team was given a number of topics about the target to research. Within a week Botes knew exactly what pseudonyms Sachs might have used, his daily routine, the layout of his house, his history and his weak and strong points. "From all the available information, I devised the assassination plan. I decided that a car bomb would be the most effective way of getting rid of him. Sachs had been on our assassination list for a long time and we did extensive surveillance on him. We knew exactly where he lived and worked, who he mixed with and what his movements were. I knew it would be easy to blow him up. I chose a highly intelligent and very dangerous black member of the CCB to plant the bomb."

A few days before the attack, the explosives were delivered to the operative in Mozambique, where the bomb was assembled. It was decided that the bomb should explode on Women's Day. Botes admitted that the operation did not altogether go according to plan as a civilian got killed. "Although it is accepted that civilians may die in the crossfire of war, it was never our intention to kill them. We did not make war against civilians. We were making war against the ANC . . . against people like Albie."

Botes said that the operative received R4 000 for blowing off Sachs's arm. When the ANC was unbanned and Sachs returned to South Africa he was told who had maimed him. His reaction was wry: "Only R4 000? I don't know if that's because he was black or because it was only an arm."

Pieter Botes was one of the men from whom the CCB gained its "civilian character". For two years he was one of the CCB's elite, entrusted with some of its inner secrets. He was well qualified to be invited into its ranks. He had been a captain in the very elitist Special Forces and held the rank of major in the Citizen Force. He had fought for some time in Angola for Jonas Savimbi's Unita guerrilla movement before leaving the Defence Force in 1982. He farmed for five years before being invited to join the CCB in September 1987. He has glowing character references from his previous commanders in Special Forces, the legendary Colonel Jan Breytenbach, founder of 32 Battalion during the Namibian bush war, and Colonel Corrie Meerholtz, his former officer commanding at 5 Reconnaissance Regiment.

Special Forces have been decribed as the operational arm of Military Intelligence. The authoritative London-based newsletter *Africa Confidential* described its task as follows: ". . . To run South Africa's secret war using techniques of clandestine activity first developed by the Portuguese authorities and perfected in Rhodesia." The "recces" can be described as South Africa's Special Air Service – highly trained specialists in unconventional warfare. They are the elite of the SADF and consist mainly of hand-picked white conscripts and former Selous Scouts from the Rhodesian war.[4]

When Botes entered the ranks of the CCB he did not know who he was working for or exactly what the work entailed. At first, people spoke simply of "the organisation" and it was only a month later that it was explained to him that it was in fact the Civil Co-operation Bureau and that his task would be the disruption and elimination of the "enemy" in Mozambique. He took an oath under the Official Secrets Act not to disclose any sensitive information about the CCB. At that time, he was committed heart and soul to its objectives.

Yet it was a disillusioned and stern-faced Pieter Botes that met me for the second time in May 1990. Next to him was a pile of papers and documents setting out the workings and structures of the CCB. Not only was Botes about to commit a criminal offence under the Official Secrets Act by revealing highly classified information, he was also set to betray his former comrades and fellow soldiers. "They haven't paid me or my men. I am going to stuff them up."

He showed me some of the official guidelines of the CCB. According to the directives the CCB could make use of any technique to discredit, manipulate or disrupt approved targets. In order to compromise a person, he had to be led into a situation where he could be manipulated. This could be done through hidden tape recorders or cameras, planting false evidence, threatening calls or letters to his family, bribery, prostitution, or the exploitation of "skeletons in his cupboard".

All new recruits into the CCB had to resign from either the Defence Force or their present employer. Their CCB personnel file would state only pseudonyms: real names would be revealed to no one. Members were requested to arrange all their insurance through a large national insurance company, where an insurance broker was sympathetic towards their cause. Even inside the organisation itself agents were instructed to address each other by their pseudonyms. The directives instructed CCB members to wear false beards, wigs and sunglasses when they talked to "indirect members".

The directives recommended that all false passports be applied for at the Johannesburg branch of the Department of Home Affairs and that new passports be provided with a few old exit and entry stamps from other countries. False signatures had to be practised thoroughly before the passport was used. Members who travelled to Europe were instructed to enter the continent through West Germany or the United Kingdom, which did not require entry visas from South Africans.

There was a very sophisticated code language that operatives had to use over the telephone when they exchanged sensitive information. During the presentation of projects telephones were unplugged, curtains drawn and a radio turned on to play in the background. A writing pad was used from the back to make indentation identification more difficult. The offices of the CCB were debugged twice yearly.

All operations had to be undertaken with foreign weapons and explosives, and weapons loaded with gloves to prevent fingerprints on ammunition. Members had to ensure that all serial numbers had been removed from the weapons.

During our conversations, Botes told me that there was something he had to warn me about. When he decided to spill the beans and talk to me, he went to a major at Military Intelligence, who was a trusted friend, and asked him for intelligence information on me and Max du Preez. He wanted to be sure that he could trust the journalists he would talk to.

There were intelligence files on both of us: Du Preez's file said he was sympathetic towards the ANC, was "politically naive", but had good intentions. My file stated categorically that I worked for the ANC's intelligence section and was a danger to state security, conclusions that had presumably been drawn as a result of my contact with Andre Zaaiman, who helped us to get Dirk Coetzee out of the country, with ANC Intelligence Chief Jacob Zuma.

I spent the next two days with Botes as he unravelled the deepest secrets of the CCB. He showed me some of his documents, among others a false passport, a so-called shopping list of Russian and East-bloc weapons he had been ordered to purchase in Mozambique, the official guidelines of the CCB, some letters and a death file, marked "Secret", on a young Mozambican academic whose life was probably saved by the exposure of the CCB and the resignation of Botes. He refused to show me other documents because they mentioned the names of operatives he did not want to expose. In contrast with the nervous and jittery man I met in the coffee bar, Botes was now confident and even assertive. I also met his wife, a quiet, attractive woman who brought us coffee from time to time. Every time she entered the dining room where we were working, Botes stopped talking. During my dealings with death squad operators, I learned that they never discussed their work with their wives.

The day before *Vrye Weekblad* was due to publish Botes's revelations, he phoned and said he wanted to see me and Max du Preez as he was uncertain whether he should go ahead with publication. In order to persuade Botes of the importance of his story, we initiated a night of heavy drinking. After many double brandies and cokes, he lifted his glass and announced: "I am going to stuff them up."

Over his half-empty glass Botes confessed that he was a born soldier and needed the excitement of hunting the "enemy" down. He said he believed totally in the concept of the CCB and that the excitement of secret warfare was still in his blood. "I miss the war. I need the action. I have asked friends what I can do to put some excitement back into my life. Somebody suggested that I should go for flying lessons. He said the sensation of freedom would still my urge for action. But what do I do when I get back on the ground and I still haven't stuffed anybody up?"

Late that night Botes took us to his house because he had a bottle of pear mampoer (a very strong traditional liqueur) he wanted us to taste. By that time, Max and I were extremely drunk. Botes, on the other hand, showed few signs of intoxication. We sat around his dinner table gulping down the mampoer. After two or three tots, we told him that we could not possibly down another one.

"I will show you what I do to people who refuse to drink my mampoer," he said. He left the room and came back with a grain bag, from which he drew a Russian-manufactured RPG rocket launcher. He put the launcher against the wall and said: "Now you will drink my pear mampoer." We finished the bottle. On the way back to Johannesburg, Du Preez was overcome by temporary blindness and stopped the car in the middle of the highway.

When I met Botes, the CCB had already been exposed and was under investigation by the Harms Commission. We had become used to nameless soldiers in clown-like disguises floating through the commission room bluntly denying responsibility for any actions, refusing to answer questions on grounds of self-incrimination and hiding vital project files. It must also be remembered that Judge Louis Harms only heard evidence on internal operations of the CCB and did not allow questions and answers on operations in neighbouring states.

Botes remains the most senior member of the CCB to have openly spoken about the organisation and as such his information was invaluable. As coordinator and at times acting regional manager for Region Two, he was in military terms probably equal to a major. He dealt frequently and directly with Joe Verster, whom he clearly hated. Botes told me that he would like to kill Verster. He gave me a passport photograph of Verster which we published. Verster had appeared heavily disguised before the Commission and Harms ordered that no photographs of him might be published. Botes and *Vrye Weekblad* shared one common view: that Joe Verster did not deserve the protection that the commission bestowed on him.

The quarrel between Botes and Verster took place on 23 August 1989 when Verster accused him of the mismanagement of R200 000. "I had just returned from Namibia where we were busy making plans for the disruption of the elections. When I walked into Verster's office to report back to him, he accused me of virtually stealing money. He threatened to kill me."

Under Verster's leadership, Botes claimed, the CCB had turned into a circus. There was little control over the actions of operatives, inadequate financial management and bad planning of murder targets. He described Verster as a power-hungry man who became very unpopular with his subordinates.

Botes himself made a mockery out of the belief that the CCB was professional and that assassinations were planned to the finest detail. There was the murder attempt on Sachs that maimed him for life. There was the attempt on the life of Joe Slovo that never materialised and a death plan for Durban attorney Kwenza Mlaba that could not possibly succeed. Botes and the CCB wasted hundreds of thousands of rands of taxpayers' money on ridiculous and far-fetched projects like buying an island off the Mozambican coast, bribing a Zimbabwean opposition politician and paying Swapo members to throw cholera bacteria into drinking water.

Pieter Botes was not the only CCB member who despised Verster. Towards the end of April 1990, I met former operative Willie van Deventer in London, where he told me that he had also left the organisation after a dispute with Verster. "I hate him," he told me.

When the CCB became a "civilian organisation" in 1988, Verster became an even more powerful person. The whole organisation, which was previously housed at Special Forces headquarters, moved to a plot outside Pretoria. All ties with the SADF were severed. All members became "civvies" with civilian jobs. They had to find their own intelligence sources, buy their own weapons and generate their own funds. Botes said this caused tremendous problems. Before the CCB became "civilian", intelligence could be obtained from the total South African intelligence community – the National Intelligence Service, the Security Police and Military Intelligence.

Now, suddenly, vital information for important operations was lacking and a whole new intelligence network had to be duplicated. Members previously issued with Defence Force weapons were now using unregistered weapons bought illegally in neighbouring states. Botes became one of the weapon purchasers for the CCB and was responsible for moving weapons between countries, including South Africa.

Before the transformation of the CCB, the organisation was an integral part of Special Forces. It operated more openly and the commander of Special Forces, General Joep Joubert, was directly in charge. Verster managed the operatives and made an assessment of operations before referring them back to Joubert for final approval. During the assessment, all relevant intelligence information was collected from the various intelligence services. Under its civilian guise, things changed dramatically. In practice, Verster was now in charge. His men had to work through him. Even Verster himself was not allowed to go to Special Forces. Joubert and later General Eddie Webb had to go to him.

When Eddie Webb became commander of Special Forces and chairman of the CCB in January 1989, things became chaotic. Botes described Webb as a good, conventional soldier who had little knowledge of the secretive warfare employed by the CCB. "Verster exploited the situation. He told Webb what he thought Webb should know. A situation developed where the tail wagged the dog. Webb had to come and see Verster, who misinformed him on certain projects and operations. Verster became a prima donna, blinded by his new-found power. I was supposed to have a meeting with him every 14 days. I had to wait for hours to see him. I once did not see him for two months. Because of this, Verster lost touch with his operatives in the field. He gave unauthorised instructions that Webb did not know about. Not all operations were referred to Webb for approval."

Botes blamed Verster for introducing civilians and hardened criminals into the ranks of the CCB. The fact that the CCB concerned itself with criminal activity is manifest in the personnel employed to carry out its tasks. The CCB made use in abundance of people with criminal records to do its dirty work. Both Ferdi Barnard and Theuns Kruger were convicted murderers; Donald Acheson and "Peaches" Gordon were known criminals.

CCB bookkeeper Theuns Kruger had blindfolded and manacled a man before murdering him in cold blood by shooting him through the head. At the time of the killing Kruger was an army sergeant commanding a mysterious SADF intelligence unit known as the "tekkie squad", presumably because its members wore civilian clothes. Kruger and his subordinate, David van den Heever, had blackened their faces to disguise themselves as Swapo guerrillas and carried AK-47 assault rifles. A night watchman, Andreas Nelomba, surprised them as they were stealing his employer's Land Rover. Nelomba was known as a supporter of the Democratic Turnhalle Alliance, Swapo's main opposition in Namibia. After blindfolding and handcuffing their captive, the two men drove him to Oshakati and murdered him at an SADF airbase.

At his trial Kruger told the judge that he had acted on orders from a parachute brigade commander who had lost his own Land Cruiser in a land mine explosion and ordered him to get another one even if he had to steal it. Kruger testified that the commander told him to eliminate the "kaffir". The commander testified behind closed doors and refuted Kruger's allegations.

The judge described the murder in his judgement as the worst case in his entire career as a jurist. Kruger was sentenced to 15 years' imprisonment but released after serving less than a third of his sentence. The CCB snapped him up.[5] "When I got out of jail I was looking for work. General [Witkop] Badenhorst recommended me to Special Forces. When I was sent to the CCB it was purely to handle the bookkeeping. I knew nothing further, not even what the aims of the CCB were. But I firmly believe what whatever was done by the CCB was not politically motivated or orientated, but was done with an eye to the security of our country and its people," Kruger said in a newspaper interview.[6]

In September 1990, a convicted bank robber who had spent 12 years in prison, Marinus Thiart, claimed that a year earlier, upon his release from jail, he had been approached by the CCB to murder Archbishop Desmond Tutu, who was on the CCB's death list. Thiart claimed in an affidavit that Eddie Webb had offered him R20 000 to murder Tutu and the general secretary of the South African Council of Churches, Frank Chikane. Shortly after his release from prison, Thiart shot a man and was charged for murder. He is currently serving an 18-year jail sentence.

Botes said that Verster employed criminals in order to perform specific clandestine jobs and operations. In some cases they were paid for jobs they never did. Verster instructed an international bank robber, a Portuguese by the name of Pinto, to eliminate an ANC official in Mozambique. All that Pinto did was to place a death notice in a Maputo newspaper, bring it back to South Africa and claim his R10 000 booty from Verster. The same Pinto was arrested by the South African Police shortly afterwards and deported back to Portugal. They found a false South African passport in his possession.

It was against this background that the tension between Botes and Verster reached breaking point. Botes told Verster that the CCB owed 18 of his operators an amount of R1,45 million. According to the account, which Botes showed to me, the CCB owed agents 11 and 12 amounts of R300 000 each. One of the amounts of R300 000 had been set apart for three senior Mozambican government officials who sold a fishing quota to a front company of the CCB. The officials did not know they were dealing with the SADF. According to Botes the CCB needed the fishing quota to give them easier access via the sea to Mozambique. He refused to tell me the names of the government officials, but I later learned that they were a Mr Sulumane at the Directorate of Fisheries and a Mr Washave at the Department of Immigration.

Botes testified before the Harms Commission that the CCB had also had plans to buy an island off the Mozambican coast. According to the evidence, which was never disputed by the SADF, he said he had paid an unidentified man to investigate development possibilities on the island. Another amount of R30 000 was owed to a Zimbabwean businesswoman who arranged a meeting between Verster and the prominent Zimbabwean opposition politician Edgar Tekere. Botes said that Verster made an assessment of the political situation in that country and concluded that Tekere was the most likely political candidate to unseat Robert Mugabe in a general election. Botes, using a pseudonym and posing as a South African businessman, met the Zimbabwean woman and appointed her as a consultant to arrange the meeting. Botes told her that his company wanted to sponsor Tekere's next election campaign. The meeting was arranged, but never took place.

During the confrontation with Verster, Botes told him that most of his operatives had not been paid for nearly a year. Verster refused to even look at the accounts. They parted with an exchange of threats. Botes told me that although he had resigned from the CCB, some of his former operatives were still extremely loyal to him and would harm Verster and his family if instructed to do so.

Six days after the meeting, on 29 August 1989, a bomb exploded outside Botes's Verwoerdburg office. It was widely reported in the media and a suspicion was created that the ANC was responsible for the blast. "The bomb exploded late at night and was not intended to harm anybody. It was a warning from Verster. If he wanted to kill me, he could have done so," Botes assured me. He decided to go and see Law and Order Minister Adriaan Vlok because the bomb had exploded in his constituency. He saw Vlok and one of his senior generals the same day, informing them about the existence of the CCB, his feud with Verster and the cholera bacteria they had put into Swapo's drinking water.

When Botes testified under oath before the Harms Commission, he was adamant that he had told Vlok about the nature and operations of the CCB and his belief that Verster was responsible for the bomb that wrecked his business premises. He said he had told Vlok that he had just returned from Nambia where they were planning the disruption of Swapo before the election. Botes said Vlok did not seem surprised.

Louis Harms sarcastically responded: "Didn't he offer you a medal?"

Vlok, through his senior counsel at the commission, admitted that he met Botes just after the bomb explosion and that the name "CCB" might have been mentioned during the interview, but that this would have meant nothing to him. The minister said Botes never mentioned Verster's name or the campaign against Swapo. But in his evidence to the commission, Floris

Mostert said that he (Mostert) had first heard about "a mysterious organisation called the CCB" as a result of a tip-off on 29 August to Vlok.

What is particularly significant about the visit to Vlok, was that the Minister of Defence, General Magnus Malan, claimed that he was only informed by Chief of Staff Intelligence General Rudolf Badenhorst about the existence of the CCB in November 1989. It thus seems that Vlok was at least informed of the existence of an organisation within the military family bent upon attacking fellow South Africans. Because Louis Harms refused to call either Malan or Vlok as witnesses, they could not be questioned about their knowledge of the CCB or their failure to take any action.

Botes had a meeting with Eddie Webb soon after his confrontation with Verster and told the general that he wanted to leave the CCB. Webb offered him a post at 5 Reconnaissance Regiment, where Botes's old friend and confidant Colonel Corrie Meerholtz – once second-in-command of the CCB – was officer commanding. Towards the end of 1989, Botes went to see Meerholtz in Phalaborwa to discuss his future in the Defence Force with him. Meerholtz mysteriously died in a car crash not long after their meeting. He received a phone call at two o'clock one morning, got up and left in his car. Ten kilometres outside Phalaborwa, his car left the road and crashed into a tree where it burst into flames. Meerholtz could only be identified by his Rolex watch. Botes decided to resign from the CCB and left the organisation in February 1990.

The evidence that Botes could present to the Harms Commission was limited because the commission's terms of reference excluded investigation of cross-border operations. The death squad Botes co-ordinated only operated in neighbouring countries and therefore his revelations about Sachs, Lubowski and his many other victims were irrelevant.

Counsels for the SADF and the SAP accused Botha of blowing up his own office. Asked why he had revealed the real names of agents to the media, thereby endangering their safety, Botes told the commission that his real identity had been blown by people within the CCB (he hinted at Verster), and he had decided to name agents in a tit-for-tat move. He said as a result of his real name being known, he was compromised in countries where he was operating under false names and where "unconscious" members did not know who he was or whom he was working for. Now they would know his true identity and what his real business activities amounted to.

Botes told me that he was especially concerned about the arms dealers in Mozambique from whom he purchased weapons. They did not know who he was or what he was buying the weapons for. While we were at his house, Botes received an anonymous phone call from somebody calling him "Bobby". Botes was extremely distressed and told me that few people knew him by that name, and those who did were not supposed to know where to contact him.

In August 1989 Botes had received a "shopping list" from the CCB listing weapons the organisation needed for its operations. The document was in the handwriting of an administrative officer. Botes claimed that he had a contact in Mozambique who could get any weapon the CCB needed. He received the money to buy the weapons in cash from Verster. The list, which he showed to me, contained the following weapons: 40 AKM assault rifles, 40 Tokarev and Makarov pistols, 20 Scorpion machine pistols with 40 magazines, 10 RPG rocket launchers with 26 rockets, 10 light machine guns, four HMG anti-air cannons, 45 blocks of TNT explosive, seven anti-tank mines, eight limpet mines and anti-personnel mines and 119 hand grenades. The "shopping list" was handed in as evidence to the commission.

Verster admitted in his evidence before Harms that Botes had been responsible for the acquisition of arms and ammunition for the CCB. He described Botes as one of the "most productive" individuals in the CCB, but that something had gone wrong with him "psychologically". He denied blowing up his office.

Verster said he had never had the power to authorise the execution of any project and had to discuss it with the chairman, who would take a written presentation to higher authority for final approval. Where the project was a matter of urgency, Verster could order its execution after having received oral authorisation from the chairman.

One CCB project exposed by Botes that was of value to the Harms Commission was the plot to murder Durban attorney Kwenza Mlaba.

Botes told the commission that poisoned razor blades were among the bizarre assassination methods conceived by the CCB. He said he was contacted by a spy handler, Shane du Plooy (an alias), who said he had been instructed by Verster to terminate Mlaba. Du Plooy had given Botes a rough draft of the assassination plan and had asked him to help draft a final presentation to Verster. Botes told the commission he refused to execute the project because his region dealt only with external operations, and it was then abandoned. The four-page proposal, which sets out how they planned to kill the lawyer, was handed in as evidence by Botes. It is dated 4 March 1989 and written in Afrikaans.

The first entry in the proposal listed Mlaba as a senior member of the ANC who provided funds to military members for operations and handled couriers from Durban to neighbouring countries. The document also stated that Mlaba had secret methods of communicating with external members and was involved with the UDF.

Botes said Shane and an operative he worked with known as Bois Nolo were to meet in Pietermaritzburg and proceed to Durban where an unnamed third person was to be involved in the assassination plot. According to the plan, Bois was to visit Mlaba and leave a bag with a razor and blades in a sealed container in his office. The hoped that Mlaba would use the razor and blades, which when used for shaving would allow the poison to penetrate the skin, with fatal results.

In the document Du Plooy said the chances were slim that Mlaba could be "murdered on the road" as he regularly changed his sleeping place and because of "previous experience" regularly looked over his shoulder. It concluded that it might be possible to find out when Mlaba was going abroad as "it could possibly be organised there". Mlaba's name appeared on a separate file of the CCB marked "Kinross Finansies" confiscated from the CCB offices by the commission. He was identified in the file as a person under CCB surveillance.

After hearing about the assassination plot, the bearded Mlaba said in an interview with *The Star*: "This goes to show how poorly informed these guys are. I don't shave, and I have never used a razor, let alone one given to me by a stranger."[7]

Verster denied giving an order to kill Mlaba. He dismissed the feasibility study as a forgery although it was in the handwriting of one of his own agents, saying Botes had a thirst for revenge after his shop in Verwoerdburg had been blown up.

An actual attempt was made to kill Mlaba in August 1986 when his Umlazi home was attacked and petrol bombed by a group of unknown men in the middle of the night. Mlaba was seriously wounded, two cars parked in the yard were gutted and his house severely damaged. The police were telephoned immediately but only arrived at ten o'clock the following morning and later issued a statement that two AK-47 shells were found outside his home. At the time, police blamed the ANC for the attack. Nearly four years later no one has been arrested.[8]

For many months, Robert Haydn Davies, researcher at the Centre for African Studies at the Eduardo Mondlane University in Maputo, lived in the shadow of death. According to CCB intelligence information, he was a member of Umkhonto we Sizwe's intelligence section. In July 1989, his name was put on the CCB's death list and an assassination plan was drawn up. Pieter Botes was given the task of devising the plan to get rid of Davies, who became CCB case number S1/8362. A death plan was compiled by CCB agent Kaelo who monitored Davies for weeks in Maputo.

The young academic's life may have been saved by the quarrel between Botes and Joe Verster. The project had still to be submitted to Verster for final approval and when Botes left the CCB, he took the yellow file, marked "Secret", with him, showed it to me and allowed me to copy the photographs and contents. "This is a classic CCB assassination plan," he said.

Davies is referred to as "the subject". The file gives a detailed description of his activities and history and is complemented by a series of maps and photographs of himself, his wife, his motor vehicle and his house. Here are some extracts:

- His activities in the ANC:
The Centre functions as part of a strategic intelligence network of the ANC. A number of ANC members work there. Believed to be involved in intelligence activities – his name has already appeared in 1986 on an ANC document that listed intelligence operators of the ANC in Mozambique. Known in Umkhonto as Rob and Adrian.
- Description of subject:
Wears a false beard and has dark brown hair. Wears dark-rimmed glasses in public. Has pale features, of average build, about 1,73 meters tall, 63 kilograms. Davies was born on 5 December 1948 in Berkirchen, West Germany. He has a British passport, number C341336. [A detailed explanation of his family history follows.]
- Place of residence:
His house is situated opposite the Italian Embassy in Maputo. It is the seventh house east of the intersection Rua Damiao de Gois, also close to the American Embassy.
- His routine:
Goes to work every morning at a quarter to eight, using his motorcycle. [The route he takes to get to the university is described in detail and illustrated by a map.] Every afternoon at 11.30, he takes the same route back home and takes his motor car to go and fetch his child at school. At two o'clock, he returns to the university with his motorcycle which he parks in front of the main building. His wife returns home at night before him.

It is the wrong time for the operation now. Because of the Fifth [Frelimo] Congress, security has been sharpened in Maputo and there are many patrols in the streets.
- His history:
Entered Rhodes University in Grahamstown in 1966. In 1969 he attracted unfavourable attention for the first time when he participated in a protest march against the Improper Interference Political Bill [legislation that prevented black people from becoming members of white political parties].

In 1968 and 1969 he attended the annual congress of the National Union of South African Students (Nusas). In 1969, he became involved with the Radical Students' Society. He was suspended as a student. On September 2, 1970, he went to England where he studied at the University of Southhampton. In 1970, an informant described him as "one of the leading radical students, Davies is clearly a Marxist". Between the years 1974 to 1977, he did his PhD at the University of Sussex.

He became an economics lecturer at Rhodes in 1975 where he mixed with radical elements. He associated himself with the Economics Commission of Nusas, which wanted to use the black working class to attain its revolutionary aims.

He left the country in 1975. From 1979 onwards, he worked with Albie Sachs and Ruth First in Mozambique. He has also been a lecturer at the University of Zimbabwe.

He is at present at the Eduardo Mondlane University. He is busy with research about a post-apartheid society in the Republic of South Africa with special reference to the role of the working class and the ruling class. Besides gathering information for the ANC, he helps the Mozambican government making decisions about South Africa.

He is married to Judith Head and they have one child. Head is a member of the ILO which gathers information about the treatment of workers in South Africa.

– Character:
He has no outstanding weak points. The fact that he can speak fluent Portuguese is to his advantage. He has also appeared on Mozambican television. He is terribly anti-South Africa and pro-ANC. Makes negative comments about the South African Government.

[A list of five acquaintances with their telephone numbers also appears in the file.]

– Political Situation:
Although it is at the present time not known whether he is busy with Umkhonto activities, there is no doubt that he is active on an intelligence level.

He had worked intimately with Albie Sachs and the research he did about a future constitutional dispensation is used by him in seminars to advance the aims of the ANC, while the present government in South Africa is put in a negative light.

– Method of destroying the subject:
On the road: He can be murdered to or from work. It is a flexible method, and a silencer should be used. This method depends on the condition of the road, the traffic and the pedestrians. He can be shot by two people on a motor cycle, or by a pedestrian when he stops at a stop street.

At his house: Somebody can wait till it gets dark, get a hiding place and do it when he is ready. During the rainy season it is very safe. There are no dogs, no night guards, no lighting at his house.

Bomb in his car: He is at his flat every lunch time. During lunch time he parks his car at his house on the left-hand side of the road. He leaves his car window open and is very careless.

End of plan.

Botes said that after studying the information on Davies, he decided that the best method to kill the academic would be to shoot him on his motorcycle during lunch time on his way back home from university. It would have been too dangerous to kill him at home because he lived in an area surrounded by guarded and well-lit embassies. Because of political considerations a car bomb was not desirable at that time.

Although the monitoring of Davies took place in July, Botes would have recommended to Verster that the killing take place later that year in the rainy season, when there would be few pedestrians around and the assassin would leave no tracks.

Botes was particularly proud of the agent who did the assessment of Davies. He said the agent gave him all the information he needed to compile an effective assassination plan. It would have been "simple" to kill Davies. He never had any doubt that the CCB had good reason to murder the academic.

From the available information, it was not clear to the CCB what Davies's role in Umkhonto had been. They believed that the Centre for African Studies was "a part" of the intelligence network of the ANC and that he was involved in intelligence activities.

Davies is back in South Africa today, lecturing at the University of the Western Cape.

Pieter Botes said many of the CCB's elimination projects in Mozambique were cancelled shortly before execution. The life of Herbert Thabo, ANC assistant chief representative in Mozambique, was saved by a telephone call to the Chief of the SADF, General Jannie Geldenhuys, who decided that the attempt could have harmed political relations between the two countries.

Botes said that the CCB had decided to kill Thabo by placing a two-litre bomb under the front seat of his motor car. The bomb was already in place when Botes was given the instruction to remove the device. It was done at the last minute.

"Some attempts were allowed to go ahead, others were stopped for political reasons. At one stage I had nine projects on the table, of which seven were stopped. In some cases, we were told to use so-called soft measures to kill opponents. It usually meant using poison, which was freely available and used by many operatives," Botes said.

The CCB also planned to kill Joe Slovo. According to Botes, they knew that every year on 17 August – the date of her death – Slovo visited the grave of his wife Ruth First in Maputo.

"It was a brilliant plan," Botes told me. A few days before the remembrance day, a CCB operator planted a bomb, consisting of plastic explosives and a detonator in a tin can, underneath the tombstone. On the day, the agent who was to detonate the bomb waited for Slovo a hundred metres away, at another grave, kneeling with a bunch of flowers in his hand. The electronic mechanism to detonate the bomb was hidden in the flowers. The agent was arrested as he awaited the arrival of the Communist Party leader.

Slovo must have been the subject of many death plans. In November 1990, a former security police agent, a woman whose name had been mentioned at the Harms Commission but who never testified, called me and said that towards the end of 1981 she had been asked by police death squad commander Dirk Coetzee to murder Slovo, who lived in London then. The plan was to smuggle poison to London, arrange a meeting with Slovo and try to put the substance in his drink. The agent refused because she thought it was too dangerous. I questioned Coetzee about the assassination plan, which he confirmed. In 1981, Slovo also narrowly escaped death during a South African army raid on ANC bases in Maputo.

Slovo, a lawyer who left South Africa in 1963 because restrictions prevented him from running his law practice, has not only been a death squad target, but also the victim of a vicious misinformation campaign in South Africa. In July 1984, *The Star* claimed that Slovo was a KGB colonel and that he had engineered his estranged wife's killing for political reasons. Slovo, who until his return to South Africa in 1990 could not be quoted in this country, instituted a defamation claim against *The Star* in the United Kingdom. High Court Judge Richard Tucker described it as a "horrendous accusation and an appalling libel" and awarded £25 000 to Slovo. *The Star* refused to submit to the jurisdiction of an English court.

In March 1990, Namibia became independent after nearly eight decades of South African rule and administration. Since the early sixties, a bitter bush war had been fought between South Africa and the South-West African People's Organisation (Swapo), which was recognised by the United Nations as the official representative of the peoples of Namibia. For many South Africans, it was a bitter pill to swallow when the government announced that it had reached an agreement with the international community on the independence of Namibia. White South Africans knew that after the UN-supervised elections the former enemy would become the new government and members of its armed wing, the People's Liberation Army of Namibia (PLAN), the new military rulers of the territory.

Botes was called to Verster's office in May 1989 to be briefed on a master plan to disrupt Swapo before the November elections. Three different CCB cells would be deployed in Namibia: Botes's Region Two, the internal region (Region Six) under the command of regional manager Staal Burger and the Namibian region under the command of Roelf van der Westhuizen. Burger, Van der Westhuizen and Botes were briefed separately. The one was not to know what the other had to do. Botes received his instructions on 11 July 1989. He was to assassinate senior Swapo officials Hidipo Hamutenya, today Nambia's Minister of Information, and Danny Tsjongerero, who became a deputy minister after independence. The murders had to look as if they were committed by fellow Swapo members unhappy with the "soft-line approach" of Hamutenya and Tsjongerero, in order to cause dissension within Swapo.

Botes was instructed to plant bombs at Swapo meetings and explode hand grenades among the spectators. The CCB devised a plan to put cholera bacteria and yellow fever viruses – provided by an army doctor – into the drinking water of Swapo refugee camps at Dobra in northern Namibia. A printing press ordered by Swapo and awaiting delivery at Walvis Bay and 54

Swapo motor vehicles were identified for sabotage. Botes said the CCB was to use a special oil that would seize the engines.

Not even Untag – the United Nations' peacekeeping force overseeing the independence process – was to be spared, although Botes was instructed not to harm officials. The cars of United Nations' Special Representative Marthi Ahtisaari and Chief Administrator Cedric Thornberry were to be fire-bombed, however.

A few days after receiving the plan, Botes deployed his team of agents and operatives in Namibia. An operative who could speak Kwanyama, one of the local languages, infiltrated Swapo camps. Tsjongerero was removed from the death list after he became ill, but the plans for Hamutenya's assassination went ahead. Botes decided to have him shot with a Russian-made pistol outside the Namibian Nights nightclub in Windhoek, frequented by Hamutenya and other Swapo members. On 20 August, a consignment of weapons arrived in Namibia, consisting of 10 hand grenades, 31 blocks of TNT explosives and an RPG rocket launcher with nine rockets and four limpet mines. Botes received and cached the weapons outside Windhoek. In the meantime, three Swapo members were recruited to assassinate Hamutenya. The assassins did not know who they were working for or why they had to murder the Swapo leader, but had been promised huge sums of money.

Botes returned to Pretoria on 23 August to report back to his superiors about the feasibility and progress of the project. He had to submit a final draft to Verster three days later. "I reported to Verster the same morning I arrived back from Namibia. As soon as I walked in, he accused me of mismanagement and the argument started. I stormed out of his office and my participation in the Namibian project ended. I withdrew, and in the end, nothing materialised," Botes told me.

Four days later, on 27 August, he received news that an agent had infected Dobra's drinking water with cholera. The bacteria did not survive, Botes explained, because the chlorine content of the water was too high. So yet another CCB project had failed.

Abram "Slang" van Zyl admitted before the Harms Commission that the CCB had planned to disrupt Swapo before the independence elections. Van Zyl had been in charge of an operation to sabotage microbuses that transported Swapo supporters to election meetings.

Joe Verster said in his evidence that the CCB had monitored Daniel Tsjongerero inside Namibia, but because the commission was precluded from investigating external operations, no further questions could be asked. CCB Region Six co-ordinator Christo Brits gave some corroborating evidence. He spoke of a project involving Swapo that started on 11 July 1989, codenamed "Doopdag" (baptism day).

A former Military Intelligence agent, Major Nico Basson, who was running a media centre in Windhoek at the time, later told me that he knew about plans to assassinate Hamutenya. Basson had in his possession an assessment of the Swapo leadership made by Military Intelligence which concluded that Hamutenya was a key person in the leadership, with wide support among the more radical elements in the organisation.

The quarrel with Verster signalled the end of Pieter Botes as an operative of the CCB. Although he stayed on until February 1990, he was "put on ice". In fighting the "enemy", Botes and his men had blown up telephone installations, sabotaged railway lines, bribed officials and cut off water and electricity supplies. In the end, Botes claimed, he had "planned six successful ANC assassinations" in Mozambique. Mozambique was his playground, he boasted.

This man's bizarre personality is perhaps best illustrated by a conversation we had just before he sold his Pretoria plot and moved down to the Cape west coast to start a new business venture. He told me that he believed that members of the CCB could constitute the core of a future rightwing revolution against State President FW de Klerk and his government.

This is nothing new, of course: the fear has been widely expressed. We know the CCB generate their own funds, have weapons and are constituted so as to be able to survive without any support from the SADF. Joe Verster had testified before the Harms Commission that the CCB felt threatened by the changes in the political situation in South Africa. But Botes had his own solution to the problem. He wanted me to arrange a meeting for him with the ANC's Intelligence Chief, Jacob Zuma, who was at one time also on his Mozambican death list. Botes had a proposal he wanted to present to the ANC: if they would pay him R250 000, he would raise, command and arm a small but very special ANC army unit consisting of trusted former operatives. He wanted to tell Zuma that the ANC would need a special person and a special unit to fight against the threat the CCB may pose in future. "I am the man they need. I would stir up the CCB," he swore.

Two weeks after Botes stormed out of Verster's office, Anton Lubowski was slain in front of his Windhoek home. According to Botes, the murder of Lubowski was a terrible mistake that should never have happened. The CCB was unaware of the fact that Lubowski was paid by the SADF for information he supplied or a service he rendered as either a conscious or unconscious agent of Military Intelligence. But a Swapo leader had to die in order to create discord in the run-up to the independence elections. Botes had been instructed to kill Daniel Tjongerero and Hidipo Hamutenya, but when he walked out the whole disruption campaign in Namibia threatened to collapse. Another Swapo leader had to be killed, and that man could have been Anton Lubowski.

We know from evidence before the Harms Commission that two days after the quarrel between Botes and Verster, operatives from Region Six started monitoring Lubowski's movements. We also know that the CCB had been cut off from state intelligence sources and would not have known of any link between him and the SADF.

Although the Namibian police are still investigating the murder of Anton Lubowski, they have virtually no hope of ever solving the case. A successful prosecution can only be achieved if both Chappie Maree and Staal Burger are extradited to Namibia to stand trial with Donald Acheson. But Namibian authorities have said it would be difficult to prosecute the two CCB operatives without the evidence of Acheson, who was deported back to Europe in March 1991. The Irishman's departure has closed the dossiers on the murder.

Just before Donald Acheson was taken into protective custody awaiting deportation, I met him in a Johannesburg hotel. The Irishman appeared terrified: the day before, another former agent of the CCB, Edward "Peaches" Gordon, had been found murdered on a highway near Cape Town. He was sure that his former comrades-in-arms in the CCB were out to kill him.

Acheson, his distinctive moustache shaved off, admitted that he was a professional murderer widely known by the codename of "The Cleaner". Yet the man I saw in the hotel did not seem like a hit-man of any kind. He was tense and nervous, wringing his hands as he said: "They are out to get me. Man, I know these people. They want to kill me." A few days before our meeting, Acheson had phoned the Afrikaans morning newspaper *Beeld* and had an off-the-record interview with a reporter. From what I gathered, he had tried to sell his story, which was to be published only after he had left South Africa and reached a safe destination. However, the next morning, *Beeld* published "in the public's interest" some of his allegations.

Now Acheson said he "had to run for it". He had been warned that former CCB agents were out to kill him because he had spoken to journalists. The CCB had given him an air ticket to Athens, but he was afraid to use it in case he was tracked down and killed in Greece. "I am the man who can nail Lubowski's murderers. I didn't pull the trigger, but I know the CCB did. If I talk, I can bring down the CCB with me," he said. He clearly wanted money for his story.

Acheson said he had been sent on a mission to Namibia to murder the editor of *The Namibian* newspaper and close friend of Anton Lubowski, Gwen Lister. He had turned out to be the decoy for another CCB operation, however: to kill Lubowski. Acheson claimed attempts were then made to frame him for the murder. He said he had also been instructed to monitor the election campaign in Namibia and confirmed that there was a plan to disrupt Swapo. Acheson said he burgled Swapo headquarters in Windhoek before the elections and stole a number of files. He said millions of dollars were handed over to Swapo Democrats, a political party opposing Swapo, to be used to destabilise the country in the run-up to the poll. "I had to spend eight months in a Namibian jail for a murder I knew nothing about. After I was released, they sent me on a holiday to Crete. They brought me back again, but I don't know why. I don't know what is going on. I have nowhere to go."

Acheson confirmed that he had been recruited by Ferdi Barnard and handled by Calla Botha and Chappie Maree. At first he did not know who he was working for, just that it was a special South African assassination squad. The CCB had promised him $200 000 to kill Lister. According to the plan, he had to put poison in her personal sanitary belongings or toothpaste. "I thought it was a ridiculous plan and that it would have been much easier to kill her with an AK-47. But they said this is how it was going to be done."

He was told to get a car, hire a flat and keep the AK-47 for a CCB operator known to him as "Roland". Shortly before the killing, he saw Roland hiding a briefcase containing about $100 000 under a bed in a Johannesburg hotel.

Acheson was not sure why he had to be in Windhoek at the time Lubowski was killed. He thought he was there to make the final arrangements to have Lister killed, but the hit was called off hours before the Lubowski slaying, and afterwards the "CCB man" rang him and told him to sit tight in his room for two days. The police arrested him the next day. He is not sure who pulled the trigger, but knows that he was set up. "I was hung out to dry," he complained.

CHAPTER ELEVEN

From teacher to apartheid assassion

A FAMOUS black South African author once said: "God does not have enough tears to wash South Africa clean."

As the story of Leslie Johannes Lesia unfolded before me these words came irresistibly to mind. It was a tale of betrayal and manipulation; of a simple middle-aged Bloemfontein bricklayer and shebeen keeper who woke one day to find himself an apartheid assassin.

The Bochabela township outside Bloemfontein is nothing more than a collection of small houses and shacks divided by dirt roads. For many years, Leslie Lesia had been one of Bochabela's most popular residents, known and loved by all. A colourful, chirpy little man, the former amateur boxing champion once ran a backyard shebeen before he decided to try and realise his dream of establishing a performing arts school for the township children of Bloemfontein. Lesia, who started life as a bricklayer and a carpenter and spent several years in jail for theft and fraud, was a jazz musician himself.

In 1985 he established Leslie's Performing Arts and Cultural Institute and started advertising his dream. "Your road to fame starts here! It's music . . . song . . . dance . . . pop . . . jazz . . . instrumentals . . . ballet . . . tap dance . . . disco . . . trampoline . . . gymnastics . . . art and painting . . . modelling . . . stay-fit and weight-trimming gym . . . drama and music . . . You could be a star!"

Within months he had received hundreds of applications from parents who wanted their children to join the school. He held auditions in the Batho community hall and soon had more than 500 children on the school's books. He quickly realised that unless he received financial aid for his project, the school would not survive. Bochabela is a poor township of mostly servants and workers who cannot afford the luxury of arts classes for their children.

Lesia wrote a letter to the United States Information Service in Johannesburg. "It is of vital importance that I first introduce the existence of this institute which is the first of its kind in this province, the Orange Free State, for black youngsters. Our main object is to promote and foster goodwill and understanding among them and young whites by forging cultural links, to build and create the right frame of mind on the basis of common interest."

He soon received a letter from the Consul General asking him to fill out an application for a human rights grant. Two American diplomats came to see him to make sure it was a non-profit scheme and not political. They assured him that they would provide the finance to build the school on condition that he set up a steering committee and get an attorney to handle all financial aspects.

Then, suddenly, Lesia received news that his late brother's son, Tebogo Lesia, had been killed in a car accident in Tanzania. Tebogo had fled South Africa years before to become a member of Umkhonto we Sizwe. Lesia's sister-in-law, who had been under constant surveillance since Tebogo had left the country, asked him to accompany her to Tanzania for the funeral. Lesia thought it wise to be on the safe side of the law and went to see a security policeman to ask for permission to attend the funeral. The policeman said there would be no problem.

Lesia and his sister-in-law flew to Swaziland in September 1986 and were met by an ANC official called Joseph. He took them to Maputo where they stayed for a week waiting for their northbound flight to Dar es Salaam. During their stay, they were introduced to the leadership of the ANC in both Mozambique and Tanzania. In Dar es Salaam the ANC, who regarded the Lesia family as friends and allies, gave them a couple of letters to deliver to ANC officials in Maputo. One of the letters was addressed to the chief representative of the ANC in Mozambique, Jacob Zuma, who later became the organisation's Chief of Intelligence.

Two days after their return to South Africa, the Bloemfontein Security Branch questioned Lesia about Tebogo's death and wanted to know whether he or his sister had a death certificate, which they produced for the police to make a photostat copy.

A week after Lesia had returned to South Africa, he received a call from a "Mr Becker" at the American Embassy who told him to immediately fly to Johannesburg. Everything was arranged and paid for. Ernie Becker met Lesia at the airport and took him to a nearby hotel where he was introduced to a "Mr Brown". Although Becker spoke with an Afrikaans accent, Lesia was not suspicious as he knew embassies often employed local people. Shortly after this meeting money was deposited into the school's trust account and a company started delivering milk to the school. Lesia was overjoyed. At last, he thought, the future of the performing arts school was no longer in jeopardy. Lesia held a meeting with all the parents informing them that the school was now funded by the generous people of the United States.

The next time Lesia saw Brown and Becker, they introduced two other men whom they said were South African businessmen willing to assist in his school project. The two men, who said they were keen to invest in

Mozambique and Tanzania, asked Lesia questions about what was happening in those countries.

"That puzzled me. I couldn't understand how they knew about my trip to the ANC because as far as I remember nobody knew about that trip with the exception of the ANC and my family and some of my friends ... and the security police. Eventually I gave them a brief account of what happened there. They threatened me that if I was not going to co-operate they were not going to let my school have that sponsorship of funds. I have greatly suffered to get funds and had promised the children. I could not let the project die."

Becker produced an album with photographs of ANC members and asked Lesia whether he recognised anyone. Lesia was questioned at length about his knowledge of the ANC and also had to describe Joseph, who had met him and his sister at the airport in Swaziland and taken them to Maputo.

Brown then revealed to Lesia: "We are not diplomats; we work for Military Intelligence. We will give you money, but you must give us something in return. We want you to keep in touch with the ANC in Mozambique and Swaziland. There will be no risks and we will look after you." Becker gave Lesia a pager number through which he could reach him.

"I was a confused person at that time," Lesia confessed. "I didn't know what to do as I have never done something pertaining to that. I fed them with what I thought was innocuous information." A while later he was instructed by Becker and Brown to make contact with Joseph, the Swaziland representative of the ANC. They told him that in order not to raise any suspicions he must make it a family trip and take his wife and his mother-in-law with him. Becker gave him R3 000 in cash for expenses.

When Lesia got to Joseph's flat in Swaziland, he was not there. The next day he went back but Joseph was still not there. He knocked at the flat next door to enquire about Joseph's whereabouts, but the person who answered the door just stood there wide-eyed without saying a word. Perturbed and apprehensive, Lesia rushed back to Johannesburg, called Becker and arranged a meeting. He told his handler that he couldn't understand why the people had not wanted to give him any information about Joseph. Brown laughed and told Lesia: "Don't worry, we have taken care of him."

Joseph had been assassinated on the strength of information supplied by Lesia, who had told his handlers exactly where the ANC man lived and what his movements were. "It frightened me really and I started realising that every bit of information I give to these people they act upon. In fact they had sent me on the mission to Swaziland to let me know I was in their power. I had been under surveillance all the time, they later told me."

Lesia had reached the point of no return. He was already implicated in the elimination of an ANC member in Swaziland and Becker told him that should he refuse to co-operate any further, they would destroy his school by withdrawing his licence and expose him to the Bochabela community as a

Defence Force agent. Lesia had to sign a contract with Military Intelligence and take an oath under the Official Secrets Act. He was paid a monthly allowance of R1 600 and Becker told him that he would work one week out of every month for the Defence Force.

In December 1986 Becker instructed Lesia to deliver a small parcel to the Russian Embassy in Gaborone. He met Lesia in Klerksdorp in the western Transvaal and he handed over two parcels and R1 000. The smaller parcel was well wrapped; the second one contained two dozen cans of beer. Lesia had to introduce himself at the embassy and say that he was a member of the ANC. He had to ask for a person by the name of "Big Jack" and hand over the parcels to him. Lesia gathered from Becker that Big Jack was an agent for Military Intelligence and that he would distribute the beer from the embassy to the ANC. Lesia said that Big Jack seemed to expect him and talked very little.

In January 1987 Lesia undertook his first trip as a Defence Force agent to Maputo to gather information on the ANC. He did not try very hard, he just sat around trying not to attract attention. He visited Jacob Zuma and told him that he was willing to work as an informant for the ANC.

Back in South Africa, Becker informed Lesia that he was to undergo a training course in the use of explosives and poison. In a hotel room he was shown how to handle and set an explosives device which booby-traps a door. The device is placed on the outside of a door with a wire with a hook attached to the key hole. The device detonates as soon as the door is opened. Becker and Brown had brought a selection of poisons with them. One, a yellowish liquid in a small glass bottle with an aluminium and rubber top, would kill within a week or two and was impossible to trace in a post mortem examination. They gave Lesia a poison ring with a hollow top in which the poison could be kept and then surreptitiously slipped into a victim's drink. He was instructed to try and poison any senior ANC official.

Lesia was given four detonators, four bottles of poison and a nine-millimetre pistol with a silencer. The spy handlers had a secret compartment built into the dashboard of his car and the engine was modified to give more power and better petrol consumption. The poison, explosives and the pistol were hidden inside the compartment.

Towards the end of January 1987 Lesia was called to Johannesburg and taken to Jan Smuts Airport where he had to try and identify certain people arriving in South Africa from the United Kingdom. According to Becker there were certain white women associated with the ANC in Maputo who could have been on that flight. While they were sitting at the airport hotel Becker pointed at a man having a meal and said to Lesia: "Do you see that man there? He's the big boss of the police. He is the man helping us to get the stuff." Becker was pointing to the head of the police forensic laboratory, General Lothar Neethling. The "stuff" was poisoned liquor.

Brown told Lesia that they had devised a plan to take booby-trapped television sets and video recorders as gifts to the ANC in Maputo. Lesia had to go to Maputo and tell his ANC friends that he had connections with gangs who stole television sets and video recorders and that he would in due course bring them some as gifts. The assistant chief representative of the ANC in Maputo, Herbert Thabo, asked Lesia to find a television set he could send to his girlfriend in Zambia.

In March 1987 Lesia accompanied Becker to a building in Pretoria where they fetched one case of brandy, one case of vodka and three cases of beer which Becker said were spiked with poison. Later in his hotel room Becker showed Lesia how the beers had been doctored. He said that the tab which is pulled off the beer tin could be lifted to insert a syringe needle to inject the poison.

Lesia fitted some of the poisoned liquor into his secret compartment and left for Maputo. When he arrived in the Mozambique capital he gave some of the liquor to a senior ANC official called Sipho. "There was nothing else I could do. Becker and Brown were dangerous and ruthless people. I felt there was no place I could hide from them." Invited to a party in Maputo, Lesia saw a young man by the name of Gibson Ncube walking into the room drinking from a can of South African beer. "It gave me a shock, you know, to see that he was drinking the poisoned liquor because I can assure you at that time in Maputo you couldn't just get that kind of beer. Mostly they were drinking locally made beer, and I couldn't do anything to stop him because while he was talking he was just finishing the beer and he had thrown the can away."

Gibson Ncube died a horrible death on 5 April 1987. Shortly after drinking the poisoned beer, his feet became paralysed. The paralysis gradually spread over his body and he died eight days later. Herbert Thabo phoned Lesia, who had in the meantime returned to Bloemfontein, informing him that Ncube had died and asking him to help them with the funeral arrangements. Lesia helped to trace the dead man's family in Johannesburg and made arrangements to fly them to Maputo to attend the funeral.

Before Lesia left for Maputo to attend Ncube's funeral, Becker gave him a booby-trapped television set to take with him and hand over to Thabo. Lesia travelled to Maputo through Swaziland and once he was in Mozambique he activated the bomb so it could be set off by a radio from a distance. Becker had told him earlier that another agent, whom Lesia did not know, would set off the bomb in the television set.

Lesia was met in Maputo by a senior ANC official, Mhlope, who asked him whether he could have the television set. Lesia explained that it was meant for Herbert Thabo, but Mhlope said he would pay Lesia well, and he could get another one later. Lesia defused the bomb before he gave it to Mhlope. On his return to South Africa, Lesia lied to Becker and said he had given the set to Thabo. A week later Becker called Lesia to Johannesburg and questioned him about why the bomb had still not exploded yet, ordering him to go back and reclaim the set. Lesia returned to Maputo on the pretext that he was on a business trip to import seafood.

Lesia arrived in Maputo unaware that the television set had already been taken to Zimbabwe, where it had exploded accidentally on 11 May 1987. An ANC member who attended Gibson Ncube's funeral, Frank Chiliza, had been asked to take the set with him back to Zimbabwe as a gift for the ANC's chief representative in that country, Reddy Mzimba. Chiliza placed the set in his flat and when he left his wife, Tsitsi, decided to switch it on. The television exploded, killing her and destroying the flat.[2]

The Zimbabwean Minister of State for Security said in a statement that the bomb was an electronically detonated device which blew up when the set was switched on. "It is quite clear that agents of the South African regime had devised a plot to kill the chief representative of the ANC, which misfired with disastrous results." South Africa denied complicity in the attack. Foreign Minister Pik Botha echoed his usual statement, saying that countries that allowed insurgents in their territories were "playing with fire". The SADF said in a statement: "It is no more than an absurd attempt to yet again try to use South Africa as a scapegoat for their [Zimbawe's] own deteriorating internal security situation."[3]

Four days after the bomb exploded, there was a knock on Lesia's hotel door in Maputo and when he opened, four men in civilian clothes burst in and started searching his room. They told Lesia to pack his clothes and warned him: "Keep your mouth shut or we'll shoot you."

The men took Lesia to their car, blindfolded him and took him to an airfield from where he was transported to Lusaka. The four plainclothes men later turned out to be members of the Zimbabwean Central Intelligence Organisation (CIO). Lesia was blindfolded again in Lusaka and taken to a room where a dozen men were waiting for him. He recognised one of them as an ANC official he had known in South Africa, called Pat.

"Why am I here?" Lesia asked his interrogators.

"Just tell us the truth. Who recruited you? Who are your bosses in the Defence Force? What information did you give to the Boers?" his interrogators demanded.

Lesia, defiant and still unaware of the television set that had exploded, told them: "Fuck you, gentlemen. I have been gathering information for the ANC. I am one of you."

Lesia tried to assure his interrogators that he was dedicated to the ANC and gave them Jacob Zuma's name as a reference. But the men knew he was lying. "You're talking bullshit! We know you're a South African spy and you're going to pay for it."

The next day Lesia was informed that the television set he had given to Mhlope had been transported to Harare where it exploded and killed a woman. He was kept for three days in Lusaka before being blindfolded again and driven to Harare, where he was taken to a police station and charged with murder. "It was a great shock to me that the innocent woman had died. First Joseph, then Gibson, now this woman. And here I was in Zimbabwe at the mercy of men I knew were going to torture me until I told them the truth."

Lesia was taken to the notorious Goromonzi detention centre, where he was stripped naked and thrown into cell number one, known as "Mugabe's cell". "My hands were manacled behind my back and attached to an iron ring on the wet cement floor and my feet to another. I lay on my back and could not move. I was left for three days without food or water. I forced my mouth to the cement floor to lick up the wetness to try and quench my thirst."

On the third day the warders carried Lesia out of his cell and threw him onto a gravel yard. His interrogators took two pick handles and thrashed him on the soles of his feet until he could take the pain no longer and passed out. After each session, he would be carried back to his cell and thrown on the wet floor, where he would regain consciousness in horrible pain. The same torture was repeated day after day until Lesia's legs had swollen up so much he could no longer walk and passed blood in his urine. Yet he maintained his innocence throughout his interrogation.

On 16 June, which is Lesia's birthday and also the commemoration of the Soweto uprising of 1976, he was taken to his car, which in the meantime had been brought from Maputo to Harare. Lesia showed his interrogators the secret compartment in which they found the pistol with the silencer, the explosives and the poison. Photographs were taken. "Now they knew I was guilty and became really vicious. I was given electric shocks on my private parts and they hit me with a Coke bottle against my head."

Although there was overwhelming evidence implicating Lesia in the bomb explosion that killed Tsitsi Chiliza, in October 1988 the state was forced to withdraw the murder charges against him. The Zimbabwean Supreme Court has a proud record of dismissing confessions made under duress or as a result of torture. Torture by the Zimbabwean authorities has led various South African spies to be either acquitted or not to be charged in the last decade.

Minutes after Lesia was acquitted, he was redetained under the State of Emergency and held at Chikurubi Maximum Security Prison in Harare. While in detention Lesia met other South African agents being held or convicted by the Zimbabwean authorities. Among them were Phillip Conjwayo, Kevin Woods and Michael Smith, all three on death row awaiting execution, Barry Bawden, sentenced to 40 years' imprisonment, Odile Harrington, sentenced to 25 years' imprisonment and Guy Bawden, who was held with Lesia under the State of Emergency.

Lesia became Zimbabwe's longest-serving black detainee. In protest against his detention and the refusal of the authorities to allow his wife,

Miriam, to visit him, he launched two hunger strikes."I could take the pain they inflicted on me, but I most worried about my wife back home. By then, my art school had been closed down and the family had very little money. From that day I was abducted from Maputo, the South African Defence Force stopped paying me my monthly allowance. My wife never got a cent while I was in jail in Harare. They just did not care."

Miriam was never allowed to visit her husband and their only means of communication became the monthly exchange of letters. Lesia's letters, written on jail paper and heavily censored by the warders, depict a man in dire need and in extreme pain. In August 1988 he wrote a letter to Miriam: "Hi there love, I beg of you to keep on fighting until the dust has settled down, love. I am sorry if what I am telling you right now is going to shock you . . . My love, I am semi-paralyzed in both legs from hips downwards. I feel somewhat that you don't or rather, yet realizes in full the seriousness of my situation. Love, I want you to pause and think.

"Love, I want you to go to the university and insist that you want to see Colonel Steyl [Lesia's contact in Bloemfontein] and explain to him my predicament and that I have insisted that he must personally introduce you to the office of the Minister of Justice or Foreign Affairs . . . I am afraid of my life.

"Gee my love, have you any idea what they have done to me? It's barbaric and I mean that in the full ugliness of the word. Otherwise my love, I am a believer and I hope and trust that my faith in God will never desert me. Though I must admit your letter made me a worried man when you mention the weight loss. But again I remembered that you once told me that letswai turns woman into fatties, remember? Lets hope my love that you are not going to fall into a trap like Mopapi. Don't forget to kiss yourself for me. Bye now my love.

And remember, Tigers don't cry."

In July 1990, Robert Mugabe lifted the State of Emergency in Zimbabwe. For Leslie Lesia it meant freedom as the authorities had no legal way of detaining him any longer. He boarded a South Africa-bound flight from Harare and flew back to Johannesburg after 39 months of hell in Zimbabwean jails. He was met at the airport by Colonel Ludwig Kemper of the SADF and taken to 1 Military Hospital at Voortrekkerhoogte, where he was treated for ten days. He was debriefed by a colonel, three majors and a captain of Military Intelligence who wanted to know how he was arrested in Maputo, what kind of treatment he received in Zimbabwe, and who his interrogators were. He was also interviewed by military psychologists.

After Lesia had spent two weeks in hospital, Military Intelligence booked him and his wife into a dingy Johannesburg hotel. After a few days he received a phone call from the military: "Mr Lesia, we are sorry, but we can only pay for your accommodation. You will have to pay for your food yourself. We are sorry, but that is all we can do."

Not only did the SADF dump Leslie Lesia in a backstreet Johannesburg hotel, they also deserted a sick man in desperate need of further medical care. It was later established by a doctor that Lesia had cancer of the testicles, probably contracted as a result of the continual electrical shocks. He could not afford to pay for the treatment himself. To the SADF, he was an expendable commodity: gullible, naive and badly trained. His handlers must have known that it was madness to send him back to Maputo after he had delivered the booby-trapped television set and the poisoned liquor. And yet, when he was arrested, they denied his existence and warned Zimbabwe that to harbour the ANC was to play with fire. The fact that he had lost his life's dream, undergone unimaginable suffering at the hands of his interrogators and became an outcast in his own community, meant nothing. There was no longer any use for Leslie Lesia.

Shortly after Lesia was released, Odile Harrington arrived back in South Africa after being detained for two years in a Zimbabwean jail. The frail-looking arts graduate had been sentenced to a 25-year term in 1987 by a Zimbabwean judge who said she was unrepentant and deserved the death sentence.[4]

Harrington was untrained and unprepared when her handler, Geoffrey Price, sent her into Zimbabwe posing as an anti-apartheid activist. She stayed at a house used by the ANC in Harare and blew her cover when she gave a Zimbabwean police guard an inadequately sealed envelope containing intelligence data to be sent to South Africa. She was arrested by Zimbabwe's CIO and for the next eleven months was tortured, starved and sexually assaulted while being held in solitary confinement.

While the homecoming of Lesia hardly attracted any attention in the media, Harrington received a heroine's welcome from Pik Botha and later had tea with the State President. She was immediately offered employment as a librarian in the Department of Foreign Affairs.

A few days after Lesia's release, I received a phone call from Pieter Botes informing me that one of his men had just arrived back in South Africa. He said Leslie Lesia was a member of Region Two of the CCB and was known in the organisation as "Tiger". Botes said Tiger's handler was Ernie Becker, co-ordinator of Region Two and a former reconnaissance soldier.

I met Lesia three months later in his Johannesburg hotel. He had contacted *Vrye Weekblad*'s lawyers to say that he might have information of value in our defamation case against Lothar Neethling. He told me he was scared, broke and extremely bitter at the Defence Force for dumping him without food in the hotel. Since his release from Zimbabwe he had been unable to return to Bloemfontein for fear of reprisals by ANC activists. He realised that his only chance to return to Bochabela would be to testify against the South African authorities and be forgiven by the ANC for betraying them. He said, however, that before he would get into the witness box, he wanted an assurance from the ANC that he was forgiven and would not be harmed.

I met with the ANC's chief of foreign affairs, Thabo Mbeki, who sent Lesia a personal message that the organisation was not looking for revenge and would welcome him back in its ranks should he testify against Neethling. For Leslie Lesia, Mbeki's message was like a second lease on life. He said his greatest ambition in life would be to start his performing arts school once again when he had regained the trust of the people of Bochabela.

Lesia was never sure who he had worked for – Military Intelligence or the Civil Co-operation Bureau. He was recruited by Military Intelligence, but in the end it seemed as though he had operated for Region Two of the CCB.

It was a stroke of luck that he never threw anything away. There was a massive collection of old air tickets, hotel vouchers, notes and diaries to corroborate his evidence. Lesia and I travelled to Bloemfontein to search for his documentation. It was the first time since his fateful visit to Maputo that he had returned home. After his exposure as a spy, activists in Bloemfontein sent messages to Miriam that they would kill the traitor should he ever return.

It was an emotional homecoming. As we climbed out of the car, his mother-in-law, who did not know he was coming home, curiously opened the front door of his brightly painted house. She embraced him with tears rolling down her cheeks while his kids stared wide-eyed at their father's sudden homecoming. After a few minutes, friends and relatives arrived with beer, food and best wishes. Lesia proudly paraded me around the small home and showed me the elaborate ceiling of the dining room – a mixture of wood and red satin decorated with golden buttons – which he had built himself.

Later that day, Lesia put on his old baseball cap and ventured out into the streets to face the residents of Bochabela. For the first time, his eyes were sparkling and he was talking non-stop. We stopped at a shebeen he used to frequent. There was a stunned silence when Lesia walked in, took off his baseball cap and announced that he was back. A woman rushed forward and pressed his face against her breasts. Old friends and drinking acquaintances shook his hand and embraced him. Someone ordered him a drink. "I think they have forgiven me," Lesia said as we left Bloemfontein later that day with a whole bag full of old air tickets, hotel vouchers and his diary. Everywhere we went, he had told people that he was going to rectify what he had done wrong and that they should watch television and read the newspapers.

We stopped in Soweto at the home of his sister to collect some more evidence. His brother-in-law refused him entry into the house and threatened to kill him if he ever saw him again. Lesia was unmoved. "He has always hated me," he explained.

Among his documents were a number of notes he made during his briefings by Becker and Brown. His main objective, according to the notes were: "All big fishes in the Communist Party must be exposed and be destroyed inside and outside the RSA. Thus we will have a meeting once or twice a month for briefing and instructions."

Two days before Lesia was due to give evidence, we chartered an aircraft to Zimbabwe to try and obtain more evidence to corroborate his story. Lesia's attorney in Zimbabwe, who was paid by the South African authorities, handed over his travel document and the brass-plated poison ring that had been found in his car. We also got hold of the photographs that the CIO had taken when Lesia showed them his secret compartment and uncovered the pistol and silencer, the poison, the explosives and the poison ring. The bottle of poison could not be found and it was only after Lesia had given evidence that we were informed that it had been traced. According to forensic tests conducted in Harare, the bottle contained an anaesthetic substance.

Leslie Lesia rose from obscurity to fame as his death squad story unfolded in the Rand Supreme Court. His revelations were the main news in the biggest newspapers. The night after his first day in the witness box, Lesia looked at himself on television and said: "I have really shown them a thing or two, haven't I?"

On the second day, as we walked out of the court building, Lesia came face to face with an ANC member he had known and betrayed in Mozambique. The man smiled at him, lifted his fist and shouted to Lesia: "Amandla!" It was a sign for Lesia that he had been forgiven and accepted back into the ranks of the ANC.

Judge Johan Kriegler later said in his judgement that he was convinced that Lesia had been recruited by Military Intelligence to undertake clandestine operations in the neighbouring states and that it was highly probable that he had been responsible for the booby-trapped television set that exploded in Zimbabwe and the poisoning of an activist in Maputo.

Since then Lesia has returned to his house with the extraordinary satin ceiling and has been accepted back into the community. He has joined the ANC and instituted a claim of R62 400 against the Minister of Defence for money owed to him while he was in detention in Zimbabwe.

CHAPTER TWELVE

The anatomy of sabotage

FOR many years South Africa waged its war in defence of apartheid far beyond its own borders. Death squads played a significant role in the strategy by which the government used the neighbouring states as buffer zones against the ANC's influence. Operatives like Pieter Botes and Leslie Lesia were vital elements in the disruption and destabilisation of southern Africa. The ANC had to be kept as far away as possible by forcing neighbouring states to expel South African refugees, making pre-emptive strikes against the ANC, setting up surrogate forces and in some cases even by means of a military presence.

Since 1980, says Dr Joseph Hanlon in his book *Beggar Your Neighbours*, South Africa has invaded three southern African capitals – Maseru, Gaborone and Maputo – and four other countries in the region – Angola, Swaziland, Zimbabwe and Zambia; sent death squads to attempt the assassination of two prime ministers – Robert Mugabe of Zimbabwe and Leabua Jonathan of Lesotho; supported dissident groups that have brought chaos to two countries – Unita in Angola and Renamo in Mozambique – and less serious disorder in two others – anti-government forces in Zimbabwe and the Lesotho Liberation Army (LLA); disrupted the oil supplies of six countries – Zimbabwe, Mozambique, Botswana, Lesotho, Angola and Malawi; and attacked railway lines in seven countries – Zimbabwe, Angola, Mozambique, Lesotho, Malawi, Zambia and Botswana.

More than one million people have been displaced in southern Africa and virtually all the states have had to care for refugees of South African attacks and destabilisation. South Africa itself has had to cope with a refugee influx from Mozambique as a result of its destabilisation policy against that country. More than 120 000 people have been killed in the region, most of them starved to death in Mozambique at least partially as a result of South African-backed rebels preventing drought relief.[1]

Destabilisation helped the South African government to foster the myth among the white electorate that blacks cannot rule themselves. To this end it was important to create turmoil around South Africa. How many times have we heard white South Africans say: "Look around you and see what's happening on South Africa's doorstep. We don't want something similar to happen here"?

In 1975 the cordon of white-ruled colonies around South Africa was broken when Angola and Mozambique became independent. Internally South Africa was faced by the Soweto uprising of 1976, the death of Steve Biko in 1977, the election of Jimmy Carter as president of the United States, the Information Scandal and an oil crisis.

The government felt compelled to build a new barrier – a ring of states that, although hostile to apartheid, could not afford economically or militarily to give active aid to the revolution.

According to researcher Diana Gammack the implementation of South Africa's regional policy can be divided into six phases. The first ran from PW Botha's assumption of power in 1978 until mid-1980 with Robert Mugabe's election victory in pre-independence Zimbabwe. The Rhodesian war had finally ended with the agreement at Lancaster House in December 1979. Mugabe's ZANU (PF) won a landslide victory at the British-supervised elections in March 1980 – to the shock of both Britain and South Africa. Bishop Abel Muzorewa, on whom South Africa had staked its regional policy, was humiliated.[2]

The second phase ran until the end of 1981 and was marked by an increase in commando raids and the sponsorship of dissident groups in neighbouring states. On 30 January 1981, just ten days after United States President Ronald Reagan took office, South African commandos hit the capital of Mozambique. They attacked three houses, killing 13 ANC members and a Portuguese technician. Named the "Matola Raid", it was South Africa's first official cross-border raid besides the war in Angola and marked an official change in South Africa's attitude towards its neighbours. "Detente" was replaced by a hard line of destabilisation. During 1981 all of South Africa's neighbouring states were attacked.

In Angola, incursions and bombing raids were stepped up, particularly after June. In August the SADF launched a full-scale motorised invasion, named Operation Protea. In November 1981 commandos attacked the oil refinery in the capital of Luanda. In Zimbabwe, the ANC's chief representative, Joe Gqabi, was assassinated in July 1981. Commandos blew up an ammunition dump in August and nearly assassinated Robert Mugabe in December. In Mozambique, South African troops came over the border again in March 1981, retreating after a clash with Mozambican soldiers. Commandos returned and blew up key bridges linking the port of Beira to Zimbabwe. In Lesotho there was a series of bomb explosions in the capital and elsewhere. In Swaziland, a South African refugee was kidnapped in February and two ANC men were killed in December. In Zambia, South African troops occupied the south-western corner of the country, mining roads and confiscating a ferry boat. In Botswana, there was a series of border incidents and incursions by South African troops.

In the third phase Pretoria focused on the removal of ANC members from neighbouring states. In this period countries that were willing to halt assistance to the ANC, like Swaziland and Malawi, were rewarded with economic aid, while those governments unwilling to compromise were ruthlessly attacked. Destabilisation involved a mix of military and economic weapons. The mix was different for each country – Angola faced a purely military assault, Mozambique a mixture of economic and military, Lesotho and Zimbabwe mainly economic with some military intervention.

Cross-border raids continued in 1982 and 1983. The most appalling occurred in December 1982 when South African commandos hit Maseru and killed 42 people. On the same day they attacked a fuel depot in Beira, causing Zimbabwe severe petrol shortages for several months. The Thornhill air force base in Zimbabwe was attacked in July 1982, the South African Air Force bombed Maputo in May 1983 killing six people and the Operation Askari invasion of Angola followed in December 1983. There was even a raid in London in March 1982 when the ANC office was bombed.

South Africa followed the Israeli example of massive raids into neighbouring states in retaliation for ANC actions and also took up the idea of using surrogates in the way Israel used the Lebanese militias. Unita was built up as a barrier to Swapo infiltration, the LLA in Lesotho was used to attack ANC targets and the so-called "Super-ZANU" in Zimbabwe was partly intended to block ANC infiltration.

Military credibility was badly dented by the May 1983 air raid on Maputo. Defence Minister Magnus Malan said that his planes had destroyed six ANC bases and a missile battery and killed 41 "terrorists". Foreign journalists who were free to tour the area found that the targets were in fact a jam factory and ordinary surburban houses, and the casualties three workers at the factory, a soldier guarding a bridge, a child playing and an ANC member washing a car. At least 40 other people, mostly women and children, were hurt by shrapnel.[3]

In 1984 the aggressive third phase ended and the fourth phase started with the signing of two accords: the Lusaka Agreement in February 1984 and the Nkomati Accord shortly afterwards. South Africa styled itself the regional peacemaker and shortly after signing the Nkomati Accord sponsored talks between Frelimo and Renamo.

The period from March to October 1984 was particularly confusing. On the one hand, South Africa was the peacemaker. In Angola, it did pull its troops back. In Mozambique, it did reduce supplies to Renamo and in Lesotho and Zimbabwe South African-sponsored dissident actions were halted. And yet in Mozambique and Angola the wars intensified. In June 1984 ANC member Jeanette Schoon was assassinated in Angola, two weeks later the oil pipeline was blown up in Cabinda and a few days after that two boats were sunk by frogmen in Luanda harbour.

Pretoria failed to capitalise on the Nkomati Accord and the fifth phase began in early 1985 with a new cycle of violence. It had been hoped that the agreement would spike the guns of the ANC and lead to a political settlement between Renamo and Frelimo and finally to the acceptance of South Africa as the region's superpower. By mid-1985, however, Pretoria had clearly failed to reach its objectives. Destabilisation and aggression, never abandoned despite the signing of formal non-aggression treaties, escalated and became the main feature of South African regional policy.

The facade of good neighbourliness suffered a blow in May 1985 when a member of the SADF's Special Forces, Captain Wynand du Toit, was captured in Cabinda during a mission to destroy the Molongo oil complex. Magnus Malan stood up in Parliament and declared that his government was not trying to destabilise Angola, but had been after the ANC and Swapo, who were plotting against South Africa from their bases deep in the north of Angola. But the hapless Du Toit said days later at a press conference: "No, this last operation was launched with the aim of destroying the storage tanks at Cabinda Gulf. We were not looking for the ANC or Swapo, we were attacking Gulf Oil."[4]

During this period South Africa was finally forced to confess to an act branded as destabilisation. The confession was made after Frelimo overran the headquarters of Renamo in the Gorongosa area of Mozambique in August 1985. During the raid diaries were found that proved that South Africa had conducted secret dealings with the rebels in Mozambique after the signing of the Nkomati Accord, which of course prohibited such dealings.

South Africa admitted its continued contact with Renamo and said that it had taken supplies to the rebels and even flown the Deputy Minister of Foreign Affairs, Louis Nel, into Mozambique to meet with their leaders. But Magnus Malan claimed that this was only a "technical violation" and that South Africa had in fact given medical aid to Renamo to "soften" it up for persuasion to go to the conference table.[5]

Shortly afterwards, South Africa launched a raid into Botswana in which outdated information led the commandos to the homes of innocent local residents. According to an American church worker, all 12 people killed were civilians. It was later established, however, that four had had links with the ANC.

In May 1986 South Africa simultaneously hit targets in Lusaka, Gaborone and Harare. The SADF reported that it had hit an ANC installation at the Makeni Refugee Transit Camp outside Lusaka, but according to the Zambian Commissioner for Refugees, at the time of the attack there were no South Africans at the centre. He said that refugees who were normally received there were only civilians. Two people, a Namibian and a Zambian, were killed and some buildings destroyed.

During March 1988 the SADF got the wrong man again when they raided a house in Gaborone. The commandos killed four sleeping people, one of whom was supposedly an ANC military commander, Solomon Molefe. However, neighbours claimed he was Chris Mokoena, a man they knew well.[7]

Meanwhile the SADF continued its covert war through Renamo bandits in Mozambique and provided considerable support for a new offensive in the southern provinces of the country. Over 1 000 civilians were murdered between June 1987 and January 1988 in this assault. Renamo attacks were launched in eastern Zimbabwe with the apparent objective of opening up a new front of destabilisation in that country in addition to Matabeleland, where the South African-backed "Super-ZAPU" continued to operate.

Although South Africa denied that it had supported the Renamo assaults, evidence of continued SADF involvement emerged from a number of sources. Several former Renamo soldiers, either captured or surrendering under the Mozambican government's amnesty programme, spoke of air- and sea-drops of supplies, SADF personnel operating with Renamo in bases in Mozambique and involvement of a special SADF commando unit sent to plant bombs in Maputo and Matola. Casualties among innocent bystanders were viewed with indifference. Most victims were not South African exiles but nationals of the countries concerned. At least part of the motivation behind the attacks was to engender fear and insecurity in local communities where exiles were living.

The fifth phase of South Africa's regional policy was marked by increased activity of death squads. Among the targeted ANC leaders were Dulcie September, chief representative in Paris, who was shot dead in March 1988, Albie Sachs, who was seriously injured in a car bomb explosion in April 1988, national executive member Cassius Make, gunned down in July 1987, Secretary-General Alfred Nzo and Treasurer-General Thomas Nkobi, who escaped assassination attempts in Lusaka in January 1988, as did Godfrey Motsepe, the ANC representative in Belgium, the following month. South African death squad members also conspired to kill Oliver Tambo in September 1987.[8]

Two bullets from a .22-calibre weapon hit Dulcie September in the head as she stood, mail in hand, opening up the ANC office near the Gare du Nord to begin another day in the difficult and lonely life that her modest French and her dedication to the struggle had bought her.

The assassination of September followed days after Belgian police defused a bomb placed outside the ANC offices in Brussels. Seven weeks earlier, an unidentified gunman had fired two shots through a window of the same office, narrowly missing Godfrey Motsepe.[9]

The influential French newspaper *Le Monde*, quoting French, Belgian, United States and British intelligence sources, said in a leading front page article that South Africa had a top secret weapon known by western intelligence services as "Z Squad Incorporated". The intelligence sources claimed to have information that "Z Squad Incorporated" – the name is a reference to the Mafia's "Murder Incorporated" – had a death list of 20 names. The names of both September and Albie Sachs appeared on the list. According to the report British intelligence had alerted their French colleagues about September but she had not been informed nor given special protection.[10]

207

The Z Squad had been operating in Europe for a few months before the death of September. It was headed by a man named by the French press as Dirk Stoffberg. He and another man had apparently been questioned by British security officers at London's Heathrow Airport and a list of ANC names had been found. In the case of September the Z Squad was supported by an extreme-rightwing Frenchman working for the South African Embassy and the Interior Ministry. He had been named by the media as Jean-Dominique Taousson, a former member of the clandestine OAS movement which fought President De Gaulle when he decided to quit Algeria. He published a far-right newsletter which was reportedly financed by South African secret funds and was distributed to European parliamentarians and businessmen with South African interests.

French intelligence sources believed that there was a connection between the slaying of September and the assassination attempt on Godfrey Motsepe in Brussels. In June the Paris-based *L'Express* reported that Belgian authorities had issued an international warrant for the arrest of a former South African defence attache in London, Sergeant-Major Joe Klue. Klue had served as a defence attache at the South African Embassy in London until 1982, when the British government threatened to expel him for "activities incompatible with his office" and he was recalled to Pretoria. Klue was dubbed "Inspector Klueless" by the British press after he was named in an Old Bailey trial in London in connection with a plot to burgle the offices of black nationalist movements in Britain and steal documents from them.[11]

The fifth phase of South Africa's war of destabilisation ended with the battle for Cuito Cuanavale. In the period between January 1987 and the end of the first quarter of 1988 the SADF became involved in what was to be probably its largest and most costly military incursion into Angola. The subsequent change in Pretoria's stance in the region was fundamentally the product of this battle. It smashed the myth of SADF invincibility and showed that its weapons and equipment were no longer technologically superior.

In the first week of May 1988 South African negotiators travelled to London for the first of several rounds of talks on Angola and Namibia with officials from Angola, Cuba and the United States. These resulted in an agreement over the withdrawal of SADF troops from Angola, followed by accords signed in Brazzaville and New York in December 1988 providing for Namibia to begin its transition to independence in accordance with United Nations Security Council Resolution 435.

The sixth phase came about because the international setting had changed, and both the United States and the Soviet Union were prepared to back peaceful initiatives in southern Africa.

South Africa also suffered a setback in Mozambique as Frelimo achieved some significant victories over Renamo towards the end of 1987. By mid-1988 the Mozambican security situation had greatly improved and a new offensive had driven Renamo from some of its bases further north. In December 1987 the Mozambican government passed a law offering amnesty to Renamo soldiers surrendering to the authorities. A year later, around 3 000 soldiers had surrendered and two senior Renamo officials had defected, two had been murdered in Malawi and a former general secretary killed in Lisbon.[12]

Pretoria's known involvement with Renamo was becoming more and more of an embarrassment to them. The extreme brutality of Renamo undermined whatever international support it might have had. In April 1988 a United States deputy assistant secretary of state, Rob Stacy, accused Renamo of "one of the most brutal holocausts against ordinary human beings since World War Two". A report commissioned by the United States government estimated that Renamo had been responsible for the deaths of at least 100 000 civilians.[13]

The era of destabilisation began with South Africa treating the region as its own backyard, mounting raids of a conventional and hit-and-run nature and supporting surrogate forces. It ended with the decolonisation of Namibia, withdrawal of South African and Cuban forces from Namibia and Angola and regional peace initiatives sponsored by the United States and the Soviet Union.

Nowhere in the region has the role of the death squads been more clearly illustrated than in Zimbabwe, which was the greatest threat to South African hegemony and dominance of the region. Zimbabwe has always been the pivot of the transport network of southern Africa and as the most developed state besides its southern neighbour, it has always had the potential to prosper and develop independently from South Africa.

The new government of Robert Mugabe posed a bizarre political threat: his policy of pragmatism and reconciliation after independence raised the prospect of a flourishing non-racial state that would further expose the ills and wrongdoings of apartheid. By early 1981, South Africa had clearly decided to hit Mugabe and destabilise his country. To white South Africans, Mugabe was portrayed as a Marxist dedicated to the overthrow of the government.

Although South Africa was more constrained in dealing with Zimbabwe than with some other states in the region, it established a highly sophisticated and well-trained death squad for operations against Zimbabwe. Largely because of the vigorous investigations by the Central Intelligence Organisation we know today who the operatives were and what their operations entailed.

At independence, at least 5 000 people with military and security links crossed the border to South Africa. Many of them joined the South African security forces and in subsequent years operated in Angola, Mozambique, Botswana, Namibia and of course Zimbabwe. Most of the former Rhodesians who joined the South African Defence Force were taken up in either Special Forces or Military Intelligence. Within Special Forces the Rhodesians were absorbed into D40, Barnacle, 3 Reconnaissance Regiment and eventually the

Civil Co-operation Bureau. Part of Barnacle's job was to recruit Rhodesians for part-time special operations. Officially they were not part of the Defence Force, enabling Magnus Malan to deny his ministry had anything to do with them if operations should go wrong, as they frequently did.

Although most whites left the Rhodesian security services and went to South Africa, some stayed to work for the new government. By the time Robert Mugabe took power, a core had already been recruited as South African agents. One of them was Geoffrey Price, who became director of close security in the CIO after independence. Price exploited Mugabe's policy of reconciliation and rose from his pre-independence position as Abel Muzorewa's campaign manager to the officer personally responsible for Mugabe's safety.

Price had a long history of co-operating with South African security officers. Promoting Abel Muzorewa's campaign, he made use of South African funds to hire helicopters, print pamphlets and organise rallies. But the new government thought that Price was a good example of a professional soldier and would serve whatever government was in power. It was also important for Mugabe to demonstrate his sincerity in reconciling the white and black in Zimbabwe and that former foes could serve together in the new armed forces.[14]

On 18 December 1981 a bomb explosion ripped through ZANU headquarters in downtown Harare, killing seven people and injuring 125. The bomb went off above the third-floor conference room where the ZANU central committee under the chairmanship of Robert Mugabe was due to meet. Mugabe and his cabinet ministers were clearly the target and would have been killed had the meeting not been delayed. The people killed were innocent bystanders in a bakery next door while the injured were mostly Christmas shoppers on the packed street outside.[15]

Price was not initially suspected of complicity, but as investigations proceeded two other white security officers were detained. Before they were interrogated, Price took urgent leave to visit relatives in the United Kingdom. A few days later, the two officers admitted to being part of a South African spy ring under his command.

Price came to South Africa where he headed the Zimbabwean desk at Security Branch headquarters. The SAP and SADF components of the network of South African agents, commandos and death squads sometimes overlapped. It later turned out that before independence Price had recruited two former Rhodesian soldiers, Alec West and Alan Trowsdale, as South African agents. They handled the first cell inside the country. The main operatives of the cell were Philip Hartlebury and Colin Evans. They did the surveillance on the ANC's chief representative in Zimbabwe, Joe Gqabi, before he was assassinated in Harare in July 1981. Gqabi was shot and killed by a death squad assassin as he came out of his home. Hartlebury and Evans were detained and charged with murder, but were acquitted in 1982 on the grounds that their confessions had been forcibly obtained. They were redetained and only released five years later. They were the first agents to be released because the Zimbabwean courts refused to prosecute on forced confessions.[16]

Security Minister Emmerson Munangagwa later said that immediately after their arrest South Africa had approached the Zimbabwean government through its trade mission in Harare and admitted that the two men had spied for it. South Africa unsuccessfully tried to include them in a prisoner exchange in which more than 100 Angolan soldiers and a Soviet national were returned to Angola.[17]

South Africa was also implicated in an explosion in August 1981 that rocked the Inkomo barracks outside Harare. Inkomo was a major weapons armoury and about $25 million of arms and ammunition were destroyed in a blast that could be felt 30 kilometres away in the capital. The CIO detained an engineer and bomb expert, Captain Patrick Gericke, claiming he had free access to the armoury and was working for South Africa. Gericke was sprung from jail in an incredible cloak-and-dagger operation by South African agents. They kidnapped the wife and children of the investigating officer, Fred Varkevisser, who was forced to release Gericke. Afterwards, however, both Gericke and Varkevisser and his whole family were flown to South Africa. It later turned out that both men worked for Graham Branfield, Deputy Inspector at Bulawayo's Special Branch, who later fled to South Africa and trained Zimbabwean agents for the South African Defence Force.[18]

South Africa was also held responsible for the destruction of a third of Zimbabwe's military air power. In July 1982 saboteurs put explosives in 13 fighters at the Thornhill air base near Gweru in central Zimbabwe, wiping out the country's strike and jet interception capabilities. The Zimbabwean authorities, blinded by anger and paranoia about ever-present South African agents, arrested six white Zimbabwean air force officers, among them Air Vice Marshall Hugh Slatter. They were eventually acquitted but expelled from Zimbabwe.[19]

South Africa was, however, caught with its pants down in August 1982 when three SADF soldiers were killed infiltrating Zimbabwe to sabotage the railway line that runs to Maputo. Pretoria admitted that the men were members of its armed forces and that they were former Rhodesian soldiers, but claimed that they were on a private and unauthorised mission.[20]

There was also a series of smaller incidents in the early eighties. Explosions damaged the railway and electricity and water installations at Beit Bridge. The South African trade mission in Harare was in all probability involved in a disinformation campaign in 1983 when threatening letters – signed by "Joe Moyo for ZIPRA High Command" – were sent to foreign airlines, embassies and white farmers. When the letters were compared with official correspondence sent out by the trade mission, it was clear that the same typewriter had been used. A South African diplomat was expelled.[21]

A major weapon in South Africa's destabilisation armoury was its support for dissident groups in neighbouring states. South African support for "Super-ZAPU" in the southern province of Matabeleland included the provision of arms and ammunition, rocket launchers, mines, medical supplies, communications equipment and logistical support in the form of bases inside South Africa, training, intelligence gathering and transport to and from South Africa. It even included the establishment of a radio station for the dissidents, Radio Truth, which beamed its anti-Mugabe messages into Zimbabwe. South Africa repeatedly denied that it was in any way involved in the broadcasts, but on 25 November 1983 the station mixed two tapes: the vernacular broadcast of Radio Truth began with the introductory music of "Voz da Africa Livre" – the South African sponsored Renamo radio station that broadcast their messages from the same location. In the Nkomati Accord South Africa later undertook to close down "Voz da Africa Livre".[22]

Dissident activity began in 1982, but had its roots in the integration of the three pre-independence forces – Robert Mugabe's Zimbabwean National Liberation Army (ZANLA), Joshua Nkomo's Zimbabwean People's Revolutionary Army (ZIPRA) and the Rhodesian armed forces – into a new national army of reconciliation. Towards the end of 1981 there were clashes between ZANLA and ZIPRA in which several hundred people were killed. Some former ZIPRA men deserted from the army and stockpiled arms.

An event in 1982 that fuelled the civil unrest and dissident problem in Zimbabwe was brilliantly masterminded by South African agents. Malcolm "Matt" Calloway, a former member of the Selous Scouts, stayed behind in Zimbabwe after independence and became a local commander of the Central Intelligence Organisation. He became close friends with a ZIPRA officer who tipped him off about the stockpile of arms in Matabeleland. Calloway in turn passed the information on to Geoffrey Price, at that time still director of close security of the CIO. Price, on instruction from his intelligence masters in South Africa, informed Robert Mugabe, adding false information to his report that implicated the former ZIPRA intelligence chief, Dumiso Dabengwa, and the former ZIPRA commander, Lookout Masuku. They were both arrested and accused of involvement in the arms caching. Dabengwa was later acquitted, but rearrested and detained for four years. However, the foundation of the dissident war in Matabeleland had been laid. It only ended in December 1987 after the unity agreement between Mugabe and Nkomo.[23]

It is highly probable that Calloway himself encouraged the hiding of the arms and that South Africa masterminded the splitting of ZANU and ZAPU after they failed to kill Robert Mugabe. Price and Calloway left Zimbabwe shortly after the discovery of the arms cache. While Price joined the South African Security Branch, Calloway joined 5 Reconnaissance Regiment in Phalaborwa, where the SADF was training former Rhodesian soldiers and Renamo guerrillas to destabilise Zimbabwe and Mozambique. It was from Phalaborwa that Calloway and other former Rhodesian officers planned commando raids and sabotage and set up the "Super-ZAPUs".[24]

"Super-ZAPU" was a small group of former guerrillas recruited by South African agents, trained and sent back to augment the existing dissident movement. Many former guerrillas fled to the Dukwe refugee camp in Botswana where they were recruited by Matt Calloway and other South African agents.

Clear evidence of South African involvement in the civil unrest in Matabeleland emerged in December 1983 when a former ZIPRA guerrilla, Hillary Vincent, was caught in Botswana and turned over to Zimbabwe. According to Vincent, he had met Calloway in Francistown in Botswana in January 1983 to talk about training and arms. Three loads of arms were brought across the border from South Africa to Botswana from where they were distributed to Zimbabwean dissidents. Among the weapons were 70 AK-47 assault rifles, ammunition, mines, rocket launchers and 258 kilograms of plastic explosives.[25]

Joseph Dube crossed the border into Botswana in early 1983 and went to Francistown where he stayed with a group of "Super-ZAPU" recruits. The recruits were addressed by Matt Calloway who told them that South Africa was ready to train and arm them to topple the Zimbabwean government. After training, Dube was part of a heavily armed group of dissidents sent back to Zimbabwe. They were involved in a clash with security forces, Dube was captured and sentenced to death.[26]

One of the South African agents who manipulated the conflict in Matabeleland was the former administration manager for the CIO in that area, Kevin Woods. He was recruited as a South African agent in 1983 by Allan Trowsdale while on holiday in South Africa. He resigned from the CIO in 1986. Woods, a former member of the Rhodesian Selous Scouts, received 400 Zimbabwean dollars per month and was given a radio to transmit messages back to South Africa.

The main role of "Super-ZAPU" was to create chaos and disruption. The dissidents attacked shops, schools, buses, villages and farms. An estimated 6 000 people died in the civil unrest in Matabeleland. At least 30 white farmers were killed, including Senator Paul Savage in 1983. In response Robert Mugabe sent in the undisciplined and ill-trained Fifth Brigade to quell the violence. There were immediately reports of brutalities and the killing of civilians; the situation deteriorated even further.

South Africa without doubt tried to create a buffer zone in Zimbabwe against ANC infiltration. "Super-ZAPU" could attack ANC infiltrators in places where the large numbers of regular Zimbabwean soldiers would make it very difficult to move through the area unseen.

But the activities of South African death squads were not restricted to the civil unrest in Matabeleland and did not come to an end in December 1987 when Robert Mugabe and Joshua Nkomo signed a unity agreement. A Zimbabwean region was created in the Civil Co-operation Bureau to sustain the terror campaign.

A field commander of the CCB, Kitt Bawden, is today Zimbabwe's most wanted man. Bawden's front was a company called Sommex in Johannesburg and among his recruits were his brother, Guy Bawden, his cousin, Barry Bawden, Kevin Woods and Michael Smith. He also gave orders to Allan Trowsdale. The cell travelled frequently to South Africa, sometimes openly and sometimes secretly in a South African Air Force helicopter, for briefings and to plan operations.[27]

In October 1987 an anti-apartheid activist, Jeremy Brickhill, was critically injured when a car bomb detonated at Harare's Avondale shopping centre. His wife, Joan, suffered blast and shrapnel wounds as glass and metal fragments were thrown up to 300 metres, and a Spanish diplomat having breakfast in a neighbouring cafe was among 20 people injured in the blast.[28]

The Zimbabwean Minister of Information, Dr Nathan Shamuyarira, accused South Africa of direct responsibility for the blast, but Pik Botha dismissed the idea, saying it was predictable that his country would once again get the blame for the internal violence in Zimbabwe.

In January 1988 Bawden and his cell of CCB operatives tried to blow up an ANC transit house in Bulawayo. An unemployed man, Obert Mwanza, was hired by Kevin Woods and Kitt Bawden to drive the car and park it in front of the suspected house. Bawden sat in another vehicle some distance away and detonated the bomb as Mwanza parked the car. Mwanza was blown to pieces and two ANC members were killed. A few days after the blast, Kitt Bawden fled to South Africa, but Kevin Woods, Michael Smith, Barry Bawden, Rory Maguire and a Zimbabwean policeman, Phillip Conjwayo, were arrested in connection with the bomb blast and charged with murder and treason.

Smith said during his trial that he had been a member of the SADF since 1980, that Kitt Bawden was his commander and that his first allegiance was to South Africa. Woods, Smith and Conjwayo were sentenced to death and are awaiting execution at Chikurubi Maximum Security Prison in Harare. Bawden was sentenced to 40 years' imprisonment and Maguire to seven years.[30]

The CCB desperately tried to free their convicted comrades. According to a report in the *Sunday Star* that quoted CCB sources, operation jailbreak in Zimbabwe was codenamed "Direction 1 and 2" and the price tag for the attempted rescue was R6 million. The planning was done by Graham Branfield, who recruited a former Rhodesian mercenary, Sammy Beahan, to execute the operation. Michael Smith's wife Eileen did the reconnaissance for the team. A Zimbabwean Air Force pilot, Lieutenant Gary Kane, was recruited to steal a military Agusta Bell helicopter and fly the convicted men back to South Africa upon their release.[31]

Fifteen CCB operatives were standing by on the day in June 1988 that the South African agents, arrested six months earlier, were due to appear in court in Harare for a monthly remand hearing. The CCB commando planned to free them on their way from prison to the court, but the operation was

214

bungled when Beahan was caught with an arsenal of weapons as he tried to enter Zimbabwe. It later turned out that the Zimbabwean security authorities had come to know of the plot in advance. The jailbreak had to be aborted and Kane and Eileen Smith fled to South Africa in a stolen light aircraft. Kane shot an 11-year-old girl in the stomach during his escape. Beahan was sentenced to 40 years' imprisonment for his abortive attempt.

There was a bizarre twist to the CCB's involvement in Zimbabwe when both Guy Bawden and Jeremy Brickhill decided to sue the South African Minister of Defence. Brickhill also sued Guy Bawden for the injuries he sustained in the explosion, while Bawden admitted in his application that he was a member of the CCB cell that planted the bomb. He also revealed in papers lodged with the Supreme Court that he had worked with SADF operatives in an attempt to assassinate Oliver Tambo in September 1987. The agents involved were named as Kitt Bawden, Kevin Woods, Barry Bawden and Michael Smith.

Bawden said that the cell planned to blow Tambo up with a home-made bomb placed next to the main Bulawayo-Harare road near Hero's Acre, a patch of consecrated ground commemorating the dead of all sides in the Rhodesian bush war. Tambo was supposed to drive past on his way to a conference in Harare. Guy helped Kitt make the bomb from materials smuggled into Zimbabwe. He hid his brother in his flat, drove him to the site of the attempted assassination and cached unused equipment. However, the plot was abandoned.[32]

The second plot mentioned by Guy Bawden was the Brickhill operation. A car bomb was planted in the parking lot of a Harare shopping centre a month after the abortive attempt on Tambo's life. Guy Bawden drove Kitt Bawden to the Brickhill house to "survey" it and at the same time showed him other houses belonging to ANC members in Harare. He also helped Kitt buy the second-hand car that was eventually blown up and again helped him to build the bomb. The car was parked and detonated by remote control.

Guy Bawden said his brother returned to South Africa after the blast. In December 1987 Barry Bawden asked Guy to go to his farm and pick up equipment which had been parachuted in by the SADF. He found clothing, grenades and firearms for six men as well as explosives and chemicals, which he hid. He disposed of the parachute. Less than a month later Guy Bawden was arrested and charged with attempted murder and espionage. He was never brought to trial, but spent over two years in Chikurubi Maximum Security Prison before eventually being released at the same time as Leslie Lesia.

Bawden is claiming compensation of more than Rl million for the loss of his farm, his home and his business in Zimbabwe, as well as for the "pain and suffering" he endured in prison. He said that he was never a member of the CCB himself, but merely helped his brother and cousin with their operations.

Jeremy Brickhill is claiming Rl,2 million from Guy and Kitt Bawden, the South African government and the ministers of Law and Order and Defence.

Brickhill, who is still undergoing medical treatment for the injuries he sustained in the blast, said he was never a member of the ANC, although he did support the organisation. Guy Bawden announced that he would be willing to testify for Brickhill in his case against the South African government.[33]

Fears that South African death squads still operated in neighbouring states were strengthened when a parcel bomb exploded in April 1990 in Harare in the hands of an Anglican priest and ANC member, Father Michael Lapsley.

A few weeks earlier Lapsley had received a letter on ANC stationery telling him to expect books from South Africa. When two parcels arrived he opened the first one and found a religious book from South Africa. The second parcel contained a bomb that blew off his left hand. He also lost an eye and three fingers on his right hand.[34]

There is no hard evidence to link the attack to the South African government, but it bears all the hallmarks of yet another death squad attack.

South Africa's military and security involvement in the neighbouring states have not been limited to brutal force alone. One of the most cunning and devious plans ever devised by the security police concerned the discrediting of the former Moderator of the Dutch Reformed Missionary Church and anti-apartheid leader Dr Allan Boesak and the abduction of a Russian diplomat from Lesotho to cause an international incident.

In May 1990 I met a former Bloemfontein security police agent, Jan Smith, who had been ordered to execute a master plan to arrange a meeting between Allan Boesak and a Soviet diplomat in Cape Town. The plan was to enable the security police to arrest the two men, discredit Boesak as a communist and cause an international diplomatic incident with the presence of the diplomat in South Africa. The plan was aborted when the agent found his loyalty divided between his friendship with the Soviets and his duty to his country.

Smith, a former Springbok judo champion, was recruited in January 1986 while working for a South African construction company in Lesotho. He was asked by his handler to take photographs of ANC transit houses that were pointed out to him, ANC training camps and airports. He received counterinsurgency training outside Pretoria and was given the assurance that he would be protected by the South African government if anything should go wrong during an operation.

Shortly after Smith was recruited, he was trapped in a luxury Maseru hotel during a South African engineered *coup d'état*. As the fighting raged in the streets of the Lesotho capital, Smith met the political officer at the Soviet Embassy in Lesotho, Yuri Popenhoff. They started talking to each other and soon became good friends.

South Africa has always believed that Soviet embassies in neighbouring states played a key role in the plotting of terrorist activities. In the first half of the eighties the ANC was particularly active in Lesotho, and Pretoria perceived that country as a key base for the organisation. Smith's handler in the security police was elated about his contact with Popenhoff and instructed him to nurture the good relationship. For the next seven months, Smith saw the Soviets on a frequent basis. In July 1987 Popenhoff was transferred to the Seychelles and replaced by Oleg D Khodyrev, with whom Smith also became friends. The South African agent was also introduced to Ambassador Stritzkov and Vassili Memonko, who Smith suspected worked for the KGB.

A bizarre situation developed when Khodyrev asked Smith to work under cover for the Russian Embassy by smuggling videos from South Africa to the Embassy in Lesotho. Smith told his handler about the request and was instructed to tape his conversations with Khodyrev. He even planted a bug in the Soviet Embassy. The security police devised a plan to embarrass the Congress of South African Trade Unions. According to the plan, Smith had to establish contact with members of Cosatu and arrange a meeting with Khodyrev in Lesotho, saying that he would meet them in Bloemfontein and smuggle them over the border.

Smith went to see his friend Khodyrev in Lesotho and proposed a meeting with Cosatu to him. Khodyrev approved and handed Smith a signed business card to give to the Cosatu officials. Smith's handler instructed him to arrange similar meetings for Archbishop Desmond Tutu and Allan Boesak.

The plan was for Smith to monitor and tape record the whole meeting in Lesotho and, as the group returned to South Africa, to have them arrested in a road block. Smith had two meetings with Boesak in his office in Cape Town where he proposed the meeting with the Soviet diplomat, which Boesak approved in principle.

In the meantime, to further win the trust of the Soviets, Smith was told to hand over plans of 5 Military Works, the Simon's Town Naval Base and the Waterkloof Air Force Base to his friends in Lesotho. The plans were altered in such a way that they could not harm South Africa.

Months went by without Smith being able to arrange the meeting with the Soviets. His handler got suspicious and took him to Pretoria where he was questioned by various security policemen about his apparent reluctance to execute the plan. He confessed that his friendship with Khodyrev had grown to such an extent that he felt he could no longer betray him. In the end, however, he was persuaded to continue with the Boesak plan.

A new plan was put forward. It was decided that Smith should go to Lesotho, drug Khodyrev and bring him back to South Africa along a secret route. The two of them, with Khodyrev presumably still fast asleep, would be stopped at a roadblock and arrested. The South Africans were aware that Khodyrev was in possession of a false British passport and that he had previously illegally visited South Africa. Smith would then admit that he had brought the diplomat to South Africa for a meeting with Allan Boesak and testify in court about his ties with Cosatu and the Soviets and that he had been a spy for the "enemy". Hopefully the whole incident would be so embarrassing to the Soviets that they would close their embassy in Lesotho.

Smith decided in the end that he could not go ahead with the plan and phoned Khodyrev from Bloemfontein to inform him about the proposed abduction. The Soviets advised him to leave South Africa immediately and seek political asylum in Botswana. Smith refused and phoned his handler, telling him that he was not going ahead with the plan and could no longer work for the security police. Smith was taken into "protective custody" and questioned for days. The police seized all his documents, diary and photographs.

This story is yet again reminiscent of a Cold War spy tale, but it appears to have been the truth. When I talked to Allan Boesak about the plan he immediately remembered two meetings he had had towards the end of 1987 with a man by the name of Smith who proposed a meeting with a Soviet diplomat in Lesotho.

"I remember him very, very well. He walked into my office dressed in his Springbok blazer and insisted on seeing me. I was a bit irritated but was soon impressed by his honesty and openness. He told me that he had ties with the Soviets in Lesotho and we talked about the church, politics and racism. I remember that he wanted to know how I feel about white people. When I saw him the second time, he asked me whether I would be prepared to meet his friend the Soviet diplomat. He said that a meeting between a person like myself and the Soviets could only foster peace in the region. Smith seemed incredibly honest and I never thought he could be a spy. I told him that I was willing to meet anybody to talk about peace," Boesak said.[35]

Cosatu officials confirmed that they had met Smith and that he showed them a signed card from a Soviet diplomat. Continued correspondence between Smith and Khodyrev confirmed their friendship, while other documents indicated that Smith must have had strong ties with the security police during the middle eighties to around May 1988.

It is significant that Ambassador Stritzkov and two senior diplomats, Vassili Memonko and Khodyrev himself, were transferred from Lesotho in June 1988 after the embassy was, according to reports, infiltrated by a South African spy. Since then, the embassy has not regained its ambassadorial status.

Looking back at the story, it is not clear whether the South Africans really intended to kidnap a Soviet diplomat from Lesotho and set up Allan Boesak, or whether it was a brilliantly devised plan to undermine the influence of the Soviet Union in southern Africa and get rid of the ambassador and his KGB agents. I suspect it was the latter.

CHAPTER THIRTEEN

To persuade a judge of murder

IT was a warm spring day and people were splashing in the fountains on Trafalgar Square as Dirk Coetzee walked into the South African Embassy in London to deliver his testimony before the Harms Commission. He faced six gruelling days of interrogation as he tried to persuade a judge, eight legal teams and an audience of lawyers, diplomats, policemen, anti-apartheid activists and journalists that he had indeed led a death squad. Opposing him were two legal teams acting for the South African Police who tried their damnedest to try and get him to admit his innocence.[1]

The scene for the hearing was the old cinema theatre, in the cellar of the embassy, decorated richly with leaping springbok, galloping wildebeest and copper proteas, that is used for church services on Sundays. Dirk Coetzee, David Tshikalange and members of the ANC who attended the hearing had been given special indemnity against detention in the embassy, which according to international law is South African territory. The commission of inquiry into the death squad allegations transferred its operations from Pretoria to the British capital for two weeks to hear the evidence of Coetzee and Tshikalange. Sitting behind a desk on the stage was Judge Louis Harms.

A month earlier Coetzee had been preceded as a witness by Almond Nofemela, who was brought from the death cells at the Pretoria Central Prison to testify before Harms in the Synodal Centre of the Dutch Reformed Church in the capital. In London, he was preceded by David.

Coetzee was ill-prepared for his evidence and emotionally devastated by his wife's affair with a Pretoria student. Shortly before his arrival in London, he had been informed that the student had moved into his house and that Karin and her newfound love had gone on holiday together. She had been supposed to fly to London to support her husband, but in the end he told her to stay in South Africa. The fact that his brother Ben was with him in London helped little to console the distraught Coetzee.

On his arrival in London from Lusaka, Coetzee had briefly been questioned by Scotland Yard detectives about the 1982 bombing of the ANC offices in London. He had been furious about the delay, demanding to know whether he was in detention. He got his entry stamp an hour or two later.

In the two weeks prior to their departure for Europe, Dirk and Ben Coetzee had worked on a lengthy statement on Dirk's life and crimes. At first, he refused to give evidence before the Harms Commission because his statement was not finished. The ANC had to persuade him to go to London and he and Tshikalange arrived only two days before they were due to start giving evidence.

Coetzee refused to speak to his wife on the telephone and went to bed early at night. One Saturday I took him on a sight-seeing tour of London to try and cheer him up. As we walked through the vaults of Westminster Abbey, Coetzee wryly remarked: "I suddenly feel at home. This reminds me of Vlakplaas."

David Tshikalange's first overseas visit had overwhelmed him. He spent his time either in his bedroom or at the embassy. At the two men's sides were the ANC guards who for the past six months had shared their twilight existence.

Coetzee followed Tshikalange to the witness table on Wednesday. He was smartly dressed in a checked jacket and dark slacks and presented a confident figure. He was led for a day by his senior counsel, Denis Kuny, and he spoke with great confidence and the sincerity of a man who had to rid himself of a terrible burden. He described in graphic detail how anti-government activists and ANC members were kidnapped, tortured, murdered and their bodies burnt; that this was part of his job as a security policeman – sanctioned at higher level – and that he had believed he was fighting for a just cause "against ANC terrorists, communists and the *swart gevaar* [black peril]".

Murder, perjury, forgery, arson, theft and assault rolled off Coetzee's tongue as he coloured his evidence with the names of senior policemen who he said played some part in the network. He described a murky world in which, at times, fact seemed to have been blended with horrible fantasy. Throughout his evidence he was watched by a row of beefy men in grey suits and matching shoes who shook their heads in disbelief as he testified about the murders of Griffiths Mxenge, Peter Dlamini, Vuyani Mavuso, Sizwe Kondile, Ace Moema, the Lesotho diamond dealer and Siphiwo Mtimkulu. He came face to face with one of his alleged co-perpetrators when Colonel Hermanus du Plessis, implicated in the murder of Sizwe Kondile, was pointed out to him.

The limitations of the Harms Commission's brief were a grave setback to Coetzee. Describing how the Vlakplaas death squad prepared for a mission into Botswana, he was brought up short in his testimony because of the extra-territorial restriction. "I just want you to understand that you cannot confine me into a water tight compartment and then expect from me to explain to you in understanding language what the security culture is all about, " he pleaded. "If I could have started from A and go right through my career, through the three years in Swaziland where I have done my so-called apprenticeship in the security police, then I think it will fall more in place."

Coetzee had chosen to testify in English as he wanted the world press to understand his evidence.It was a grave mistake as he fumbled and struggled to express himself.

The senior counsel for the police, Sam Maritz, subjected Coetzee to three days of fierce cross-examination as he probed the contradictions between his account and those of Nofemela and Tshikalange. There were heated exchanges between Coetzee and Maritz, a skilled and aggressive cross-examiner.

Maritz arrived in London in a welter of papers and documents for his cross-examination, the result of months of preparation for the task of breaking Coetzee's evidence down and discrediting him in the face of the world. Police strategy was clear when Maritz told him: "It must be plain even to you, Mr Coetzee, that your stories are totally ridiculous ... Those members of the South African Police that you have scurrilously involved in all these supposed enterprises of yours will deny your allegations, every one of them."

Coetzee responded: "I believe so, Mr Maritz, they have got no option ... It's all lies, sir, and if I [had remained] home in South Africa, I would have done exactly the same."

Soon after the cross-examination started, Louis Harms responded sharply to the fact that Coetzee had not even read through the statement he made in Mauritius or the transcript of the tape recordings. Harms told Denis Kuny: "I cannot believe ... we provided your side, I believe, long ago with these transcripts and if the witness now says he hasn't read it and he came unprepared, I find it difficult to know how we are going to handle this matter. I would have thought that a witness of Mr Coetzee's standing would have read his statement prior to getting into the witness box." The few days that Coetzee and his legal team spent together in London had simply not been enough to prepare him properly. Two days before the cross-examination was completed, Kuny had to return to South Africa and Coetzee's junior counsel, De Wet Marais, had to handle the re-examination, to scathing criticism from Harms.

Coetzee insisted that he was telling the truth to the commission, whatever lies he might have peddled in the past, saying that he had decided to spill the beans because he wanted to clear his conscience once and for all.

Maritz told Coetzee that by his own admission he was a liar, a perjurer, a burglar and a murderer. "In fact, you're not a very pretty person, are you?" he goaded.

Coetzee: "No, like all of us in the security police ... My skills were misused in the security police, in the security family ... I've never murdered again. I've never stolen cars again."

221

Harms: "Since you've left the security police, have you become a good man again?"

Coetzee: "Well, normal in my sense. Not a murderer and a car thief. Not a, what I would call a you know, angel, but the authentic Dirk Coetzee . . ."

Maritz: ". . . So in this war . . . anything went?"

Coetzee: "Anything went."

Maritz: "Then explain the incident with the diamond dealer."

Coetzee: "It was a private enterprise, sure. It had nothing to do with fighting the war . . . It is a question that if you could do it for a nation and for a country, illegal things that are not lawful, why not for yourself?"

Maritz: "Why did you mention it?"

Coetzee: "To get my conscience clear for once and for all. I've spoken out about every single thing in my life that I've done wrong."

Maritz: "And that's the big conundrum that I can't work out . . . I've not heard one word of sorrow from you."

Coetzee: "Of sorrow? Do you want me to sit down crying? I went to the enemy . . . I took that calculated risk. I went to the ANC. And I went and I said I've done wrong to you guys."

Maritz: "What disgusts me, is that you would say: 'This table cloth is white' and 'I burnt Peter and Vusi' in exactly the same fashion."

Coetzee: "What disgusts me is that you defend dishonest policemen that are lying in South Africa."

Maritz: "The worst part of it is that one could still forgive you, but the only way in which you can save yourself is by drawing all around you and everybody around you into your own cesspit."

Coetzee told the commission that the security police were an elite force and had good relations with other branches of the police force, who respected and admired the secrecy and close loyalty within the units. This enabled them to operate above the law. He said: "They were seen as the front line against the onslaught against South Africa. They worked in secrecy, they performed an honourable task against the enemy of South Africa and it was a small family. Not everyone was selected to join them. So, it was an honour to be with them."

Maritz repudiated Coetzee's claim that the security police operated above the law. A telex was urgently sent to security police headquarters in Pretoria to obtain some figures to show that security policemen had in the past been investigated, charged and convicted. Maritz came back the next day with some statistics. He told Coetzee: ". . . Now it may interest you to know that during the period from 1981 to 1989 there were 288 criminal cases brought against members of the security branch . . . to do with the execution of their duties . . . In that time 21 of them were found guilty."

Coetzee: "Only . . . Of the 288 . . . ?"

Maritz: "That is not a picture of a force which is beyond the law."

Coetzee was slammed by Maritz for implicating respected senior policemen in his "death squad fantasies" without any hard evidence and even simply on hearsay. Maritz said to Coetzee: "But I want you to realise what you are doing ... General [Lothar] Neethling, one of the most respected criminologists in the world today. You reduce him to a common poisoner."

Coetzee: "That is exactly what he is." Harms: "Or a bad poisoner . . ."

Maritz: "But it goes further than that. He's not just a bad poisoner, but an idiot."

The judge was severely criticised for his attitude to Coetzee, at times interjecting sharply and sometimes commenting unfavourably on his claims. When the rogue policeman could not remember how long his squad had stayed with Peter Dlamini and Vuyani Mavuso at Zeerust and Groblersdal before they took them to Komatipoort to have them killed Harms said: "What I find amazing, Mr Coetzee, is that you can remember the number of drops which were in a bottle ten years ago, but you cannot remember the number of days."

Coetzee: "But, sir, I didn't prepare at that time to come and give evidence in the court. There were certain things that made a greater and [more] permanent impression on me than other things."

Harms: "So the number of drops was to you more important than the number of people killed or when they were killed, or the sequence in which they were killed?"

Harms was slammed by the British press for his behaviour when in an amazing outburst he told Coetzee that he was talking "crap". In a deviation from his statement to *Vrye Weekblad*, Coetzee told the Harms Commission that he had lied when he said that Mxenge's car radio had been put into Brigadier Willem Schoon's car. It was in fact installed into Brigadier Jan du Preez's car. Coetzee explained: "Brigadier Jan was always very, very special . . . Okay, I tried to protect Brigadier Jan."

Harms: "But you didn't protect him, because you involved him in that statement, but you also involved an innocent man. So you didn't protect Du Preez. You involved him in the Mxenge murder and the car radio. That's a lot of crap."

Coetzee was extensively cross-examined from the records of his police trial in 1985. The police used all the available evidence against him, including the foul language recorded from his tapped telephone. He admitted that he had given false information to the doctor who testified on his behalf at his police trial because he felt the disciplinary hearing was a farce, and that he had exaggerated his diabetic condition in order to ensure early medical retirement. Harms found him difficult to believe: "My problem is then, Mr

Coetzee, it is a very simple problem, where does the fabrication begin and where does it end?"

Coetzee's evidence underscored his transition from self-confessed death squad commander to a dedicated ANC neophyte. Every time the other senior counsel for the police, Louis Visser, spoke about terrorists, Coetzee would set the record straight by reminding him that he was in fact referring to freedom fighters.

Visser started a political skirmish when he asked: "Would you agree with the fact that the ANC has since at least 1986 waged a revolutionary war in South Africa?"

"Would you deny that since 1912 the ANC has been trying to negotiate till up to 1962 when Comrade Nelson Mandela was standing in the dock and addressed the court and he said – he was quoting from Chief Albert Luthuli – saying for thirty years in vain I have been knocking moderately, patiently at a barred and closed door?" was Coetzee's prompt answer.

The letter Coetzee wrote to a family member and gave to James Stevens in Lusaka (see Chapter 6) had been intercepted when Stevens handed himself over to the police. Its embarrassing contents were read out at the hearing. The letter revealed that Coetzee had nurtured hopes of being appointed as chief investigator in a post-war Nuremberg trial in South Africa.

Les Roberts, senior counsel for the commission: "You see yourself as the chief investigator in what you call South Africa's own Nuremberg trial."

Coetzee: "I said that could happen in the future if the truth doesn't come out at this stage."

Roberts: ". . . And at the end of this Nuremberg procedure which you think is a possibility, after you have flushed everybody out are you going to turn yourself in so that you can be prosecuted along with the rest?"

Coetzee: "That's right. Accused [number] one."

Roberts: "That makes about as much sense as it would be if at the original Nuremberg they'd made Rudolf Hess the chief investigator."

In the end, the police had painted Coetzee as a mentally unstable man who bitterly hated the police force and dreamed about returning to South Africa as a general under an ANC government. Maritz summed up: ". . . I want to put it to you that you saw in the revelations of Nofemela the opportunity to vent your hate towards the police. That is the *fons et origo* of your whole attack, of all your stories, of all the nonsense that you have been spouting over the past months and there is not a word of truth in it."

Coetzee: "I had the opportunity . . . or the choice to just sit put and lie, as everyone else is doing now, or to come out with the truth. So if there is an opportunity to go back one day, I can go back with a complete, clear conscience and start a new life."

After his evidence Coetzee said giving evidence to the commission had been like trying to play rugby in a squash court. Every time you tried to run a yard you hit a brick wall. Coetzee was worried that Harms was not going to believe his evidence, and his life on the run began again.[2]

It was disturbing but not surprising that little or no documentary evidence of any significance adverse to the South African Police was produced by the commission's investigation team. By far the greatest part of the evidence against the police was produced by the Independent Board of Inquiry into Informal Repression. Human rights lawyers agreed that a major purpose of the investigative team appeared to have been to provide exculpatory evidence for the police.[3]

The human rights lawyers investigating the activities of the Vlakplaas squad experienced problems similar to those of their counterparts digging into the activities of the CCB. Several police witnesses refused to answer questions; other witnesses refused to testify unless their identity was protected; a number of material documents either disappeared or were not produced, or their existence was flatly denied. On several occasions the human rights lawyers requested copies of certain documents through the commission and from the police only to have their requests refused or not complied with. These documents included the personal files of several policemen implicated in the atrocities. The police also refused to provide the records of arrests made by Vlakplaas members. Dirk Coetzee's successor, Colonel Jan Coetzee, said there had been no time to keep records of operations because they were "looking for terrorists". Brigadier Willem Schoon, on the other hand, stated that there was a file on Vlakplaas and that all written reports went to Security Headquarters. When these documents were requested, the police simply responded that none had ever existed.[4]

In the end, the police drew a veil of secrecy across the activities of the Vlakplaas squads and Louis Harms was faced with blank and bare denials by a battery of police witnesses. The policemen serving at Vlakplaas were covered in a coat of white paint and presented as knights in shining armour. It was astounding to hear them telling the commission that they had never made use of any unconventional or unlawful methods in attempting to deal with problems presented by revolutionary activities. By contrast, Dirk Coetzee, David Tshikalange and Almond Nofemela were subjected to relentless, lengthy and at times contemptuous cross-examination. They were treated as accused instead of being listened to as witnesses trying to help the commission unravel the web of atrocities. In the end, Harms was faced with a mass of conflicting, contradictory and in some respects very unsatisfactory evidence. As with the CCB, he refused to call the political head of the police, Adriaan Vlok, to explain what orders had been given to his subordinates.[5]

The terms of reference of the commission were far too narrow, preventing many important questions from being asked and answered, and preventing the commission from investigating some of the most controversial and sinister aspects of the scandal. A number of policemen who testified before the commission vehemently denied that the Vlakplaas squads had ever operated outside the borders of the Republic. There was, however, undeniable evidence of cross-border activity, like the Botswana raid, the kidnapping of Joe Pillay and the Swaziland atrocities committed by Dirk Coetzee. If it could be proved that the police had lied about this, why should their evidence in respect to internal acts of violence be believed?

Lawyers for Human Rights said in argument: "The limitation is highly artificial and totally illogical ... It has become perfectly clear, from documents, affidavits and oral evidence tendered to the Commissioner that various acts of violence ... were committed from time to time outside the borders of the Republic in neighbouring countries such as Swaziland, Lesotho, Botswana and Mozambique by or at the instance of members of the Vlakplaas Squad and by members of the CCB. How can such a report, limited by its geographical boundaries, ever be seen to constitute a full, accurate or satisfactory report? ... The Commissioner was only able to obtain a truncated picture of the acts and activities. Evidence concerning external acts of violence may have constituted vital corroboration of evidence concerning internal acts of violence."

However, despite the difficulty in cross-examining the police witnesses, it became clear that Vlakplaas had achieved very little of what it was set up to do – identify and arrest insurgents. It was difficult to believe that this could have been the sole function and object of the unit. If Vlakplaas was established to carry out acts which were perfectly lawful, there could have been no reason why proper records were not kept, and why pocket-books were not carried by individual policemen. Jan Coetzee had spent three years at Vlakplaas and said only six insurgents were apprehended by the askari units, Paul van Dyk spent seven years at Vlakplaas and testified that only between two and five arrests were made, while Koos Vermeulen said that in his five years at the unit, one or two arrests were made. Willem Schoon said he was commander of Section C for eight years and could not recall the exact numbers, but that only 20 arrests were made. Eugene de Kock declined to say how many arrests there had been in his time at Vlakplaas. About 20 people had been shot, he admitted.

Almond Nofemela had given his evidence to the commission a month before Coetzee. He was taken from Pretoria Central Prison's death row to testify before Harms in the Synodal Centre of the Dutch Reformed Church in the capital. Wearing olive-green prison overalls, slippers and brown socks and speaking in a slightly hoarse and emotionless voice, Nofemela undertook to tell the truth but refused to take the oath because he had stopped believing in God when he was convicted of murder. Calm and unemotional as always, he told the judge that he had joined the death squad because it paid according to the importance of the person eliminated and that in his eight years in the force he had made just one arrest. "I don't arrest anyone, I kidnap or assassinate them, " he stated.

226

In a week of intensive cross-examination Nofemela demonstrated what appeared to be a phenomenal memory for the details of particular missions but often stumbled over actual dates – a factor which was seized on by the opposing legal teams. They called Nofemela an outright liar and a common car thief.

Maritz told him: "There has never been a hit squad in the police, not then, not now, not ever . . . You have made the most hideous untruthful accusations against members of the police . . ."

The murder of Griffiths Mxenge had become central and crucial to the death squad controversy. There were a number of discrepancies in the accounts of the murder as given by Tshikalange, Coetzee and Nofemela. Although their accounts agreed more than they diverged, there were discrepancies about who had prepared the poisoned meat for the dogs, the wounds that were inflicted during the murder, the bar in which Coetzee met the assassins afterwards and the disposal of Mxenge's car.

The discrepancies between the evidence of Coetzee and Nofemela might have been attributed to the lapse of time since the murder: it was possible that Nofemela resorted to a certain amount of reconstruction and possibly used his imagination where his memory for detail had failed him.

Maritz pounced on Nofemela: "As a matter of fact you know that you had nothing to do with the murder whatsoever . . . You sat in jail, death row and . . . you thought up a story and you took the Mxenge murder and you decided this happened nine years ago, the trail is so dead and cold now that nobody can catch me up, I latch on to this one and tell this story and save my neck."

Nofemela: "I had something to do with the murder because I was told to do that . . . Who then killed him if I did not?"

Another victim who featured prominently in the heated exchanges between Nofemela and Sam Maritz was Ernest Dipale, a man Nofemela claimed he had to "steal" from Soweto in 1985. Maritz told Nofemela that the man he referred to as Moabi was in fact Ernest Moabi Dipale who, according to police records, was a young Soweto man detained in October 1981 for three months and again in August 1982. He died in detention three months after he was interned. The man Nofemela referred to, Maritz told the commission, was not on record anywhere in the entire police files.

However, Bob Nugent, counsel for the Independent Board, asked Nofemela under re-examination if he could perhaps recall the registration number of his previous motor car. "FGR 245 T, " came the reply.

Nugent responded: "Mr Chairman, we have a piece of paper here with the registration number of Mr Nofemela's car written on it. The registration number is FRG 245 T. The number was taken down by someone who saw Mr Moabi being taken from his house, and the paper was given to a Johannesburg lawyer, who had as a matter of course investigated the number and ascertained who owned the vehicle. It has been in her possession since 1981."

This meant that Nofemela had been telling the truth when he told the commission about the Moabi abduction, and appeared to have demolished the police case on that particular point.

Maritz told Nofemela that Major Eugene de Kock would deny having shot Japie Maponya point-blank to prevent him identifying Nofemela afterwards. Maritz said: "I am telling you again that you are lying. That your whole story regarding Japie Maponya is a concocted lie. I am going to prove it to you . . . So here is the man [De Kock] who is supposed to have committed this abduction with you, he denies it."

Nofemela: "I am not surprised when he denies it . . . A planted lie. He [Maponya] was kidnapped in order to tell us more about his brother. It is what has been suggested to me that I must go and kidnap him so that he can tell us more about his brother . . ."

Nofemela stated that there was never a written report on work he and the team undertook. They reported back verbally to their superiors. He told the commission there was once an occurrence book on the farm they had to fill in, but it eventually fell into disuse.

On another occasion the Independent Board handed in some documents about the theft of a motor vehicle in Port Elizabeth literally a couple of hours after the police had said that they had been unable to find any evidence of such a theft and that Nofemela was lying. Maritz responded to the document: "We do not know either whether you and Coetzee and Tshikalange organised yourselves into a car stealing gang for your own ends as in the case of the diamond dealer . . . Were you a car stealing gang, the three of you? You went around the country stealing cars, taking them across the border, selling them and pocketing the proceeds, is that what you did?"

Nofemela: "I do not remember having done so . . . I was instructed to steal."

In the end, it seemed as though the police had succeeded at least partially in discrediting Almond Nofemela. Harms himself had given numerous indications that his assessment of Nofemela's evidence was far from favourable. Inconsistencies and memory lapses had been exposed and sufficient doubt had been sown to place question marks over the truth of his claims.

Aspects of the testimonies of Nofemela and Coetzee were corroborated by David Tshikalange, who gave evidence before Harms in the South African Embassy in London. He repeated under oath that he had participated in the murder of Mxenge and described the wounds he inflicted on the attorney, but counsel for the police accused him of fabricating a "horror story". He also described how the Vlakplaas death squad prepared for a mission into Botswana. But after saying how they prepared for the operation by blackening their faces, he was stopped by Kuny, who told him that nothing further could be told about it because of the restrictions on the commission. Had he been allowed to continue, he would have described the raid into Botswana in which Joyce Dipale was shot by Joe Mamasela. It was this particular incident which later exposed a massive cover-up by the police.

Back in Johannesburg, Joseph Mamasela, who was implicated by Coetzee in the killings of Griffiths Mxenge, Peter Dlamini and Vuyani Mavuso, told the commission that he had not had any involvement with Vlakplaas before 1982. He and several senior security policemen testified that until 1982 he was only a police informer who was personally handled by Colonel Jan Coetzee. He could therefore not have known Dirk Coetzee or Almond Nofemela in 1981 and could not have participated in the killing of Griffiths Mxenge, the raid into Botswana, the murder of Peter Dlamini and Vuyani Mavuso or the killing of the Lesotho diamond dealer. The fact that Mamasela only came to Vlakplaas in 1982 was used extensively by the police to discredit Coetzee and Nofemela.

Counsel for the Independent Board, Paul Pretorius, shot a missile into the legal melting pot when he informed the commission that the Independent Board had obtained immigration documents from the Botswana government which revealed without a shadow of doubt that Mamasela was lying when he denied that he had known Coetzee before 1982 and never participated in the Botswana raid. According to the customs documentation, three men entered Botswana on 26 November 1981 in a vehicle which the Independent Board established was registered at security police headquarters. The three men were Mamasela, Dirk Coetzee and Anderson Paul Gumede, an alias used by Nofemela. It was the same night that Joyce Dipale opened the door of her house in Gaborone and was shot point-blank by an attacker whom she identified as Joe Mamasela.

It was not only a police cover-up that had been exposed, but the date of the raid was also very important. The police cross-examined Coetzee in London on the assumption that the Botswana raid took place between 4 and 21 November 1981. That was when the Vlakplaas squad was in Durban and Griffiths Mxenge was murdered. Maritz told Coetzee that he was lying about the raid as the men could not have been in Botswana and Durban at the same time.

Mamasela tried to wriggle out of his predicament as he was taken under severe cross-examination by Pretorius. Claiming that the Botswana documents were forged, he said: "Yes, it is the work of a genius who is very sick in his mind. I can assure you that because I was not on that day in Botswana with any kind of travel document."

Pretorus: "A genius?"

Mamasela: "It is possible. I said this is the work of a genius with a sick mind because really if you look at this thing it looks so convincing, but if you look at it thoroughly you can see that there are flaws, there are genuine flaws."

Pretorius: ". . . So, are you saying that Dirk Coetzee went across the border in the company of an ANC person who knew you? Is that what your version comes out to?"

Mamasela: "Ja, I mean I have got my own speculations and suspicions. My suspicions are that Dirk Coetzee may have been a double agent for all his life in the police force. It is possible. People can laugh but it is possible . . . Much of the allegations that is put in front of this commission is farfetched . . . I am not a liar. I am prepared to put my head on a guillotine. I am prepared to suffer the dire consequences of the truth. If I wanted to lie I would have joined all those who ran away from the truth . . . And I will die for the truth I am standing for."

Jan Coetzee, questioned about the documents and his part in the cover-up, said: "Looking at these documents, I have to accept that these persons went into Botswana that day. I don't think there can be any question about that . . . I must have been misled by these persons, because I don't know anything about this." Pretorius suggested to him that the police had denied that Mamasela and Dirk Coetzee knew each other in 1981 not only to conceal the truth about the Botswana raid, but also to try and convince the commission that Coetzee, Nofemela and Tshikalange must have lied about the Mxenge murder. It was a strong indication of a police conspiracy to prevent disclosure of unlawful acts to the commission and to discredit Dirk Coetzee. Jan Coetzee denied the allegations.

The exposure of the police cover-up to protect Mamasela was the only real break-through the human rights lawyers achieved. Although they had appointed investigators to search for clues and evidence, it had always been known that the Vlakplaas death squad never left any traces and that all possible evidence would have been destroyed. The blunt denials by the policemen appearing before Harms made proper cross-examination impossible.

After months of tiring and expensive commission work, South Africa knew very little more about the existence of a death squad in the South African Police. In their final argument before Judge Louis Harms, the human rights lawyers suggested that in a situation of combating terrorism and the "total onslaught" it would not be surprising to find that very often normal lawful and generally accepted forms of conduct on the part of the police would be discarded in favour of more drastic action. At a time when a revolution was in progress which the police were determined to curb and curtail, things might have been done that were not carried out according to the book. Harms was asked not to be so naive as to believe that policemen never lie, never commit unlawful acts, and that in combating terrorism and insurgency they would not resort to any method which they considered necessary, even though in so doing they would be breaking the law. It made no sense, nor could it possibly be true, that the section of the police force that constituted a counterinsurgency unit would fight a war with kid gloves on and strictly according to the "Marquis of Queensberry" rules.[7]

The Independent Board argued: "The public interest . . . goes far beyond the factual question of whether the acts alleged occurred and, if so, who committed these acts . . . The public interest goes further even than the personal safety and security of citizens and their property . . . The public interest at issue goes to very root of the existence of South African citizens in a society subject to law and justice and under a Government accountable to its citizens."[8]

CHAPTER FOURTEEN

Blessed is he who can recognise the truth . . .

ON 13 November 1990, after more than 70 days of hearings both inside and outside South Africa, the State President released the Harms Commission's findings. The report raised more questions than it answered. It had been an exercise in futility.

At the opening of the commission the Ministry of Justice had submitted a list of 71 unsolved and politically motivated murders; the Independent Board of Inquiry into Informal Repression had presented for special consideration a list of 42 murders allegedly perpetrated by agents of the state against opponents of apartheid, as well as details of seven disappearances of persons in suspicious circumstances and information regarding over 200 other instances of state-inspired violence; the police had submitted a total of 2 851 murders recorded by them as being allegedly politically motivated.

These dossiers contain the political history of a South Africa engulfed for decades by a wave of violence. The files of the human rights organisations tell a tale of a government that usurped the licence to kill those it viewed as enemies of the existing order. The police list showed how a voteless and frustrated majority took to violence and killed those they viewed as perpetrators of the apartheid system and enemies of their struggle for freedom.

Judge Louis Harms only investigated the alleged existence of state-sanctioned death squads. Atrocities committed by members and supporters of the ANC and the PAC were nothing new and did not warrant any judicial investigation. There was ample evidence – led in South African courts and through statements by ANC leaders in exile – of the nature and magnitude of the ANC's armed struggle. The organisation has in fact had a policy of claiming responsibility for most acts of violence committed against apartheid targets in South Africa.

Nobody expected a single judge or a single commission to solve a substantial number of murders. The commission's brief was to establish whether the government or specific organs of the state had followed a policy of eliminating opponents. If that was not the case, why then were political assassinations never solved? Was it possible that a death squad might have existed without official sanction?

Political philosophers and human rights lawyers agreed that the Harms Commission was one of the most important judicial investigations in South African legal history. It would be difficult to imagine an issue of greater public interest than the one with which the commission was dealing. Why? The respected American jurist and United States Supreme Court judge, Louis Brandeis, once said: "If government becomes a law-breaker, it breeds contempt for law; it invites every man to become a law unto himself; it invites anarchy."[1]

The Harms Commission had a duty to at long last bring state atrocities into the public domain and thereby show the way to prevent a similar scenario in future. Knowledge of the atrocities committed under National Party rule would help South Africans prevent a new government from using similar methods and fostering a similar evil. However, at the end of the day, South Africans still did not know what had happened.

Harms unearthed ten incidents he thought warranted further action:

- Two murders, those of Mamelodi medical docter and activist Dr Fabian Ribeiro and his wife Florence.
- Conspiracy to murder three anti-apartheid activists: journalist Gavin Evans, Cape Town lawyer Dullah Omar and Natal lawyer Kwenza Mlaba. In none of these instances was any serious damage done.
- One bombing, that of the Early Learning Centre in Athlone. Again nobody was hurt although substantial damage was done.
- One motor car theft.
- One arson attack in Johannesburg.
- The theft of documentation and perjury by one of the witnesses.[2]

That's all. It was not an impressive tally given the scale of the problem that the commission was meant to be addressing. Louis Harms admitted in his report: "The commission has been unable to achieve one of its main purposes, namely to restore public confidence in a part of the State administration."[3]

In the end, Harms found that the Civil Co-operation Bureau had been involved in death squad activities. On the other hand, he exonerated the South African Police, drawing accusations that he had ignored aspects of the evidence that had been placed before him of a police death squad that operated beyond the law and committed a series of shocking and brutal acts.[4]

With the exception of the killing of Fabian and Florence Ribeiro, the trail was still littered with unsolved murders. It was a valuable opportunity lost. Professor John Dugard concluded that the commission's failure to deal convincingly with the issues had merely opened the door to future recrimination, retribution, and possible Nuremberg-style trials under a post-apartheid government. "The State have let an opportunity slip to establish their good faith. Future actions against apartheid criminals are likely to be far harsher, " he said.[5]

Yet, ironically, Harms chose to introduce his report with a Latin expression: *Felix qui potuit verum cognoscere causas* – Blessed is he who can recognise the truth.

Despite its limitations, the report did deliver a scathing denunciation of the CCB, which Harms said ". . . had arrogated itself the power to try, sentence and punish people without the persons knowing of the allegations against them or having had the opportunity to defend themselves. The information on which the verdict is based is inherently suspect and untestified. The penalty imposed is also out of proportion to what would have been imposed in a civil court."[6]

The judge also said that it was more than likely that members of the CCB participated in crimes that did not form part of the commission's hearings. These actions had "contaminated the whole security arm of the State" and the CCB's conduct before and during the commission "creates suspicions that they have been involved in more crimes of violence than the evidence shows. These suspicions are not necessarily unfounded."[7]

The judge failed, however, to determine political accountability for the actions of Magnus Malan and other SADF officials. Harms said in his report that he had not concerned himself with the nature and extent of Magnus Malan's responsibility, nor even with how much the minister knew, though he did point out that Malan was politically responsible for his department – which included the CCB. Harms said there were no facts available that indicated Malan needed to be called as a witness before the commission – "in fact a consultation with him did not produce anything of assistance to the commission." By the same token, the commission had also not called for Minister of Law and Order Adriaan Vlok to give testimony. Harms found "the request bordered on the absurd and was therefore rejected."[8]

The judge said there had been "a basic lack of evidential material that might put some flesh on the bones" as regards the testimony given to him in general. "Victims failed to furnish information. Willing, trustworthy witnesses did not come to the fore. It appeared relevant documentation had either been destroyed or concealed by members of the CCB – intervention by the State President, Minister of Defence and the Chief of the Defence Force was to no avail." Those responsible for the disappearance, he added, were probably Joe Verster, Braam Cilliers and Christo Brits.[9]

Harms found that the CCB had its own political agenda which did not correspond with the "expressed agenda of the political authority . . . there are also indications that the CCB put its own interests and those of its members above the public interest of the State." There was a suspicion that the CCB might have been involved in the murder of David Webster. "The CCB has done nothing to allay this suspicion," Harms declared.[10]

Commenting on the criticism levelled at the composition of the commission, Harms said the dedication and conduct of the officials had been exemplary and they had acted fearlessly whoever the "opponent" was.[11]

A full-scale government public relations exercise was brought into operation on the eve of the release of the report. Parliamentary and special correspondents were briefed by government officials and State President FW de Klerk and three cabinet ministers had carefully prepared statements ready.

FW de Klerk supported his Minister of Defence's denial of responsibility and said that after careful study of the report he could find "no reason to condemn the politicians in charge for the way in which they carried out their duties and responsibilities."[12]

Malan was eager to convey a message that it was only a few rotten apples in his department that had caused the unnecessary controversy. He said it was the "unauthorised activity of five or six people" whose alleged actions had blemished the image of the armed forces. What the minister failed to explain away was that the Harms Commission, hampered by its severely circumscribed brief, had only been allowed to investigate a very small and very recently established segment of the CCB. And the one segment it did investigate, despite the lack of evidence and the concealment of documents, was found to have arrogated itself the role of executioner.[13]

According to the Westminster parliamentary tradition which South Africa inherited it is simply not good enough for Malan to claim innocence on the grounds of ignorance. Ministers must accept full liability for whatever happens in their departments – whether or not they know about it or are personally responsible. The irony is that if Malan really did not know, he is guilty of monumental incompetence, in any case.

But what was even more disturbing about the reaction of the Government was the total lack of regret or repentance. The best that De Klerk could come up with was: "The events dealt with in the report took place in an era of serious conflict, now belonging to the past. We should act with a view to our future and take conciliatory steps which are necessary to again create a peaceful South Africa."[14]

Colleague Philip van Niekerk remarked in the *Weekly Mail:* "For the people of South Africa that remembered or were touched by the corpses, the deafening silence is all they have."[15]

The former South African Secretary of Information – today a high-powered political consultant in the United States, Dr Eschel Rhoodie, once remarked: "[What South African commissions of inquiry] investigate is not the truth of the matter, but any person that might dare to publish or reveal information that implicates the government."[16]

In the end, what was investigated was not police death squads, but the mental state of Dirk Coetzee and Almond Nofemela. While the police miserably failed to produce any documents of substance relating to police atrocities, they had no problem in finding evidence relating to the personality and conduct of their accusers. Without a single shred of psychiatric evidence to support his finding, Harms declared Coetzee to have strong psychopathic tendencies. Yet he admitted at the same time that it was very difficult to evaluate Coetzee.

Lawyers and psychologists agreed that Harms was unjust and unfair when he made a finding about Coetzee's mental state in the absence of any psychological evidence. Although Coetzee's own legal team said in argument that he was not a shining example of what is right and wrong and there were many unsatisfactory features about his evidence, nobody, not even the South African Police, had suggested that the man might be a psychopath. What made Harms's finding even worse was that Coetzee was not an accused, but merely a witness assisting the commission in establishing the truth. He was never given the opportunity to defend himself against accusations that he might suffer from a mental disorder. Coetzee was in a way more prejudiced than an accused in a criminal trial who would in all probability have received an opportunity to be examined by a psychiatrist or a psychologist before judgement was passed on his mental state.

There was no evidence before the court pertaining to Coetzee's mental state when he committed the crimes, his childhood, his relationship with his wife and his family or other factors that may have had an important influence on his state of mind. In fact, when Coetzee tried to tell the commission early on in his evidence about his bizarre divorce, the judge told him that he was not interested in his personal relationships. Harms did not even hear the full story of Coetzee's death squad experiences because evidence on cross-border activities was not allowed.

Although very little or no research has been done on the mental states and personalities of death squad operatives, extensive psychological research has been done on torturers. There are of course a lot of similarities in that torturers also hurt, maim or sometimes kill their victims, deny their actions, see themselves as above the law and are a united brotherhood.

The Institute of Criminology at the University of Cape Town's 1986 study concludes: "A widely held hypothesis argues that torturers must be grossly disturbed personalities . . . Available evidence however tends to point in an alternative direction; the torturers are not particularly abnormal. They are far more likely to be quite ordinary people in an extraordinary, abnormal situation."[17]

An analysis of Nazi war criminals found that most torturers attributed their actions to obedience to a figure of authority. The great majority of participants in the study, quite ordinary, balanced people, went along with the horrific situation, despite evidence of substantial internal conflicts. The results strongly suggested that personality factors played a less significant role than expected in explaining such grim behaviour. In widely acclaimed research Greek military policemen were interviewed after the fall of the Greek military dictatorship (1967-1974). All the policemen interviewed had been involved in

236

atrocities. The study concludes by saying: "To believe that only sadists can perform such violent acts is a fallacy and a comfortable rationalisation to ease our liberal minds . . . If the proper learning procedures are applied under the right circumstances, any individual is a potential torturer."[18]

Harms considered Coetzee highly intelligent, with a remarkable memory, but also a strong imagination, seeing himself emerge as the victor from the battle. Coetzee claimed to have remorse about what he did, but never showed any signs, Harms found. Although he regarded himself as the leader of a death squad, he distanced himself time and time again from the actual crimes.

Harms found that the rogue policeman believed that because he had confessed his past, he could no longer be called to account. His conscience was now clear and he was entitled to a new life. He had blamed other people for his deeds even if he initiated or committed the crime.[19]

Louis Harms misjudged Coetzee. But what is even more disturbing is that the judge ascribed evidence and actions to Coetzee that the rogue policeman had never said or done. Coetzee did not see himself emerge as the victor from his cross-examination before the commission. At a press conference afterwards he said that Harms had not believed him and that he knew that the legal teams for the police had succeeded in discrediting him.[20]

Coetzee was extensively questioned by the commission on his lack of remorse yet he maintained that he deeply regretted what he did. The presence or absence of remorse is an important aspect in the evaluation of mental disorders. Only through psychological evaluation could it really have been established whether Coetzee showed remorse. Then again, if he did not show remorse, why not? Was it a sign of a mental disorder, or was it because he honestly believed that he was involved in a just war for his people and his country? The atrocities Coetzee participated in were committed under exceptional circumstances during a period of unprecedented upheaval in South African history.

Harms was wrong when he found that Coetzee had distanced himself from his actions. Coetzee admitted that he was a murderer, a thief, a kidnapper, an arsonist and whatever else. He even admitted that he was an accessory to a murder that was "a private enterprise", a crime he could easily have concealed.

Coetzee never said he could no longer be called to account. What he did say was that he was perfectly prepared to return to South Africa and stand trial on condition that his co-conspirators were charged with him. He does think that he is entitled to a new life, but that is mainly the result of assurances like that of Archbishop Desmond Tutu: "Our people have demonstrated that they are ready to forgive if someone expresses sorrow."[21]

Harms also found that it was very difficult to distinguish between fact and fiction, as Coetzee had for some time been busy collecting material on his atrocities because he wanted to write a novel. This is incorrect: I was the one who wanted to write a novel based on Coetzee's life story. I discussed the possibility with him once and never again. Nobody collected material until after he had left the country and told his life story.

I do not suggest that Coetzee should have been believed on face value, as he had often lied in the past and fabricated evidence to suit his own purposes. It is doubtful that any judge would have accepted each and every aspect of his evidence. Neither can I give an unequivocal assurance that Coetzee does not suffer from a mental disorder. It is just unfortunate that the evidence before Harms was clouded by this misdirected attack.

Both Nofemela and Tshikalange were discredited by Harms. He found that Nofemela had fabricated evidence and lied in the past and that he had nothing to lose by implicating himself in the atrocities as he tried to save his own life. Tshikalange was a bad witness who inspired no confidence. Harms said it was important to note that Tshikalange had never implicated himself in any crime until he joined up with Coetzee in Lusaka, implying that Coetzee influenced Tshikalange to admit that he actively participated in the killing of Griffiths Mxenge. That was not true: Tshikalange admitted his part in the killing long before he left South Africa to join the ANC.

Harms found that the police had also lied to him when they claimed that the askari Joe Mamasela did not know Dirk Coetzee before February 1982. Harms found that the police's version was false and that they had lied to him. But then the judge left the whole matter there: he never explored or commented on the fact that there was police conspiracy to mislead him and to fabricate evidence. He did find that a police colonel had committed blatant perjury when he denied that Mamasela could have known Coetzee in 1981.[22]

Harms found that the raid into Botswana did take place, but came to the conclusion that it must have been an unauthorised operation in which Coetzee and Nofemela assisted Mamasela in a revenge attack on his former ANC captors. Harms said that this incident did not contribute to either Coetzee's or Nofemela's credibility.

The Independent Board of Inquiry into Informal Repression slammed Harms for his reluctance to judge the police in their conspiracy to mislead him. If the act of attacking a neighbouring state for the purpose of killing people is not that of a death squad, then they did not know what would constitute a death squad operation, the Board said.[23]

Harms also found that there was a suspicion that the kidnapping of Joe Pillay was planned by Coetzee and not authorised by higher command, but said that because this incident fell outside the terms of reference of the commission, he was not going to deal with it. He rejected Coetzee's allegations that Peter Dlamini, Vuyani Mavuso, Isaac Moema, Gonisizwe Kondile and Siphiwo Mtimkulu were murdered by the security police. He found that the fact that all these activists disappeared in 1981 and 1982 never to be seen again was not significant or an indication that Coetzee might have spoken the truth.[24]

Harms said that with the single exception of Mtimkulu, all the other activists would have been regarded as traitors by the ANC and therefore targets for elimination by the organisation. He was mistaken yet again: it is not true that an activist like Mavuso, who was highly trained and participated in Umkhonto operations, would have been eliminated by the ANC if he returned to the organisation. He refused to co-operate with the security police and had an attitude of "charge me or shoot me". If it is true, as the police claimed, that he was released and went back to the ANC, he would have received a hero's welcome.

Peter Dlamini could have been a target for elimination by the ANC because he walked over to the "enemy" and joined forces with the security police. But then, if Dlamini had been released by the police, he would certainly not have gone back to the ANC as he must have known that he was a target for elimination. That means he is either still alive in South Africa, or was killed by the ANC inside the country. Where is Dlamini?

It is significant that the askaris who escaped from Vlakplaas and went back to the ANC are alive and well and living with the organisation in the neighbouring states. I have personally met two of them in Lusaka. Therefore it is highly improbable that Ace Moema would have been eliminated if, as Captain Koos Vermeulen claimed, he escaped and went back to the ANC.

Harms said in his report that there was no evidence that either Dlamini or Mavuso had disappeared or was dead. We only know that their current addresses are not known to the police, Harms said. He did not deal with the fact that the police would have done everything in their power to prove that at least one of the disappeared activists is still alive. In doing so, they could have discredited Coetzee completely.

Harms found that there was no clear-cut answer to who murdered Griffiths Mxenge. He said there were five possibilities, the first being that Nofemela and Coetzee had both lied, the second that they had performed the killing as a "private enterprise" and the third that Coetzee gave the order to kill of his own accord. A fourth possibility was that Mxenge was murdered by someone else and the fifth was that a group had done so "on the instructions of higher authority and with a political motive ... There is no reason to prefer the evidence given by Mr Coetzee, Nofemela and Mr Tshikalange (with their shortcomings) above that given by the respective members of the security police (with their shortcomings). This does not mean to say that parts of the disputed evidence given by the three cannot be true; it is just that those facts could not be established on a preponderance of probabilities," Harms said.[25]

In the end Harms found that although security police members based at Vlakplaas had been guilty of common-law offences, no death squad had ever existed on the farm. He said that some of the events described by Coetzee and Nofemela did take place, but that there was a lack of documentation to prove the allegations. It was probable that in the security situation members of the South African Police had perpetrated acts of violence. If one considered the fact that the ANC and PAC had declared war on the police, the probability even increased.[26]

Despite wide-ranging criticism of the report, Lawyers for Human Rights national director Brian Currin said that something good did result from the commission: "In a sense the whole country has lost its innocence about sinister activities conducted by members of the security forces. And both the SADF and the SAP now know that their covert activities cannot go undetected . . . I expected that at least Judge Harms would have found that there was a Coetzee death squad, although I still believe that there was a police death squad beyond Coetzee. I concede that both Coetzee and Nofemela were not good witnesses, but there was a substantial amount of corroborative evidence which supported their evidence."[27]

Both the government-supporting and the liberal newspapers criticised the findings. *The Star* said: "The ghosts of death squads have not been laid to rest. The culprits are out there untouched and capable of striking again . . . the commission washed its hands of assigning the nature and extent of political responsibility. The probe must go on. Obstacles to uncovering the truth must be removed."[28]

State President FW de Klerk took nearly two months to study the Harms report. The release of the 207-page document conspicuously coincided with the testimony of the head of scientific and technical services of the South African Police, General Lothar Neethling, in the Johannesburg Supreme Court. Neethling was giving testimony in his million-rand libel suit against *Vrye Weekblad* for publishing Coetzee's revelation that he had received poison from the general.

Lothar Paul Neethling is a formidable, feared and highly decorated policeman. He came to South Africa in 1948 as a 13-year-old German war orphan. He rose frow the ashes of a war-torn Europe to become the third highest ranking policeman in South Africa and achieved fame and respect as a forensic scientist. He obtained two doctorates and holds membership of various local and international scientific associations.[29]

He was described by character witnesses as a man of God, a family man whose most valuable anchors in his life are his family and his Creator. Under his command the police's forensic laboratory expanded from a small beginning in the early seventies to be a mighty weapon in the combat against crime. The laboratory handled 26 000 cases in 1989. Neethling himself has made 13 000 affidavits over the past 20 years and conducted 50 000 forensic analyses.

But in the latter half of 1989 the ghost of Joseph Mengele rose in South Africa when Lothar Neethling was exposed as a poisoner – and a lousy one. Despite his scientific expertise and high reputation, his poison did not work.

Challenging the general was Dirk Coetzee, the rogue policeman who only hours before Neethling's testimony had been described by Louis Harms as a man with strong psychopathic tendencies, who had lied when he said that Lothar Neethling supplied poison to him to murder three kidnapped ANC activists.

As we anticipated when we published Coetzee's story, Neethling reacted with anger against the allegations and instituted the biggest defamation suit in South African legal history. He demanded restitution of R1 million from *Vrye Weekblad* and another R500 000 from the *Weekly Mail* for republishing Coetzee's allegations. It was an impressive sum of money, but then Neethling not only felt he had been grossly defamed, but also feared that his own life and the lives of his family had been put in jeopardy. The general claimed that he could not travel overseas any longer to attend international conferences.

The survival and credibility of *Vrye Weekblad* hung on the outcome of the case. During a South African conference in Paris the European Economic Community and the French government pledged their support and promised a sponsorship of R500 000 towards our legal costs. It enabled us to appoint the very best legal team available to present our case. The state sponsored Neethling's case, appointing two advocates and a firm of attorneys to represent him.

Vrye Weekblad's legal costs in the end exceeded R800 000 and I suspect Neethling's costs were in the same region. The case was decided on cost, which meant that the defeated party would pay the other's legal costs. Despite the foreign aid, we could never hope to pay the total legal costs if we lost. We realised that if the judge ruled against us, Max du Preez, as the first defendant, would have to declare himself and *Vrye Weekblad* bankrupt. Furthermore, the judgement would determine whether the controversy surrounding police death squads would fall into oblivion, with Dirk Coetzee finally branded a liar and the security police getting off scot-free.

On the face of it, we were in for an uphill battle. Lothar Neethling was part of the security establishment, a respected scientist with an international reputation, while there were a number of improbabilities in Coetzee's version, the most important being that a person of Neethling's reputation and apparent integrity would supply poison to kill people, and if he did, that the poison might fail. On the other hand, Coetzee's version was strengthened by the fact that he had no reason to implicate Neethling. If his story of the killing of Peter Dlamini and Vuyani Mavuso had been a fabrication, would he really have told the world that he got poison from Lothar Neethling that did not work and expect them to believe him? When *Vrye Weekblad* published Dirk Coetzee's allegations in November 1989 we never suspected in our wildest dreams that in the end we would experience so much anguish, anxiety and even fear that the newspaper would not survive the massive onslaught on its credibility and sheer existence.

There was one major difference between the Harms Commission and our defamation case. A commission of inquiry and a court of law are governed by different rules and regulations. There was no reason why the findings should be the same, since the information available to each, despite significant overlap, was different. The trial judge was not hamstrung by the same rules as Louis Harms. He was free to explore and investigate external operations and therefore had access to material that the Harms Commission did not have.

Coetzee was well prepared for his testimony in the defamation case and by that time, vital new evidence had emerged that we knew could prove his allegations. For each and every incident he described, there was some corroborative evidence we could present to the judge. Although the case centred around the supply of poison, it was important to lead evidence on Coetzee's complete story in order to establish his credibility.

Presiding over the defamation case was Judge Johan Kriegler, recognised as one of South Africa's finest and most skilled jurists. Kriegler said during the proceedings that it was the most special case he had ever presided over and that the allegations concerning death squads were of such a serious nature that it would hopefully never be repeated.

Unlike Louis Harms, Kriegler had wide experience in criminal litigation, both as a judge and as an advocate. He had frequently dealt with state corruption and, as an advocate, had appeared for as wide a diversity of people as Eschel Rhoodie, the leader of the neo-Nazi Afikaner Weerstands-beweging Eugene Terre'Blanche, and the Afrikaans poet and philosopher Breyten Breytenbach.

In his classic jail novel *The True Confessions of an Albino Terrorist*, Breytenbach wrote: "For now I just want to enter the remark that if, as happened supposedly when God wanted to destroy Sodom and Gomorrah, if it ever were to become necessary to find three just and good men among the Afrikaners to save the tribe from extinction, I would have no qualms in proposing Van Zyl Slabbert and Johan Kriegler and, – this may surprise you – Charles de Fortier as candidates." (De Fortier was the head of the Pollsmoor Prison where Breytenbach was interned.)[30]

Three new and very important pieces of evidence that further corroborated Coetzee's allegations emerged before and during the court case. The first was a small green police notebook dating back to 1980 in which Coetzee wrote contacts' names and telephone numbers.

The notebook was discovered by Coetzee's son, Dirk, after his father had left the country. He gave it to a friend who claims to have handed photostated copies to a human rights lawyer who appeared at the Harms Commission. The lawyer must have forgotten about the notebook because it was never produced at the commission. It was sent to London two days before Coetzee started giving evidence in the defamation case.

Coetzee had not seen the notebook for years and could not remember what it contained. It was only in London that he and our lawyers noticed that the name and telephone numbers of Lothar Neethling were there.

There were many other names and numbers of people implicated by Coetzee in the notebook: Military Intelligence officers who provided the explosives to blow up the transit house in Swaziland in 1980, the Defence Force officers who interrogated Joe Pillay, the advocates who defended Peter Casselton in London, the car dealer in Swaziland who bought the car of the murdered Lesotho diamond dealer, the officer at Special Forces who provided foreign weapons and silencers to the Vlakplaas squads, the two agents in Swaziland who assisted Coetzee in the attempted kidnapping of General, the agent in Swaziland who bought the Eastern Cape labour union's stolen microbus, members of the security police's explosives unit who manufactured bombs and other devices for the death squads. The notebook would have been invaluable evidence before the Harms Commission.

That it contained Lothar Neethling's telephone numbers was of particular importance for our defamation case. What was significant was that there were two work telephone numbers in the notebook, one of which was the number of the police Quartermaster General, where Neethling had a special extension. That number never appeared in any internal telephone directory and ordinary policemen would not have known that he could be reached there.

Neethling tried desperately to discredit the notebook by accusing Coetzee of falsification. The general secretly lifted the notebook from the registrar's office to conduct tests in his laboratory over the weekend. Back in court he told the judge that he had no doubt that the notebook had been treated. "Something happened to this book. It was treated with steam and ironed afterwards. It was done to make further examination [of the book] impossible. One wonders what the history of this notebook really is."

Bobby Levin, *Vrye Weekblad's* senior counsel, objected to Neethling's evidence and the manner in which he had obtained and conducted tests on the book. Neethling was forced to withdraw his evidence and undertook not to lead further evidence on the state or appearance of the book. In his judgement Kriegler said that Levin had probably made a mistake by objecting to Neethling's evidence. Had Neethling been allowed to continue with his allegations about the book, he would have discredited himself even further.

Kriegler said the suggestion that the notebook was a recent fabrication was absurd. The book was without doubt what Coetzee described it to be. If the former policeman had previously remembered about the book, he would certainly have used it before the Harms Commission. Kriegler accepted the evidence that Neethling's name was entered between October and December 1981 and that he personally gave the numbers to Coetzee.[31]

After the notebook's evidence Neethling was in a serious predicament. He had already told the court that he had never met Coetzee before and certainly never had any dealings with him in 1981 – the year that Coetzee was commander at Vlakplaas. The notebook established that there must have been contact between the two during that year.

The second piece of evidence that emerged was the statement signed by Vuyani Mavuso after he was kidnapped from Mozambique and brought to South Africa to be interrogated by the security police. In the statement he admitted that he was a highly trained member of Umkhonto we Sizwe and had participated in military operations in South Africa. And yet, despite his admission, the police claimed that they had released him. The file containing the document was available to the investigators at the Harms Commission, but they never regarded it as important. Kriegler said that it was highly unlikely that the police would have released an ANC suspect as highly trained and dangerous as Mavuso. It became much more probable that the police had not had enough evidence to charge their captive – his admissions and signed statement might have been made under duress – and decided to kill him rather than set him free and run the risk of him participating in ANC military operations again.

The third piece of evidence was a police document relating to the release date of Sizwe Kondile, the young ANC activist who dived through the window while under interrogation by the Port Elizabeth Security Branch. Coetzee had said he saw Kondile manacled to a bed at the Jeffrey's Bay Police Station shortly after the Vlakplaas squad had stolen an activist's car. He had been badly discredited at the Harms Commission when the police produced documentation showing that the activist's car had been stolen more than a month after Kondile was officially released from police custody.

The official security police document was found by Bobby Levin among the bundle of official exhibits before the Harms Commission. It stated that Kondile was in fact still in police custody in October 1981 – two months after police claimed they had released him and a month after Coetzee said he had seen him. It became clear that the police had again fabricated evidence when they said that the activist was released on 10 August 1981.

Dirk Coetzee, well prepared by a skilled and dedicated legal team, testified for five days in October 1990 in London in front of a British barrister. He was determined not to let *Vrye Weekblad* down and knew it might be his final opportunity to convince the world that he was telling the truth.

Kriegler said in his judgement that because he had never had the opportunity to evaluate Coetzee personally in the witness box, he would be extremely cautious in evaluating his evidence. He evaluated the former security policeman as he would an accessory in a criminal case, considering not only the evidence before him, but also the evidence before Louis Harms, the interviews we did in Mauritius and a British television programme on death squads.

Referring to the gripping lectures that Coetzee and the other candidate officers received at the Police College, Kriegler said it was clear that the

South African security forces were involved in a life-or-death struggle on various fronts against an enemy who used terror and sabotage against innocent people. Referring to the ideology of the total onslaught, he said it was presented as a battle against the forces of darkness and communism, which were intent on destroying the religious and material values of white South Africans. Therefore the use of poison to get to the otherwise untouchable enemy would not be unthinkable.

Kriegler said Coetzee's story was far-reaching and in many ways bizarre. It was further clear that he had frequently been dishonest in the past and was capable of fabricating evidence. His dishonesty did, however, have to be evaluated in context. All the false affidavits he made were with the full knowledge of his superiors and he was never taken to task. In fact, a short while after he furnished Rika Lourens-Botes with a false alibi, he was promoted to the rank of captain and received a police medal for faithful service.

Kriegler found that Coetzee was not a habitual liar and had not lied that many times in the past. What his lies really showed was that he honoured the Eleventh Commandment: don't get caught. Kriegler said that it was important to look at why and under what circumstances Coetzee had lied in the past.

Neethling's senior counsel argued that it was highly improbable that a man of his client's standing would supply poison to kill people and that a man with his expertise could prepare poison that did not work. He said that the story of driving halfway around the Transvaal to try and poison the two activists while they could have been shot reminded him of a fairy tale. Coetzee had fabricated the poison story to give extra spice to his tale.

Kriegler admitted that it was a strange story from a strange man. He said it was important to remember that Coetzee had left the force at the end of 1985 and that four years had expired before he told his story to me. When I interviewed him in Mauritius, he had no notes or diaries with him, Later on, as his story was challenged, he ordered his thoughts and could remember more and more detail. The interview he gave in Mauritius did not differ in essence from his evidence now, Kriegler found. What was even more remarkable was that it was in many ways similar to what he told Martin Welz in 1984.

The judge referred to Coetzee's decision to leave the country and said it was unthinkable that he would have fled if there was no truth in Nofemela's allegations, He had too much to lose: his new job, his aged parents and his family, his house, his country – and he knew that he might not be able to return. He left because he knew that some of Nofemela's allegations were true and he feared that he might become the scapegoat.

If he was willing to sacrifice everything, it was unthinkable that he would then fabricate a story that nobody was going to believe. He must have known that it would be crazy to tell a story as bizarre as the murders of Peter Dlamini and Vuyani Mavuso. Only a hardened criminal who did not want to be believed would tell such a story. Kriegler said it was one of those cases in which the truth lay in the improbability of the story. He said it was significant that Coetzee did not implicate those policemen he had a grudge against in atrocities like kidnapping or murder. One of the people he hated was the former Commissioner of Police, General Johan Coetzee, and yet he didn't implicate the man in any of his murders. Instead he implicated friends and trusted colleagues: Nick van Rensburg, Koos Vermeulen, Paul van Dyk, David Tshikalange and even his guardian angel, Jan du Preez.

Kriegler said the documentation about Kondile and Mavuso supported Coetzee's story. In Kondile's case it was even more remarkable that the three persons that Coetzee implicated in the murder were indeed the officers that investigated Kondile's case. Coetzee's knowledge of Kondile was remarkable if taken into account that he had never dealt with the man. If his story was false, how did he know that the man was in detention? He knew what kind of car he drove and what he looked like. Police documents stating that the activist was released in August 1981 had been proved false.

Kriegler said that Coetzee's information and detail about the murder of Griffiths Mxenge were so detailed in regard to names, dates, places, times and events that it could not be a fabricated story. He again implicated friends and not enemies. The raid into Botswana turned out to be a failure and not a triumph. Why fabricate the event when there was no honour to be gained? His presence in Botswana on the day of the attack was proved by Botswana's customs documents. There was no reason to suspect that the Botswana raid was not authorised by higher authority, Kriegler said. There was not a single instance where Coetzee was shown to have lied. There were not even serious contradictions in his long and tiring evidence and he was a credible and trustworthy witness.

On the other hand, Kriegler found, Neethling had misled both him and the Harms Commission. "I must admit that it hit me like a thunderbolt because it was unbelievable that a person of the plaintiff's [Neethling's] esteem could descend to such a devious stunt . . . It wrote Ichabod over his chances of success," Kriegler found. He referred to a passage that Neethling deliberately misread from his own evidence before the Harms Commission to try and escape from a lie he had told.[32]

Evaluating Coetzee's description of Neethling's house, where he and Koos Vermeulen had gone one Sunday morning to fetch some more poison, Kriegler said he had tested Coetzee's evidence against the facts and found that "quantitively, he must pass *cum laude*. Qualitatively, he fares even better. Not one mistake he made is of real importance." Coetzee described 22 characteristics of Neethling's house of which only two were completely wrong. His evidence about Neethling's place of work was tested on 26 points, such as the layout of the office and what was hanging on the walls. "It is remarkable that Coetzee was correct on 22 of these points – remembering a certificate testifying that General Neethling had flown on the Concorde and a photograph of the 1963 Oostelikes rugby team, in which the general appeared third from the left in the middle row, " Kriegler said. He found that Neethling had lied to him and the Harms Commission when he testified that Coetzee had got his description of his house from the television programme "Dispatches". Neethling had lied to Louis Harms about what characteristics of his house could be seen on the video.[33]

Unfortunately for Neethling, the television programme was shown in court and the lies exposed. Kriegler remarked that it was incredible that Coetzee's legal team, who had a copy of the video, had never used the material to prove this point to the Harms Commission.

The judge found that Major Archie Flemington, former security police commander at Komatipoort, who vehemently denied having been present when ANC activists were killed on the banks of the Komati River, had been an unreliable, "slippery" and dishonest witness. Kriegler also pointed a finger at the former Commissioner of Police, General Mike Geldenhuys, who testified on behalf of Neethling. The general had displayed a "remarkable lapse of memory" while testifying before him, Kriegler said.

Kriegler's judgement also gave a significant extension to press freedom when he established the duty of the media in South Africa to expose very serious state corruption. He said that seen against the background of a public debate about the misuse of power by public servants, the public had the right to be informed about Coetzee's allegations.

Vrye Weekblad and the *Weekly Mail* alleged in an alternative defence that even if Coetzee's allegations were not true and correct in every aspect, the information was in any event so important that the right of the public to know outweighed the possible damage to the reputation of the defamed person. The right of the public to know was therefore more important than the plaintiff's right not to be defamed.

My former colleague at *Rapport*, Martin Welz, testified before Kriegler: ". . . when you are confronted with what appears to be a credible account of a top-level security force involvement in general homicide, I think the public is entitled to know what is being said in private so that they actually politically react to that."[34]

Kriegler's acceptance of Welz's argument removed many of the reasons newspapers have to fear defamation cases and opened up new avenues for them to explore. It will make it far easier in future for newspapers to expose corruption in the public service, with less fear of retribution.

We lived through anxious moments during Kriegler's judgement. We knew that Coetzee spoke the truth and we had a right and a duty to publish, but could we possibly win against a person as powerful as Lothar Neethling? The courtroom in which for the past three weeks we had battled for our survival was packed, as it had been nearly every day during the trial.

In the end, after more than 20 days in court, Kriegler delivered his 240-page judgement, destroying Neethling's and reinstating Coetzee's credibility.

He found that the remarkable and sometimes bizarre tale that Dirk Coetzee had told the world was the truth and that police death squads did exist. Neethling, Kriegler found, had misled and lied to both him and Louis Harms and had indeed supplied poison to kill anti-apartheid activists. His final words were: "Neither of the defendants [*Vrye Weekblad* and *Weekly Mail*] had acted in an unlawful manner." He instructed Neethling to pay the legal costs of our two advocates.[35]

As Neethling sat shaking his head, devastated, in his bench behind his legal team, I was on my way to phone Dirk Coetzee in London. That night, there was the mother of all parties in a Johannesburg restaurant.

In January 1991 the *Sunday Times* said in an editorial: "So it's true. The death squads do exist. The police do use poison. General Lothar Neethling has been found by a judge of the Supreme Court to have misled the Harms Commission, whose work lies in shreds.[36]

"Mr Justice Kriegler's judgement has not only vindicated *Vrye Weekblad* . . . but it has established the credibility of Captain Dirk Coetzee. He may be a ruffian and a self-confessed assassin, but on the subject of the death squads he has been telling the truth.

"The SAP, like the SADF, has become a degenerate organisation, the haven of gangsters. The Harms Commission, artificially constricted by its terms of reference, fed evidence tainted by prejudice and misled by a police general, produced nothing but rubbish. It is utterly discredited.

"Mr De Klerk can rescue his own reputation from the condemnation of history only if he appoints a new commission, with an open brief, to penetrate the cover-up so that the murderers of the State can be brought to trial, " the newspaper said.

The bizarre phenomenon of a former security police captain begging the world to believe that he was an assassin, with the South African authorities trying equally desperately to persuade the public that he was lying about his heinous crimes had finally come to an end.

It was the first time that a South African court had found that the government had assassinated its political opponents. It was a severe blow to the morale of the South African Police, already undermined by continual allegations of death squads, partiality and inability to stop the growing wave of political violence. The judgement coincided with an advertising campaign to boost the police's image as a peacemaker.

In his reaction, John Dugard said that the judgement clearly placed the credibility of the Harms Commission report in question. "It suggests there has been a police cover-up of the activities of death squads. It also begs the question as to why the so-called independent prosecutors in the Harms Commission did not probe police irregularities more fully. The underlying assumption throughout [the Harms Commission] was that Mr Coetzee was not credible. No attempt was made to corroborate any of his evidence and the question now is what other police irregularities have been covered up. There has been a tendency in South African judicial history for judges to accept the word of senior police officers without question. Thankfully this has not happened in this case, " Dugard said.[37]

In July 1991, in an unprecedented admission by the South African government, Foreign Affairs Minister Pik Botha said that the Harms Commission had been a complete and utter failure. "We have experienced a number of extremely unfortunate, if not reprehensible, incidents: Mr Webster's murderer was never found or arrested; the Harms Commission eventually ended in a very frustrating and unsatisfactory manner due to the fact, apparently, that some files and documents were stolen and the police could not complete their investigation. Certain individual instances of policemen gave rise to a suspicion that the police were, indeed, partial in taking sides."[38]

CHAPTER FIFTEEN

A country's madness[1]

A S the new non-racial South Africa struggled to emerge after more than
40 years of apartheid rule, attacks on anti-apartheid activists continued,
many of them bearing the death squad stamp. The senseless murder of a
Johannesburg attorney confirmed that while death squads had been partly
exposed, they had by no means been exorcised.

In February 1991, a woman phoned human rights lawyer Bheki Mlangeni
at his Soweto home to tell him to collect a parcel from a Johannesburg city
post office. The parcel was eventually delivered to the law offices where
Mlangeni worked. Unwrapping the package, he found a walkman tape
player with headphones and a tape marked "Evidence of hit squads".[1]

For the previous 18 months, Mlangeni had been investigating death
squads. In 1990 he had been seconded to the Independent Board of Inquiry
into Informal Repression, on which one of his duties was to serve as a link
between the investigative team and Dirk Coetzee. His work led to a number
of Coetzee's allegations being substantiated as well as uncovering a
considerable amount of corroborative evidence.

Mlangeni had been detained on three separate occasions, once under the
State of Emergency for a year. He was a well-known activist and had been
chairperson of the Jabulani branch of the ANC since 1990. In April that year
he had received a telephone call from an unknown person informing him
that a death squad had been despatched to Lusaka to kill Dirk Coetzee. He
also received telephonic threats to his life.

Mlangeni took the tape player home and walked into his bedroom. He put
the tape into the player, put the earphones on his head and pushed the
"play" button. The next moment, a bomb hidden inside the earphones of the
walkman exploded and Mlangeni died instantly as two holes were punched
by the explosive charges into the base of his skull.

Four months earlier, in October 1990, I was sitting at Lusaka's international
airport waiting for Dirk Coetzee and his two boys to join me for a London-
bound flight where he was to testify in General Lothar Neethling's defamation
case against *Vrye Weekblad*.

When Coetzee arrived at the airport, he told me that he had just had a
terrific row with a Zambian post office worker who refused to hand him a

parcel from Bheki Mlangeni in South Africa. Weeks earlier he had been informed by the ANC that there was a parcel for him waiting to be collected at a Lusaka post office, but he had no transport and was living in a motel eight kilometres outside town. En route to the airport he stopped off with his sons at the post office to collect the parcel. Coetzee refused to pay the high import duty on the item and after a heated exchange of words with the post office worker he stormed out of the building, telling the officials to return the parcel, about the size of a book, to the senders. The address, typewritten and incorrectly spelt, was Mlangeni's law firm in Johannesburg. Next to the address was written: "From Bheki".

"Why would Bheki send me a parcel without informing me about it?" Coetzee wondered. He told me he thought the parcel might be a trap and had asked the ANC intelligence officer who brought him to the airport to warn Bheki that the parcel was on its way and that he should be careful. That warning never reached the lawyer. The ANC's oversight cost him his life.

The assassin clearly took advantage of the working relationship between Mlangeni and Coetzee and used his name to allay possible suspicions about the parcel.

Coetzee was extremely upset when he heard the news about his friend. "Those vicious hooligans! They could have blown my sons up as well. Bheki died in my place. Knowing that, I can't even begin to express my shock. I only hope that his death, in the end, won't be for nothing."

Bheki Mlangeni certainly did not deserve to die in this way. He was a cheerful, dedicated little man whom I got to know well during the death squad investigations. He also became a good friend of Coetzee's as he frequently had to fly to Lusaka to interview and question the rogue policeman.

One night in December 1990, Bheki and I chased after an askari right through the night up to the Botswana border in Bophuthatswana. As we drove through a dusty village looking for the liquor store belonging to the askari's parents, where we thought he might hide, Bheki said to me: "Hey man, I hope I survive all this to see where it ends."

When will my country's madness come to an end?

The way in which the South African government has handled the death squad allegations has been both disturbing and disappointing. Its failure to respond to the revelations of rampant state brutality and to "cut to the bone" has created the impression that it has something deeply sinister and evil to hide. Death squads raise the most profound philosophical, ethical, religious and political questions imaginable regarding the nature of South African statehood and statecraft. The present government will not and can never admit that its agents have assassinated political opponents of the apartheid regime.

As far as I can establish, no government has ever admitted its complicity in death squads. The former Chilean military ruler, General Augusto Pinochet, remains unrepentant and defiant about his dictatorship during which 2 300 people were executed and assassinated. Responding to Amnesty International' s charge that more than 700 people disappeared during his rule, Pinochet said: "I can emphatically declare that there are no such cases, except for some unresolved denouncements dating back to the years 1973 and 1974, an era in which the Government found itself up against paramilitary forces of some 15 000 guerrillas supported by international terrorism . . . Those people who wanted me to apologise and ask for forgiveness are just creating stumbling blocks on the road to reconciliation."[2] The attitude of the South African government is similar. An apology or an acknowledgement of guilt is therefore inappropriate.

The SAP's first reaction to the death squad allegations was one of categorical denial. Former police commissioner General Johan Coetzee dismissed the allegations as "unadulterated nonsense" while Law and Order Minister Adriaan Vlok said: "The South African Police does not kill people, they arrest them and bring them before the courts."[3] This was followed by the so-called "rotten-apple" approach. If their allegations were true, then Dirk Coetzee, Almond Nofemela and David Tshikalange had acted on their own motives in defiance of official police policy. Although the authorities lodged an enquiry, the allegations were dismissed before they could be investigated. The standard police practice of investigating all allegations before coming to a conclusion was ignored. The investigators had nothing to investigate!

The SAP has throughout maintained this position, which mirrors its attitude for decades now in regard to the torture and death of detainees and other police atrocities. Despite irrefutable evidence, torture has always been denied by the authorities. Even after the finding of Judge Johan Kriegler that death squads did exist, Vlok said: "We've got the Harms report . . . we don't believe that death squads in the South African Police ever existed." Magnus Malan has remained equally defiant about the responsibility he has to bear for the atrocities committed by the CCB.

Magnus Malan came into his job saying his aim was: "Victory, victory at all costs, victory in spite of all terror, victory however long and hard the road may be, for without victory there is no survival."[4]

PW Botha, then Prime Minister, found in Malan a military commander willing and able to make the SADF the mightiest military machine in Africa. Malan was only 43 when he was made Chief of the Army in 1973, and became Chief of the SADF three years later. It came as no surprise when he was appointed Minister of Defence less than two years after Botha became Prime Minister.[5]

Behind him lies a highly controversial and clouded political career. This "soldier's man", who still insists on being called "general", has been called the world's worst minister of defence. The man who deceived South Africa with his total onslaught ideology is, after many years in Parliament, all too conspicuously at ease as a politician.

When Frederik van Zyl Slabbert left Parliament in 1985, he said in his farewell speech, "My problem with the Minister of Defence is a simple yet disturbing one: I cannot believe him any more."[6] Six years later he described Malan as follows: "As general Norman Schwartzkopf said of Saddam Hussein: As a parliamentarian he understands little of Parliamentary procedure, he disregards the democratic process, he is impatient with regard to any critical questioning and has been blessed with a terrible inability for debate – but otherwise he is a wonderful and extraordinary Minister of Defence."[7]

As South Africa enters the post-apartheid era, Malan's "total onslaught" has been exposed as "total fraud", and he has been held responsible for the CCB controversy. For someone who has so fearlessly abolished apartheid laws and cleared obstacles from the road to a post-apartheid South Africa, State President FW de Klerk has been remarkably restrained in his handling of the legacy of murders carried out by security forces in defence of apartheid.

Malan has accepted responsibility for the CCB, but claims his conscience is clear. "With the CCB, the position is almost as simple as that of a chairman of a rugby club who is informed beforehand of tactics, but cannot take responsibility whenever a player or two delivers unacceptable play on the field."[8] On television he owns to being extremely proud of the achievements of the CCB, which were an essential element in safeguarding all of South Africa's people. ". . . It was a good organisation . . . they did terrific work . . . We must lash the ANC, not the CCB who did such praiseworthy work," he said.[9]

Malan, like his senior officers, disclaims responsibility for anything the CCB might have done. His defence – that he did not know troops under his command were committing crimes – is reminiscent of the defence which failed the commander of the Japanese forces in the Philippines, General Tomayuki Yamashita, when he appeared before a war crimes tribunal at the end of World War II. Although it was never found that Yamashita ordered or approved of their atrocities and crimes, he was sentenced to death and executed because "he failed to provide effective control of his troops." General Douglas MacArthur, confirming the sentence, said that Yamashita had "failed utterly his soldier faith". According to international law, military commanders remain responsible for the crimes of their subordinates, no matter how diligently they preserved their ignorance.[10]

Magnus Malan said in a statement on 5 March 1990 that he had been informed about the existence of the CCB in November 1989. However, according to documents handed to the Pretoria Supreme Court in March 1991, he was briefed on the CCB and on retirement benefits promised to its members at least as long ago as November 1988. On 5 December 1988 Malan signed a document approving early retirement of an SADF member to enable him to join the CCB while retaining his state pension. The documents were produced as part of an urgent application brought by three former CCB members to force the SADF to pay out retirement benefits promised to them in accordance with their employment contracts.[11]

The documents were supported by a copy of a handwritten note signed by General Joep Joubert, then commander of Special Forces (which included the CCB). The note, dated November 1988, certified that the Chief of the SADF, then General Jannie Geldenhuys, and the Minister of Defence had been informed about the CCB and its personnel plan. Asked about the discrepancies between his earlier statement and the court evidence, Malan made an about turn and said: "The CCB concept comes from the mid-eighties and I have already said I approved this concept in principle . . . In November 1989 I became aware of a small element of the CCB which carried out operations inside South Africa."[12]

It is, of course, irrelevant when Malan became aware of the existence or operations of the CCB. People like Magnus Malan and PW Botha were responsible for creating the climate in which the CCB was created and allowed to function: they must take ultimate responsibility.

In April 1991, Malan fired CCB managing director Joe Verster and 27 other operatives who had refused the offer of a retirement package or a transfer to other branches of the SADF. Malan has sued Verster for the return of the missing files of the CCB's controversial internal operations. Speaking during the budget debate in Parliament, he announced that these and other "firm measures" had been taken to wind up the CCB affair. He also offered to help former CCB agents receive indemnity for their acts, claiming that as ANC members were being granted indemnity, it was "only right that our people should be looked after." Malan's offer has been described as an implied admission that the CCB had committed criminal offences.[13]

Democratic Party Law and Order spokesman Tian van der Merwe said: "The real issue, and the real concern of decent South Africans, is that a murderous band of criminals, some of them recruited from the ranks of criminals, had been constituted and let loose to harass and kill South Africans . . . they had plenty of money and resources to indulge their wildest fancies. Soldiers or members of the defence establishment in any country do not need indemnity or applications for indemnity. It is their legitimate function to destroy enemies of the State. Indemnity only comes into play when their actions constitute crimes. In other words, when they operate completely outside the ambit of their job as soldiers and defenders of the State."[14]

In a dramatic and significant cabinet reshuffle in July 1991 FW de Klerk demoted Malan to Minister of Water Affairs and Forestry. Law and Order Minister Adriaan Vlok was demoted to Minister of Correctional Services. The State President made it clear that the demotions of Malan and Vlok were not admissions of wrongdoing but the removal of obstacles to negotiations.

The dismissal of Malan brought to an end an era, stretching over a quarter of a century, in which the defence portfolio was held by "hawks" who represented first and foremost the military. In came the young Roelf Meyer, a reformist who has the massive task of dismantling the counter-insurgency machine, creating a depoliticised and professional army and incorporating members of Umkhonto we Sizwe into the military.

Millions of South Africans rightly feel extremely nervous about entering a post-apartheid South Africa in which the guardians of peace and order have provided havens for former hitmen.

CCB operatives have been given a choice of either accepting the retrenchment packages offered to them by the Minister of Defence, or being transferred back into SADF units as ordinary soldiers. A number have found their way back into the SADF's Special Forces.[15]

At the time of writing, a legal task force headed by the Attorney-General of the western Cape was compiling a dossier on the criminal activities of the CCB. Its inquiries may lead to charges being laid in connection with numerous crimes, including murder, terrorism, sabotage, conspiracy to murder and corruption. A number of CCB commanders and operatives could be prosecuted as a result of the investigation.[16]

Not a single policeman has been charged or suspended for any death squad atrocity, although the Minister of Justice has recently reissued a murder warrant for Dirk Coetzee's arrest. In a move reminiscent of the promotion of Brigadier Piet "Biko" Goosen after the death of Steve Biko, Eugene de Kock was recently promoted from the rank of major to lieutenant-colonel.

General Lothar Neethling, who has been found guilty of gross irregularities, remains the head of scientific and technical services of the SAP. He has not been suspended. Neethling remains the one hot potato the government cannot drop. Either it will have to use taxpayers' money to pay his legal costs and therefore condone his behaviour – lying in court and supplying death squads with poison – or abandon South Africa's third most senior policeman. At the time of writing, Neethling has been granted leave to appeal against the judgement. The police are yet to respond to Johan Kriegler's finding. After the judgement, they said they were studying the finding. Three months later, when the Supreme Court refused to allow Neethling to seek a hearing at the Appeal Court, a police spokesman said their legal experts were now studying the new judgement. In the meantime, Neethling remains in charge of the police laboratory.

Instead of winding down the Vlakplaas squads, police architects are busy drawing up plans for a new police farm with 400 sleeping units on which to house a new police unit consisting of Vlakplaas and former Koevoet soldiers who came to South Africa after Namibian independence. Overall in command of the new unit is Brigadier Krappies Engelbrecht, who told me that the askaris have been retrained and are now fine, disciplined policemen. The former Koevoet policemen, who were accused of numerous atrocities during the Namibian bush war, have also been retrained, the brigadier said.[17]

However seriously the SAP takes its new image, it is unthinkable that the askari units and the former Koevoet policemen will ever be acceptable to the majority of South Africans. With Vlakplaas intact, the SAP will remain a partial and politicised force which can never be described as a friend of the black community. Instead, they will continue to be seen as racists in uniform.

In an effort to get the support of the general public the Security Branch was disbanded in April 1991, merging with the CID. Announcing the formation of the new Crime Combating and Investigation (CCI) force, Adriaan Vlok said this step would "remove the police from the political playing field".[18] With a stroke of the pen the once terrifying security policeman is now, according to the SAP, just a bobby on the beat; your friendly neighbourhood cop, catching thieves and fighting crime. However, security police structures – like Vlakplaas, for example – remain intact, and a police spokesman said the new CCI would use the intelligence network of the security police against organised crime. The Democratic Party's Tian van der Merwe said: "I am not sure what the significance of the move is, frankly. The CID guys will still do CID work and the security police will do security police work. There may be a flow from one to the other, but I cannot see the same police will both do the same work."[19]

It is essential that the truth be told and justice be done, but it is also virtually impossible for that to happen without profound changes in our political order. However, the fact that the truth about death squads is beginning to unravel is perhaps the best indicator that change in South Africa is for real.

Most South Africans agree that the truth must be allowed out. The killers must be brought to justice and sentenced for their crimes. People may have to kill each other in times of war or revolution, but that does not mean that everything is morally permissible or justifiable. The international rules of war view attacks on the military as legitimate, but not against innocent civilians.

Human Rights Commission commissioner and lawyer Geoff Budlender exposes the dangerous fallacy in the "logical" assumption that death squad activities may in some instances be forgiven. This book describes four sorts of murder, the first arising out of the bombing of what are said to be ANC houses or the killing of guerrillas in neighbouring states. The assumption is, says Budlender, that the house accommodates people who may be armed insurgents planning to enter South Africa. The bombing is thus justified as an act of war – a sort of anticipatory hot pursuit. But the bombing of houses easily slides into the second sort of murder: the assassination of people outside South Africa who are political leaders within or close to the ANC. Ruth First was murdered in Maputo, Jeanette Schoon and her little daughter blown up in Angola, Albie Sachs maimed in Mozambique, Joe Gqabi shot dead in Zimbabwe. None of these people were actually involved in the military activities of the ANC, but the logic is inexorable: if it is justifiable to kill people outside South Africa who are about to engage in a terrorist attack, why not those who support their organisation politically?

This kind of justification slides almost unnoticeably into the third sort of murder: the killing of people who are said to be captured members. Even the "realists", says Budlender, may start to be uncomfortable here, because the courts are supposed to deal with unlawful ANC activities.

By force of logic we arrive at the fourth sort of murder: the killing of people inside South Africa who are engaged in non-violent support of the ANC, and against whom the police do not have enough evidence to obtain a conviction. Of course, says Budlender, only the truly psychopathic could justify this murder.

"Notice how inexorably the logic has flowed, from the bombing of ANC houses in Swaziland to the murder of an ANC supporter in South Africa. Once you accept the premise – that it is acceptable for the state to murder people in Swaziland who may be prospective armed insurgents – the consequence is logically inevitable ... If this sort of execution of people believed to be ANC activists is justifiable, then on the same basis so is the necklace murder of people believed to be police informers ... And why only political murders? Why should a woman not be allowed to kill a man who she knows – but cannot prove – raped her?" argues Budlender.[20]

Albert Camus, writing of Algeria at a time when the French authorities were seeking to justify torture, said: "The fact that such things could take place amongst us is a humiliation we must henceforth face. Meanwhile, we must at least refuse to justify such methods, even on the score of efficacy. The moment they are justified, even indirectly, there are no more rules or values; all causes are equally good, and war without aims or laws sanctions the triumph of nihilism. Willy-nilly, we go back in that case to the jungle where the sole principle is violence."[21]

White South Africans love to call their country a member of the Western community of states, a land of civilised Christian standards where democracy prevails, while in fact, for the last four decades it has been one of the band of pariah states cast out by the world community.

South Africa has always had a notoriously bad record on human rights, rubbing shoulders with countries like Chile, El Salvador and Rumania. And even while the old order is dying, the past endures and continues to spread its influence. However, the death squads of the military regimes of South and Central America had a much more devastating effect on political opposition than the squads of the South African Police and Defence Force back home. If one accepts the widely held definition that death squads are organised units within the armed forces whose actions include assassinations and other clandestine acts of violence against persons and property in the pursuance of organisational objectives,[22] it is safe to conclude that probably a total of 230 anti-apartheid activists were the victims of South African death squads. If we also include the deaths of political detainees under the heading of death squad activities or at least consider them part of the phenomenon of informal state repression, the number of victims rises by a further 74.

According to Amnesty International and the Americas Watch Committee, between 1978 and 1986 more than 19 000 people were murdered by state-sanctioned death squads in Guatemala, while a further 2 400 people disappeared. In El Salvador, 48 000 opponents of the regime were murdered during the same period, while 6 800 people disappeared. In the Honduras, 356 people were murdered between 1979 and 1987 while 190 people disappeared.[23] Since 1980 more than 60 000 people have been killed by death squads and security forces in the military dictatorship in El Salvador.[24]

In South America, many more people were killed and disappeared. In Argentina, the military coup of 1976 brought the federal police under the direction of the army. During this joint action between the armed forces, which lasted until 1982, more than 10 000 people disappeared.[25]

During the years of repression in South America the South African government established close ties with Argentina and Chile. Ties between them were fostered by their shared unpopularity – South Africa because of its apartheid policy and Chile because it is seen as a fascist dictatorship. They had a mutual enemy – communism – and used a similar method in responding to the threat – repression. They all waged their national wars for the "survival of Western Civilisation".[26]

There were especially close ties between the armed forces. In 1981 the then Commissioner of the SAP, General Mike Geldenhuys, secretly visited Argentina and Chile. During a meeting with his Argentinian counterpart, it was "explained that both police forces were fighting a mutual enemy, Communism, and that the exchange of knowledge was absolutely essential". A year later, after a visit to South Africa by the Chilean Commissioner of Police, Geldenhuys decided that "both organisations would exchange information of mutual interest and priority should be given to training and information concerning terrorist organisations".[27]

According to the Commission for Truth and Reconciliation in Chile, 2 300 people were killed by the Pinochet regime. Between 1983 and 1986, when the Chilean economy collapsed and Pinochet was faced with mass demonstrations in the streets of Santiago, the dictatorship sent 18 000 troops into combat. There were days when up to a hundred people died. Bodies turned up with their throats cut and there were mass disappearances.[28]

While many more thousands of people were killed by death squads in small countries like Guatemala or El Salvador, the international outcry against repression was always aimed more intensely towards South Africa. In a country like Guatemala, death squads operated openly to prevent "the spread of guerrilla movements". Their tactics included the publication of lists and posters with names of supposed "communists", many of whom were soon killed or simply disappeared. There were periods in which more

258

than 40 people were kidnapped each week, most of whom would permanently disappear. Politicians and trade unionists were intimidated and killed by the thousand, and many left the country. Large groups of people were killed or herded into specially designed "strategic villages".[29]

Intensive psychological research has been conducted in Chile on the effects of Pinochet's death squads and the repressive methods of the regime. It was found that they had left lasting psychological scars on the Chilean people. The most striking story is that of the women of Calama, some thousand miles from Santiago. It is a poor community where the men are miners and the women work the land. Twenty-six men were taken by the military in October 1973 and shot on the orders of an army general. The military returned to the houses of the men they had shot and threatened the women. They were told that they must never speak about what had happened. If they did, their children would be killed.[30]

The women of Calama organised their lives around silence. Once a year they would take their children to imaginary graves to keep their memories alive, but never dared to tell the youngsters what had really happened to their fathers. Some mothers simply told their children to be patient, because their fathers had left in search of work. Every so often a military officer would return to check that the women of Calama never broke their silence.

The first outside person to hear what had happened at Calama was a psychologist who treated one of the women at a social service clinic. When psychologists unravelled the mystery of Calama they discovered an unresolved fear of mourning and the fear of more horror in the future. And yet the case of the women of Calama was not unique. Their passivity, their fear that the soldiers might return and the creating of illusory graves have been repeated elsewhere in Chile.

The psychologists investigating the executions went in search of the widows. A slow, difficult process of therapy began. Distrust had to be overcome, safety guaranteed and the truth had to be shared with the children. The rite of mourning had to be observed, the family unit had to be reconstructed and fear had to be eliminated. Psychologists discovered that the women felt resentment towards their children because they had maintained silence to protect the children's lives, and then internalised this resentment as a betrayal of their husbands.

The women of Calama were partly healed and reconciled with the murder of their menfolk during a ceremony in the cemetery during which there was a symbolic burial of the murdered men. Children, friends, neighbours and the psychologists attended the ceremony. They told stories to each other, they shared food prepared by the women themselves and musicians accompanied the singing. Death ceased to be an ending and became a beginning.

In retrospect, it is fitting that four decades of apartheid rule under Hendrik Verwoerd, John Vorster and PW Botha should culminate in ignominy. As

259

Ken Owen, the editor of the *Sunday Times*, pointed out: "This, after all, is the republic of Nico Diederichs and Fanie Botha, bankrupts; of liars like Connie Mulder and Jimmy Kruger, born Jones, who lied even about his humble Welsh origins; of Hennie van der Walt, the cabinet minister who later graduated to, and then from, prison.

"It is also the republic of the CCB, of murder cases quashed by high authority, of police killers, of unpunished deaths in the cells, and of harsh punishment for such crimes as the dissemination of thought."[31]

It therefore came as no surprise that as the National Party and the ANC were preparing themselves for "real" negotiations to create a new constitution, a majority-ruled government and hopefully a new social order, the state's dirty tricks and conspiracies against "the enemy" continued.

As I was finishing this book, the government was severely embarrassed after documents, produced by the *Weekly Mail* and *The Guardian*, showed that it had financed Inkatha rallies in 1989 and 1990 in a campaign to counter the ANC's influence. In a desperate attempt to explain the security police's subversion of Inkatha using taxpayers' money, the government alleged that the money was used to counter sanctions.[32]

This was the latest in a succession of allegations which at first seemed incredible but have proved to be true. Ken Owen commented: "There is a history to all this. When the fantastic allegations of the Information scandal finally came to light, after years of deceit and untruthfulness, the *Rand Daily Mail* carried a simple headline: It's all true.

"Similarly, the allegations of hit squads seemed fantastic, and turned out to be true. The allegation of police collusion with Inkatha seemed far-fetched, and proved to be true. The idea that military officers would defy President de Klerk by concealing and destroying evidence seemed incredible, and proved true. As the *Rand Daily Mail* said, it's all true.

"But other allegations, more dreadful wait to be proven. Did the government, or any of its agencies, assassinate Lubowski? Did the CCB assassinate Webster, as a senior police officer at first suspected? Did the police protect the 'impis' that attacked ANC supporters? Did the Casspirs guard the 'rooidoeke' (a vigilante group)? If a fund to fight sanctions was misused, as plainly happened, to drum up support for Inkatha, what other misappropriations might have occurred?"[33]

There were further allegations of security force collusion in the political violence when a former member of 5 Reconnaissance Regiment, Sergeant Felix Ndimene, claimed that four reconnaissance soldiers were involved in the cold-blooded murder of six commuters on a Johannesburg-bound train in Soweto in June 1991. Ndimene, who used the alias Bob Dickson, named a corporal and three sergeants as the men who pumped bullets into men, women and children. Operatives were initially given "urban training" at the Phalaborwa camp and were provided with an assortment of weapons including AK-47 rifles. According to Ndimene they were responsible for a large number of massacres in Natal and townships on the Reef.[34]

Allegations of security force complicity in attacks by Inkatha members on ANC-supporting communities have gushed forth since violence erupted between the two organisations. In some cases the SAP and SADF have been accused of turning a blind eye to the presence of armed Inkatha groups, neglecting to disarm them, or escorting them to and from their hostel bases. In other cases they have been accused of more direct support. Security force spokespeople have routinely denied these allegations – often in the face of eyewitness affidavits. In most cases no-one has been arrested because of "lack of evidence".[35]

People rightfully ask: Can we trust the government to lead South Africa into the era of majority-ruled government and non-racialism? Can the beast change its spots? Can we ever trust the politicians who devised and justified the "total onslaught" ideology, the generals who unleashed crack "recce" regiments on hapless populations and governments in southern Africa, the policemen who assassinated political "undesirables".

This points to the crucial need for an interm government; no political party will trust a government with a monopoly of power during a period of transition. There is widespread fear that the National Party will use its monopoly to influence the political process in the country.

It also illustrates the dire need to transform the SAP and the SADF into a non-political and truly representative security force. Members of Umkhonto we Sizwe should be incorporated into the security forces and "hawks" such as SADF Chief Kat Liebenberg, Chief of Staff Intelligence Rudolf Badenhorst, Commissioner of Police Johan van der Merwe, and National Intelligence Director Dr Niel Barnard, should be dismissed.

Instead, not only do these men retain their positions, but the SADF and the SAP maintain those units and its men that spearheaded the elimination of political opposition and the destabilisation of the subcontinent during the years of the "total onslaught": the reconnaissance regiments, 32 Battalion, Military Intelligence, the security police (albeit under another name), the askaris, Koevoet and Vlakplaas.

In the absence of any foreign threat to South Africa and in view of the government's assurance that the political process is irreversible, it is difficult to understand why these forces of repression are maintained during a time of drastic cutbacks in defence expenditure. There are only two logical explanations; either the government needs its reconnaissance soldiers and security policemen in case something goes wrong during the negotiating process, or it is better to have disaffected military men on the inside than rallying on the outside. Whatever the reason, the presence of these men in the security forces is hardly conducive to establishing mutual trust, which explains why the ANC finds it necessary to maintain its own armed forces.

One senses some sort of alliance between the government and the ANC that involves a general bilateral amnesty: the safety and non-prosecution of ANC guerrillas in return for dropping charges against the death squads and their political superiors, letting go of Griffiths Mxenge's killers in compensation for the perpetration of the Pretoria bomb blast.

In August 1991, the ANC brought back a group of 32 alleged South African agents captured during the years of the armed struggle who had been held in camps throughout southern Africa. On his return, a member of the group claimed that he had been tortured and mistreated by the ANC. Intense negotiations followed between the returnees and the ANC, after which a statement was released saying that no more accusations would be levelled at one another.

A day later, a top member of the ANC's National Executive Committee revealed to me that among the returned agents were the killers of Victoria Mxenge, Cassius Make and Joe Gqabi. According to him, the ANC had solid evidence to this effect and the agents made lengthy statements admitting their complicity in the murders. Their confessions were not made under duress. However the ANC refused either to reveal the identities of the murderers or to announce in public that they had brought back some of South Africa's most wanted killers. According to the ANC, they could not reveal the information as it would have endangered the lives of the killers whom they have forgiven and want to reintegrate into society. In part, I believe that the ANC was honest in their claim. Yet, I also believe that the stories of torture that their former captives had to tell was embarrassing enough to the ANC that they were willing to strike a deal with Victoria Mxenge's murderers.

Political philosopher André du Toit warned against this: "This may amount to an unholy alliance of the killers, on both sides, to protect their own interests. That is surely not the way to lay the foundations of a new South Africa. Should we be prepared to let the killers go free, if that is the price for ending the violence and ensuring the prospects for a just and democratic South Africa? There are some historical accounts which have to be settled if our society is to come to terms with itself at all."[36]

I want to conclude this chapter by saying how deeply I have been convinced of the desperate need South Africans have of an equivalent healing process after being brutalised by four decades of apartheid rule.

As much as the victims of apartheid need healing, so do those who had to enforce this ideology through violence and force. Underneath the bloody bravado of a Pieter Botes and the gleeful torture talk of a James Stevens I have found men of moral straw.

As I was finishing this book, I was called to the Weskoppies Psychiatric Hospital in Pretoria by Ronald Desmond Bezuidenhout, former security police operative. He is a small, nervous man with a body and a life full of scars, having spent the last 13 years on the edge of society in the underworld and on South Africa's secret but official business.

The police dismissed him as merely a police informant issued with a pistol and some police identity documents who had spent 18 months on Vlakplaas. Whether he was a fully fledged policeman, an askari or an informant, is not really important. The life story of Ronald Bezuidenhout is a testimony of a South Africa of the last decades where life was cheap, where dignity and humanity were difficult to find.

CHAPTER SIXTEEN

In the heart of darkness

HELL, we hated that duckfucker of a Dirk Coetzee. I swore then I would never split on my buddies like he did. But things have changed, and now I am also spilling my guts.[1]

You see, I am on the run. The police want to silence me.

Since the last time you saw me, I have shaved my beard, dyed my hair and hacked it into a different shape and changed my style. It is easy for me to change my appearance, as I have been many different people before.

I have not slept for some time. I need more than one sleeping pill to knock me out. If I do sleep, I suffer from terrible nightmares. I jump up at night and scream and cry. Sometimes I am very scared, at other times my mood changes into a terrible rage.

I need medical help. I slug my wife, I drink up to half a litre of cough medicine per day, I see no future for myself. I am bitter and I hate. I've got too much dirt in my head.

I have just been released from the maximum security section of the Weskoppies psychiatric hospital where I had to stay for 30 days because I assaulted my wife, Marylin. A magistrate sent me here to find out whether I am mad or not. But I am not mad.

I am scared to death of my former colleagues at Vlakplaas. I know that Duiwel [Devil] Brits is looking for me. But not one of them on the farm has the pluck to do what I have already gone through. They are nothing more than a bloody bunch of jam thieves.

I am talking, so help me God.

I am 38 years of age. My name is Ronald Desmond Bezuidenhout, alias Desmond Barkhuizen, or Ronnie Daniels, or Duncan Smith, or Stallone or Tokarev. Most of my friends and colleagues just call me Tokkie.

I have been a spy, a double agent, killer, mercenary, fugitive, security policeman. I have been kept in a hole in the ground by the ANC, I have been shot, I have been tortured. I have been in the underworld. I have been in many strange places. I have also been on Vlakplaas. I have been in places where life is cheap and humanity has no place.

Look, my body is full of wounds and scars that bear testimony to my existence in the darkest places of life. You say my eyes are fired up too brightly by the cough medicine I am addicted to. Well, that stuff's given by the police to members of the death squad at Vlakplaas to fire them up before an operation.

Now I cannot live without it any more. It helps me to forget about the young boy I shot. It helps me to cope with my frightful life that has fallen to pieces.

I have endured all this for my God, my Country and my People.

As a child I grew up on the pavements and I know the other side of life. My mother was a teenager when I was born in Port Elizabeth. She was only 15 when she married my father, but it didn't last. She was divorced and married again.

My stepfather died last year. I was the only person who wept at his funeral, but I will never forgive him for a truly miserable childhood. I grew up in Welkom among the empty booze bottles. I was beaten, I was neglected, I was the scum in the house. My parents were always sodden with liquor. Of course I landed up in reform school. I ran away. I was sent back. My step-sister and half-brother committed suicide.

Sometimes I wondered why I had to endure all this punishment, but it was as though there was some strength coming from above and then I just carried on.

I went to the army in 1973. I soon got the nickname of Short Shit Meany because I was fit and tough and did not take any shit. I was taken up in a special unit and sent to Angola to hunt for terrorists. I was dropped by parachute at night into enemy territory where we had to hide and rest during the day and moved around silently at night looking for terrorists.

I never saw bugger all, no Swapo, no terrs, no Angolan soldiers, no Cubans, no Russians, just the bloody bush. It was here, during my training, and as a member of a recce unit in northern Namibia at a base called Sodelite, that I learned to hate kaffirs. We were told that black people are the enemy. They would say: "Do you want them to take the country?"

You ask me why I call black people wooden shoulders? Well, I have used that name for a very long time now. Believe me, they are as hard as wood.

After army I led a normal life for a short period of time. I worked, I got a pay slip, I had civilian friends, a wife. But it didn't last very long.

I started living a lie again. I was paid in cash from secret funds. My pay was equated with the considered worth of my information. I was employed in the small-parts machine room of an industrial company in Port Elizabeth where I had to snoop on members of the union.

It was a time of unrest in the eastern Cape and my duty at the time was to identify agitators among the workforce. I went to work on a gold mine in the

Free State where I did exactly the same thing. I snooped well enough to secure a few arrests.

But I went back to the bush as a mercenary. They are called dogs, and they are. But I joined. I subscribed to the magazine *Soldier of Fortune*, through which I landed a job as a Renamo rebels instructor.

I travelled through the Kruger National Park to a South African Defence Force supplied camp across the border in Mozambique in the Pafuri District. I had no concern for Renamo or their war, but the money was good. Most of the people I trained were kids, aged between 10 and 15. About a thousand went through my hands. One day I handed my unloaded gun to this kid of about 12 and told him to pull the trigger. He couldn't because he was not strong enough. I took the gun, put the magazine in, and shot the child because we were told he was a Frelimo spy. He fell and died before my eyes.

I returned to South Africa in 1985, and went back to National Intelligence, where I snooped again on the South African Railways and Harbour Workers' Union. But I could not infiltrate them. No white could.

I was then living in Vryheid, where the ANC was very active and recruiting members for its military wing. It was there, with two ANC members, that I slipped across the border to Swaziland. I was detained at a jail near Matsapa and deported to Lusaka.

I endured three years with them and was kept in a hole in the ground on and off for 14 months. I was frequently tortured by a sadist within the ANC's intelligence ranks known as JJ. I was a spy, and they never believed me, no matter what I said about their struggle. I was starved on a diet of only water for 29 days, my foot was broken by a rifle butt and I was accidentally shot in my right arm. Look, here is the scar where they removed the bullet without any anaesthesia.

I was eventually sent to the ANC training camp Vienna in Angola where I underwent guerrilla bushwar training. It was a relief to be away from Lusaka and in the bush again. But conditions were horrible. I got very sick, started vomiting blood and contracted malaria. The ANC still didn't trust me. During that time, the ANC was heavily infiltrated by South African agents. A lot of trainees were accused of being agents and tortured from time to time. One of the instructors, thought to be an agent, was shot point-blank before our eyes.

Chris Hani at one stage saved my life by preventing members of the security department from further assaulting me. I believe I would have died if Chris Hani hadn't intervened.

From Angola I was transferred to the Tetoreff military base in East Germany, where I underwent specialised military training. After completion of my training I went back to the ANC in Lusaka where I was kept under house arrest with other Umkhonto guerrillas.

One day Hani and Joe Modise (Military Commander of the ANC) approached me and told me that they would give me an opportunity to prove my allegiance to the ANC by sending me on a military mission to South Africa to sabotage an oil pipeline in Natal.

I arrived back in South Africa in March 1990 and tried to contact my handler, but failed to get hold of him. I was later arrested by the security police and detained and questioned until they could clear my position.

Major Eugene de Kock, Sergeant Stephen Bosch and a white askari came to pick me up and took me to Vlakplaas.

It was here on Vlakplaas that I slotted into cough medicine and another potent brew, courtesy of the South African Police Forensic Laboratory, put false number plates onto police vehicles, learned to despise Dirk Coetzee, drove around with an arsenal of weapons and tailed anyone and everyone suspected of being a member of the ANC.

The brew at Vlakplaas was given mainly to the askaris to drink before we went into the townships on operations. But I also drank the potion and became addicted. It gave me an unlimited amount of guts and made me bloodthirsty. Sometimes I could hardly remember what we did on operations in the townships.

I was goofed out of my mind when we raided the house of the parents of a political detainee who escaped from a prison on the East Rand. We knocked at their door late at night and burst into the house. We threatened to kill his mother and tried to force her to admit that her son had phoned her that same day. The family didn't even have a telephone, but that didn't matter. We slapped the daughter through the face and assaulted another person in the house. We pulled a plastic bag over his face and slapped and kicked him. We also threatened to kill him and hit him with a sewing machine on his back.

I arrived back home early that morning, took a sip of cough medicine and fell down and tried to sleep. It was only when I saw reports in the newspapers that the events of the previous night came back to me.

I operated mainly in Soweto and the East Rand and did some investigations into Winnie Mandela, who was really hated by the security police. I remember one night how we kicked her door open to search her house. As she confronted us, she looked me in the eyes and said: "Don't I know your face from somewhere? "

Oh God, how we hated Coetzee when he spoke. He was our enemy number one. Those who worked and operated with him nine or ten years ago said he had always been a coward. He never had the heart to do the job and could never pull the trigger himself.

Coetzee was a traitor and had to die. Myself and five other security policemen came together one night to decide how we were going to eliminate Coetzee. One of the men volunteered: "I'll go to Lusaka and do the duck-fucker." But we decided, no, that would be too risky. We decided to send a case of South African red wine via London to Coetzee in Zambia.

In the end the local explosives expert at Vlakplaas, who has a safe full of explosives and other beautiful devices, volunteered to pack a bomb and send it to the traitor in Zambia. That was the bomb that exploded when Bheki Mlangeni opened the parcel in his house in Soweto.

The men at Vlakplaas were devastated by the news that the State President decided to unban the ANC and the South African Communist Party. I remember how I lay on my wife's lap that night and cried like a small child. Why, I asked her, did I have to go through all that hell in the ANC camps in Angola and Zambia? I was tortured, I threw my whole life away to clean my country of communists. What for? Most of the men on the farm shared my feelings.

We were also extremely bitter about the appointment of the Harms Commission. We acted upon the instructions of our superiors and now that very government whom we served and protected wanted to clean us out. No ways, we decided. We moved the Russian armoury from Vlakplaas to Daisy, we burnt all the documentation that could be harmful and removed the rest to Daisy. We had to hand in our false passports and remove the false registration numbers from the official vehicles and replace them with the original ones.

We were instructed to deny everything to the commission. We were told to create the impression that Vlakplaas is nothing more than a normal police unit. We were not really worried about the commission. As one officer assured us: "It takes a terr to catch a terr." Another was walking around on the farm saying: "They will search for ever to find the body of the Krugersdorp security guard lying somewhere down a mine shaft. Underground the rats are as big as cats . . . and without a body there is no case."

He was of course referring to the poor Japie Maponya, who was shot point-blank because he could have recognised Almond Nofemela. Hell, he might have been a wooden shoulder, but he was innocent.

I still suffer from extreme nightmares because of all the people I tortured with a car tube at Vlakplaas. I pulled the tube tightly over their faces and just before they suffocated, I released it again. It is not a pleasant sight to see somebody nearly entering the gates, lying in front of you fighting to get air in his lungs. Next to you somebody will laugh or another would say: "Tube the bastard again."

Suddenly, in August last year, Vlakplaas decided they didn't need me any longer. They thought I was a spy for the Harms Commission. My god, can you ever believe that! Me, a spy for the commission?

I was transferred to police intelligence where I again had to infiltrate various organisations. But I was fed up with police work and Marylin said she would leave me unless I resigned from the force.

At that time, my nightmares were worse than ever before. I was drinking five bottles of cough medicine a day. When I drank the cough medicine, I couldn't sleep, which saved me from my nightmares. At two o'clock at night, the time at which we conducted most of our operations, I would walk around in the garden, sometimes simulating a night attack.

If I did sleep, I would wake up, shouting at Marylin to duck and hide and get away. At other times, I would shout at her about the body I once had to stay a night with.

But I don't want to talk about that; there are many things I do not wish to talk about.

After I resigned from the police force, I went to see a Pretoria psychiatrist. I told him I could no longer face and live with my past.

And then I terribly assaulted Marylin. I am not sure what happened on that day in April 1991, but I know I threatened to kill her and blow up the whole house. And then I hit her. She became so petrified of me that she tried to commit suicide by drinking rat poison.

She laid a charge against me and I was sent to the psychiatric institution where I had to stay for 30 days. It was pure and utter hell. The only good thing about my stay behind the high grey walls was that I could not get hold of any cough medicine.

They decided I was sane enough to be released. But since then I have been on the run, because I dared to talk.

I do not know what the future holds for me. But for the meantime, I have a bottle of cough medicine.

Political assassinations of anti-apartheid activists

(February 1971-February 1991)[1]

Details of killing	Alleged killers

1974

Abraham Tiro

Former South African Students Organisation (SASO) leader, killed in February by a parcel bomb while in exile in Botswana. — Unknown

John Dube

ANC activist, killed in Zambia when a parcel delivered to him exploded. — Unknown

1978

Rick Turner

University of Natal political science lecturer, shot dead on 8 January when he answered a knock at his front door. — Unknown

John Majola

ANC activist, killed after being abducted from Swaziland. — Unknown

Khela (codename)

ANC activist who was kidnapped from Swaziland by South African security policemen who ambushed an ANC vehicle carrying ANC guerrillas to the border. According to Dirk Coetzee, Khela was killed by his abductors. — Various Security Branches in Natal and Eastern Transvaal.

1980

Patrick Nkosi, Patrick Makau

Nkosi, 9 years old, and Makau, an ANC guerrilla, were killed on 4 June when two bombs, provided by the technical division of Security Branch Headquarters and Military Intelligence, exploded at ANC transit houses in Manzini in Swaziland. The bombs were planted by a security police death squad led by Captain Dirk Coetzee. The bombs were planted in a revenge attack after the ANC bombing of a Sasol petroleum plant.

Dirk Coetzee claimed he was instructed by brigadiers Jan van der Hoven and Nick van Rensburg. Coetzee's squad included various members of the Ermelo Security Branch.

1981

Matola Raid – 13 ANC members and 1 civilian killed

On 13 January, SADF commandos crossed the Mozambique border and drove 70 kilometres to Matola, a suburb of Maputo. They destroyed three houses, killed 13 ANC guerrillas and a Portuguese passer-by. At one house, the ANC fought back, killing two commandos and injuring others. One of the dead was wearing a helmet painted with swastikas; he turned out to be a British mercenary, who had left the British Army to join the Rhodesian SAS and then moved to South Africa after independence.

Planned by Brigadier JJ Viktor, former head of the ANC/PAC desk at Security Branch Headquarters. Information for the operation was supplied by a "turned" ANC guerrilla, Steven Mashamba, and the attack was carried out by SADF Special Forces.

Joe Gqabi

Gqabi, ANC Chief Representative in Zimbabwe, was killed on 1 August by a car bomb outside his home. Several attempts had previously been made on his life.

Two South African agents were charged with murder, but acquitted because their confessions had been forcibly obtained. It later turned out that the two agents were part of a South African spy ring set up by the director of close security, Geoffrey Price. He later fled to South Africa and joined the Security Branch.

Sizwe Kondile

ANC activist captured, detained and tortured by the Port Elizabeth Security Branch. He was killed in October and burnt to avoid a second "Steve Biko" incident in the Eastern Cape.

According to Coetzee, Kondile was brought to Komatipoort where he was murdered by Dirk Coetzee, Nick van Rensburg, Colonel Hermanus du Plessis and members of the Komatipoort and Port Elizabeth Security Branches.

Peter Dlamini, Vuyani Mavuso

Both ANC activists. Dlamini handed himself over to the Security Branch and was brought to Vlakplaas, while Mavuso, a highly trained soldier, was captured in the Matola raid. He refused to co-operate with security police. Both were shot and burnt in October, Mavuso because the SAP did not have enough evidence to charge him, and Dlamini because he was of no use to Vlakplaas.

According to Coetzee, Willem Schoon instructed him to get rid of the two activists. Major Koos Vermeulen shot them. Also involved in the killing were Joe Mamasela and Major Archie Flemington of the Komatipoort Security Branch.

Griffiths Mxenge

Prominent human rights lawyer and political activist who was killed on 19 November after being stabbed more than 40 times. The day before he was killed, his dogs were poisoned.

Captain Dirk Coetzee and his Vlakplaas death squad (David Tshikalange, Almond Nofemela, Brian Nqulunga, Joe Mamasela), instructed by brigadiers Jan van der Hoven and Willem Schoon.

7 Zimbabwean civilians

On 18 December, as people were busy with their Christmas shopping, a bomb exploded above the conference room of ZANU's headquarters in Harare, where Prime Minister Robert Mugabe and his cabinet were due to meet. Mugabe's life was saved by the fact that the cabinet meeting had been postponed, but seven innocent civilians were killed and 125 people injured.

The director of close security at Zimbabwe's Central Intelligence Organisation, Geoffrey Price, fled to South Africa after the bomb blast and joined the Security Branch. It was later established that he had set up a South African spy ring that was allegedly responsible for the killing.

ANC member, SACTU official

The two men were killed by a car bomb in Botswana.

Unknown

1982

Petros Nzima, Jabu Nzima

ANC representatives in Swaziland. Killed on 4 June when their car was blown up. The askaris Joe Mamasela, David Tshikalange and Almond Nofemela did the reconnaissance for the operation.

Vlakplaas death squad

Z Mbali

ANC representative in Lesotho who went missing on 27 June. He was later found decapitated.

Unknown

Ruth First

Wife of South African Communist Party leader Joe Slovo and researcher at the Eduardo Mondlane University in Maputo. Killed by a letter bomb on 17 August.

According to Coetzee, First was killed by a letter bomb prepared by the security police. The SAP's involvement was confirmed to him by Major Craig Williamson.

42 killed in SADF Lesotho raid

On 9 December, SADF commandos raided a residential area of Maseru, killing 42 people of whom at least 12 were civilians, including women and children. Some were ANC, including the Lesotho representative, Zola Nguini, but there was no evidence to support the claim that these were terrorist bases.

SADF Special Forces

1983

Saul Mkhize

Driefontein community leader shot dead while addressing a crowd.

Unknown

Keith McFadden, Zwelakhe Nyanda

ANC members shot dead on 22 November in an attack on an ANC house in Swaziland. The raiders hurled a grenade into the room and fired with automatic rifles.

In an affidavit, Almond Nofemela said he was part of a security police death squad under the command of Major Eugene de Kock that attacked the house.

1984

Jeanette Schoon, Katryn Schoon

ANC activist and lecturer Jeanette Schoon and her six-year old daughter, Katryn, were blown up on 28 June.

Dirk Coetzee claimed he was sent in 1981 to kill Jeanette's activist husband, Marius, but the operation was eventually abandoned. Shortly after the bomb exploded, Major Craig Williamson told Coetzee that the Security Branch was involved in the killing.

Bongani Khumalo

Secretary of the Soweto Branch of the Congress of South African Students (Cosas) was shot dead outside his home.

Unknown

1985

Alex Pilane

An East Rand member of Cosas was abducted and beaten to death in April.

Unknown

Vernon Nkadimeng

On 14 May, Nkadimeng, son of the general secretary of the SA Congress of Trade Unions, was killed in a car bomb explosion in Botswana.

Unknown, but a strong suspicion that SADF Special Forces or the CCB were involved.

12 killed in SADF Botswana raid

On 14 June, South African commandos drove to Gaborone here they attacked ten houses and fired at passing cars. Nine of those killed were SA refugees, including three woman, a 6-year-old child and a 71-year-old man. Five of the dead had ANC links. The SADF claimed they had attacked the nerve centre of ANC machinery.

SADF Special Forces

Mathew Goniwe, Sparrow Mkhonto, Ford Calata, Sicelo Mhlawuli

Goniwe, rural organiser of the UDF, Mkhonto, chairperson of the Cradock Residents' Association, Calata, UDF regional executive member, and Mhlawuli, UDF member, all went missing on 27 June on their way to Cradock. Prior to leaving, Goniwe said he would stop only for a uniformed policeman. The night they disappeared, there was a roadblock on their way. It was later discovered that they were all abducted and killed.

Unknown, but a strong suspicion remains that members of the Port Elizabeth Security Branch were responsible for the murders.

Brian Mazibuko

Anti-apartheid activist and former Robben Island prisoner, Mazibuko was stabbed to death on the East Rand in August.

Unknown

Gasuebe Hubhuli

Anti-apartheid activist who was shot dead in broad daylight in Vryburg in the Northern Cape.

Unknown

Victoria Mxenge

On 1 August, prominent human rights lawyer, political activist and the wife of the assassinated Griffiths Mxenge was shot and stabbed to death outside her home.

Unknown

274

Toto Dweba

Dweba, Natal Freedom Charter Committee member, was found on 25 August with his neck almost severed and both hands cut off at the wrist.

Unknown

Thabo Mokoena

National Federation of Workers Union organiser and UDF member who was abducted and killed in September 1985.

Unknown

Godfrey Phuso

On 19 September, this standard 7 pupil at Thabo-Jabula High School in Pimville was shot dead. The assassin, a white motorist, fired into a group of pupils who had gathered outside the school premises.

Unknown

Bathandwa Ndondo

ANC activist and student leader who was shot dead on 24 September by two SA and two Transkei security policemen. Ndondo was shot 8 times, at least 6 bullets entering his body at point-blank range.

Two Vlakplaas askaris: Captain Silumami Mose and Xolelwa Sosha. Two Transkei policemen were charged with murder, but the trial never got underway.

Lefu Rasego

A member of Cosas who was abducted in December. He was later found burnt to death.

Unknown

Ian Zamisa

A South African Allied Workers Union (SAAWU) organiser who was abducted and shot dead in December.

Unknown

Zalisile Matyholo

A former member of SASO, killed near East London.

Unknown

9 killed in SADF Lesotho raid

On 20 December, a death squad of eight men, some white, using hand guns with silencers, attacked houses in Maseru. Six ANC members and three Lesotho nationals were killed.

SADF Special Forces

1986

Esther Masuku

On 5 March, a hand grenade was thrown into the   Unknown
home of a political activist, Oupa Masuku, killing
his mother and severely injuring him.

Frank Martin

In April, Martin was killed and four members of   Unknown
his family injured when petrol bombs were thrown
into his home in Atteridgeville, Pretoria.

Joyce Modimoeng

She was killed on 28 May and her trade unionist   Unknown
husband seriously injured when a sophisticated
bomb was thrown into their Oukasie home near
Brits

Antonio Pateguana, Suzana de Souza, Joao Chavane

Pateguana, director of a Mozambican enter-   Unknown, but probably SADF
tainment company, his wife, Suzana, and night   Special Forces.
watchman Chavane were killed when unidentified
attackers raided the Polana suburb in Maputo.
Mozambique authorities believed that the
attackers meant to strike at a nearby house used by
South African exiles, but missed. An ANC
storehouse was raided the same evening.

Pansu Smith, Sipho Dlamini, Busi Majola

Three ANC members who were found shot dead   In all probability, a Vlakplaas death
on 2 June outside Mbabane in an attack during   squad.
which armour-piercing ammunition was used. In
his affidavit, Almond Nofemela described an
attack in May 1986 by the Vlakplaas squad led by
Major Eugene de Kock during which three people
were killed. Later on his passport showed that he
entered Swaziland on 31 May.

Stanley Nhlapo

Allegedly kidnapped in Kwaggafontein by se-   Unknown
curity force members at a night vigil. His body
was found in June at the Bronkhorstspruit
mortuary.

Matsela Polokela

Killed on 14 June in a raid on Botswana by SA commandos. Two more people were injured in the attack.

In 1990, a former CCB operative, Willie van Deventer, admitted that he was a member of a CCB death squad that attacked the ANC in Botswana.

Joseph Mothopeng

Abducted from his home on 19 June and taken to the Lesotho border in the boot of his car. He escaped, but was murdered the same day.

Unknown

Muntu Khanyile, Joseph Mthembu, Sandile Khawula, Russel Mnomezulu

On 20 June the four young men, all members of the Chesterville Youth Organisation, were killed by a Vlakplaas squad under the command of Major Eugene de Kock. According to police evidence at the inquest, a group of seven askaris lured the activists into a small backyard room and fired 68 rounds at them at close range. Police claimed that one of the youths fired first, but it was established at the inquest that no shots were fired from inside the room at the askaris waiting outside.

Nofemela claimed in his affidavit that after the shootout, the askaris reported to Eugene de Kock that the mission was successful. The investigating officer told the askaris that they had nothing to fear and that he would sort out the problem.

Sidney Mbisi

Mbisi, a former bodyguard of ANC President Oliver Tambo, was abducted from Swaziland in July and detained by the police. He was gunned down after his release from detention.

Unknown

Sonwabo Ngxala

Regional executive member of Azapo who was kidnapped when his taxi was forced off the road. He was later found stabbed and shot near Port Elizabeth.

Unknown

Fuzile Lupulwana

Local executive member of Azapo in Port Elizabeth was abducted, stabbed and burnt to death in August.

Unknown

Walter Ledwaba

Died on 19 September when a powerful explosion ripped through his home in Atteridgeville, Pretoria.

Unknown

Fabian Ribeiro, Florence Ribeiro

Prominent anti-apartheid activist and medical practitioner Fabian and his wife were gunned down in their home in Mamelodi, Pretoria on 1 December.

CCB operative Noel Robey, who has in the meantime fled South Africa, was found by the Harms Commission to have been involved in the murder of the couple in his official SADF capacity.

Jomo Mkize

A detainee support group worker who was abducted from a shopping centre, beaten and hacked to death.

Unknown

Leon Myers, Jackie Quinn, Harold Dentile, Midian Zulu, Joseph Mayoli, Nonkosi Mini, Morris (surname unknown)

A raiding party burst into a house in Maseru and killed seven of the nine people present.

Unknown, but probably SADF Special Forces.

1987

Gibson Ncube

ANC activist in Mozambique who died on 5 April of poisoning after drinking South African beer brought to Maputo by CCB operative Leslie Lesia, who later admitted poisoning Ncube.

CCB operative Leslie Lesia, on the instructions of his handler, Ernie Becker (a pseudonym).

Tsitsi Chiliza

She was killed on 14 May when a television set exploded in her Harare flat. The television set was meant for the ANC's chief representative in Zimbabwe, Reddy Mzimba.

CCB operative Leslie Lesia, on the instructions of Ernie Becker.

Mildred Msomi, Tutu Nkwanyane, Theopholis Dlodlo

Three ANC members were shot dead in a car outside Mbabane in Swaziland on 24 May. Askari Glory "September" Sidebe, "turned" by the SAP in August 1986, was recognised by an eyewitness as one of the attackers.

In all probability, a Vlakplaas death squad.

Yvonne Ntsele

In May, Ntsele, a standard 7 pupil at the Senaoane High School in Soweto, was shot dead outside her parents' home.

Unknown

Nkosinathi Shabangu

On 5 June, Shabangu, a standard 9 pupil at the Senaoane School, was shot dead by an unknown gunman in front of his teachers and fellow pupils. He was an SRC member and an active member of the Soweto Students' Congress.

Unknown

Eric Mntonga

Idasa's Border Region regional director, who was found on 24 July with his hands and feet tied. The post mortem revealed that despite a knife wound to the heart, Mntonga died from a haemorrhage as a result of a severe blow. This is the only death squad assassination where the perpetrators were brought to trial, convicted and jailed. They were six senior Ciskei police officials. Their conviction followed a tip-off from within the Ciskei police. The information was detailed and could not be ignored.

Six senior Ciskei policemen, convicted in the Ciskei Supreme Court.

Cassius Make, Paul Dikalede, Eliza Tsinini

ANC executive member and Umkhonto we Sizwe senior commander Make was gunned down along with ANC officials Dikaledi and Tsinini on 29 July. They were travelling in a taxi from Matsapa airport when the vehicle was sprayed with machine gun fire. In 1988, policeman Robert van der Merwe testified that he overheard four security policemen at the Oshoek Border Post planning the murders. During a visit by Dirk Coetzee to Swaziland after the attack, his former colleagues from Ermelo Security Branch told him they shot the three activists.

Members of the Errnelo Security Branch.

Caiphus Nyoka

An anti-apartheid student leader who was shot nine times while lying in his bed on 23 August. Three policemen testified that they went to his house to arrest him, but shot him when he moved his hands towards the bottom of the bed. A magistrate exonerated the police, saying they had acted reasonably.

Three members of the Benoni Security Branch.

Samuel Ndlovu

Vice-president of the Daliwonga High School SRC and executive member of the Soweto Students' Congress died after being shot on 2 September.

Unknown

Mtosana (first name not known)

Executive member of the Western Cape Civic Association who was found shot dead on 14 November 1987.

Unknown

Amos Tshabala

Member of the Tsakane Civic Association and union organiser who was stabbed and killed on 17 November 1987.

Unknown

Petros Mnisi

A regional educator of the Unemployed Workers Co-ordinating Committee was stabbed to death in the Vaal Triangle in November 1987.

Unknown

1988

Sipho Ngema

An ANC member who was assassinated on 13 January in Swaziland while eating in a restaurant.

Unknown

Linda Brakvis

UDF member who was killed in Allanridge in the Free State on 29 January, only three days after being released from detention.

Unknown

Jacob Molokwane

An ANC member who was shot dead in his car outside Francistown in Botswana in January.

Unknown, but SADF Special Forces accused of masterminding the murder.

Sicelo Dhlomo

An ex-detainee working in the offices of the Detainees' Parents Support Committee was shot dead. His body was found in the veld near his home in January.

Unknown

Amos Boshomane

A shop steward with the Steel, Engineering and Allied Workers' Union who was shot in the head but survived the attack. However, three months later, on 25 February, he was shot and killed.

Unknown

Dulcie September

ANC Chief Representative in France who was assassinated on 19 March in Paris. Belgian police subsequently named a SADF sergeant major, Joseph Klue, as one of the alleged assassins.

Unknown, but a strong suspicion that the CCB was involved.

Mazizi Maqekeza

ANC member who was shot dead on 22 March by unknown gunmen while in hospital in Maseru in Lesotho.

Unknown

Charles Makoona and 3 others

SADF commandos attacked a house in Gaborone on 28 March during the night, killing four people, dousing their bodies in petrol and setting them on fire, totally gutting the house. South Africa claimed that Makoona was a regional commander of the ANC. The other three victims undisputedly innocent civilians.

SADF Special Forces

Makhosi Nyoka, Lindiwe Mthembu, Surendra Naidu, June-Rose Cothoza

Four ANC members were shot on 8 June by a Vlakplaas squad under the command of Eugene de Kock. The police claimed the infiltrators were killed in an act of self-defence, but evidence emerged that the infiltrators were unarmed and were shot in cold blood.

Vlakplaas squad, members of the Piet Retief Security Branch.

Jabulani Sibisi, Joseph Mthembu, Sifiso Nxumalo, Nkosi Thenjekwayo

Four days after Nyoka and three ANC members were killed, on 12 June, another four ANC members were killed at Piet Retief in similar circumstances.

Members of the Piet Retief Security Branch.

Mthuthuzeli Payi

A Cape Youth Congress and Food and Allied Workers' Union activist who disappeared in June during a three-day stayaway. His mutilated body was found a month after his disappearance.

Unknown

Michael Banda

Post and Telecommunications Workers' Association member who was assassinated on 1 July.

Unknown

Mzuzwana Ndyogolo

Ndyogolo, general secretary of the National Education and Health Workers' Union, fell to his death in mysterious circumstances in November.

Unknown

Sipho Tshabala

A form one pupil at Pimville Secondary School who was shot dead by unknown gunmen.

Unknown

Gladstone Sewela

A former member of the Mandela United Football Club, Sewela was found hanging from a tree near Zeerust on 23 December. He had been released from custody that day by Bophuthatswana security police.

Unknown

14-year-old Botswana boy

The unknown child was killed on 28 December when a bomb exploded next to a house in Gaborone.

Unknown

1989

Thabo Mohale, Derrick Mashobane, Porta Shabangu

Members of the restricted SA National Students' Congress. Their bodies were found riddled with bullets in a forest in Swaziland on 12 February.

Unknown

Sawutini Booi

President of the Adelaide Youth Congress who died following a petrol bomb attack on his home in February.

Unknown

Christy Ntuli

Stabbed to death on 14 April after reporting to Imbali police in terms of a restriction order imposed on him at the time of his release from detention.

Unknown

David Webster

University of the Witwatersrand anthropology lecturer who was shot dead on 1 May outside his Troyeville, Johannesburg home. At the time of his death, he was allegedly investigating the training of Renamo guerrillas by members of the SADF.

Unknown, but a strong suspicion remains that the CCB or some of its operatives acting in their "private capacity" killed Webster.

Zolani Dala

Khayelitsha Committee of Ten member who was shot dead near Cape Town in May.

Unknown

Bofana Sigasa

East Rand regional secretary of the Food, Beverage   Unknown
and Allied Workers' Union, found floating in a
dam between Katlehong and Vosloorus. His hands
and feet were bound. He was last seen alive on
19 July.

Bashi Gugushe

Former Robben Island prisoner and member of the   Unknown
Azanian Students' Movement who was stabbed to
death in Ikageng, Potchefstroom, in July.

Stanford Mazikwana

SA Chemical Workers' Union member, who died   Unknown
as a result of injuries sustained when he was
attacked by four white men in Kempton Park in
July.

Andile Sapotela

The house of Joe Sapotela, NUMSA's chief shop   Unknown
steward at Uitenhage's Goodyear Tyre Company,
was fire-bombed in July. He escaped, but his
brother Andile was burnt to death. At the time of
the bombing the Goodyear workers were on strike.

David Gayisa

SRC president at the CN Pathudi College of   Unknown
Education in Sekhukhuneland, Gayisa was found
dead at the beginning of July with a stab wound at
the back of his neck. Police only informed his
parents on 24 July. Gayisa's assassination followed
protracted student protest at the college.

Eric Gumede

A KwaMashu Youth League activist who was   Unknown
gunned down on 11 August by a death squad in a
cream-coloured car. Shortly before his death he
had been released from detention.

Samson Godola

Cookhouse youth activist who was shot dead in   Unknown
August by two men, one wearing a balaclava.

Anton Lubowski

Advocate and Swapo leader who was shot with an   Members of the CCB's Region Six.
AK-47 rifle at his Windhoek home on 12 September.
He died during a CCB campaign in Namibia to
disrupt the independence elections. CCB agent
Donald Acheson was arrested and charged with
his murder, but had to be released because of
South Africa's refusal to extradite the alleged CCB
murderers to Namibia. Amongst them were CCB
Regional Manager Staal Burger and operative
Chappie Maree. Police brigadier Floris Mostert
also believed Burger and Maree were involved in
the killing.

Themba Myapi

The mutilated body of Myapi, a Witwatersrand   Unknown
Council of Churches field worker, was found in
the veld at Phonla Park on 4 November.

Eric Liberty

A Witbank civic leader, stabbed to death on 28   Unknown
December after receiving numerous death threats.

1990

Aldo Mogano

An executive member of the Alexandra Youth   Unknown
Congress, shot dead by two unknown gunmen
outside his home in Alexandra, Johannesburg on
7 April.

Sam Chand, his wife and 2 sons

PAC activist Chand, his wife Hajira and their sons   Unknown
Redwan and Amina were shot dead in Botswana
on 22 April 1990.

Simon Maswanganye

Maswanganye, an executive member of the Soweto   Unknown
Civic Association, was shot in the chest on 23 May
in Naledi, Soweto. Residents alleged that a group
of men in a white minibus without registration
plates were responsible for the shooting.

Sidwell Nonno

The mutilated body of Nonno, a shop steward of   Unknown
the South African Railways and Harbours
Workers' Union, was found in Langa, Cape Town,
on 26 May.

Lindiwe Maziya, Elizabeth Maziya, 9-month-old baby

Lindiwe, wife of Vosloorus Crisis Committee   Unknown
chairman Ali Maziya, their 9-month-old baby
Zwelakhe and Ali's mother Elizabeth, were shot
by unknown gunmen on 1 June.

Abel Molokwane

Molokwane, former executive member of the Brits   Unknown
Action Committee, was shot dead by unknown
gunmen on 15 June 1990. Three weeks before he
was killed, Molokwane had confronted two
alleged askaris with a death list containing his
name.

Clement Msome

The body of Msome, a NUMSA shop steward, was   Unknown
found on 3 August. He was shot dead by unknown
gunmen in Johannesburg.

Abram Mabele

Mabele, a NACTU organiser, was shot dead   Unknown
outside his Soweto home on 13 December 1990.

1991

Bheki Mlangeni

Mlangeni, human rights lawyer and ANC branch   Unknown, but a strong suspicion
chairman, was killed by a bomb built into a   remains that this was a Vlakplaas
walkman cassette player and sent to Dirk Coetzee   squad revenge attack on Dirk
in Lusaka. Coetzee refused to accept the parcel   Coetzee.
and it was sent back to Mlangeni, whose address
appeared on the parcel. A former Vlakplaas
operative, Ronald Bezuidenhout, said he was part
of a Vlakplaas group that planned to murder
Coetzee. The bomb exploded in Mlangeni's home
on 15 February.

Mhlabunzima Maphumulo

Chief Maphumulo, leader of the Congress of Traditional Leaders of South Africa, (Contralesa), was shot dead outside his Pietermaritzburg home on 26 February. Two months after the killing, a man claiming to be a Military Intelligence agent, Sipho Madlala, confessed to being a member of a death squad that assassinated the chief. Madlala, who claimed he was MI agent 810, said he received R5 000 for the killing. He said the security police participated in the murder. The SADF denied any complicity, but admitted that Madlala was an MI informant.	An SADF informer/operative, Sipho Madlala, claimed that he was a member of the death squad that murdered the chief.

Number killed:

Inside South Africa	87
Outside South Africa **(including cross-border raids)**	138
Total	**225**

Disappearances of anti-apartheid activists

(April 1982-December 1988)[1]

Details of disappearance	Alleged perpetrators

Siphiwo Mtimkulu, Topsy Mdaka

Congress of South African Students leader Mtimkulu was detained by the Port Elizabeth Security Branch on 31 May 1981. Immediately after his release five months later, he showed signs of thallium poisoning. He disappeared with Mdaka in the Eastern Cape in 1982 after filing a claim against the police for torturing and poisoning him. Although police alleged that they might have joined the ANC, Dirk Coetzee testified that Mtimkulu was killed and his body disposed of by the security police.

Unknown, but according to Dirk Coetzee, the security police killed Mtimkulu.

Isaac Moema

Trained ANC guerrilla who was captured by the security police. He was "turned" and sent to Vlakplaas in 1981 but was never trusted by his colleagues, who suspected him of being loyal to the ANC. Disappeared at the end of 1981 while on a mission with Major Koos Vermeulen.

According to Dirk Coetzee, Brigadier Willem Schoon instructed him and Koos Vermeulen to get rid of Moema. Vermeulen reported to Coetzee after the mission that he had got rid of Moema.

Japie Maponya

Building society security guard Maponya disappeared in March 1985 and was never seen again. In 1989, Almond Nofemela claimed that he abducted Maponya to question him in connection with the ANC activities of his brother. Eugene de Kock shot Maponya to prevent him from later indentifying Nofemela as his captor. The guard's body was wrapped in plastic and put in the boot of De Kock's car.

According to Almond Nofemela, Vlakplaas commander Major Eugene de Kock shot Maponya.

Qaqawuli Godolozi, Sipho Hashe, Champion Galela

Godolozi, president of the Port Elizabeth Black Civic Organisation (PEBCO), Hashe, secretary-general of PEBCO and Galela, organising secretary, disappeared on the night of 8 May 1985 after they had gone to the airport to meet somebody. The three men were never seen again, although police claimed they left the country.

Unknown

Stanza Bopape

Bopape, general secretary of the Mamelodi Civic Association, was detained on 9 June 1988. Police claimed that he escaped three days later while travelling by road in the custody of three policemen. Despite a search by his family, the UDF and human rights lawyers, nothing has since been seen or heard of the missing man.

Unknown

David Maswai

Young East Rand activist alleged to have been involved in Umkhonto we Sizwe underground structures. He mysteriously disappeared at the end of 1988. In 1990, a former riot police sergeant, Barney Horn, claimed that he witnessed Maswai lying dead in the back of a police car. His body was thrown down a mine shaft by members of the East Rand Security Branch.

Allegedly killed by members of the East Rand Security Branch.

References

Chapter 1

1. The murders of Vuyani Mavuso and Peter Dlamini were described by Dirk Coetzee in personal interviews (November 1989). The events were later also related before the Harms Commission of Inquiry into Certain Alleged Murders, Pretoria (1990), and in the case Neethling v Du Preez and Others, Rand Supreme Court, Johannesburg (1990).
2. *Daily News*, 20 November 1981; *Natal Mercury*, 21 November 1981.
3. Griffiths Mxenge's murder was described by Almond Nofemela in an affidavit (20 October 1989) and before the Harms Commission, by Dirk Coetzee in personal interviews (November 1989), and before the Harms Commission and in the Rand Supreme Court (1990), and by David Tshikalange in a personal interview (November 1989) and before the Harms Commission.
4. *Natal Mercury*, 21 November 1989.
5. *Drum*, October 1982; *City Press*, 8 April 1984.
6. *Daily Despatch*, 25 November 1981; *Daily News*, 24 November 1981.
7. *Daily News*, 11 December 1981.
8. *Daily News*, 23 November 1981.
9. *City Press*, 18 August 1985.
10. *Natal Mercury*, 28 November 1981.
11. *Daily Despatch*, 30 November 1981; *Pace*, February 1982.
12. *Daily Despatch*, 30 November 1981; *Eastern Province Herald*, 30 November 1981.
13. *Rand Daily Mail*, 30 November 1981.
14. *Sunday Tribune*, 4 August 1985.
15. Record of the inquest into the death of Griffiths Mxenge, Umlazi Magistrate's Court (1982, 1983).
16. *Probe*, September 1985.
17. *Ibid.*
18. *Sunday Times Extra*, 4 August 1985; *City Press*, 4 August 1985.
19. *Cape Times*, 3 August 1985.
20. *City Press*, 4 August 1985.
21. *The Guardian*, 11 August 1985.
22. *Weekly Mail*, 9 August 1985.
23. *Probe*, September 1985.
24. Patrick Lawrence, *Death Squads: Apartheid's Secret Weapon*, Johannesburg: Penguin Forum Series, 1990.

Chapter 2

1. The information in this chapter, except where indicated otherwise, is based on personal interviews with Dirk Coetzee in Mauritius (November 1989) which were published in *Vrye Weekblad* (17 November 1989). This information was repeated before the Harms Commission of Inquiry into Certain Alleged Murders, Pretoria (1990) and in the case of Neethling v Du Preez and Others, Rand Supreme Court, Johannesburg (1990).
2. *Weekly Mail*, 20 October 1989.
3. Affidavit by Almond Nofemela (19 October 1989). He later repeated his allegations before the Harms Commission.
4. *Vrye Weekblad*, 17 November 1989.
5. *The Star*, 17 November 1989; South African Broadcasting Corporation, TV1 News Bulletin, 17 November 1989.

Chapter 3

1. The information in this chapter is, except where indicated otherwise, based on personal interviews with Dirk Coetzee (1989 and 1990), the record of the Harms Commission of Inquiry into Certain Alleged Murders, Pretoria (1990), the record of the case Neethling v Du Preez and Others, Rand Supreme Court, Johannesburg (1990) and Dirk Coetzee, "Death Squads: The Testimony of a South African Security Policeman" (Unpublished manuscript, 1990).
2. Statement made by Vuyani Mavuso to the Security Branch (1981) and handed in at the Rand Supreme Court (1990) as evidence in the case Neethling v Du Preez and Others.
3. Evidence before the Harms Commission of Inquiry into Certain Alleged Murders (1990).
4. Comment made by Mr Justice Johan Kriegler in the case Neethling v Du Preez and Others, Rand Supreme Court, Johannesburg (1990).
5. *Weekly Mail*, 24 May 1989.
6. *The Sunday Tribune*, 22 June 1980.
7. *The Swazi Times*, 7 August 1978.
8. ANC Intelligence Report on Death Squad Atrocities, 1990.
9. *The Swazi Times*, 9 March 1980.
10. *Servamus*, May 1980.
11. *The Sunday Tribune*, 22 June 1980.

Chapter 4

1. The information in this chapter is, except where indicated otherwise, based on personal interviews with Dirk Coetzee (1989 and 1990), the record of the Harms Commission of Inquiry into Certain Alleged Murders, Pretoria (1990), the record of the case Neethling v Du Preez and Others, Rand Supreme Court, Johannesburg (1990), and Dirk Coetzee, "Death Squads: The Testimony of a South African Security Policeman" (Unpublished manuscript, 1990).
2. Almond Nofemela, Evidence before the Harms Commission (1990).

3.   Joe Mamasela, Evidence before the Harms Commission (1990).
4.   Brian Ngqulunga, Evidence before the Harms Commission (1990).
5.   David Tshikalange, Evidence before the Harms Commission (1990).
6.   The South African Police admitted in their evidence before the Harms Commission that this incident had occurred, but claimed that Dirk Coetzee and his squad had acted without permission from their superiors.
7.   Joseph Hanlon, *Beggar Your Neighbours*, London: Catholic Institute for International Relations, 1986.
8.   *The Star*, 28 January 1990.
9.   This incident is also referred to in ANC intelligence files and by Almond Nofemela in his affidavit (19 October 1989).
10.   Evidence of the South African Police before the Harms Commission.
11.   *The Star*, 29 April 1990.
12.   Affidavit by Edward Apolosi Maepi submitted to the Harms Commission.
13.   Evidence of Colonel Hermanus du Plessis before the Harms Commission.
14.   The document referred to was submitted by the South African Police to the Harms Commission, but its relevance was discovered only six months later in the case of Neethling v Du Preez and Others.
15.   Customs Documents of the Botswana Government (November 1981) submitted to the Harms Commission.
16.   Affidavit by Joyce Dipale (November 1981) submitted to the Harms Commission.
17.   The fate of Isaac Moema is also referred to by Almond Nofemela before the Harms Commission and in a statement by Chris Mnisi to the ANC (1990).
18.   *South*, 15 March 1990.
19.   *New Nation*, 4 May 1990.
20.   *Rand Daily Mail*, 23 December 1981.
21.   *The Sunday Tribune*, 20 June 1982.
22.   Statement made by Robert Sacco and submitted to the Harms Commission.
23.   Affidavit made by Frederick Sauls of the National Automobile and Allied Workers' Union, submitted to the Harms Commission.
24.   This incident was corroborated by Almond Nofemela and David Tshikalange before the Harms Commission.
25.   Interview with Marius Schoon, Johannesburg (1991).
26.   *Vrye Weekblad*, 24 November 1989.
27.   *The Guardian*, 17 November 1989.

Chapter 5
1.   The information in this chapter is, except where indicated otherwise, based on personal interviews with Dirk Coetzee (1989 and 1990), the record of the Harms Commission of Inquiry into Certain Alleged Murders, Pretoria (1990), the record of the case Neethling v Du Preez and Others, Rand Supreme Court, Johannesburg (1990), and Dirk Coetzee, "Death Squads: The Testimony of a South African Security Policeman" (Unpublished manuscript, 1990).

2. *Servamus*, October 1981.
3. Don Foster, Dennis Davis and Diane Sandler, *Detention and Torture in South Africa*, London: James Currey, 1987.
4. Evidence by the South African Police before the Harms Commission.
5. *Rapport*, 3 March 1985.
6. Statement by Dirk Coetzee, Pretoria (1984).
7. Interview with Tian van der Merwe, Cape Town (1989).
8. Interview with Frans Whelpton, Pretoria (1991).
9. Interview with Martin Welz, Johannesburg (1990).
10. Record of the Interdepartmental Police Trial of Dirk Coetzee before the President of the Regional Court, Pretoria (1985).
11. Interview with Ben Coetzee, Johannesburg (1989).
12. *Rapport*, 17 December 1989.

Chapter 6
1. Evidence before the Harms Commission of Inquiry into Certain Alleged Murders, Pretoria (1990), and the Record of the Inquest into the Killing of Four Alleged ANC Infiltrators on 8 June 1988, Piet Retief Magistrate's Court (1989).
2. Evidence of Almond Nofemela before the Harms Commission.
3. Interviews with Marthinus Grobler and James Stevens, Johannesburg (1990), published in *Vrye Weekblad*, 26 January 1990, and in *Weekly Mail*, 2 February 1990.
4. *South*, 9 February 1989.
5. Record of the Inquest into the Killing of Four Alleged ANC Infiltrators on 8 June 1988, Piet Retief Magistrate's Court (1989).
6. *Vrye Weekblad*, 26 January 1990; *Weekly Mail*, 2 February 1990.
7. Patrick Lawrence, *Death Squads: Apartheid's Secret Weapon*, Johannesburg: Penguin Forum Series, 1990.
8. Record of the Inquest into the Death of the Chesterville Four, Durban Magistrate's Court (1989, 1990).
9. Affidavit by Almond Nofemela, Pretoria (22 November 1989). He repeated his allegations before the Harms Commission.
10. Record of the Inquest into the Death of the Chesterville Four, Durban Magistrate's Court (1989, 1990).
11. Affidavit by Almond Nofemela, Pretoria (22 November 1989).
12. Records of Lawyers for Human Rights, the Independent Board of Inquiry into Informal Repression and the Human Rights Commission.
13. *SA Barometer*, Vol. 2, No. 7, 22 April 1988.
14. Record of the evidence of General Mike Geldenhuys in the case of Neethling v Du Preez and Others, Rand Supreme Court, Johannesburg (1990).
15. *The Sunday Star*, 3 March 1991.
16. Affidavit by Almond Nofemela, Pretoria (22 November 1989).
17. Lawyers for Human Rights, Argument before the Harms Commission of Inquiry

into Certain Alleged Murders, Pretoria (1990).

18. *The Sunday Star*, 28 January 1990.
19. *The Sunday Star*, 3 March 1991.
20. Dirk Coetzee, "Death Squads: Testimony of a South African Security Policeman" (Unpublished manuscript, 1990).
21. *The Citizen*, 4 April 1988.
22. *Vrye Weekblad*, 24 November 1989.
23. *Beeld*, 10 July 1987.
24. *New African*, September 1987.
25. *The Sunday Tribune*, 28 January 1990.
26. Barney Horn, Affidavit made in Durban (3 January 1990).
27. Robert Thornton, "The shooting in Uitenhage, 1985: The Context and Interpretation of Violence", in N. Chibani Manganyi and André du Toit (Eds), *Political Violence and the Struggle in South Africa*, Johannesburg: Southern Book Publishers, 1990.
28. *Ibid.*
29. Evidence by the South African Police before the Harms Commission of Inquiry into Certain Alleged Murders (1990).
30. *Vrye Weekblad*, 12 January 1990.
31. *The Sunday Star*, 24 February 1991.
32. *Ibid.*
33. The build-up and expansion of Vlakplaas were revealed in a statement by Godfrey Ndaowana to the ANC, Zimbabwe (1990), a statement by Ronald Bezuidenhout, Pretoria (1991), evidence before the Harms Commission and statements by the South African Police.
34. Godfrey Ndaowana, Statement to the ANC.

Chapter 7
1. David Webster and Maggie Friedman, "Repression and the State of Emergency: June 1987 – March 1988", in Glenn Moss and Ingrid Obery (Eds), *South African Review 5*, Johannesburg: Ravan Press, 1989.
2. *Ibid.*
3. Patrick Lawrence, *Death Squads: Apartheid's Secret Weapon*, Johannesburg: Penguin Forum Series, 1990.
4. Brian Lapping, *Apartheid: A history*, London: Paladin Grafton Books, 1987.
5. *Ibid.*
6. Don Foster, Dennis Davis and Diane Sandler, *Detention and Torture in South Africa*, London: James Currey, 1987.
7. *Ibid.*
8. *Ibid.*
9. *Ibid.*
10. N. Chabani Manganyi and André du Toit (Eds), *Political Violence and the Struggle in South Africa*, Johannesburg: Southern Book Publishers, 1990.

11. Don Foster, Dennis Davis and Diane Sandler, *Detention and Torture in South Africa*.

12. Mary Rayner, "From Biko to Wendy Orr: The Problem of Medical Accountability in Contexts of Political Violence and Torture", in N. Chabani Manganyi and André du Toit (Eds), *Political Violence and the Struggle in South Africa*, Johannesburg: Southern Book Publishers, 1990.

13. Jacklyn Cock, "Political Violence", in Brian McKendrick and Wilma Hoffmann (Eds), *People and Violence in South Africa*, Cape Town: Oxford University Press, 1990.

14. Adèle Thomas, "Violence and Child Detainees", in Brian McKendrick and Wilma Hoffmann, *People and Violence in South Africa*.

15. Institute of Race Relations, *Race Relations Survey: 1989/90*, Johannesburg: South African Institute of Race Relations, 1990.

16. *Ibid.*

17. Patrick Lawrence, *Death Squads: Apartheid's Secret Weapon*.

18. Mary Rayner, "From Biko to Wendy Orr: The Problem of Medical Accountability in Contexts of Political Violence and Torture", in N. Chabani Manganyi and André du Toit (Eds), *Political Violence and the Struggle in South Africa*.

19. Human Rights Commission, "Violence in Detention", in Brian McKendrick and Wilma Hoffmann (Eds), *People and Violence in South Africa*.

20. *Ibid.*

21. Brian Lapping, *Apartheid: A history*.

22. Donald Woods, *Biko*, London: Penguin, 1987.

23. Mary Rayner, "From Biko to Wendy Orr: The Problem of Medical Accountability in Contexts of Political Violence and Torture", in N. Chabani Manganyi and André du Toit (Eds), *Political Violence and the Struggle in South Africa*.

24. *Ibid.*

25. *Ibid.*

26. Donald Woods, *Biko*.

27. *Ibid.*

28. Mary Rayner, "From Biko to Wendy Orr: The Problem of Medical Accountability in Contexts of Political Violence and Torture", in N. Chabani Manganyi and André du Toit (Eds), *Political Violence and the Struggle in South Africa*.

29. Donald Woods, *Biko*.

30. *Ibid.*

31. *Ibid.*

32. Patrick Lawrence, *Death Squads: Apartheid's Secret Weapon*.

33. *The Daily News*, 15 February 1989.

34. *The Star*, 25 October 1990.

35. Nicholas Haysom, "Policing the Police: A Comparative Study Survey of Police Control Mechanisms in the United States, South Africa and the United Kingdom", in *Acta Juridica*, "Policing and the Law", Law School: University of Cape Town, 1989.

36. Donald Woods, *Biko*.

37. Elrena van der Spuy, "Political Discourse and the History of the South African Police", in Desirée Hansson and Dirk van Zyl Smit (Eds), *Towards Justice? Crime and State Control in South Africa*, Cape Town: Oxford University Press, 1990.

38. Jacklyn Cock, "Political Violence", in Brian McKendrick and Wilma Hoffmann (Eds), *People and Violence in South Africa*.

39. *Ibid.*

40. *Vrye Weekblad*, 20 July 1990.

41. John Brewer, "The Police in South African Politics", in Shaun Johnson (Ed), *South Africa: No Turning Back,* London: The MacMillan Press, 1988.

42. Institute of Race Relations, *Race Relations Survey: 1989/90.*

43. Elrena van der Spuy, "Political Discourse and the History of the South African Police", in Desirée Hansson and Dirk van Zyl Smit (Eds), *Towards Justice? Crime and State Control in South Africa.*

44. Institute of Race Relations, *Race Relations Survey: 1989/90.*

45. John Brewer, "The Police in South African Politics", in Shaun Johnson (Ed), *South Africa: No Turning Back.*

46. Elrena van der Spuy, "Political Discourse and the History of the South African Police", in Desirée Hansson and Dirk van Zyl Smit (Eds), *Towards Justice? Crime and State Control in South Africa.*

47. John Brewer, "The Police in South African Politics", in Shaun Johnson (Ed), *South Africa: No Turning Back.*

48. *Ibid.*

49. J.H.P. Serfontein, *Apartheid, Change and the N.G. Kerk,* Johannesburg: Taurus, 1982.

50. M. Dippenaar, *Die Geskiedenis van die Suid-Afrikaanse Polisie, 1913–1988,* Silverton: Promedia, 1988.

51. Elrena van der Spuy, "Political Discourse and the History of the South African Police", in Desirée Hansson and Dirk van Zyl Smit (Eds), *Towards Justice? Crime and State Control in South Africa.*

52. *Ibid.*

53. *Ibid.*

54. *Ibid.*

55. D.S. Hansson, "Trigger Happy? An Evaluation of Fatal Police Shootings in the Greater Cape Town Area from 1984 to 1986", in *Acta Juridica,* "Policing and the Law".

56. *Ibid.*

57. Nicholas Haysom, "Policing the Police: A Comparative Survey of Police Control Mechanisms in the United States, South Africa and the United Kingdom", in *Acta Juridica,* "Policing and the Law".

58. Nico Steytler, "Policing Political Opponents: Death Squads and Cop Culture", in Desirée Hansson and Dirk van Zyl Smit, *Towards Justice? Crime and State Control in South Africa.*

59. *Ibid.*

60. John Brewer, "The Police in South African Politics", in Shaun Johnson (Ed), *South Africa: No Turning Back*.

61. Nico Steytler, "Policing Political Opponents: Death Squads and Cop Culture", in Desirée Hansson and Dirk van Zyl Smit, (Eds) *Towards Justice? Crime and State Control in South Africa*.

62. *The Sunday Star*, 11 March 1990.

63. Jacklyn Cock, "Political Violence", in Brian McKendrick and Wilma Hoffmann (Eds), *People and Violence in South Africa*.

64. *The Weekly Mail*, 24 November 1989.

65. *The Star*, 6 April 1990.

66. Gordon Winter, *Inside Boss*, London: Penguin, 1981.

67. Patrick Lawrence, *Death Squads: Apartheid's Secret Weapon*.

68. *The Weekly Mail*, 24 November 1989.

69. *The Argus*, 2 June 1989; *The Weekly Mail*, 24 November 1989.

70. *The Weekly Mail*, 2 June 1989.

71. *The Argus*, 2 June 1989.

72. *Ibid.*

73. *The Argus*, 14 June 1989.

74. *Vrye Weekblad*, 23 November 1989.

75. Gordon Winter, *Inside Boss*.

76. Nicholas Haysom, "Vigilantism and the Policing of African Townships: Manufacturing Violent Stability", in Desirée Hansson and Dirk van Zyl Smit, *Towards Justice? Crime and State Control in South Africa*.

77. David Webster and Maggie Friedman, "Repression and the State of Emergency: June 1987–March 1989", in Glenn Moss and Ingrid Obery, *South African Review (5)*, Johannesburg: Ravan Press, 1989.

78. Clive Plasket, "Sub-Contracting the Dirty Work", in *Acta Juridica*, "Policing and the Law".

79. Nicholas Haysom, "Vigilantism and the Policing of African Townships: Manufacturing Violent Stability", in Desirée Hansson and Dirk van Zyl Smit, *Towards Justice? Crime and State Control in South Africa*.

80. *Cape Times*, 8 November 1988.

81. Mark Phillips, "Divide and Repress: Vigilantes and State Objectives in Crossroads", in Catholic Institute for International Relations, *States of Terror: Death Squads or Development*, London: CUR, 1989.

82. Catholic Institute for International Relations, *States of Terror: Death Squads or Development?*

83. Donald Woods: *Biko*.

84. *Ibid.*

85. Independent Board of Inquiry into Informal Repression, Arguments before the Harms Commission of Inquiry into Certain Alleged Murders, Pretoria (1990).

86. *Ibid.*

87. *Ibid.*

88. *The Sunday Times*, 13 February 1977.

89. *Ibid.*

90. *The Star*, 10 September 1977.

91. Kenneth W. Grundy, *The Militarization of South African Politics*, London: Oxford University Press, 1988.

92. *Ibid.*

93. *Ibid.*

94. *Ibid.*

95. The David Webster Trust and The Human Rights Commission, *The Civil Co-Operation Bureau*, Johannesburg: HRC, 1990.

96. Shula Marks and Stanley Trapido, "South Africa since 1976: an Historical Perspective", in Shaun Johnson (Ed), *South Africa: No Turning Back*.

97. Kenneth W. Grundy, *The Militarization of South African Politics*.

98. *The Weekly Mail*, 1 February 1989.

99. *Christian Science Monitor*, 11 May 1988.

100. Jacklyn Cock, "Political Violence", in Brian McKendrick and Wilma Hoffmann (Eds), *People and Violence in South Africa*.

101. *Ibid.*

102. *The Sunday Times*, 6 May 1990.

103. *The Sunday Star*, 11 March 1990.

104. *Ibid.*

105. Patrick Lawrence, *Death Squads: Apartheid's Secret Weapon*.

Chapter 8

1. *Weekly Mail*, 5 May 1989.

2. *Ibid.*

3. *Sunday Times*, 7 May 1989; *Vrye Weekblad*, 30 June 1989.

4. *Cape Times*, 3 May 1989.

5. Patrick Lawrence, *Death Squads: Apartheid's Secret Weapon*, Johannesburg: Penguin Forum Series, 1990.

6. *Weekly Mail*, 16 March 1990.

7. *The Sunday Star*, 11 March 1990.

8. *Sunday Times*, 18 February 1990.

9. *The Evening Post*, 9 March 1990.

10. *The Sunday Star*, 13 May 1990.

11. *The Star*, 25 February 1990.

12. Personal interview with Donald Acheson, Johannesburg (1991).

13. Record of the Harms Commission of Inquiry into Certain Alleged Murders, Pretoria (1990).

14. *The Sunday Star*, 13 May 1990.

15. *Vrye Weekblad*, 15 September 1989.

16. *The Sunday Tribune*, 4 March 1990.

17. *Vrye Weekblad*, 22 September 1989.
18. Anton Lubowski writing in *Stet*, 1985, as quoted in *Vrye Weekblad*, 22 September 1989.
19. *The Sunday Tribune*, 4 March 1990.
20. *The Sunday Star*, 13 May 1990; *The Saturday Star*, 12 May 1990.
21. Patrick Lawrence, *Death Squads: Apartheid's Secret Weapon*.
22. *Ibid*.
23. Affidavit by Brigadier Floris Mostert, handed in at the Rand Supreme Court (1990).
24. *The Sunday Star*, 11 February 1990.
25. *Cape Times*, 27 February 1990.
26. *The Star*, 27 February 1990.
27. *The Star*, 21 February 1990.
28. *The Argus*, 3 March 1990.
29. *Ibid*.
30. *The Sunday Tribune*, 7 January 1990; *The Natal Mercury*, 5 January 1990.
31. *The Evening Post*, 9 December 1989.
32. *Natal Witness*, 5 January 1990.
33. *Financial Mail*, 29 November 1989.
34. *The Evening Post*, 9 December 1989.
35. *Financial Mail*, 29 November 1989.
36. *The Argus*, 3 February 1990; *Cape Times*, 31 January 1990.
37. *The Argus*, 3 February 1990.
38. *Sunday Times*, 4 March 1990.
39. *Business Day*, 24 January 1989.
40. *The Sunday Star*, 11 November 1990.
41. *The Weekly Mail*, 11 May 1990.
42. Patrick Lawrence, *Death Squads: Apartheid's Secret Weapon*.
43. *Ibid*.

Chapter 9

1. The information in this chapter was, except where indicated otherwise, obtained from the records of the Harms Commission of Inquiry into Certain Alleged Murders, Pretoria (1991).
2. *The Argus*, 8 March 1990.
3. The David Webster Trust and the Human Rights Commission, *The Civil Co-operation Bureau*, Johannesburg: HRC, 1990.
4. Independent Board of Inquiry into Informal Repression Report for the month of January 1991. Johannesburg.
5. The David Webster Trust and the Human Rights Commission, *The Civil Co-operation Bureau*.
6. *Ibid*.
7. *The Star*, 25 February 1990.

8. *The Sunday Star,* 2 February 1990.
9. *Sunday Times,* 11 March 1990.
10. *Ibid.*
11. *The Star,* 10 June 1990.
12. *The Star,* 28 April 1990; *The Weekly Mail,* 27 April 1990.
13. Patrick Lawrence, *Death Squads: Apartheid's Secret Weapon,* Johannesburg: Penguin Forum Series, 1990.
14. Statement by the Lubowski family, Cape Town (1990).
15. *Sunday Times,* 14 April 1991.
16. Affidavit by Brian Currin, handed in at the Harms Commission (1990).
17. *The Star,* 25 April 1987; *The Sowetan,* 24 June 1990.
18. *The Star,* 1 June 1990; *The Sowetan,* 9 December 1987.

Chapter 10
1. The information for this chapter, except where indicated otherwise, was obtained from interviews with Pieter Botes, an affidavit made by him (May 1990) and his evidence before the Harms Commission of Inquiry into Certain Alleged Murders, Pretoria, 1990.
2. Albie Sachs, *The Soft Vengeance of a Freedom Fighter,* Cape Town: David Philip, 1990.
3. *The Star,* 8 April 1988.
4. *The Weekly Mail,* 8 December 1989.
5. *The Sunday Star,* 18 March 1990.
6. *Beeld,* 15 March 1990.
7. *The Star,* 27 May 1990.
8. *Echo,* 23 May 1990.
9. *The Star,* 30 January 1989.

Chapter 11
1. The information in this chapter, except where indicated otherwise, is based on personal interviews with Leslie Lesia (1990) and evidence he gave in the case of Neethling v Du Preez and Others, Rand Supreme Court (1990).
2. *The Star,* 18 September 1987.
3. *Eastern Province Herald,* 16 May 1987.
4. *The Sunday Times,* 31 March 1991.

Chapter 12
1. Joseph Hanlon, *Beggar Your Neighbours,* London: Catholic Institute for International Relations, 1987.
2. Diana Gammack, "South Africa's War of Destabilisation", in Glenn Moss and Ingrid Obery (Eds), *South African Review,* (5), Johannesburg: Ravan Press, 1989.
3. Joseph Hanlon, *Beggar Your Neighbours.*
4. *Business Day,* 30 May 1985.

5. *The Citizen,* 21 September 1985; *Rand Daily Mail,* 24 May 1984.
6. Joseph Hanlon, *Beggar Your Neighbours.*
7. Report by the Human Rights Commission, 1989.
8. Records of the Human Rights Commission, The Independent Board of Inquiry into Informal Repression and Lawyers for Human Rights.
9. *Business Day,* 30 March 1988.
10. *The Argus,* 9 April 1988; *The Star,* 10 April 1988.
11. *Sunday Times,* 12 June 1988; *The Sunday Tribune,* 12 June 1988.
12. *The Star,* 23 April 1988; *The New York Times,* 31 July 1988.
13. *The Star,* 28 April 1988.
14. Joseph Hanlon, *Beggar Your Neighbours.*
15. *The Herald of Zimbabwe,* 19 December 1981.
16. *Parade,* June 1990.
17. *Ibid.*
18. Joseph Hanlon, *Beggar Your Neighbours; Parade,* June 1990.
19. Joseph Hanlon, *Beggar Your Neighbours.*
20. Gerald L'Ange, "Countries in the Cross-fire", in Al J. Venter (Ed), *Challenge: Southern Africa within the African Revolutionary Context,* Johannesburg: Ashanti Publishing, 1989.
21. Joseph Hanlon, *Beggar Your Neighbours.*
22. Diana Gammack, "South Africa's War of Destabilisation", in Glenn Moss and Ingrid Obery (Eds), *South African Review.*
23. *Parade,* June 1990.
24. *Ibid.*
25. Joseph Hanlon, *Beggar Your Neighbours.*
26. *Ibid.*
27. *Parade,* June 1990.
28. *Natal Mercury,* 14 October 1987.
29. *Ibid.*
30. *Parade,* June 1990.
31. *The Sunday Star,* 2 September 1990; *Vrye Weekblad,* 30 April 1990.
32. *Sunday Times,* 4 November 1990.
33. *Sunday Times,* 28 October 1990.
34. *The Weekly Mail,* April 1990.
35. *Vrye Weekblad,* 25 May 1990.

Chapter 13
1. Information for this chapter was, except where indicated otherwise, obtained from the record of the Harms Commission of Inquiry into Certain Alleged Murders, Pretoria (1990).
2. *The Star,* 4 May 1990.
3. The Independent Board of Inquiry into Informal Repression and Lawyers for Human Rights, Argument before the Harms Commission of Inquiry into Certain

Alleged Murders, Pretoria (1990).

4. *Ibid.*
5. *Ibid.*
6. Lawyers for Human Rights, Argument before the Harms Commission of Inquiry into Certain Alleged Murders, Pretoria (1990).
7. *Ibid.*
8. The Independent Board of Inquiry into Informal Repression, Argument before the Harms Commission of Inquiry into Certain Alleged Murders, Pretoria (1990).

Chapter 14

1. *The Sunday Star*, 26 November 1989.
2. LTC Harms, Report of the Harms Commission of Inquiry into Certain Alleged Murders, Pretoria (1990).
3. *Ibid.*
4. *Ibid.*
5. *The Star*, 14 November 1990.
6. LTC Harms, Report of the Harms Commission of Inquiry into Certain Alleged Murders.
7. *Ibid.*
8. *Ibid.*
9. *Ibid.*
10. *Ibid.*
11. *Ibid.*
12. *The Star*, 14 November 1990.
13. *Weekly Mail*, 16 November 1990; *The Star*, 14 November 1990.
14. *The Star*, 14 November 1990.
15. *Weekly Mail*, 16 November 1990.
16. *Vrye Weekblad*, 16 November 1990.
17. Don Foster, Dennis Davis and Diane Sandler, *Detention and Torture in South Africa*, London: James Currey, 1987.
18. *Ibid.*
19. LTC Harms, Report of the Harms Commission of Inquiry into Certain Alleged Murders, Pretoria (1990).
20. *The Citizen*, 4 May 1990; *The Sunday Times*, 6 May 1990.
21. *The Citizen*, 4 May 1990.
22. LTC Harms, Report of the Harms Commission of Inquiry into Certain Alleged Murders, Pretoria (1990).
23. *Vrye Weekblad*, 16 November 1990.
24. LTC Harms, Report of the Harms Commission of Inquiry into Certain Alleged Murders, Pretoria (1990).
25. *Ibid.*
26. *Ibid.*

27. *The Sunday Times*, 18 November 1990.
28. *The Star*, 14 November 1990.
29. Evidence in the defamation case of Neethling v Du Preez and Others before Mr Justice Johan Kriegler, Rand Supreme Court, Johannesburg (1990).
30. Breyten Breytenbach, *The True Confessions of an Albino Terrorist*, New York: Farrar, 1983.
31. Johan Kriegler, Judgment in the defamation case of Neethling v Du Preez and Others in the Rand Supreme Court, Johannesburg (1991).
32. *Ibid.*
33. *Ibid.*
34. Martin Welz, Evidence in the defamation case of Neethling v Du Preez and Others in the Rand Supreme Court, Johannesburg (1990).
35. Johan Kriegler, Judgment in the defamation case of Neethling v Du Preez and Others in the Rand Supreme Court, Johannesburg (1990).
36. *The Sunday Times*, 20 January 1991.
37. *Ibid.*
38. SABC, Agenda, 25 July 1991.

Chapter 15
1. Report of the Independent Board of Inquiry into Informal Repression for the month of March 1991.
2. *Vrye Weekblad*, 5 April 1991.
3. *The Independent*, 20 November 1989.
4. *Sunday Tribune*, 27 March 1983.
5. *Weekly Mail*, 9 March 1990.
6. *Hansard*, 1985.
7. *Vrye Weekblad*, 15 March 1991.
8. *The Star*, 11 April 1991.
9. Magnus Malan, interview with the SABC, 11 March 1991.
10. *The Sunday Times*, 10 March 1991.
11. *The Sunday Star*, 11 March 1991.
12. *Ibid.*
13. *The Star*, 11 April 1991.
14. *The Sunday Star*, 14 April 1991.
15. *The Star*, 12 March 1991.
16. *The Saturday Star*, 25 May 1991.
17. *Vrye Weekblad*, 10 May 1991.
18. Report of the Independent Board of Inquiry into Informal Repression for the month of March 1991.
19. *The Sunday Star*, 3 March 1991.
20. *The Sunday Star*, 24 November 1991.
21. *Ibid.*
22. Nico Steytler, "Policing Political Opponents: Death Squads and Cop Culture",

in Desirée Hansson and Dirk van Zyl Smit (Ed), *Towards Justice? Crime and State Control in South Africa,* Cape Town: Oxford University Press, 1990.

23. Jorge Caceres, "Violence, National Security and Democratisation in Central America", in Catholic Institute for International Relations, *States of Terror: Death Squads or Development?* London: Catholic Institute for International Relations, 1989.

24. Nico Steytler, "Policing Political Opponents: Death Squads and Cop Culture".

25. *Ibid.*

26. *Ibid.*

27. *Ibid.*

28. Jacobo Timerman, *Chile: Death in the South,* London: Picador, 1987.

29. Jorge Caceres, "Violence, National Security and Democratisation in Central America."

30. Jacobo Timerman, *Chile: Death in the South.*

31. *The Sunday Times,* 21 July 1991.

32. *The Weekly Mail,* 26 July 1991.

33. *The Sunday Times,* 21 July 1991.

34. *The Sunday Star,* 21 July 1991.

35. *The Weekly Mail,* 2 August 1991.

36. *The Star,* 2 May 1990.

Chapter 16

1. The information for this chapter was obtained through interviews with Ronald Bezuidenhout in the Weskoppies Psychiatric Hospital in Pretoria, and a personal account he wrote for this book.

Annexure A and B

1. It is difficult to determine when a killing is a political assassination. The information for these annexures was obtained from the files of the Independent Board of Inquiry into Informal Repression, Lawyers for Human Rights, the Human Rights Commission, various newspaper articles and evidence before the Harms Commission of Inquiry into Certain Alleged Murders, Pretoria (1990). The murders committed inside South Africa, except for the murder of Eric Mntonga, remain unsolved by the South African authorities. The only explanation for the killing is that they were committed with a political motive. South African commando raids into neighbouring states have also been included. Although some people may argue that ANC members in neighbouring states were legitimate targets, an astounding number of innocent civilians died in the raids. This list is by no means complete, there are probably many more political activists who have been killed or who have disappeared in southern Africa. I remain uncertain about the spelling of certain names, although I have used various sources and tried to be as accurate as possible.

Index